COMPUTERS IN SOCIETY

COMPUTERS IN SOCIETY

Nancy Stern
Hofstra University

Robert A. Stern
Nassau Community College

Prentice-Hall, Inc. Englewood Cliffs, N.J. 07632

Library of Congress Cataloging in Publication Data

STERN, NANCY B.
 Computers in society.

 Bibliography: p.
 Includes index.
 1. Computers and civilization. 2. Electronic
data processing. I. Stern, Robert A. II. Title.
QA76.9.C66S83   304.4′834   82-7488
ISBN 0-13-165282-6   AACR2

Editorial/production supervision
 by *Aliza Greenblatt*

Interior design
 by *Aliza Greenblatt, Anne T. Bonanno,* and *Dawn Stanley*

Cover design
 by *Anne T. Bonanno*

Manufacturing buyer
 Gordon Osbourne

Printed in the United States of America
10 9 8 7 6 5 4 3 2

ISBN 0-13-165282-6

PRENTICE-HALL INTERNATIONAL, INC., *London*
PRENTICE-HALL OF AUSTRALIA PTY. Limited, *Sydney*
PRENTICE-HALL CANADA INC., *Toronto*
PRENTICE-HALL OF INDIA PRIVATE LIMITED, *New Delhi*
PRENTICE-HALL OF JAPAN, INC., *Tokyo*
PRENTICE-HALL OF SOUTHEAST ASIA PTE. LTD., *Singapore*
WHITEHALL BOOKS LIMITED, *Wellington, New Zealand*

To Lori and Melanie

Courtesy List for Figures

ADT   13.3
Apple Computers, Inc.   6.13
BASF   4.14
Bell Labs   3.17, 3.19, 3.20, 15.1, 15.2, 15.4
Coastal Data Services, Inc.   13.2
Control Data Corp.   8.15, 9.6, 9.8, 9.10, 11.5
Cray Research   6.7
Data General   3.18, 6.3
DEC   6.8
A. B. Dick Company   14.1
Digital Equipment Corp.   8.7, 9.9, 10.9
Eastman Kodak   4.19
General Dynamics   8.10
Goodyear Aerospace Corp.   8.13
Graphic Sciences, Inc.   8.6
Hewlett-Packard   4.18, 8.9
Honeywell   4.21, 6.11
IBM   2.1, 2.2, 2.3, 2.4, 2.6, 2.9, 3.9, 4.5, 4.6, 4.7, 4.8, 4.9, 4.15, 4.22, 4.23, 9.4, 10.2, 10.4, 12.1
Intermec   10.3, 12.7
Interstate Electronics   8.14
London Science Museum   2.5
Mohawk Data Sciences   6.9
Moore School Computer Museum   2.7
NASA   11.6
NCR   1.1, 3.2, 3.6, 4.13, 4.23, 6.4, 6.5, 12.2, 12.10
Norand Corp.   12.8
Radio Shack   9.5
Rusco   13.1
Spatial Data System   15.5
Talos Systems, Inc.   10.10
Wang Laboratories   8.5
Watson-Manning   15.3

Contents

Preface

I COMPUTERS: AN OVERVIEW   1

1   *Introduction to Computer Literacy*   3

1.1 Introduction 3

1.1.1 The Need for Computer Literacy 3   1.1.2 Computer Professionals and Users 2   1.1.3 Scope of This Book 8

1.2 An Introduction to Computer Concepts 9

1.2.1 The Processing of Data by Computer 9   1.2.2 The Computer System 10   1.2.3 The Stored-Program Concept 12   1.2.4 Computer Operations: An Overview 12   1.2.5 Types of Computers 13   1.2.6 The Limitations of Computers 14   1.2.7 The Advantages and Disadvantages of Computers 17   1.2.8 And, Finally, What Is a Computer? 19   1.2.9 Problem Areas 20

Key Terms 23

Review Questions 24

Discussion Questions 24

2   *Computers: From the Past to the Present*   26

2.1 Introduction 26

2.1.1 What is History? 27

2.2 The Pre-Modern Era 27

2.2.1 Abacus 29

2.3 The Emergence of the Modern Era 30

2.3.1 Blaise Pascal 31   2.3.2 Gottfried Leibniz 32

2.4 The Industrial Revolution 33

2.4.1 Joseph Marie Jacquard 35   2.4.2 Charles Babbage 36   2.4.3 Babbage and the Countess of Lovelace 39

2.5 The Industrial Revolution in the United States 40

2.5.1 Herman Hollerith 41

2.6 Digital Computers in the Twentieth Century 43

2.6.1 Introduction 43   2.6.2 Electromechanical Computers 44   2.6.3 Electronic Computers 45   2.6.4 The Stored-Program Concept 47

Key Terms 50

Review Questions 51

Discussion Questions 51

3   Computer Concepts   59

3.1 The Computer System 59

3.1.1 Input Units 56   3.1.2 Output Units 56   3.1.3 The Central Processing Unit 56   3.1.4 Auxiliary Storage Units 63

3.2 Methods of Processing Data 65

3.2.1 Batch Processing 65   3.2.2 On-line Processing 66   3.2.3 Real-Time Processing 66   3.2.4 Off-line Operations for Future Batch Processing 68

3.3 Introduction to Computer Technology 70

3.3.1 Data Representation 70   3.3.2 Types of CPU Memory 77   3.3.3 Features of Primary Storage 82

Key Terms 83

Review Questions 85

Application 86

II COMPUTER HARDWARE AND SOFTWARE   89

4   Hardware   91

4.1 Equipment and Media Generally Used for File Processing 92

4.1.1 Punched Card Files and Punched Card Devices 92   4.1.2 Magnetic Tape Files and Magnetic Tape Drives 97   4.1.3 Magnetic Disk Files and Magnetic Disk Drives 103

4.2 Devices Used for Reporting or Inquiring about the Status of a File 107

4.2.1 The Printer 108   4.2.2 The Use of Terminals as an Alternative to Punched Card Processing and Printer-Generated Reports 114   4.2.3 Computer Output Microfilm: An Alternative to Printed Output 117

4.3 Specialized Equipment and Media Used to Update a File 119

4.3.1 Magnetic Ink Character Recognition 120   4.3.2 Optical Character Recognition 120   4.3.3 Punched Paper Tape Read/Punch 123

Key Terms 124

Review Questions 125

Discussion Questions 125

Application 126

5   A Guide to Software   127

5.1 Application Programs 129

5.1.1 Planning the System That Incorporates the Program 129   5.1.2 Program Preparation 130 5.1.3 Coding the Program 133   5.1.4 Getting the Program to Work 139   5.1.5 Implementing the Program 142 5.1.6 Documenting the Program 143   5.1.7 Major High-Level Programming Languages 144   5.1.8 Evaluating Application Software 150

5.2 Operating System Features 152

5.2.1 The Supervisor 154   5.2.2 Communicating with the Supervisor 156   5.2.3 Input/Output Control through Multiprogramming 156   5.2.4 Virtual Storage 158   5.2.5 Multiprocessing 158

5.3 Firmware: Where Hardware and Software Merge 159

Key Terms 160

Review Questions 161

Discussion Questions 162

Application 163

6   Computer Systems: With a Focus on Minis and Micros   166

6.1 Evaluating Computer Systems 168

6.1.1 Memory Size 168   6.1.2 Cost 168   6.1.3 Available Hardware 169   6.1.4 Speed 169   6.1.5 Available Software 169   6.1.6 Compatibility 169

6.2 Traditional Computer Systems: Small-, Medium-, Large-Scale and Supercomputers 170

6.2.1 Small-Scale Computers 171   6.2.2 Medium-Scale Computers 172   6.2.3 Large-Scale Computers 172   6.2.4 Supercomputers 174

6.3 Minis: The Computer Revolution in Miniature 174

*6.3.1 Defining a Mini 174   6.3.2 Applications of
Minis 177   6.3.3 Input/Output Devices Used with
Minis 180*

6.4 Micros: The Personal Computers 182

Key Terms 188

Review Questions 189

Discussion Questions 190

Application 190

7   Programming in BASIC   194

7.1 An Overview 194

*7.1.1 Why Learn to Program at All? 194   7.1.2 Why
BASIC? 195   7.1.3 The Two Facets to Programming in
BASIC 195*

7.2 Interacting with a Computer System Using a
      Terminal 196

*7.2.1 Log-On Procedures 196   7.2.2 Correcting
Typographical Errors 198   7.2.3 Running a
Program 199   7.2.4 Listing a Program 199   7.2.5 Saving
a Program 200*

7.3 Essential Elements of a BASIC Program 201

*7.3.1 An Overview 201   7.3.2 Fundamental Rules for
BASIC Programs 202   7.3.3 Variations on a
Theme 209   7.3.4 Conditional Statements 212
7.3.5 Other Uses of* IF-THEN *Statements 217   7.3.6* REM
Statements 219   7.3.7 Summary 219   7.3.8 READ *and*
DATA *Statements 220*

7.4 Advanced Concepts in BASIC 222

7.4.1 Loops and ON-GO TO *Statement 222
7.4.2 Arrays 226*

7.5 Versions of BASIC 229

7.6 A Summary of the BASIC Language 230

Key Terms 230

Review Questions 231

III COMPUTERS IN SOCIETY   235

8   *Computers in Business and Industry*   *237*

8.1 Computers in Business 237

8.1.1 Types of Computers Used in Business 238
8.1.2 How Business Operations Are Computerized 239
8.1.3 Facets of Computerized Business Applications 241
8.1.4 Systems Analysis: Science or Art? 245
8.1.5 Traditional Systems Approach versus Management
Information Systems Approach 246   8.1.6 Centralized
versus Decentralized Computer: Types of Computer
Facilities 248   8.1.7 Automating the Office 251

8.2 Computers in Industry 253

8.2.1 Computers in Manufacturing 254
8.2.2 Transportation Control 262   8.2.3 Computer-Aided
Design 263

8.3 Computers and Automation: Effects on Workers 266

8.3.1 Automation: A Brief Background 266   8.3.2 The
Hawthorne Experiments 267   8.3.3 Computers and
Automation 268

Key Terms 270

Review Questions 271

Discussion Questions 272

Application 272

9   Computers in Education   275

9.1 Computer-Assisted Instruction: Hardware
Considerations 275

9.2 CAI: Software Considerations 280

*9.2.1 Elements of a CAI Sequence 280   9.2.2 Types of CAI
Lessons 285   9.2.3 Who Writes the CAI Lessons? 288*

9.3 Controversies and Debates over CAI 290

*9.3.1 CAI: A Supplement to Classroom Teaching or a
Replacement for It? 290   9.3.2 Advantages of
CAI 290   9.3.3 Disadvantages of CAI 293*

9.4 Computer-Managed Instruction (CMI) 295

9.5 Major CAI Systems 297

9.5.1 PLATO 297   9.5.2 TICCIT 300

Key Terms 301

Review Questions 301

Discussion Questions 302

Application 303

10   Computers and Health   305

10.1 Hospital Information Systems 306

*10.1.1 Basic Objectives 306   10.1.2 Reasons Why Hospital
Information Systems Are Scarce 311*

10.2 Medical Information Systems: Focusing on
Computers in Diagnosis, Treatment, Clinical
Evaluation, and Research 314

*10.2.1 Computers as Diagnostic Tools in Medical
Information Systems 315   10.2.2 Examples 318*

10.3 The Health Information System 319

10.3.1 Characteristics of a Health Information System 319

10.4 Other Health-Related Uses of Computers 320

10.4.1 Mini Medical Systems 320   10.4.2 Computers for Treatment and Evaluation 321   10.4.3 Computers in Medical Research 322   10.4.4 Computers for Simulation 323   10.4.5 The Use of CAT Scanners 324   10.4.6 And Many More Possibilities 324

10.5 Is a Hospital Negligent for Failing to Use a Computer? 327

Key Terms 328

Review Questions 328

Discussion Questions 329

Application 329

11 **Computers as Scientific Tools: A Focus on Artificial Intelligence   331**

11.1 Controversies over Artificial Intelligence 331

11.2 Alan Turing and His Definition of Machine Intelligence 333

11.3 Heuristic Programming: A Major AI Technique 335

11.3.1 Game Playing Using Heuristics 336
11.3.2 Theorem Proving Using Heuristics 338
11.3.3 General Problem Solving Using Heuristics 338

11.4 Robotics 339

11.5 Language and Linguistics 340

11.6 Cybernetics and Other Areas of Computer Research 342

11.7 Artificial Intelligence: The Larger Issues 343

11.7.1 Do AI Techniques Provide Machines with the Capability to "Learn"? 343   11.7.2 Can Machines

Simulate Human Behavior? 343 11.7.3 Is the Human Brain a Computing Machine? 346

11.8 Computers in the Sciences: A General Overview 348

11.8.1 Passive Role 349 11.8.2 Active Role 349

Key Terms 351

Review Questions 351

Discussion Questions 351

Application 352

12 **Computers and the Consumer 353**

12.1 Point-of-Sale Systems 353

12.1.1 Types of POS Systems 355 12.1.2 POS Terminals 355 12.1.3 How Supermarket Products Are Marked for POS Systems 359

12.2 Electronic Funds Transfer Systems 363

12.2.1 Types of EFT Systems 364 12.2.2 Basic Concepts of EFT 364 12.2.3 Major Social Issues Concerning EFT 368

12.3 Security: A Critical Problem for POS and EFT Applications 374

12.3.1 Methods Used to Minimize Computer Breakdown and the Losses Resulting from Such a Breakdown 375 12.3.2 Methods Used to Minimize Manual Errors or Fraud 376 12.3.3 Dealing with Power Outages 376 12.3.4 What to Do about Natural Disasters 376

Key Terms 377

Review Questions 377

Discussion Questions 378

Application 378

13   Computer Crime and Security   381

13.1 Computer Crimes and Specific Laws That Have Been Enacted to Prosecute or Prevent Them 382

13.1.1 The Dearth of Precedence in Dealing with Computer Crimes 382   13.1.2 The Prevalence of Computer-Related Crimes 382   13.1.3 Types of Computer Crimes 383   13.1.4 Computer Crime Laws 389

13.2 Major Aspects of Computer Security 391

13.2.1 Techniques Used to Ensure the Security of a Computer System 393

Key Terms 399

Review Questions 399

Discussion Questions 399

Application 400

14   The Privacy Question and Other Legal Issues   404

14.1 The Issue of Privacy 404

14.1.1 The National Crime Information Center 405   14.1.2 The National Security Agency and Computers 406   14.1.3 Federal Computer Matching Programs 407   14.1.4 Financial Data Banks 407   14.1.5 The Social Security Number Controversy 408   14.1.6 The Privacy of Medical Information 409   14.1.7 Privacy Legislation 411

14.2 Other Legal Issues 414

Key Terms 416

Review Questions 416

Discussion Questions 416

Application 417

15   *Computers in the Arts and the Humanities*   *419*

15.1 Computers in the Arts 420

15.1.1 The Computer as Artist 420   15.1.2 Computers and Music 428

15.2 Research in the Humanities 432

15.3 Computers and Museums 434

    Key Terms 435

    Discussion Questions 435

    Application 436

IV COMPUTERS: THE YEARS AHEAD   439

16   *The Computer Professional*   *440*

16.1 Opportunities in the Computing Field 441

16.1.1 Programming 441   16.1.2 Job Requirements for Programmers 441   16.1.3 Programming Languages 442   16.1.4 The Next Step 442

16.2 The Computing Field: Science or Art? 445

16.3 Structured Design: An Effort to Formalize Computing as a Science 446

16.4 Ethics within the Computing Field 448

16.5 Certification of Computer Professionals 449

16.6 Major Computer Societies 453

    Key Terms 454

    Discussion Questions 455

    Application 455

17   A Look to the Future   457

17.1 Introduction 457

17.2 The "Office of the Future" 457

17.2.1 Facsimile Devices 458   17.2.2 Word-Processing Systems 458

17.3 Management Information Systems 459

17.4 The Changing Nature of the Workplace 460

17.4.1 Effects on the Workplace and the Worker 461   17.4.2 Effects on Society as a Whole 462

17.5 The Future of Personal Computers 463

*17.5.1 Microcomputers in the Home 463
17.5.2 Microcomputers as Educational Tools 464
17.5.3 Microcomputers in Business 465*

17.6 Hardware and Software in General 466

17.7 The Future of the Computer Profession 467

17.8 Human-Machine Interface 468

17.9 Other Issues to Be Considered 469

Key Terms 471

Discussion Questions 471

Application 471

A   Appendix–Glossary   474

B   Appendix–Resources in the Computing Field: a Bibliographic Review   490

Index   505

Preface

Objectives

The importance of computers in society today simply cannot be overstated. Virtually every sphere of activity is in some way affected by the computer and there is every reason to believe that computer use will increase in the future. Because of the tremendous impact that computers have had and will continue to have on society, it is essential that people—regardless of their major field of interest—understand how the computer can be used effectively for social applications.

It is the primary purpose of this book to provide students with an understanding of how computers can be utilized for a wide variety of applications—business, scientific, industrial, educational, legal, and so on—and to provide an assessment of their effectiveness in these areas. Our intention is to consider—realistically as opposed to ideally—the past, present, and future significance of the so-called Computer Revolution.

The book is designed to be used by liberal arts students as well as computer majors. The text focuses on the need for users as well as computer professionals to work closely in automating an application. We point out that unless users understand how computers are best employed, as well as the pitfalls associated with their use, computerization will not be entirely satisfactory. Similarly, computer professionals must be made aware of the needs of the user, and the concerns that many people have about computerization. Thus the book has two primary goals: (1) to provide nonmajors with an appreciation for computers but, at the same time, indicate the main problem areas that arise when computers are used; and (2) to provide computer majors with an awareness of the social uses of computers and of the philosophical, legal, and even moral issues that some computer applications raise.

Note that this is *not* an introductory text on the principles of information processing. It considers the principles of information processing only insofar as those principles provide an understanding of how computers are applied to social problems.

It is the objective of this book, then, to provide students—both majors and nonmajors—with the following:

1. An understanding of how computers are utilized effectively for solving business, scientific, industrial, and social problems
2. An understanding of the potential problems inherent in computer processing
3. An understanding of computer capabilities, from the user's point of view
4. An understanding of how computers actually process data by focusing on programming in BASIC
5. An understanding of some of the crucial philosophical, social, economic, and political issues—past, present, and future—that relate to information processing

Market

This book can be used in a wide variety of computer courses. It can serve as a computer literacy textbook in a liberal arts or an interdisciplinary program, designed to familiarize non-computer-oriented students with information processing, the ways in which computers are currently being used, and the ways in which they are apt to be used in the future.

This book can also be used in a computer course in the computer science or business department. Such a course would be designed to familiarize computer majors with the more general applications and issues related to their field.

The text presents the computer professional's perspective as well as the humanistic perspective. Classroom discussion drawing out individual opinions on these perspectives will add to the course and help bridge the communication gap that exists between users and computer professionals.

How This Book Differs from Other Books in the Field

Most Computers in Society books can be separated into two main categories: those that devote approximately half the text to computer concepts and those that deliberately avoid computer concepts and provide, instead, general descriptions of computer use and misuse.

Our book combines the major advantages of both these approaches while minimizing the disadvantages. Specifically:

1. Our book includes technical features, but from a user-oriented point of view. It describes enough of the concepts and the terminology to enable a noncomputer person to communicate effectively with a computer professional.
2. It is our philosophy that to understand how computers process data, one needs to understand at least the fundamentals of programming. Hence we have provided a chapter on programming in BASIC. This is an inclusive chapter that teaches the fundamentals of the BASIC language. Students will be able to write and debug simple and intermediate-level programs after studying the chapter.
3. Most Computers in Society books contain a short section of several pages on minicomputers and microcomputers. We feel that this subject merits much greater attention, not only in light of their current utilization, but because of their future potential as well. Hence we have included an entire chapter on minis and micros, one that focuses on their application as well as their technical features.
4. The pedagogic approach used in this text is appropriate for an introductory course. The perspective used is not to idealize computing as some books do, nor to present an unsophisticated and overly simplified point of view as other texts do. Rather, we have included a very realistic, user-oriented perspective that explores the social issues relating to computer utilization.
5. We have incorporated into this text our traditional approach—attention to the organizational flow of material focus on pedagogy rather than on length and breadth of material, and frequent reinforcement of material.

About the Authors

Each of the authors has expertise in a liberal arts field as well as in computers and draws on that background to provide the proper balance between technical concepts as well as humanistic issues. Nancy Stern has a Ph.D. in the history of science and technology, with a specialization in the history of computers, and has a considerable background in that field as well as in technological assessment and the sociology of science. Robert Stern has a J.D. degree and has considerable experience in the legal field, specifically in the areas relating to privacy and security.

COMPUTERS IN SOCIETY

COMPUTERS: AN OVERVIEW

Introduction to computer literacy

1.1 INTRODUCTION

1.1.1 The Need for Computer Literacy

This book has been written for two groups of students:

1. Liberal arts majors who wish to learn a little about computers and a lot about how these machines are actually used in business, science and, most important, in society in general
2. Business and science majors, many of whom have had some experience with computers, who wish to learn more about the actual applications of these devices in society and the social issues which they raise

With computers significantly affecting numerous functions in society, it is increasingly important for all individuals to possess at least a conceptual understanding of the processing involved. The list of activities and functions that make use of the computer grows each day. From registration procedures in schools, to checkout counters in retail establishments, to banking transactions, the effects of these machines on our day-to-day lives are clearly of great magnitude and significance.

Computers have become so important and pervasive that many colleges and universities require students to possess at least a working knowledge of how these devices function. **Computer literacy**, then, has become a main objective of many schools. It is the major goal of this book, as well.

The main objectives of this chapter are:

1. To make the student aware of why there is a need for computer literacy
2. To provide an introduction to computer concepts
3. To examine the capabilities and limitations of computers
4. To discuss some of the major social issues that have arisen with regard to computer utilization

All of these topics are discussed more fully in subsequent chapters.

1.1.1.1   The Communication Gap

This text attempts to bridge a fundamental communication gap that exists between computer professionals and those who may use computer services but are not computer specialists. This communication gap has had an adverse effect on the effectiveness of computer processing.

Many computer professionals are very technically oriented and tend to ignore or disregard the actual effects of computers on the individuals who will use them. They often have no real concern about the impact of computers on society in general; instead, their major objective is typically the immediate computerization of a particular function, with little or no regard to long-term consequences.

The communication gap is in part a result of the tendency of computer professionals to ignore the need for a proper interface between people and machines. Often, the computer professional will proceed to computerize a particular function according to his or her perception of the user's needs, without having adequately understood and confirmed what is desired. On the other hand, the nonspecialist, who is frequently a computer "user," is also partly responsible for this communication problem. Users are often so uninformed about how computers are actually applied that they cannot adequately communicate their needs to the professional. Moreover, they tend to distrust the computer as well as the people associated with it.

What results from this conflict is a critical communication problem between those who view computers as a positive social force and those who view machines as a serious threat to society. A major objective of this book is to bring these two viewpoints into perspective and thus closer together; in this way, we hope to ease the communication problem.

1.1.1.2   The Two Cultures

The dual perspectives outlined above are symptomatic of an even more widespread social conflict. In 1957, C. P. Snow, the late British philosopher, published a book entitled *The Two Cultures*. This monograph suggested that society was developing into two separate spheres, one with a scientific, technological orientation and one with a more humanistic or liberal arts focus. According to Snow, those who are more scientifically minded have values, viewpoints, and perspectives that are vastly different from those who lean toward the humanities. Moreover, Snow viewed this split as unhealthy and a potentially divisive cultural force.

One can almost equate the scientific, technologically oriented forces of Snow's era with the computer specialists of today. Similarly, one can equate the humanists of 25 years ago with those who currently fear and distrust the widespread use of computers in society.

This book will examine the orientations of the pro-computer forces as well as the anti-computer forces in an effort to bridge the ever-widening communication gap and, by so doing, move us closer to a single culture.

1.1.2   Computer Professionals and Users

There are two broad categories of computer studies at the college level: business data processing and computer science. They may not always be called by these terms, but college courses are easily identifiable as belonging to one or the other grouping.

Business data processing is usually taught by the business faculty and is typically part of a business department or school. Computer science is usually offered in a liberal arts program. Schools may have computer science departments or may teach computer science as part of a mathematics or electrical engineering curriculum. Let us consider the two specializations in some detail.

Business data processing is a field of study that focuses on the computer as a business or management tool. The program examines, for example, the ways in which computers are used for inventory control, accounts receivable, payroll, and so on. The use of computers to integrate departmental functions in a business is also explored. On a more advanced level, business data processing is concerned with how computers can be used for forecasting, for improving the decision-making process for management, and for data base management.

Note that there is only minimal attention in such a program to actual machine construction and internal components. Business data processing professionals are not interested in designing a computer or maximizing its efficiency; rather, they focus on the ways computers can best be used by businesses.

Students enrolled in degree-granting business data processing programs can expect to have the following career objectives:

Programmer: one who actually writes the sets of instructions (programs) to accomplish various business objectives

Systems analyst: one who serves as an "efficiency expert," specializing in techniques designed to maximize the effective use of computers in a business environment

Such data processing programs usually require a broad exposure to business subjects such as accounting, finance, management, marketing, and so on. In addition, students in this program should have some knowledge of statistics and statistical methodology.

There are managerial-level positions in many businesses that require a data processing background, so that students enrolled in such programs may well have a sound future in management as well.

Computer science is a course of study that focuses on understanding computer technology and theory and on techniques used for maximizing the overall design efficiency of the machine. It often emphasizes numerical analysis and mathematical programming.

Computer scientists are concerned with internal machine organization more than with actual applications. They possess a strong background in mathematics so that they can understand logical design theory. Sometimes a background in electrical engineering is required so that they can understand machine operations. Students enrolled in computer science programs are required to take a wide variety of computer processing courses, many of which are highly technical.

Students enrolled in degree-granting computer science programs can expect to have the following career objectives:

Scientific programmer: one who actually writes the set of instructions that the computer will use to perform technical or scientific tasks

Systems programmer: one who designs programs that will be utilized by computer installations to maximize the efficiency of the computer

Computer scientists are much in demand in today's market. There are a wide variety of technical positions which they can hope to fill.

Many universities offer a *single* computer major where students can elect to specialize in business-oriented courses or focus on the more scientific program. In an effort to combine both specializations under one heading, such a program is sometimes referred to as an "Information Sciences" program.

Despite their shared area of interest, computer scientists and business data processing professionals tend to have dual, and not always compatible, perspectives. Computer scientists tend to view business data processing as somewhat less professional and less specialized. They have a scientific view of their discipline which considers a business orientation to be less significant. On the other hand, business data processing professionals sometimes view computer scientists as too technical and not pragmatic enough.

In considering computer concepts, we will make every effort to present a relatively unbiased account, emphasizing both the data processing and computer science concepts. In this way, we hope to provide a broader perspective of precisely how computers are used in society.

A summary of the computer science and business data processing disciplines is given in Table 1.1.

A computer professional, then, may be a business data processing specialist or a computer scientist. Computer professionals will thus have differing perspectives depending on their area of specialization.

There is another category of people who are *not* computer professionals but who are nonetheless directly affected by this technology. These people are commonly referred to as computer **users**. A user is usually a nonspecialist who works with computer professionals in an effort to obtain the proper information for a specific computer application.

Table 1.1. *Business Data Processing as compared to Computer Science.*

Discipline	Meaning	Typical Responsibilities	Perspective
Business data processing	Focuses on the computer as a business tool: Used for inventory control, payroll, accounts receivable, etc. Used to integrate departmental functions Used for forecasting and improving decision-making process	Programmer: writes sets of instructions to accomplish business objectives Systems analyst: seeks to maximize the effective use of the computer in a business environment	Tends to view computer scientists as too technical and not pragmatic enough
Computer science	Focuses on: Internal machine organization and design Problem-oriented and machine-level programming Numerical methods and scientific applications	Scientific programmer: writes instructions to perform technical/scientific tasks Systems programmer: designs programs to maximize the efficiency of the computer	Tends to view business data processing as somewhat less professional and less specialized

Computer professionals and computer users often have problems communicating with one another. Users know what they want the computers to produce but do not necessarily know how to state these requirements technically; and computer professionals often have difficulty understanding the needs of users. Therein lies another major communication problem.

It must be borne in mind that computer professionals and users alike have a joint obligation to develop systems that consider the computer's impact on the individual in society. The user must consider, for example, whether the creation and maintenance of data banks of credit information will infringe on an individual's right to privacy if improperly utilized. The computer professional, on the other hand, must anticipate how computer crimes might be committed and then design a secure computer system to maintain the integrity of confidential data stored in its memory.

1.1.3   Scope of This Book

1.1.3.1   *What Will Be Covered*

A major objective will be to focus on what computers can reasonably be expected to do and what tasks are, or should be, outside the range of computer-related activities. To achieve this objective, it is necessary to examine the features of computer processing. We cannot expect to understand computer applications without having some idea of how computers function. In addition, there will be significant emphasis on actual social applications, expectations for the future, and on how negative consequences may be avoided. In each case an attempt is made to explore the attitudes and philosophies of both computer specialists and nonspecialists.

1.1.3.2   *What Will Not Be Covered*

Having indicated what this text will include, it is equally important to indicate what it will expressly omit. It will *not* emphasize terminology or complex computer concepts. The objective is not to train specialists—other texts and courses serve this purpose; rather, we hope to provide an understanding of how computers can be used and how their use can be evaluated in a social context. Therefore, we make no attempt to be encyclopedic; we do not emphasize current "buzz" words which are fashionable today but may become obsolete tomorrow. The intent here is to provide a conceptual foundation that will be helpful to students in understanding and assessing computer applications.

1.2 AN INTRODUCTION TO COMPUTER CONCEPTS

1.2.1 The Processing of Data by Computer

The actual operation of a computer can be depicted quite simply as follows:

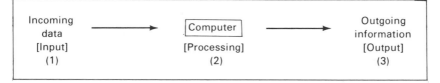

Of course, there are hidden complexities in this schematic, but it does provide an overview of the subject:

INPUT

> 1. Incoming data (input) consists of a set of facts that need to be processed.

Example A: A scientist enters several numbers that are to be used as variables in calculating the trajectory of a rocket.

Example B: A businessperson enters a series of prices and quantities that will be used for calculating the total amount due for items sold.

PROCESSING

> 2. The computer is instructed to perform a series of prescribed operations on the data. The primary reasons for using the computer to process this data are that it is extremely fast and, when instructed properly, it is highly accurate.

Example A: The computer is instructed to take a set of variables that have been entered and, using a prescribed formula, to calculate a trajectory.

Example B: The computer is instructed to take a series of prices and quantities that have been entered and, using a prescribed formula, to calculate a total price.

OUTPUT

> 3. The result of these computer operations is outgoing information called output.

The term **information** has come to mean data that has been processed so that it is meaningful and useful. **Data processing**, then, is the set of operations required to produce meaningful information. **Electronic data processing** (EDP) uses electronic devices such as computers to produce information.

9

1.2.2 The Computer System

In the schematic in Section 1.2.1, it may appear as if a computer is a single device. In fact, a **computer system** is a series of devices that read input data, process it, and produce output information. The devices within the computer system function interactively to process data. There are three types of devices that comprise a computer system:

1. **An input device:** reads input data
2. **A central processing unit (CPU):** actually processes the data
3. **An output device:** produces output information

A modification of the preceding schematic will provide a more comprehensive picture of a computer system:

Computer System

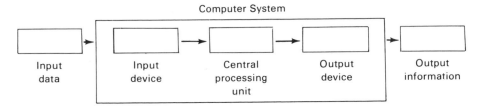

1.2.2.1 Input Devices

Note that a computer system can accept input data in a wide variety of forms. Data can be entered on punched cards, magnetic tape, tape cassettes, typewriter keyboards, and other media. Each form of input requires an input device uniquely designed to read that form of data and transmit the data, at high speeds, to the central processing unit.

Typically, a computer system has many input devices, enabling the system to accept several different forms of input data. Thus it is not uncommon for a system to have several punched card readers, numerous typewriter keyboards, cassette units, and other devices.

When an organization acquires a computer system it decides precisely what forms of input would be most beneficial; it then orders those units that can read the desired forms of input. Acquiring computer devices these days is a little like acquiring a wardrobe—you can mix styles and patterns very easily.

1.2.2.2 The Central Processing Unit

There is usually one device of a computer system that serves as the central processing unit (CPU). The CPU must be capable of:

1. Controlling the high-speed reading of input data
2. Storing the necessary data
3. Processing the data
4. Controlling the high-speed creation of output information

A CPU requires significant storage capability for holding data, complex circuitry for performing high-speed arithmetic and other data manipulation operations, and a control section for supervising the activities of the entire system.

1.2.2.3   Output Devices

You will recall that input data can be entered in many different forms and that there are many different input devices which can read that data. Similarly, output can be produced by a computer system in many forms. Printed reports, punched cards, magnetic tapes, TV-like screen images, and so on, are all output forms. Each form of output requires a special device to create it.

A computer system, then, is not a single device but a group of devices that function interactively. It is not uncommon, therefore, to see a computer system with dozens of independent units that are linked together. See Figure 1.1 for an illustration of a typical computer system.

Figure 1.1.   Typical computer system.

1.2.3 The Stored-Program Concept

You will recall that a computer must be programmed in order for it to perform particular operations. A **program** is a set of instructions that enables the computer to read input data, process it, and produce output information: the program for a particular application must be entered into the central processing unit (CPU) before any data can be processed. We can thus modify our schematic of a computer system as follows:

Computer System

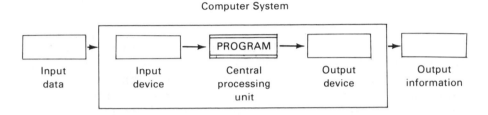

| Input data | Input device | Central processing unit | Output device | Output information |

Because a program must be stored or located inside the CPU in order for various operations to be performed, we call a computer a **stored-program device.**

1.2.4 Computer Operations: An Overview

A computer system is capable of only a fixed number of functions. All tasks performed by a computer can be characterized as follows:

> **Types of Computer Operations**
> 1. **Input:** The computer can read data from some input form and store the data.
> 2. **Data manipulation:** Data can be moved from one section of the central processing unit to another for different types of processing. Data can also be edited (i.e., a number read in as 1005 can be printed as $10.05).
> 3. **Arithmetic:** The computer can perform arithmetic operations such as addition, subtraction, multiplication, division, and exponentiation. More complex math must be defined in terms of these operations.
> 4. **Logical control:** The computer can test entries for specified quantities or can compare entries (i.e., does the item number in record 1 = the item number in record 2?). The computer can then perform different procedures based on the results.
> 5. **Output:** The computer can produce, as output, any information stored in the central processing unit.

In short, there are five basic operations that a computer can do, and that is all it can do! It becomes, then, the computer professional's task to define all jobs in terms of these five basic operations. Having the computer calculate a rocket's trajectory, for example, means defining the functions in terms of reading in numbers, performing arithmetic operations, and producing a result. You will see that accomplishing such tasks is not as complex as it might seem.

1.2.5 Types of Computers

1.2.5.1 Analog and Digital Computers

a. *Analog Functions.* An **analog device** is one that measures or processes data in a continuous form. A traditional watch or clock, as opposed to a digital timepiece, is an analog device. Time is represented in a continuous fashion. A slide rule, as opposed to a calculator, is an analog device. Quantities are represented on a continuous scale. Similarly, fuel gauges are usually analog devices.

Physical quantities are best measured in a continuous fashion and thus are ideally suited for analog computation. Voltage, temperature, and pressure, for example, are frequently computed using analog devices. Hence voltmeters, thermometers, and barometers are additional examples of analog devices.

A disadvantage of analog computation is that when data is represented in continuous form, readouts can only approximate actual results.

Analog computers, which process data in continuous form at very high speeds, are frequently used for scientific, engineering, and process control applications. A computer that controls an assembly line or a manufacturing operation, for example, is apt to be analog.

b. *Digital Functions.* Analog devices were used extensively (indeed, almost exclusively) for scientific computations in the 1930s and early 1940s. Now, however, the term "computer" is most frequently used to denote a digital device.

A **digital device** is one that measures and represents quantities as discrete digits. On an analog device, 1.5 is represented as the midpoint between 1 and 2. On a digital device, 1.5 is represented as two digits, 1 and 5, with a decimal point between them. Note the difference between the representation of time on analog and digital devices:

Analog clock

Digital clock

The term "computer" usually refers to an "electronic digital computer," which represents numbers as a series of "on" and "off" pulses:

represents the digit 1		[1-pulse is "on"]
represents the digit 0		[0-pulse is "off"]

The overwhelming majority of computers in use today for both scientific and business problems are electronic digital computers. Hence this text will focus exclusively on this type; analog computers were mentioned simply to remind the reader of their existence.

1.2.5.2   General-Purpose and Special-Purpose Computers

Both digital and analog computers can be categorized as general purpose or special purpose, the former being the most widely used.

The terms are really self-explanatory. A **special-purpose computer** is one that performs a specific set of functions. It has, in other words, a dedicated use. Such computers are constructed to function for one set of operations, but they can sometimes be programmed to modify the original functions.

A **general-purpose computer** is one that can be programmed to perform a wide variety of functions. In this text, we focus on general-purpose electronic digital computers.

Types of Computers: Summary

Digital	*Analog*
Operates on data in discrete form; used for a wide range of business and scientific applications	Operates on data in continuous form; used mostly for scientific and process control applications

General Purpose	*Special Purpose*
Can perform any number of functions; must be programmed	Wired or preprogrammed to perform a limited range of operations

---

Having described, in the broadest possible terms, a computer system and its basic operations, let us now consider what computers can and cannot be expected to do.

1.2.6   The Limitations of Computers

Because this book is intended for the skeptics as well as the believers in computer technology, we begin this section with a discussion of what computers cannot do so that when we next consider their capabilities, we will not appear to be overselling their advantages.

1.2.6.1 Computers Need Programs

First, and most important, a computer cannot do anything at all unless it receives a set of instructions which indicate, in very precise terms, exactly what its functions are for a specific job. The set of instructions to the computer is called a **program**. To say it another way, a computer operates on input data only if it has been properly programmed by a person called a **programmer**. We will see later that programming simplified problems does not take any special talent—in fact, it is really very easy to code elementary programs. Of course, more complex procedures require the skills of a computer professional.

To pursue this point even further, a computer really cannot do anything more than people can do since it receives its instructions from people. Hence the benefit of a computer is *not* its ability to perform operations beyond the capability of people; rather, it is its speed, which permits far greater flexibility in the range of tasks that can be performed.

Getting rockets to the moon may have been made possible by computers, but *not* because these machines can solve problems that were previously unsolvable. Our space program was possible because computers could perform the calculations in a finite period of time with a greater degree of accuracy than people could. In short, computers should not be credited with a "higher intelligence," but rather with an ability to perform more functions in less time than would be feasible otherwise.

1.2.6.2 Do Computers Make Mistakes?

Similarly, an electronic device cannot process data accurately unless its instructions are correct and unless it has been provided with correct input. This last point is fundamental to an understanding of machine processing.

Surely you can cite numerous instances where a computer error caused major problems for users. Note that such errors are only rarely a result of machine malfunction. In the overwhelming majority of cases, inaccuracies are the result of human errors, which are usually of two types:

Common Causes of Errors

1. **Input errors**: Something is wrong with the data.
2. **Programming errors**: The program or set of instructions has errors in logic.

Unlike many conscientious people who perform arithmetic and logical operations, a computer will not itself examine data for reasonableness unless specifically instructed to do so. It simply executes the instructions that have been provided. If either the instructions or the data have flaws, even obvious ones, the computer simply proceeds from step to step as best as it can.

Suppose, for example, that a program has been developed to complete an income tax form. Suppose, in addition, that the data that is to specify "number of dependents" is entered as 59—clearly an error, since no one can reasonably be expected to have 59 dependents. The computer will process the form, calculating deductions based on 59 dependents, despite the unreasonableness of that figure, unless instructed to do otherwise. One would hope that a conscientious accountant or clerk who might prepare the same form by hand would at least question the number 59 as requiring verification. Hence the judgmental factor which can be expected of intelligent people cannot be similated by a machine except insofar as that type of human factor can be logically delineated and programmed using the computer's five basic operations.

Suppose, as another example, that the computer has been programmed to expect a *single integer* to represent "number of dependents." If 11, a figure that might be entered for a person with a large family, were entered, the computer would probably accept that as "1" since the programmer did not provide for families larger than nine people. Such an error would again not be detected by the machine, which, in and of itself, cannot judge reasonableness in any sense.

1.2.6.3 Can Computers Make Decisions?

For social applications where tasks may require judgment, experience, intuition, or even an emotional element, computers are, at best, of limited value and sometimes of no value at all.

If, on the other hand, some elements of judgment, intuition, or emotion can be depicted as a series of logical instructions, the computer may have more value. One area where major attempts have been made to simulate human factors is in decision making. Many psychologists, physical scientists, and computer professionals have undertaken to design programs and applications so that a computer can assume a decision-making role.

In general, a competent and experienced individual can, in the end, make more effective decisions regarding various tasks than a machine. This is true mainly for the reasons already mentioned—it is difficult, if not impossible, to instruct a computer to simulate judgment, experience, or intuition.

But there are abilities of a computer that *do* facilitate the decision-making process. These include its speed and accuracy. Hence, it might be better to have a machine make minor-level decisions for a manager, for example, even if these decisions are at best uninspired. This would then free the manager to make more significant decisions or respond to specified exceptions. Similarly, because of its speed, one machine can make as many decisions as literally scores of people and with fewer errors. Even if these decisions are not always the best ones, the cost and time factors alone may make use of a computer worthwhile.

1.2.6.4   Do Computers Save Money?

Computers cannot be guaranteed to be cost-effective. Too often, organizations are so impressed with a computer's capabilities that they acquire one without even considering the efficiency factor. If one considers the cost of staffing a computer facility, the equipment costs, and the time it takes to get it operational, one finds that it is not always advantageous to acquire a computer. A special study called a **feasibility study** should be undertaken by any group considering the acquisition of a computer system. This study is used to determine whether such a system is justifiable.

1.2.6.5   The Last Word

Lastly, computers cannot function effectively as the final authority. Computers are tools—they need to be managed. Hence results provided by machines must be checked by people; moreover, judgments regarding those results must be made by people. It is inappropriate for any organization to use computers as the final authority. When discrepancies exist or questions are raised, there needs to be a "feedback" mechanism for making necessary changes.

1.2.7   The Advantages and Disadvantages of Computers

Despite the caveats outlines above, computers have been known to serve exceedingly useful functions as problem-solving tools. The reasons for their widespread use are diverse and have basically already been discussed in some form. We now formally consider each major benefit.

1.2.7.1   Iterative Operations

Computers are best utilized to perform a series of fixed operations numerous times. That is, an ideal use of a computer is to produce 100,000 payroll checks, each of which requires a series of computations.

1.2.7.2   Speed

Unquestionably, the most important factor in computer utilization is speed. Table 1.2 illustrates the increase in computer speeds over the years. Note that speed is really a significant factor in two types of applications:

Applications in Which Speed Is a Significant Factor
1. *Applications that have very large amounts of data to be processed.* These tend to be business-oriented applications—e.g., calculating the payroll checks for 100,000 employees. 2. *Applications that have a very significant number of arithmetic operations to be performed on data.* These tend to be scientifically oriented applications—e.g., testing the flight pattern of a new airplane.

Table 1.2.   *Increase in Computer Speed over Time.*

Generation	Measure of Processing Speed
First (1951–1958)	milliseconds (thousandths of a second)
Second (1958–1964)	microseconds (millionths of a second)
Third (1964–1971)	nanoseconds (billionths of a second)
Fourth (1971–)	nanoseconds and picoseconds (trillionths of a second)

1.2.7.3 Accuracy and Reliability

Computer equipment itself is highly accurate. Built-in design features virtually assure the correct processing of data.

That is not to say, of course, that all computer-produced results are error-free; when errors do occur, however, they can usually be traced to mistakes made by people in programming the computer or in entering input.

1.2.7.4 Cost

Presumably, since computers are so very fast and so very accurate, they have the potential of effecting substantial cost benefits, particularly in business organizations.

Whether they are actually cost-effective or not has been a matter of considerable controversy. It is exceedingly difficult to compare the actual cost factors of a computerized application to the same activity performed manually. On the one hand, computers usually enable the user to process more functions and more data than can be processed manually. In addition, there may be intangible benefits, such as more timely reports, that are hard to measure. Thus, comparing costs of manual operations with computerized operations is not entirely fair. Moreover, it has traditionally been difficult to assess the financial impact of computer acquisition since it often takes many years before the system begins to function efficiently.

Hence, measuring the actual costs associated with a computer can be difficult. In many instances where cost-effectiveness studies have been made, it has developed that the cost of a computer has been much more than anticipated and more than the organization could justify.

The reasons for these negative findings have been diverse.

1. The anticipated cost savings were more than offset by the cost associated with acquiring an experienced staff of computer professionals and data-entry personnel.
2. The equipment was not being used properly or to its full potential. Frequently, organizations acquire more equipment or more powerful machinery than they actually need or are able to use.
3. The error rate—resulting either from faulty equipment or human errors— was so high that additional staff was necessary to process corrections.

Minicomputers have become a less costly alternative to large-scale systems. We consider minis in some detail throughout the text.

1.2.7.5   *Storage Capacity*

The computer has the ability to store vast amounts of data and make it available to users instantaneously.

For example, an airline reservation system enables users to obtain updated flight information and to purchase tickets at any time. Such a system would simply not be feasible without this storage capacity.

The computer's ability to store data may, however, result in an invasion of privacy and produce security problems. The fact that the FBI, for example, has a computerized file means that they can access information that may infringe on the rights of individuals. Similarly, credit organizations that have amassed information on consumer purchasing habits have the potential for invasion of an individual's right to privacy.

Moreover, when an organization maintains computerized files of a sensitive nature, there is always the risk of a security breakdown. That is, some unscrupulous person may gain access to that file and may even possess the ability to alter it. More on this in Chapter 13.

1.2.8   And, Finally, What Is a Computer?

Thus far, we have considered the features of a computer system, the operations it can perform, and its basic advantages. But what *is* a computer? Do you think you can define it?

In fact, there is no consensus about what a computer is and what sets it apart from other devices, such as a calculator. With more and more devices being manufactured that contain miniature computers, the distinction becomes even less clear.

Based on our previous discussions, we will utilize the following criteria for defining a computer:

What Is a Computer?

1. It operates on data at high speeds.
2. It is highly reliable.
3. It can store vast amounts of data for present and future processing.
4. It may be programmed—that is, the set of instructions to obtain output is entered by a programmer.
5. The program is stored or loaded into the central processor for each run as required.

A typical calculator, therefore, would not qualify as a computer because it does not satisfy points 3, 4, and 5. A calculator's functions are usually wired and most often cannot be altered by a program.

Note that although the criteria above will suffice for our purposes, the controversy surrounding the precise definition remains.

1.2.9   Problem Areas

Despite the widespread use of computers in business, education, hospitals, and the sciences, to name just a few, there has been a great deal of concern about the problems these computers can, and in many cases, have, caused.

Computer professionals, as well as users, need to be aware of these problems and, to some extent at least, must take some responsibility for avoiding them.

Some of these potential problems are:

1. *Computers Can Be Dehumanizing.*   People can become just numbers, or entities, and feel as if they are losing their uniqueness. This can be avoided if respect for individuals is a major concern of the computer professional as well as the user.

2. *Computers Can Result in Mass Unemployment.*   Most studies suggest that unemployment has occurred in some areas as a result of computerization; but the need for computer professionals has, in total, more than compensated for this unemployment. Nonetheless, most computerized procedures have the potential for reducing the size of the work force. Computer professionals and users must work closely to avoid displacement of employees by encouraging retraining programs.

3. *Computers Inhibit Creativity and Originality.* If the computer professional and user do not build enough flexibility into a computerized system, it can be too restrictive and constraining, minimizing the user's ability to be creative or original. For example, if a computerized learning module requires a specific response from a student,

this may inhibit the student; that is, he or she may be told that a creative response is wrong because it does not conform precisely to the program's expectations.

   4. *Computers Are a Threat to Our Privacy.*   A recent poll indicated that 54% of the American public considers the present use of computers to be a threat to personal privacy. The growing concern for an individual's right to privacy has raised numerous philosophical and legal questions about limits that should be placed on the use of computers in society. This is especially true in light of the increasing number of computerized data banks that are being maintained throughout the country by various organizations, such as credit bureaus, governmental agencies (the IRS, FBI, etc.), and the health insurance industry.

   Although information in a particular data bank may be accurate and relevant for the purpose of the organization maintaining that data bank, it may be misinterpreted or taken out of proper context when entered into another organization's data bank.

   To illustrate how the issue of privacy can be involved with the maintenance of data banks, consider the following case in point. Recently, government researchers investigating the long-term effects of abortions examined the medical records of 48,000 women, without their consent. Inadvertently, the names of some of the women were disclosed in a preliminary report. This is a clear violation of an individual's privacy.

   5. *Computers Are Vulnerable to Crime.*   Computer crime is the act of stealing, embezzling, or otherwise defrauding an organization with the use of a computer. The average loss from a computer crime has been estimated at $600,000. In one scheme involving the Equity Funding Corporation, a $2 billion computer fraud was perpetrated. In this case, the chairman and some of the executive officers of the company used terminals to enter fictitious data into the computer to increase the company's assets by $2 billion. Since these officers were large share-holders of the company's shares which were traded on Wall Street, they were able to benefit by selling their shares at grossly inflated prices.

   It should be noted that many computer crimes frequently go either undetected or unreported. Often, when an organization finds that a computer crime has been committed and discovers the perpetrator, it refuses to bring criminal charges against the person involved. There are two primary reasons for a company's unwillingness to disclose the crime:

   1.   The adverse publicity received by the company may destroy consumer confidence in the organization. This is especially true if the organization involved is a bank, for example.

2. Frequently, the organization actually hires the perpetrator as a computer security consultant to make the computer system secure!

One major type of computer crime is the *theft of business funds by computer*. There are several reasons that help explain how this could have happened.

1. Much of the computer data used by businesses is stored on media such as magnetic tape or disk. This data cannot be "read" by an individual without the use of a computer and a program to interpret the data. Hence it is possible for unauthorized changes to go undetected for a long time.
2. Computer users often have little understanding of how a computer operates and rely to a great extent on the expertise of computer professionals. It is thus relatively easy for computer professionals to commit computer crimes in such an environment if adequate safeguards are not implemented.
3. Auditors frequently have little computer experience and rely on computer printouts for assisting them in their audits. It is possible for the computer professional to steal funds from the company and program the computer in such a way that the computer printouts would not reflect the crime.

As you proceed through this book, keep in mind that the negative effects of computers described above can result if the computer professional and the user do not take steps to prevent them. With the computer having the potential for such a profound effect on business, science, education, health, and on the economic and political structure of this country, it is imperative for students to understand how this equipment can be effectively and efficiently used.

What's in a Name?

The meaning of the word "computer" has changed over the last 30 years. It was around 1960 . . . we drew the line this way: computers were machines in which stored instructions could operate on other instructions to modify or alter them. . . .

With the arrival on the scene a few years ago of sophisticated pocket programmable machines, the distinction between computers and calculators began to get quite fuzzy. (Notice, however, that those companies that make both devices . . . see fit to preserve the distinction.)

It is, in fact, difficult now to cite the specific attributes that relegate the TI-58 to the class "calculator" and the PDP-11 to the class "computer."

Looking at it the other way, in the years prior to about 1953 the trouble went the other way; that is, anything and everything could legitimately be called a computer, because (a) there was no confusion among those who knew; (b) the total number of people who could possibly care was perhaps 250; and (c) there was nothing to be gained by mislabeling any machine. Hence the term "computer" and "calculator" were *at that time* synonymous.

It is discouraging we can't, as a profession, get simple things like definitions straight. Perhaps we will never be able to fabricate a decent definition of a term like "systems analyst" but we ought to be able to pinpoint a term like "computer."[1]

KEY TERMS

Be sure you understand each of these terms. Write down a definition for each and check your definition with the one provided in the Glossary at the end of this book.

Analog computer
Business data processing
Central processing unit (CPU)
Computer science
Computer system
Data
Digital computer
Electronic data processing (EDP)
Feasibility study
General-purpose computer
Information
Input
Nanosecond
Output
Program
Programmer
Scientific programmer
Special-purpose computer
Stored-program concept
Systems analyst
Systems programmer

[1]Fred Gruenberger, in response to an article by Nancy Stern, "The ENIAC," *Datamation*, May 1979. Reprinted with permission of *Datamation®* magazine, ©copyright by Technical Publishing Company, a Dun & Bradstreet Company, 1979. All rights reserved.

REVIEW QUESTIONS

1. What are the main differences between the fields of business data processing and computer science?
2. What are typical job descriptions for each of the following?
   a. Programmer (business)
   b. Systems analyst
   c. Scientific programmer
   d. Systems programmer
3. Why do computer users often have difficulty communicating with computer professionals?
4. Define the following terms:
   a. Data
   b. Information
   c. Computer system
   d. Program
5. What is the stored-program concept?
6. Explain the five basic operations that can be performed by a computer.
7. What is the main difference between an analog computer and a digital computer?
8. What are major limitations of computers?
9. What are some of the major reasons for computer errors?
10. What are some of the key social issues relating to computer utilization?

DISCUSSION QUESTIONS

1. For a computer to be efficient and effective, must it result in a cost savings? Explain.
2. Do you think the computer has had more effect on society than television has had? Than the airplane? Than the car?
3. Provide some examples of systems that would simply not be possible without computers.
4. Suppose that you are the manager of a department and you want an aspect of your procedures computerized. You outline your requirements to a computer professional. After some study, the computer professional tells you: "I can give you exactly what you want, or I can give you 95% of what you want for 50% of the cost." How would you respond?
5. Why do so many computer applications fail to satisfy the user?
6. We have considered, in an introductory way, the effect of computer technology on society. In turn, does society ever affect technology? Can you provide some examples?
7. If one is to believe the pessimists, what is likely to be the result of rampant computerization?
8. Computers have been depicted in films and science fiction books with increasing frequency. What types of attributes are ascribed to computers in these works?

9. How do the potential dangers of computers compare with the potential dangers of other technologies?
10. Give some examples of special-purpose computers.
11. A company representative states: "We are currently leasing a large-scale computer. According to our estimates, the computer will save us $70,000 a year."

    Such statements should be viewed with some skepticism. What questions would you ask the company representative to determine if, in fact, the computer results in a savings of that magnitude?
12. A company representative states: "We purchased a medium-sized computer two years ago. Comparing previous manual costs to computer costs, we estimate that the equipment is costing us $300,000 a year. This is excessive and we are, therefore, going to sell our computer and fire our computer staff."

    This, too, should be viewed with some skepticism. What questions would you ask the company representative to determine if, in fact, the computer results in a cost of that magnitude?
13. The complaint department of a retail establishment is asked to count the number of complaints made by customers regarding their bills, which have recently been processed by computer. What would you regard as an acceptable error rate and what would you view as excessive? Suppose that the error rate is considered too high. How would you proceed to determine what is responsible for the errors?
14. Indicate some of the reasons why noncomputer majors should take a course in computer processing.

Computers: from the past to the present

2.1 INTRODUCTION

It is frequently difficult for some people, especially computer specialists, to understand why the study of history is so important. Indeed, most technologically oriented individuals are so intent on keeping up with their fast-paced disciplines that they hardly have any time for, or recognize the value of, historical study.

It is the purpose of this chapter to demonstrate to students, regardless of their perspective, that tracing the history of the computational field will add a dimension to their understanding of technological development.

The words of George Santayana, a nineteenth-century philosopher, best describe the importance of historical study:

Those who do not learn from history are destined to repeat it.

This admonition serves to remind us that if we fail to learn from the lessons of the past, we will make no progress at all. That is, without a keen understanding of past developments, we will find ourselves continually reinventing the wheel.

The purpose of studying history is not simply to amass a long list of dates, facts, and events. That is not history—it is data collection. Rather, history is a study of the *processes of change or development.*

Understanding how change occurs in any discipline is extremely useful in understanding the discipline itself, as well as its future potential. That is one reason why government agencies that perform technology assessments call on historians for counsel.

There is still another important dimension to the study of history. Technological developments must be viewed within a social context. These developments are really responses to social forces; moreover, they frequently have a profound impact on these same social forces. Thus the history of technology really tells us something about societies themselves and how they respond to change. We live in an era in which controversy surrounds the use of many technologies, such as nuclear energy, genetic experimentation, and even computers themselves. Historical studies can help to explain what can and cannot be reasonably expected from technological developments. For our purposes, the study of how various computational devices affected past societies will undoubtedly shed some light on how computers are likely to affect our society in the future.

In summary, then, this chapter on the history of computing will provide an understanding of how and why:

1. Computational devices evolved during specific periods in history, and why such devices were neither developed nor in demand during other periods
2. Changing views about science and technology throughout history had a profound impact on the development of computational devices
3. The development of computational equipment was affected by, and in turn responded to, changing social norms

2.1.1   What Is History?

Having provided some indication of why history should be studied, it is important that we emphasize the way it should be studied.

To reiterate a point made in the previous section—history is not simply the study of dates, events, and places, despite the fact that many texts treat it as such. There is nothing more tedious or of less educational value than reading about a series of isolated inventions of the past several hundred years, with no explanation of the society in which they developed or of their relationship to one another.

Thus this chapter focuses on specific key historical periods and the types of computational devices developed during those periods.

2.2   THE PRE-MODERN ERA

The modern world, as we know it today, began to emerge in Europe in the sixteenth and seventeenth centuries. Prior to this period, the Western world was characterized by a set of social, economic, political, and intellectual ideas that were very different from what we now consider to be the norm. Some of the changing values that emerged during the sixteenth and seventeenth centuries can be deduced from the comparison in Table 2.1 of societal conditions that existed during each period.

These changes, which evolved over centuries, resulted in a virtual revolution in people's lives and their social values. With these changes came a reorientation in academic and philosophical values as well. Because scientific values, specifically, changed so radically during the sixteenth and seventeenth centuries, this period is referred to as the **Scientific Revolution**.

Both modern and pre-modern views about science encompass the way people see themselves in a changing universe; for this reason, such scientific views are extremely significant cultural forces.

During the Scientific Revolution, modern views about science replaced the Greek perceptions which, despite some significant modifications, had existed for almost 2000 years. Table 2.2 lists some of the more important distinctions between Greek and modern science.

At first glance, you might be tempted to dismiss the Greek values as naive or even mystical. Note, however, that such views were popular for many centuries and produced some very significant scientific advances, particularly in astronomy, geometry, and even biology.

But despite the advances made in some scientific areas, the climate of opinion that existed during the Greek period was *not* conducive to the development of computational equipment. The following represents some reasons why the Greek view of science did not foster such devices:

1.   Since science was not a discipline that was normally applied to real-world problems, there was no need for scientific equipment to facilitate the solving of mathematical problems.

Table 2.1.   *Changing Conditions of the Sixteenth and Seventeenth Centuries.*

Pre-Modern	Modern
1. Rural existence	1. A shift in population—increasing numbers move to urban areas; a middle class emerges
2. Farming was the main source of living—farms were largely self-sufficient	2. A widening of trade, creating a heavy emphasis on commerce, exploration, and cultural diversification
3. Feudal social structure—nobility rules; serfs belong to the land	3. Centralized government; nationalism becomes a force, equal in many ways to religion
4. Property could be owned only by nobility	4. Tenant farmers allowed to purchase land
5. The Christian Church had one main set of doctrines	5. The Protestant Reformation has a profound impact on Christianity

Table 2.2. *Changing Perceptions during the Scientific Revolution.*

Greek View	Modern View
1. Scientific knowledge was acquired through observations.	1. Scientific knowledge is acquired through deduction *and* experimentation.
2. Astronomy and geometry were the major scientific disciplines. Astronomy, as the study of the heavens, and geometry, as the study of ideal forms, both had religious significance.	2. Physics, chemistry, and biology became important scientific disciplines. The study of the natural world and life on earth took on added significance.
3. Science was a purely intellectual pursuit with no real applicability. Only the independently wealthy could afford to spend their time studying science.	3. Science is seen as a useful discipline which can improve civilization. A growth in scientific knowledge is one method of achieving social progress.
4. Technology was a craft or art; it was not based on universal or scientific laws.	4. Technology is the application of scientific laws to real-world problems.
5. According to the Greeks, the world functioned as if it were a vital, living organism. Understanding scientific disciplines meant realizing that each element has a vital, living facet.	5. The world functions as a machine, with all parts operating together. To understand each cog in the machine is to know the machine in its entirety.

2. Since technologists and scientists rarely worked together, technologists focused their attention on building devices that the average person might need. This usually meant farm equipment or some handcrafted tools.
3. Mathematics was seen as an ideal, almost mystical science, not the sort of discipline for which laborsaving devices would be deemed beneficial.

With this in mind, it is not at all surprising that almost no attention was paid in the Western world to computational devices during the entire 2000 years when Greek science was the norm. Keep in mind that scientific and technological developments tend to be responses to existing needs. If there is no apparent need, there is usually no development.

This is not to say that computational tools—tools used for counting—were nonexistent. Rather, they tended to be adapted from other civilizations. One such device, which is *still* probably the most widely used computational tool in existence, is the **abacus**.

2.2.1 Abacus

Since the abacus (see Figure 2.1) dates back to about 3500 B.C., it is difficult to say which civilization actually invented it. It was used by the Semitic tribes and in India originally, and later spread east to China and Japan. By 1000 B.C., the abacus was a tool used in the West.

The original abacus consisted of a slab (called an abax in Greek)

Figure 2.1. An abacus.

that was divided into sections. Pebbles, called "calculi" in Greek, were used for counters.

Merchants in most societies were, by the modern era, familiar with the abacus. Scientists in the West did not, however, employ any sophisticated computational devices, except in astronomy, where instruments were available for navigational use. But aside from these devices, computational equipment was not a major focus for scientists or technologists.

2.3 THE EMERGENCE OF THE MODERN ERA

The Scientific Revolution resulted in many new values that fostered an interest in computation and computational devices. The following is a partial list of reasons that explain this:

1. Science was fast becoming an important discipline, one that could benefit mankind. Hence any tools that could assist the scientist were seen as valuable and important.
2. Technology was becoming a discipline that could assist scientists; instrument makers, for example, began to work closely with scientists. Hence it was only a matter of time before technologists recognized the scientist's need for computational devices.
3. The growth of commerce and a middle class resulted in a need for computational devices for businesspeople as well.

With the emerging values of modern scientists and the growing need for some calculating tools, it should not be surprising that some of the most important figures in the Scientific Revolution were not only influential scientists, but inventors of calculating equipment as well.

There are numerous examples of scientists and technologists who focused on computational devices; we will consider only a few.

2.3.1   Blaise Pascal (1623–1662)

Pascal was a French scientist who made some very significant contributions to the Scientific Revolution. He was an influential mathematician as well as an experimental physicist.

Pascal is a pivotal figure in the history of computing because he was one of the first modern scientists to develop and build a calculator. Pascal developed this machine to assist his father, a civil servant, with bookkeeping calculations. His machine, which was capable of adding and subtracting numbers, was constructed in 1645. Because Pascal thought he might want to market this device, he applied for and received a patent. He realized that a calculating device could have widespread applicability not only for businesspeople, but for computing navigational tables, and for scientific measurement as well.

Pascal's machine was, of course, very crude (see Figure 2.2). It used gears and wheels that could be set and turned individually by hand. It employed the technique of rotating wheels for carrying numbers from one positional value to another. This is still the basic technique for carrying integers on desk calculators.

Pascal did not, however, have very much success in marketing his calculating machine. First, the device itself was not very reliable.

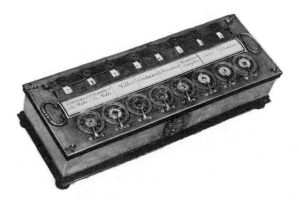

Figure 2.2.   Pascal's calculator.

Second, since this was a new concept, Pascal was the only person who could adjust and repair the device; maintenance, then, was a very serious problem. Third, and probably most important, despite the emerging uses for such devices, the need was not critical or even really evident to most people. It remained, then, for future generations to draw on Pascal's work once the need for computational equipment was clearer.

2.3.2   Gottfried Leibniz (1646–1716)

Like Pascal, Leibniz was a very important figure of the Scientific Revolution. Also like Pascal, Leibniz made significant contributions to both physics and mathematics.

Leibniz, a Prussian, designed his calculator in 1671; it was completed in 1694 (see Figure 2.3). This machine was significantly more advanced than Pascal's. It employed the same techniques for addition and subtraction as Pascal's device, but it could also perform multiplication and division. Leibniz himself acknowledged the fact that his machine used techniques similar to Pascal's:

> In the first place it should be understood that there are two parts of the machine, one designed for addition (subtraction), the other for multiplication (division) and that they should fit together. The adding (subtraction) mechanism coincides completely with the calculating box of Pascal.

Leibniz, like Pascal, recognized the value and potential of his device for scientists and businesspeople. In addition, Leibniz recognized that his device could have implications for society in general. He sent a copy of his machine to Peter the Great of Russia and to the Emperor of China. He also sought to convince astronomers of its applicability:

> The astronomers surely will not have to continue to exercise the patience which is required for computation. . . . For it is unworthy of excellent men to lose hours like slaves in the labor of calculations which could safely be relegated to anyone else if machines were used.

Like Pascal's device, however, Leibniz's machine was somewhat ahead of its time. In its day, it did not receive the kind of attention he had hoped for.

Pascal and Leibniz were not the only mathematicians concerned with developing computational devices. John Napier, who invented logarithms, also invented a mechanical aid for computation called "Napier's bones." The bones were rods on which logarithms were

Figure 2.3. Leibniz's calculator.

represented. By manipulating these rods, division and square-root operations could be performed. In addition, slide rules were invented and improved upon during this period as well. Thus, the focus on computational devices was clearly evident at this time.

Summary

The Scientific Revolution of the sixteenth and seventeenth centuries resulted in a new model for science, one that was machine-oriented and focused on the application of science to real-world situations. It was during this era that the computational device, as we know it today, evolved.

We have focused on two mathematicians, both established and important scientists, who developed calculators designed to serve as laborsaving devices. Both Pascal and Leibniz were successful in their design, but they failed to convince society that a need really existed. Despite the significant changes that occurred in the scientific field, society was not yet ready for calculating devices designed to save labor.

2.4 THE INDUSTRIAL REVOLUTION

The period in which modern science emerged produced not only changes in ideas but in the social setting as well. But despite the truly revolutionary changes that occurred, society was still essentially rural, with manufacturing and commerce very much limited. Technological changes of great magnitude were not in evidence.

The Industrial Revolution began in Great Britain about 1760 and was essentially completed by 1830. Spreading rapidly to other nations, it had a tremendous impact on the population as a whole. In fact, it is probably safe to say that no single period in history resulted in such a

Table 2.3. *Major Changes Brought About by the Industrial Revolution.*

Pre-Industrial Revolution	Industrial Revolution 1760–1830
1. Predominantly rural society (although the number of urban areas was always increasing).	1. Predominantly urban society. Because of the rapidity with which this change occurred, poor, overcrowded, and unsanitary conditions characterized most urban areas.
2. Products produced by the cottage system—people working by hand at home.	2. Manufacturing emerges—the factory system results.
3. Handcrafted products are highly valued.	3. Laborsaving machinery becomes a main focus—the artisan class is displaced.
4. A large class of tenant farmers exists. As a result of weather conditions and market fluctuations, there are many famines.	4. A large working class emerges.
5. Society is regional; commerce is limited.	5. Mass transportation develops; commerce expands.

profound and widespread social change. Some of the radical changes that resulted during this period in Great Britian are given in Table 2.3.

The Industrial Revolution, which began in Great Britain, spread rapidly to Germany, France, and the United States, and later to other Western countries. Historians and philosophers usually evaluate its impact in one of two ways—optimistically or pessimistically.

The **pessimistic view** of the Industrial Revolution focuses on the profound changes and displacement caused by rapidly expanding technologies. Mass unemployment resulted from the widespread use of laborsaving machinery, young children were sent to work at factories for 12 to 14 hours per day, and urban areas were crowded, unsanitary, and profoundly unpleasant. This focus tends to view technology as the cause for radical, reckless, and even immoral change. Industrialization is presented as a threat to civilization. This pessimistic view is very similar to the way in which some people today see computer development. When the emphasis is on negative effects of a technology and on the need for restraints and controls, the perspective is clearly pessimistic.

The **optimistic view** of the Industrial Revolution associates technology with progress. That is, despite initial displacements and difficulties, the overall, long-term result of technology is improved living conditions. In the end, industrialization in Great Britain resulted in better schools, improved housing, improvements in health care, and so on.

In the preceding section we indicated that the Scientific Revolution produced a climate of opinion conducive to the development of computational equipment; although such devices were indeed developed, the society as a whole was not really ready for the marketing of these machines as laborsaving devices. The Industrial Revolution, however, resulted in an era in which laborsaving equipment was seen as integrally related to success in business and in scientific pursuits as well. Let us consider a few examples of this.

2.4.1   Joseph Marie Jacquard (1752-1834)

Jacquard was born in Lyon, a large, silk-producing center in France. As an adult, he witnessed the radical changes wrought by the French Revolution, as well as the emergence of the Industrial Revolution.

As a member of a family with many silk weavers, Jacquard himself was attuned to the needs of the silk industry. In 1801, he built an attachment to the weaving loom that resulted in automated pattern weaving. His device used a system of rectangular, punched holes in cards which would direct the movement of threads so that a specific weave or design could be produced. Wire hooks would fall through the rectangular holes to grasp the threads. Where there were no holes in the cards, there would be no contact between the hook and the thread. Using holes in specific areas of the cards, the device could control the pattern woven by a loom.

At first glance, this weaving loom attachment might seem representative of the Industrial Revolution but of no significance to the computing field. Note, however, that the use of rectangular punched holes in a card to control machine operations is essentially the technique employed by punched cards today. Moreover, the holes in Jacquard's cards functioned just like a *program*, providing its set of instructions to the machine, which in this instance was a weaving loom.

Jacquard's attachment to the weaving loom met with resistance by the silk weavers because they feared that it would result in unemployment. Despite this resistance, the device was exceedingly successful. By 1812, there were 11,000 Jacquard looms in France alone, and significant numbers in other areas of Europe as well.

Thus the climate of opinion was vastly different from that which existed about 100 years before, when Pascal and Leibniz attempted to market their devices. Jacquard's machine was developed during a period in which laborsaving machinery was very much in demand. In addition, inventors themselves received much more attention in Jacquard's era than 100 years before. Jacquard was honored by the Napoleonic government for his achievement and received a pension as well. This was the beginning of an age in which government felt the need to support or reward inventors, hoping that such support would encourage other developments.

2.4.2 Charles Babbage (1791–1871)

Charles Babbage is considered by many to be the father of the modern computer. Although he did not actually build an operational computer himself, he did outline the ideas that have become the basis for modern computational devices. A brief discussion of Babbage's work will provide insight into nineteenth-century British society, which gave rise to ideas for the modern computer, and to the perspective and viewpoints of a very colorful and farsighted historical figure.

Babbage was born in England into an upper-middle-class family. He graduated from Cambridge University, where he studied mathematics. During his college years, he formed a close working relationship with John Herschel, the British astronomer, who was attempting, at the time, to produce reliable astronomical tables. Because the existing tables were replete with errors, navigational measurements were subject to frequent errors, a problem of considerable magnitude, especially for the British Navy.

While at Cambridge, Babbage conceived the idea for developing a machine that could produce astronomical tables accurately and quickly. The device, begun in 1822, was to be powered by a steam engine, which was the primary form of power during the Industrial Revolution. Steam was used extensively during the nineteenth century to provide power for weaving looms, spinning jennies, locomotives, and so on; it was not surprising, then, that Babbage thought of this type of engine for his calculating device.

In fact, Babbage's focus on a laborsaving device was itself characteristic of this period in England:

> I think the application of machinery in aid of the most complicated and abstruse calculations can no longer be deemed unworthy of the attention of the country. In fact, there is no reason why mental as well as bodily labor should not be economized by the aid of machines.

Babbage's device, called the Difference Engine, was a special-purpose machine designed to automate a standard procedure used to calculate the roots of polynomials (see Figure 2.4). This sort of calculation was frequently necessary for producing astronomical tables; because it required numerous arithmetic operations, it was a common source of errors.

Babbage began the construction of his Difference Engine in 1822 using his own funds as necessary. During this period, scientists and technologists were dependent on their own personal incomes for support. Babbage, a man who was really ahead of his time, thought he might be able to persuade the British government to assist him.

Figure 2.4. Babbage's Difference Engine.

In today's era, it is common practice for scientists to receive government support for projects that seek to apply scientific principles to real-world situations. In the last few decades, governments have come to recognize that advances in science often have a significant impact on society and ought, therefore, to be actively encouraged. In Babbage's time, however, when modern science had begun to take shape but had not yet been fully realized as a social pursuit, such government support was not known. To be a scientist, one needed to have independent means or be employed in a laboratory.

To his credit, Babbage was able to convince the British government to support him. He received the equivalent of $7000 for his device.

But, despite Babbage's foresight and his keen ideas, he made very little progress with his device. As a result, the government cut off his funding in 1827.

The reasons for Babbage's lack of success are diverse. Many books attribute it simply to a lack of precision instruments in England. This is difficult to accept if one considers the fact that only 27 years later, in 1854, Pehr George Scheutz, a Swede, was able to build an operating Difference Engine based on Babbage's work.

Babbage was a unique thinker, a gifted individual with truly inspired ideas, but he lacked the perseverence to follow through on his ideas. Instead, while he was working on the Difference Engine, he conceived a far more powerful computer; as a result, he virtually abandoned the former project.

Still at Cambridge, but now Lucasian Professor of Mathematics (Sir Isaac Newton's former position), Babbage began work on this new device called the Analytical Engine (see Figure 2.5). This machine was strikingly similar in concept to twentieth-century digital computers.

The Analytical Engine was to use two types of cards—one, called operation cards, for indicating the specific functions to be performed and the other, called variable cards, for specifying the actual data. This is the same concept used for stored-program computers, which were developed in the late 1940s. Entering a program, or set of instructions, on cards, followed by data cards, is one method used by modern computers for implementing the stored-program concept.

Jacquard's punched cards, which were used to control the weaving pattern on a loom, formed the basis of Babbage's operation and

Figure 2.5. Babbage's Analytical Engine.

variable cards. The use of one development for an entirely different application is a very common aspect of invention.

Babbage outlined two main units for his Analytical Engine:

Store: an area within the device in which instructions and variables are maintained

Mill: an area within the device in which arithmetic operations are performed

We will see in Chapter 3 that *both* of these units are used in modern digital computers.

Babbage's machine was to be capable of storing 1000 numbers. The speed with which it was to perform addition was one operation per second; multiplication was to be performed at the rate of one per minute. This was significantly faster than any existing device.

2.4.3   Babbage and the Countess of Lovelace

Babbage's Analytical Engine received a significant amount of attention in Europe. In 1842, Menabrea, a French mathematician, published a treatise on Babbage's work.

In England, a young woman, the Countess Augusta Ada Lovelace, became very interested in Babbage's work. She translated Menabrea's treatise into English and then began publishing articles on Babbage's work on her own:

We may say most aptly that the Analytical Engine weaves algebraic patterns just as the Jacquard loom weaves flowers and leaves.

Augusta Ada Lovelace, the only daughter of Lord Byron, studied mathematics with Auguste De Morgan, a famous French mathematician known for his work in logic. The Countess of Lovelace learned of Babbage's work while attending a lecture at a London Mechanics Institute. Later, she worked closely with Babbage himself in developing ideas for the Analytical Engine. She wrote a demonstration program for Babbage's device, prompting many to categorize her as the first programmer.

Publishing scientific treatises was most unusual for a woman during the nineteenth century. The Countess of Lovelace deserves our attention not only as a proponent of Babbage's ideas but for her keen understanding of computing concepts. In addition, her ability to ignore and resist the existing social norms concerning women was itself a significant achievement.

Despite the ingenuity of Babbage's ideas and their use in modern computers, Babbage himself never actually constructed a working device. He was clearly an innovative thinker, but not the sort of man skilled in bringing ideas to fruition. Nevertheless, Babbage is to be remembered for many "firsts":

1. Utilizing the technology of the Industrial Revolution to develop his ideas for mechanical computational equipment
2. Developing ideas for the stored-program computer, many of which are still in use today
3. Encouraging government support of science

2.5 THE INDUSTRIAL REVOLUTION IN THE UNITED STATES

The Industrial Revolution in Great Britain resulted in a virtual transformation of society. The radical changes in social conditions began about 1760 and were largely completed by 1830.

There were, and still are, many differences of opinion regarding the effects of that transformation. Many view the overall results of industrialization with its changes to the economy, the population distribution, the family structure, and so on, as positive. On the other hand, there are many who view rampant and fast-paced technological change as harmful to society.

The Industrial Revolution, which began in Great Britain, spread rapidly to other countries in Europe and to the United States. It had perhaps its greatest effect on the American people.

In the nineteenth century, the United States had several characteristics that set it apart from Great Britain and actually facilitated the process of industrialization. Because the United States is geographically so large and diverse, and was only sparsely populated in the nineteenth century, there was a vast amount of natural resources which were essential to the process of industrialization. Land, coal, forests, waterways, minerals, and so on, were all in abundance, making the raw materials necessary for industrialization readily available.

Moreover, unlike Great Britain, Americans had the option of owning farmland or working in the cities. Because of the availability of land, there always existed a shortage of labor. This shortage meant that, in general, workers were treated well and that the use of laborsaving machinery was *not* interpreted as a threat to the working class; workers were confident that they could always find jobs.

In addition, because of the pioneering efforts of early Americans, U.S. society always valued the ingenuity and innovativeness of people intent on constructing laborsaving devices. The term "Yankee ingenuity" is frequently used to characterize this pioneering spirit of Americans who focused on creativity, ingenuity, and new design.

Indeed, the notion of progress in the United States is integrally related to the concept of Yankee ingenuity and to technological development. The position of strength that the United States holds today is largely a result of its fundamental emphasis on technology. It was this emphasis, beginning in the nineteenth century, which led to its preeminence in the computing field as well.

2.5.1   Herman Hollerith (1860–1926)

The United States' entry into the computational field began in the late nineteenth century, when the belief in Yankee ingenuity was firmly established and the effects of industrialization produced a need for even more laborsaving equipment.

The U.S. census, which is produced every 10 years, has always required a significant amount of labor. This task is even more cumbersome in the United States than elsewhere because of the tremendous expanse of land to be covered. In 1880, the census task was undertaken by John Shaw Billings, who immediately recognized the critical need for mechanical tabulating equipment.

He encouraged his assistant, Herman Hollerith, to investigate this need. Hollerith had just received his Ph.D. in engineering from the Columbia University School of Mines and was eager to pursue this problem.

By 1884, Hollerith had developed reliable tabulating machines which utilized the punched card concept that is still an important aspect of the data processing industry today. There is some disagreement among historians as to how Hollerith actually came to utilize this punched card concept. Some claim that Billings suggested to Hollerith that he examine the Jacquard card principle; others claim that Hollerith conceived the idea while observing a rail conductor punch passengers' tickets. In either case it is clear that ideas generally do not "fall from the skies," but are usually based, to some extent, on prior invention.

Hollerith used a card punched with holes to represent an individual's vital statistics, such as birth date, sex, and citizenship. The cards measured $3\frac{1}{4}$ by $6\frac{5}{8}$ inches, the exact size of the dollar bill at that time. Hollerith reasoned that it would be easier to develop machines that operated on conventionally sized input.

Hollerith developed a specific code for representing data with the use of punched holes. This code, aptly called the Hollerith Code, is still used for punched card systems.

In addition, Hollerith designed and constructed two machines—a sorter and a tabulator—for performing the required operations.

To tabulate the punched data, the cards would pass a set of contact brushes. If there was a hole in a specified position of the card, the contact brush would complete an electric circuit with the metal supporting the card. If no hole was present, the circuit would not be completed.

Each complete circuit activated a counting mechanism so that a "1" would be added to an appropriate counter every time the circuit was completed. The sorter automatically positioned cards in various slots depending on where the holes were punched (see Figure 2.6). This ingenious system was able to save a significant amount of labor and was very reliable as well.

In 1886, having just completed his machines, Hollerith left the Census Bureau to form his own tabulating machine company. He began by supplying the city of Baltimore, and later other municipalities, with devices for calculating mortality rates.

By the late 1880s, the Census Bureau began preparation for the 1890 Census. Accordingly, it sought bids from manufacturers who might be able to supply appropriate calculating equipment. Hollerith was asked to make a bid; his equipment was judged the most suitable and he received a contract. As a result, the 1890 U.S. Census was

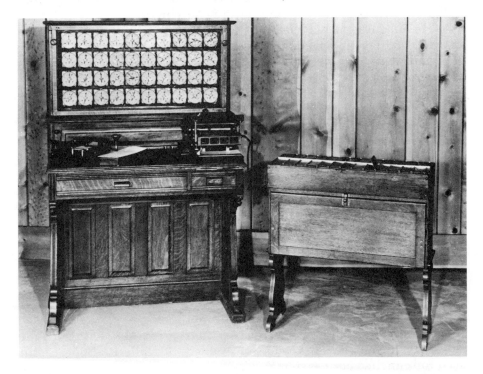

Figure 2.6.   Hollerith's tabulating machine.

completed in two years, compared to six years the decade before. It required the punching of approximately 60,000,000 cards, one for each American.

Hollerith's system spread rapidly to other organizations in the United States and Europe. It was used for the 1900 U.S. Census as well. But, after 1900, the Census Bureau felt that Hollerith's devices were too expensive; as a result, it undertook its own research and development project. James Powers, a Census Bureau employee, developed his own version of punched card tabulating equipment, which he later marketed for his own company.

The emergence of this second organization in the tabulating field is very characteristic of our capitalist system of free enterprise. Of course, Hollerith did not think so; he felt that his patent was being infringed upon and a bitter patent fight resulted. Both men continued to develop their machines and a new industry began to emerge.

It is interesting to follow the careers of Hollerith and Powers, since they relate to the status of the current computational field. In 1911, Hollerith sold his company, the Tabulating Machine Company, to the Computing-Tabulating-Recording Company (C-T-R). In 1914, Thomas J. Watson became director of C-T-R, which in 1924 became the International Business Machines Corporation (IBM).

Powers' company was acquired by Remington Rand, which in 1955 became Sperry Rand. Even today, IBM and the Sperry-Univac division of Sperry Rand are vigorous competitors for the computer market.

2.6   DIGITAL COMPUTERS IN THE TWENTIETH CENTURY

2.6.1   Introduction

During the nineteenth century, Great Britain emerged as the most powerful nation in the world, politically, economically, and technologically. This was largely a result of the Industrial Revolution.

During the twentieth century, the United States emerged as the most powerful nation in the world politically, economically, and technologically. Similarly, this was a result of American industrialization.

The United States was seen as a leader in many technological fields, and the computational area was no exception. Adding machines, cash registers, and tabulating equipment became successful commercial products during the twentieth century.

2.6.2 Electromechanical Computers

But it was during and after World War II that the computing field, as we know it today, really began to take shape. There are several reasons why the 1940s was such a fruitful time for computing devices:

1. Wartime, in general, tends to be a particularly ripe period for invention. During a war, people and industry tend to focus on the needs of the country; this focus results in an emphasis on invention. Moreover, individuals and organizations are willing to subordinate their competitive instincts in a spirit of wartime cooperation.
2. The need for better computational equipment had grown over the past century. The needs of scientists who were working in the fields of astronomy, meteorology, and mathematics were most critical. During World War II many of these scientists were engaged in government work and made their needs known to government officials. The result was a series of computer projects, at various institutions, funded by the government.
3. Advances in radar, electronic counter, and vacuum-tube technology made the time particularly ripe for the development of electronic digital computers.

What resulted was a veritable revolution in the computing field. In 1938, there were no devices in existence that one would categorize as a computer. Twenty years later, there were hundreds of computer manufacturers and thousands of users clamoring for more machines.

As is the case in most revolutionary periods, the computer was not the idea of a single individual or the result of any one effort. Rather, there were numerous computer projects under development. Some were even begun before the onset of World War II.

> 1. Machine: Mark I
>   Institution: Harvard University
>   Designer: Howard Aiken
>   Dates: 1939–1944

In 1937, Howard Aiken, a mathematician at Harvard University, developed the idea for an electromechanical computer which used relays for completing circuits and adding to specific counters. He stated:

> There exist problems beyond our ability to solve, not because of theoretical difficulties, but because of insufficient means of mechanical computation.

In 1938, he was able to convince Thomas J. Watson, Sr., of IBM that his ideas were worth supporting. IBM provided funding and engineering support for this computer, which was begun in 1939 and completed in 1944 for Harvard University. Its official name was

"Automatic Sequence Controlled Calculator" but it later became known as the Mark I. Many of Babbage's original ideas for an Analytical Engine were incorporated in Aiken's design but, strangely enough, Aiken was not at the time even aware of Babbage's work. This is a case of independent invention approximately 100 years later.

> 2. Machines: Models I–V
> Institution: Bell Telephone Laboratories
> Designer: George R. Stibitz
> Dates: 1939–1946

These were really five electromechanical, relay computers for wartime use. Stibitz's machines used telephone relays for adding to specific counters. He, too, was unaware of Babbage's work.

At the same time that these devices were being built in the United States, there were similar developments in Europe. In Germany, Konrad Zuse, without any institutional support, constructed his own computers. Similarly, in Great Britain, there were several secret wartime projects for developing computers to decipher enemy codes.

Thus by the time that World War II was under way, there were numerous efforts already in progress. Most of these were electromechanical devices which used mechanical means for representing data and for counting.

Current computers are *electronic*, as opposed to electromechanical. Electromechanical devices, although much faster than previous desk calculators, are themselves significantly slower than electronic machines. Electronic computers initially made use of vacuum tubes, transistors, and then other solid-state components. Because there are no moving parts, these devices are faster and experience fewer breakdowns.

2.6.3 Electronic Computers

> 3. Machines: ENIAC and EDVAC
> Institution: Moore School of Electrical Engineering.
> University of Pennsylvania
> Designer: J. Presper Eckert and John Mauchly
> Dates: 1943–1946

The first U.S. electronic digital computer was undertaken in 1943 at the Moore School of Electrical Engineering of the University of Pennsylvania for the Army Ordnance Department. The machine was to compute range tables for the government's newly developed artillery. The contract was for $500,000, a decided bargain, even in those days.

J. Presper Eckert, Jr., was chief engineer and John Mauchly was

Figure 2.7. The ENIAC.

principal consultant on this project, called ENIAC, an acronym for Electronic Numerical Integrator and Computer.

The ENIAC, completed in 1946, was several times faster than any existing equipment. It contained 18,000 vacuum tubes, 30 panels, and occupied an entire room. By today's standards, it had one main deficiency: no stored-program concept. The instructions to the machine were entered by setting a series of external switches (see Figure 2.7).

Most texts and articles point to the ENIAC as the first electronic digital computer. Note, however, that no single invention is without its precursors or antecedents. The ENIAC is no exception.

John Mauchly, the man credited with the original idea for the ENIAC, was familiar with a research effort at Iowa State College under the direction of John V. Atanasoff to construct an electronic digital computer. Atanasoff's electronic machine was, however, special purpose, designed to solve some specific mathematical problems and was never really operational.

Despite the obvious differences between Atanasoff's work and Mauchly's, many have attempted to claim that Atanasoff, and not Mauchly, was the actual inventor of the first U.S. electronic digital computer. A 1973 court case[1] held that the ENIAC patent was invalid because of, among other things, the existence of Atanasoff's works.

Such claims are not really valid if one realizes that *all* inventions have, in some sense, precursors. The actual construction of an opera-

---

[1] *Honeywell* v. *Sperry Rand.*

tional device, along with the ability to convince some financial supporters of its significance, are really two important criteria for judging priority. Mauchly, with Eckert and others at the Moore School, was able to construct a working computer and Atanasoff was not.

2.6.4   The Stored-Program Concept

The stored-program concept was conceived of, and developed by, the Moore School staff. The same engineers and scientists who developed the ENIAC recognized that the setting of external switches for issuing instructions was slow and inefficient. Eckert and Mauchly and their associates developed the idea in 1944, and received another government contract for a machine called EDVAC to incorporate the stored-program concept. John von Neumann, one of the United States' most prestigious mathematicians, provided the logical design theory for this concept. Instructions were to be entered into a computer, like data, and were to occupy storage positions like data.

See Table 2.4 for a summary of these early modern digital computers.

Beginning in 1946, after the war was over, several other institutions undertook stored-program computer projects. Mauchly and Eckert left the Moore School to form their own company to build UNIVACs for

Table 2.4.   *Early Digital Computers.*

Computer	Where Developed	Pioneers	Dates	Features
MARK I	Harvard Computation Laboratory (IBM-supported project)	Howard Aiken	1939–1944	Electromechanical computer; not stored-program
RELAY COMPUTER MOD I	Bell Telephone Laboratories	George Stibitz and Sam Williams	1939–1943	Electromechanical computer
ABC COMPUTER	Iowa State College	John Vincent Atanasoff and Clifford Berry	1939–1942	Electronic vacuum-tube computer; special-purpose; never completed
ENIAC	Moore School of Electrical Engineering, University of Pennsylvania	John Mauchly and J. Presper Eckert	1943–1946	First operational electronic digital computer; programmable by manual setting of switches
EDVAC	Moore School of Electrical Engineering, University of Pennsylvania	Begun by Mauchly and Eckert (they left to build UNIVACs for commercial use)	1944–1951	First electronic digital computer designed to have stored-program capability

the government and for business. The UNIVAC, an acronym for Universal Automatic Computer, was the first commercial computer. Von Neumann returned to the Institute for Advanced Study in Princeton, New Jersey, where he and his associates built a stored-program computer. That computer became the prototype for several other academic computers.

The Moore School ran a series of lecture courses on computers for government, academic, and commercial organizations, as well as for representatives from European countries.

Thus, by 1950, the computer field had spread to Europe and to a wide variety of governmental, academic, and small commercial institutions in the United States as well. In 1950, the Eckert-Mauchly Computer Corporation was in financial difficulty and was acquired by the Remington Rand Company, which as the result of a merger became Sperry Rand.

With the entrance of Remington Rand into the computer field in the early 1950s, the era of the large computer corporation began. In just a few years, IBM, NCR, Burroughs, and GE, to name a few, became actively involved in the design and construction of electronic digital computers. By 1955, a multimillion-dollar industry had emerged. See Figure 2.8 for an illustration of total computer expenditures in the United States in the last 15 years.

Electronic digital computer technology is best described as a series of generations. See Table 2.5 for a full description. Figure 2.9 illustrates the components that have been used in computers. The

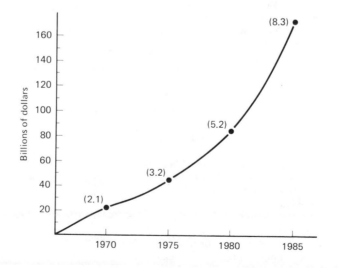

Figure 2.8. Total computer expenditures in the United States. Numbers in parentheses represent percent of gross national product.

Table 2.5. *Characteristics of the Various Computer Generations.*

	First Generation (1951–1958)	Second Generation (1958–1964)	Third Generation (1964–1971)	Fourth Generation (1971–)
Technology	Vacuum tubes; mercury delay lines; card-oriented	Transistors; tape-oriented	Integrated circuits; time-sharing; disk-oriented	Very large scale integrated circuits; bubble memory; charge-coupled devices; mini-computer-oriented
Operation time	Milliseconds (thousandths of a second)	Microseconds (millionths of a second)	Nanoseconds (billionths of a second)	Nanoseconds or picoseconds (trillionths of a second)
Cost	$5/function	$0.50/function	$0.05/function	$0.01 to $0.0001/function
Processing speed	2000 instructions/second	1 million instructions/second	10 million instructions/second	100 million to 1 billion instructions/second
Memory size (bytes)	1000–4000	4000–32,000	32,000–3,000,000	3,000,000+
Mean time between failures	Minutes–hours	Days	Days–weeks	Weeks
Auxiliary units	Punched card-oriented	Tape-oriented	Disk-oriented	Disk and mass storage

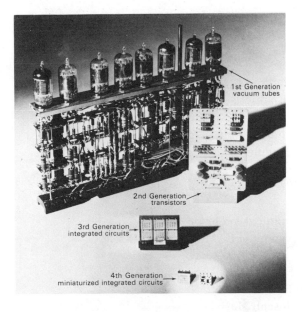

Figure 2.9. Components that have been used in computers.

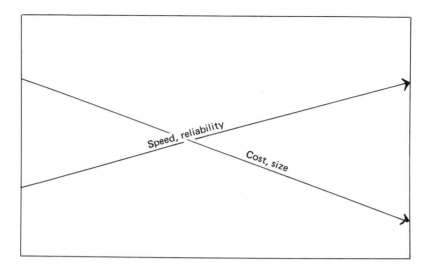

Figure 2.10. Current trends in computer technology.

technical features of third- and fourth-generation computers are considered in detail in Chapter 3.

See Figure 2.10 for an illustration of the current trends in computer technology.

KEY TERMS

Abacus
Aiken, Howard
Analytical Engine
Atanasoff, John
Babbage, Charles
Difference Engine
Digital computer
Eckert, J. Presper, Jr.
EDVAC
Electromechanical computer
Electronic computer
ENIAC
Hollerith, Herman
Industrial Revolution
Jacquard, Joseph Marie
Leibniz, Gottfried

Lovelace, Augusta Ada
Mark I
Mauchly, John
Pascal, Blaise
Powers, James
Scientific Revolution
Stibitz, George
Stored program concept
von Neumann, John

REVIEW QUESTIONS

1. How did the Scientific Revolution lead to an increased interest in computation and computational devices?
2. Although both Pascal and Leibniz were successful in designing calculators in the seventeenth century, why were they unable to convince society that a need existed?
3. How do the pessimistic and optimistic views of the Industrial Revolution relate to the issues surrounding computer development today?
4. How does Jacquard's weaving loom attachment have significance relative to the computing field?
5. Why is Charles Babbage considered the father of the modern computer?
6. Why is Herman Hollerith important in the history of computing?
7. Why was the period of the 1940s especially conducive to the development of computers?
8. What is the major difference between an electromechanical computer and an electronic computer?
9. What are the major characteristics of the various generations of computers?

DISCUSSION QUESTIONS

1. What is the relevance of historical study?
2. Indicate some of the reasons why the modern approach to scientific study did not really take shape until the seventeenth century.
3. What aspects of American society make it particularly ripe for technological advance?
4. In what ways do wars foster technological development? Can you think of some arguments for the position that wars inhibit rather than foster technological development?
5. The legal issues relating to the invention of the first electronic digital computer have been provided in this chapter. What criteria would you use for determining priority?
6. There is the so-called "serendipity" theory of invention, which indicates

that luck or chance plays a large role in invention. There is another theory that underplays the importance of chance by stating that "chance favors the prepared mind." Which theory do you think is closer to the "truth"? Explain your answer.

7.   Do you think that technological developments occur in an *evolutionary* fashion, where one invention builds on the next, and so on? Or do you think that there are *revolutions* in technology where a class of inventions that have developed in an evolutionary fashion are rendered obsolete by a revolutionary change that causes a totally different class of inventions to become relevant?

8.   Scientists have been, as a group, relatively uninterested in the history of their subject. Can you explain why this is so?

9.   Do you think it is important for professionals in *any field* to understand the historical roots of their profession? Explain your answer. What about the importance of history for the computer professional specifically?

10.   There is evidence to suggest that the United States' faith in technology has been waning in recent years. Can you explain why and hypothesize on some of the possible consequences of this change in attitude?

11.   The following is an excerpt from a Reader Response to *Interface*, a computer journal.[1] ACM is an abbreviation for the Association for Computing Machinery, the largest computing organization:

> Granted, ACM suggests a course on the impact of computers on society, but we disagree with the suggested contents. Computers have revolutionized our society. So, exactly so, did cars, electricity, steam engines, paper and movable type, the wheel. . . . The impact of computers on society can be better assessed, scaled down and, more important, controlled, if the college graduates of the 80's are made aware of how, exactly how, similar revolutionary impacts of the past became taken-for-granted routine in our lives. As an amusement, the ACM proposed elective topic on "futurists view of computing" may be as appealing as science fiction. The best way to look into the future is, however, quite often to look critically, knowledgeably and comparatively at the past.

Summary and Conclusion

I believe that Mathematics, Engineering and Computer Science should neither clash against each other nor diverge and lose contact. Their strength and growth are enhanced by mutual influence and stimulation.

For a computer expert to help as such in the shaping of human individual and community life in the future, liberal arts training

[1]J. M. S. Simoes-Pereira, A Reader Response, Computer Engineering Corner, Harold S. Stone, *Interface, The Computer Education Quarterly*, Vol. 2, No. 1, Mar. 1980, p. 14.

or background is already a must. Particularly important is the awareness of historical or societal phenomena similar to, or related with, the impact of the computer in our lives. Important also, is the less traditional field of Operations Research where, however, many traditional scientific approaches are used well along with other new, less orthodox ones. Operations Research deals with the study of complex systems; firstly, the computer itself is a system and secondly, it is a tool to study systems, including itself.

J. M. S. SIMÕES-PEREIRA
CUNY-Hunter College & Graduate Center
and University of Coimbra,
Portugal

a. Indicate in your own words the point of view expressed by the author.
b. Do you agree or disagree with the author's points?

3

Computer concepts

3.1 THE COMPUTER SYSTEM

Each computer installation consists of a series of devices, which together operate as an integrated unit or **computer system**. Each computer system consists of separate machines that include the following:

Elements of a Computer System

1. **Input units**: read input data and transmit it to the central processing unit
2. **Central processing unit (CPU)**: controls all operations of the computer system; provides primary storage
3. **Auxiliary or secondary storage units**: provide auxiliary storage to augment primary storage
4. **Output units**: transmit processed data from the CPU to output form

---

The schematic in Figure 3.1 illustrates the integration of the basic elements in a computer system. See Figure 3.2 for an illustration of a typical computer system.

Note that a computer system consists of a series of independent machines or **hardware** that functions in an integrated manner to produce desired output. Note, too, that computer systems have a wide variety of input/output (I/O) devices which can be hooked up to the **mainframe** or CPU.

In this chapter we discuss the basic characteristics of a computer system. Keep in mind that in order to process data at any given time, a computer system must be under the control of a **program**, a set of instructions indicating which units are to be used and precisely how

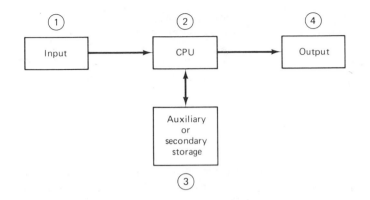

Figure 3.1. The basic elements in a computer system.

the data is to be processed. This program, written by a programmer, is read into the CPU.

The objectives of this chapter are to familiarize the student with:

1. The elements of a computer system
2. How computers operate on input data to produce output
3. Various methods for processing data

Figure 3.2. Typical computer system.

4. How data is represented internally within a computer
5. The technological features of a computer system

Do not become overconcerned about the many terms discussed; each of them will be redefined, reinforced, and expanded in subsequent chapters.

3.1.1 Input Units

Each input unit of a computer system reads data from a specific form and converts it into electrical pulses. It then transmits these pulses to an input area in the CPU. A card reader, for example, is an input unit that reads punched cards, converts the holes sensed to pulses, and transmits the pulses to an input storage area in the CPU. There are, of course, many other input units that can perform the same electrical conversions and transmissions with other forms of input.

Chapter 4 considers in depth the input units shown in Figure 3.3.

Each of these devices has its own features but they all are capable of reading a form of input called an **input medium** and transmitting it to the CPU.

3.1.2   Output Units

Each output unit of a computer system transmits information from the CPU and converts the electrical pulses to an appropriate output form. A printer, for example, is an output unit that transmits output from the CPU and converts it to a printed form. There are, of course, many other output devices that can perform the same electrical transmissions and conversions to produce other **output media**: in Chapter 4 we discuss the devices in Figure 3.4 which can serve as output units. You will note that some computer media can serve as both input from and output to a computer system. Figure 3.5 illustrates some of these devices in operation.

Figure 3.6 is the same as Figure 3.2, but in addition to illustrating a full computer system, it includes the names of the various devices.

3.1.3   The Central Processing Unit

The **central processing unit** (CPU) is the physical device that controls the computer operations. It is the "brains" of the computer system. Each program specifies the functions required for a particular problem.

Device	Form of input	Description

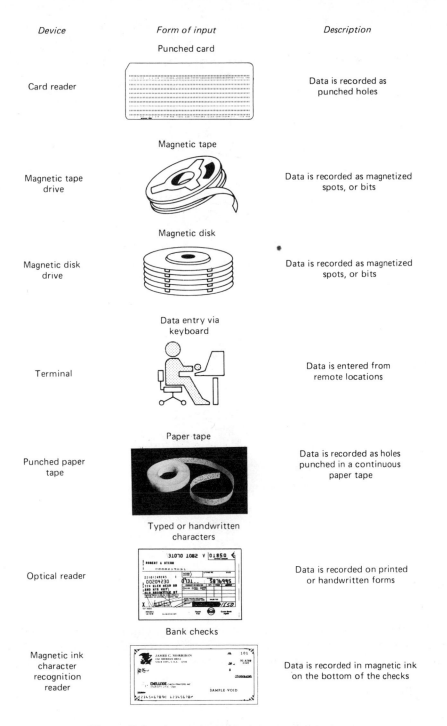

	Punched card	
Card reader		Data is recorded as punched holes
	Magnetic tape	
Magnetic tape drive		Data is recorded as magnetized spots, or bits
	Magnetic disk	
Magnetic disk drive		Data is recorded as magnetized spots, or bits
	Data entry via keyboard	
Terminal		Data is entered from remote locations
	Paper tape	
Punched paper tape		Data is recorded as holes punched in a continuous paper tape
	Typed or handwritten characters	
Optical reader		Data is recorded on printed or handwritten forms
	Bank checks	
Magnetic ink character recognition reader		Data is recorded in magnetic ink on the bottom of the checks

Figure 3.3. Input devices of a computer system.

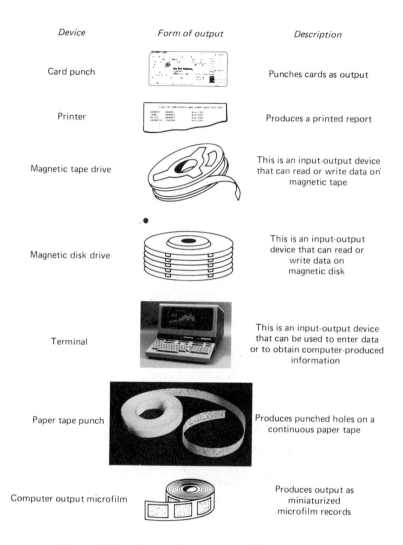

Device	Form of output	Description
Card punch		Punches cards as output
Printer		Produces a printed report
Magnetic tape drive		This is an input-output device that can read or write data on magnetic tape
Magnetic disk drive		This is an input-output device that can read or write data on magnetic disk
Terminal		This is an input-output device that can be used to enter data or to obtain computer-produced information
Paper tape punch		Produces punched holes on a continuous paper tape
Computer output microfilm		Produces output as miniaturized microfilm records

Figure 3.4. Output devices of a computer system.

All operations performed by the computer system are controlled by the central processing unit. The CPU is connected by cable to each of the input/output devices and can control the I/O operations of each.

Thus the CPU controls:

1. The reading of input from an input device
2. The processing of that input data
3. The writing of output using one of the computer output devices

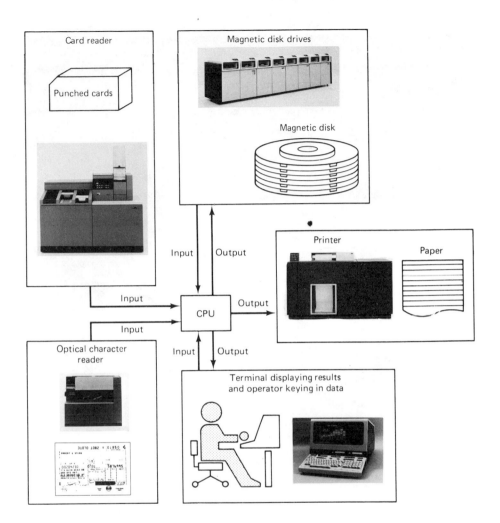

Figure 3.5. Some examples of input and output devices.

3.1.3.1 *Operations Performed by the CPU*

The operations performed by the CPU can be categorized as follows:

Operations Performed by CPU

Input
Data transfer ⎫
Arithmetic   ⎬ Processing
Logic   ⎭
Output

Figure 3.6. Devices of a typical computer system.

These operations are performed as called for by the programmer's instructions.

a. *Input Operation.* An **input operation** is one that signals an input device to read data; it then automatically transmits that data to the central processing unit. That is, each program provides an area of computer storage within the CPU to hold an input record. Thus input operations perform two functions:

Input Operations
1. Cause an input device to physically *read* the data.
2. *Transmit* the data from the input device to an input area of the CPU.

b. *Processing Operations.* Data transfer, arithmetic, and logic operations are **processing functions** that operate on the input data. These are the *only* operations that a computer can perform.

For information to be written, it must appear in an output area within the CPU that is set up by each program. The **data transfer operation** can, for example, *move* data from the input area to the output area. The **arithmetic operations** can add, multiply, subtract, and divide fields. The **logic operations** can test or perform simple decisions such as: Is one field less than, equal to, or greater than another?

    c. *Output Operation.*   An **output operation** causes information to be transmitted from the output area, provided for by each program, to an output device, where it is then written out or recorded.

In short, each program that is read into the CPU generally provides for the following:

Summary: Operations Performed by the CPU

1. Input
   a. Data is read by an input device.
   b. Input data is transmitted to the CPU for processing.
2. Processing
   a. Data can be transferred from one area to another.
   b. Data can be added, subtracted, multiplied, and divided.
   c. Logical tests can be performed on the data.
3. Output
   a. Information is transmitted from the CPU to an output device.
   b. Information is written by the output device.

3.1.3.2   *Elements of the Central Processing Unit*

The central processing unit is composed of three sections:

Sections of CPU

1. Primary storage
2. Control
3. Arithmetic-logic

---

    a. *Primary Storage.*   The **primary storage** section within the CPU contains the stored program. The program, you will recall, consists of the set of instructions necessary to read input data and convert it to output. Thus if a program reads card data and converts it to printed output, storage areas will be required for the instructions, plus a storage area for card data and a storage area for accumulating the print output.

Instructions, as well as input/output areas, occupy storage positions. Each element of an instruction or element of data is placed in a storage position which is identified by an **address**. On most computers, each address can hold a single character, such as a letter or a digit. Whereas the addresses remain constant, the contents of the addresses vary depending on the data or the instruction. A storage position is typically referred to as a **byte**.

The primary storage capacity of very small computers ranges from as few as 4000 bytes or characters to as high as 256,000 bytes. Small computer systems range from approximately 32,000 bytes to 512,000 bytes, with large-scale computers possessing a primary storage capacity well in excess of 1 million bytes; 1 million bytes is called a **megabyte** of storage.

Thus on average- or medium-sized computers, we can have programs with thousands of instructions, in addition to many input/output areas. The notation K is often used as an abbreviation for approximately 1000 storage positions (actually 1024 bytes). Thus one can say that small computers possess primary storage capacity of from 32K to 512K.

b. *Control.*   The control unit of the CPU supervises or monitors the functions performed by the entire computer system. A special program called a **supervisor** is responsible for controlling the operations of the system. This supervisor calls in each application program and integrates the processing of each step. Instructions in each program are transferred, one at a time, to the control unit. The circuitry in the control unit in turn interprets and executes the instructions.

c. *Arithmetic-Logic Unit.*   Whenever the computer performs arithmetic operations or makes a comparison, the CPU activates the arithmetic-logic section. Special accumulators, or **registers**, necessary for performing arithmetic operations are located in this unit. These registers are internal areas used to temporarily hold data that is being processed.

Logic operations are performed on a computer by a series of comparisons activated by this unit. Electronic circuits called **gates**

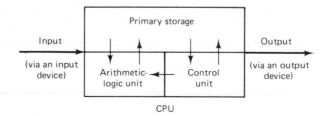

Figure 3.7.   Basic components of a CPU.

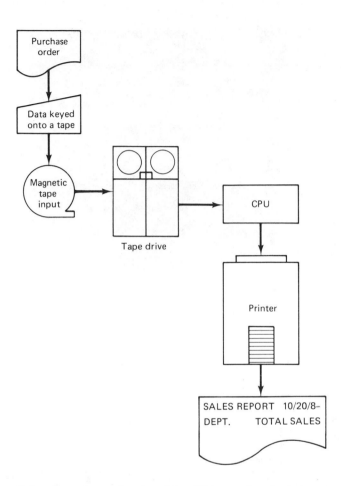

Figure 3.8. Sample application. The CPU contains the program that reads the purchase order data from magnetic tape, processes the data, and produces a sales report by department.

can direct the path taken by a computer program. Depending on whether an item being tested is less than, equal to, or greater than another value, specific gates or circuits are opened or closed.

Figure 3.7 illustrates the basic CPU components. Figure 3.8 provides a sample application.

3.1.4 Auxiliary Storage Units

The total storage of a computer system is called its **memory size**. Often, the memory size required is too large to be completely housed in the CPU. In such a case, auxiliary or secondary storage devices, linked by cables to the CPU, are used for supplemental storage. Auxiliary

Figure 3.9. Mass storage device. Each cartridge holds 50 million bytes of data.

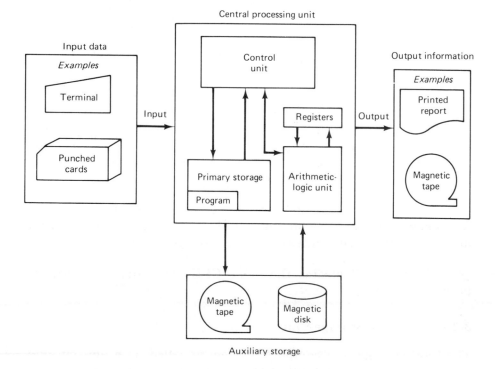

Figure 3.10. Computer system illustration.

storage units are usually provided on tape or disk drives or on a magnetic drum.

Primary storage provides high-speed access of data for CPU processing. But such storage is very expensive. Disk storage is frequently used to supplement primary storage, but disks are limited in terms of the amount of data that can be stored.

Mass storage devices have been developed that can greatly enhance the memory capacity of a computer system. Many different types of mass storage devices are available. See Figure 3.9 for an illustration of an IBM mass storage device.

When an auxiliary storage device is linked to the CPU for supplemental storage, the CPU itself maintains control. That is, there is no need for the programmer to keep track of whether instructions or data are in primary or auxiliary storage.

Figure 3.10 illustrates a computer system in operation.

Summary: Computer System

1. Input Devices
   Examples: Card reader
               Terminal
               Magnetic tape drive
               Magnetic disk drive
2. Central processing unit (CPU) or mainframe
   a. Primary storage: consists of addressable locations; memory size—the number of addressable locations, is described in terms of K (1000's of locations or **bytes**) or **megabytes** (millions of bytes)
   b. Control unit: provides central control for the CPU
   c. Arithmetic-logic unit: performs all arithmetic and logical control operations with the use of registers
3. Auxiliary storage
   a. Provides additional memory for processing
   b. Linked to CPU
   c. Usually on magnetic tape, disk, or a mass storage device
4. Output units
   Examples: Card punch
               Printer
               Terminal
               Magnetic tape drive
               Magnetic disk drive

3.2   Methods of Processing Data

3.2.1   Batch Processing

With this method, data is entered into the information flow in large volumes, or batches. That is, the processing by computer is performed periodically, at specified time intervals (weekly, monthly, etc.) when large volumes are accumulated. Daily accounts receivable tickets, for example, may be **batch processed** on a weekly basis. Instead of being processed as they are received, the tickets are processed periodically when a sufficient volume has been accumulated.

There are several inherent disadvantages to batch processing. The system that utilizes batch processing is not especially timely, since it takes a fixed time interval before current data is added. That is, the main or master accounts receivable file, in our example, does not contain the current accounts receivable data for a full week. For this reason, a system that utilizes batch processing cannot effectively answer inquiries *between* processing intervals. The accounts receivable file in our example is only current on the day of the processing cycle; after that, current data will not be processed until the following week's run.

3.2.2   On-line Processing

Batch operations as described above frequently process data that has been punched into cards or coded on magnetic tape. This data is then transported to the CPU, where it is processed.

Sometimes, however, the physical transportation of data in this way is too time consuming. Moreover, data can be lost or misplaced. It is more efficient, in some instances, to use terminals at the point where the data is generated. The terminals are connected directly to the CPU. As transactions are made, the data is recorded using the terminal. That data is then directly transmitted to the CPU, typically by telephone lines or cables.

An **on-line** operation, then, is one that uses devices directly connected to the CPU either for data entry or inquiry purposes. That is, with a terminal we can either enter data, as described above, or inquire about the status of a record or file that is stored by the computer.

3.2.3   Real-Time Processing

We have seen that on-line processing can be used for entering data from a terminal. That data can update a file at a later time in batch mode or immediately upon entry. If the processing of data is done immediately, this is a real-time operation.

Airline reservation systems, for example, require immediate processing. Each time a ticket is issued or canceled, or a plane's schedule is altered, the data must be immediately entered into a computer, processed, and made available.

Batch Processing

1. Periodic processing.
2. Input data usually sequenced.

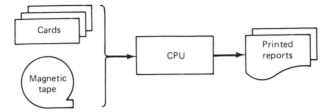

On-line Processing

1. Input can be entered at point of transaction.
2. Input data usually not sequenced.
3. Responses to inquiries can be made immediately.

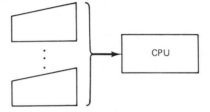

Numerous on-line input stations

Real-Time Processing

1. Immediate processing of data entered.
2. Results can be produced quickly enough to affect decision making.

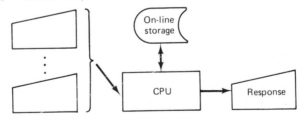

Numerous on-line input stations

Figure 3.11. Comparison of batch processing, on-line processing, and real-time processing.

Such systems utilize devices that can be manually activated, that have immediate access to a computer, and that instantaneously receive messages. This form of processing usually uses terminals linked to a CPU via telecommunication lines and is called **real-time processing**. We discuss this further in Chapter 12. Figure 3.11 shows a comparison of batch processing, on-line processing, and real-time processing.

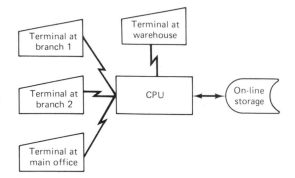

Figure 3.12. Real-time inventory system.

Thus when an on-line computer system operates quickly enough to facilitate the decision-making process in an organization, we call it a **real-time system**. For example, if an inventory system that functions on-line allows us to obtain the correct status of an item at any time and distribute products or write purchase orders accordingly, we call it a real-time system (see Figure 3.12).

3.2.4 Off-line Operations for Future Batch Processing

Computer processing is, without question, expensive. Thus any operation that can avoid inefficient utilization of computer equipment can save a company a great deal of money. **Off-line processing** is the processing of data that is *not* directly under the control of the main CPU.

A terminal may, for example, be used for keying data *not* directly into the CPU but onto a small cassette tape or a small magnetic disk called a floppy disk. At the end of the day, or at any fixed interval, the tape or disk is then entered, at high speeds and in batch mode, to the CPU. The key-to-tape or key-to-disk operation is called an *off-line* process; it is used for data entry. This data is then batched for reading by the CPU at a future date.

We noted in Chapter 1 that minicomputers have become very important tools and are used for a wide variety of applications. One area where minis are frequently used is to facilitate an off-line procedure. That is, numerous terminal devices may be linked to a minicomputer, which produces output on a tape or disk, for example, and in addition validates the data to minimize errors, formats it so that it can be processed quickly, sorts it into sequence if necessary, and so on. Then the tape or disk can be entered, at high speeds, into a main computer system in a batch mode. The minicomputer would, then, be controlling an off-line procedure (see Figure 3.13). Some terminals are themselves capable of maintaining data in a buffer area off-line.

In Chapter 6 we focus on the various types and sizes of computer systems, and pay particular attention to the increasing use of minicomputers either to replace large-scale systems or, as in Figure 3.13, to assist or supplement them.

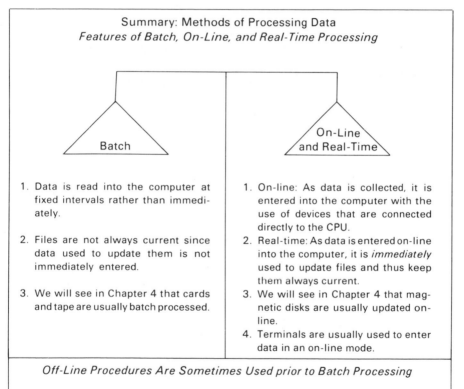

Summary: Methods of Processing Data
Features of Batch, On-Line, and Real-Time Processing

Batch

1. Data is read into the computer at fixed intervals rather than immediately.

2. Files are not always current since data used to update them is not immediately entered.

3. We will see in Chapter 4 that cards and tape are usually batch processed.

On-Line and Real-Time

1. On-line: As data is collected, it is entered into the computer with the use of devices that are connected directly to the CPU.

2. Real-time: As data is entered on-line into the computer, it is *immediately* used to update files and thus keep them always current.

3. We will see in Chapter 4 that magnetic disks are usually updated on-line.

4. Terminals are usually used to enter data in an on-line mode.

Off-Line Procedures Are Sometimes Used prior to Batch Processing

1. Data is entered via a terminal or other device, but does not go directly to the main CPU.
2. Instead, the data is placed on a high-speed medium such as tape or disk for future processing.
3. Since this operation is not itself under the control of the main CPU, it is called an off-line procedure.
4. Data that has been collected off-line is usually entered, at a later date, into the computer in batch mode.
5. Minicomputers are frequently used for off-line procedures for formatting, editing, and verifying data before it enters the main CPU.

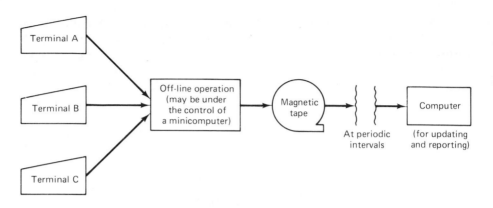

Figure 3.13. Off-line operation for future batch processing.

3.3 INTRODUCTION TO COMPUTER TECHNOLOGY

3.3.1 Data Representation

People commonly communicate with one another using words that consist of letters of the alphabet (A through Z), digits (0 through 9), and special symbols such as $, ., and -. Computers are capable of reading such symbols into primary storage, but this data must be converted into a form that permits high-speed internal processing.

All computers use some variation of the **binary numbering system** for representing every character, where a character is defined as a letter, digit, or special symbol.

In the binary numbering system, there are only two possible digits: 0 and 1. This is ideal for computer processing because the "1" is used to denote the presence of an electrical pulse or signal in the computer circuitry, and a "0" is used to denote the absence of such a signal. See Figure 3.14 for an illustration of how the computer utilizes the binary numbering system.

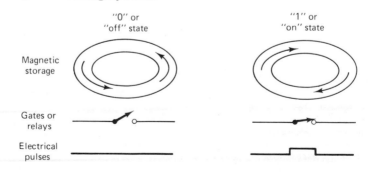

Figure 3.14. Binary representation as used in computers.

We begin by considering how binary and decimal numbers can be converted one to the other. Then we focus on how the computer actually represents characters internally, using a form of binary representation.

3.3.1.1 *Binary Representation*

You will recall that the decimal or base 10 system has the following positional values:

...	10^3	10^2	10^1	10^0	Exponential Value of Position
	1000	100	10	1	Decimal Value of Position

A 1 in the second position and a 0 in the units position (10) is the number after 9. When there are no more single digits, we proceed to the next position, initializing the first position with 0.

Since this system has a base 10, each position has a value that is a factor of 10. The first position is 10^0 or 1, the second is 10^1 or 10, . . ., and the seventh position is 10^6 or 1,000,000.

The binary numbering system has a base of 2. Thus each position has a value that is a factor of 2. We have, then:

...	2^4	2^3	2^2	2^1	2^0	Exponential Value of Position
	16	8	4	2	1	Decimal Value of Position

You will recall that any number raised to the zero power is 1; 2^1 is 2; 2^2 is 2×2 or 4; 2^3 is $2 \times 2 \times 2$ or 8, and so on.

The two binary digits are 0 and 1. To represent the number 2 we must use the position next to the units position. Thus 10 in binary is 2 in decimal. That is:

```
    2 │ 1   ← Decimal Value of Position
   ───────
    1 │ 0   ← Binary Number
    │   └────────→ 0 × 1 = 0
    └────────────→ 1 × 2 = 2
                          ─
                   2   Decimal Equivalent
```

Thus $10_2 = 2_{10}$ (10 in base 2 = 2 in base 10).

A 3 would be 11; to represent a 4 we must initialize these two first positions and place a 1 in the third position. Thus 100 in binary is a 4 in decimal. A 5 would be 101. Notice that the sequence is 0, 1; then proceed to the next position and initialize (10, 11, 100, and so on).

Binary	Decimal
0	0
1	1
10	2
11	3
100	4
101	5
110	6
111	7
1000	8
.	.
.	.
.	.

Thus using a variation of the binary numbering system, the computer can represent *any* decimal number using a series of on-off circuits, where "on" denotes a binary 1 and "off" denotes a binary 0.

3.3.1.2   *Determining the Decimal Equivalent of a Binary Number*

All positional numbering systems have similar structures. To obtain the decimal equivalent of a number in any base, multiply the digits by their positional values and add the results.

Example 1: $1001_2 = (?)_{10}$.

Find the decimal equivalent of 1001 in binary (represented as 1001_2, where the subscript denotes the base).

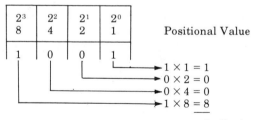

9   Decimal Equivalent

Thus $1001_2 = 9_{10}$. We can simplify this calculation by eliminating all multiplications in which 0 is a factor. Thus we have

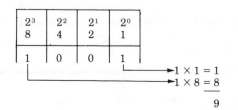

9

In short, the binary digit 8 and the binary digit 1 are "on," the others are "off." That is, the 8-bit and the 1-bit are on, where **bit** is an abbreviation for *bi*nary dig*it*.

Example 2: $1110_2 = (?)_{10}$.

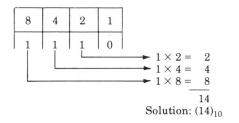

Solution: $(14)_{10}$

Example 3: $11101_2 = (?)_{10}$.

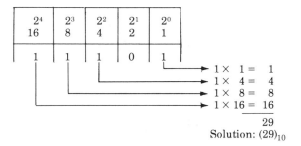

Solution: $(29)_{10}$

Thus, given any binary number, we can find its decimal equivalent by the following technique.

Given Binary Number—Find Decimal Equivalent

1. Determine the positional value of each digit.
2. Add the positional values for all positions that contain a 1.

3.3.1.3   *Determining the Binary Equivalent of a Decimal Number*

Thus far, we have some idea of the way in which binary numbers are converted to decimal numbers. In this section we will learn the manner in which the binary equivalent of a decimal number may be determined.

This conversion process is a relatively simple task when small numbers are used. That is, we merely employ the positional values of binary numbers to find the right combination of digits.

Example 1: $10_{10} = (?)_2$.

This example concerns itself with determining what combination of 1, 2, 4, 8, 16, 32, . . . will equal 10.

It is clear that we do not need to use more than four binary digits to represent 10_{10}, since the fifth positional value is 16, which is greater than 10_{10}. Hence we must determine what combination of 8, 4, 2, 1 will equal 10.

There is only one such combination. The numbers $8 + 2 = 10$. Thus our binary equivalent is

8	4	2	1
1	0	1	0

In order to represent the decimal number 10 in binary form, the 8-bit and the 2-bit are on, whereas the others are off.

Thus $10_{10} = 1010_2$.

Example 2: $(14)_{10} = (?)_2$.

Here, again, we use four binary digits since the next position has value 16, which exceeds the required quantity. Again, we must determine what combination of 8, 4, 2, 1 will produce 14.

There is only one such combination: 8, 4, 2 bits are on $(8 + 4 + 2 = 14)$, whereas the 1-bit is off.

Thus $(14)_{10} = (1110)_2$.

Example 3: $(23)_{10} = (?)_2$.

Here we must use a combination of the numbers 16, 8, 4, 2, 1 that will produce 23. We must determine which bits are "on." The 16-bit must be on, since 8, 4, 2, 1 bits can produce a maximum decimal number of 15. Thus the 16-bit must be on to obtain a number larger than 15. The 8-bit is off since 16-8 produces 24, which exceeds the required number. Thus the 16-4-2-1 bits are on and only the 8-bit is off. We have, then,

$$(23)_{10} = (10111)_2$$

This method of determining the combination of positional values that produces the required number is useful only with small numbers. Consider the task of finding the combination of binary numbers for the decimal number 1087, for example. In short, the method described above is too cumbersome for larger decimal numbers.

3.3.1.4   Representation of Characters in Storage

We have seen that through a combination of on-off pulses, it is possible to represent any decimal digit. These on-off pulses are called **bits**, which is an abbreviation for *binary digits*.

Table 3.1. *The Binary Equivalent of Decimal Digits 0 through 9.*

Decimal Equivalent	Bits			
	Place Value			
	8	*4*	*2*	*1*
0	0	0	0	0
1	0	0	0	1
2	0	0	1	0
3	0	0	1	1
4	0	1	0	0
5	0	1	0	1
6	0	1	1	0
7	0	1	1	1
8	1	0	0	0
9	1	0	0	1

Note that if each storage position, or byte, contained 4 digit bits, representing the decimal numbers 8-4-2-1, it would be possible to represent any of the decimal digits 0 through 9. See Table 3.1 for an illustration.

Most computers use 4 digit bits to represent each decimal digit. Since 4 bits can represent numbers 0 through 15, this code is referred to as the **hexadecimal**, or base 16, **code**.

In short, 4 bits in each byte are used to represent numbers. An "on" bit means that an electric pulse is "on" and an "off" bit means that no current is present.

But what about the representation of alphabetic characters or special symbols? How can they be represented using binary digits or bits? To accommodate these characters, the computer frequently uses an 8-bit code:

The 4 leftmost bits are called **zone** bits.
The 4 rightmost bits are called **digit** bits.

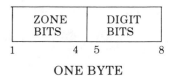

ONE BYTE

Thus each storage position or byte consists of 8 bits; 4 are used for zone representation and 4 are used for digit representation. A commonly used code is called EBCDIC (for Extended Binary Coded Decimal Interchange Code). See Table 3.2 for an illustration of this code. Figure 3.15 provides an example of how this code might be used to represent data in storage.

Table 3.2. *EBCDIC Representation: A through Z; 0 through 9.*

Character	EBCDIC Bit Configuration		Character	EBCDIC Bit Configuration	
A	1100	0001	S	1110	0010
B	1100	0010	T	1110	0011
C	1100	0011	U	1110	0100
D	1100	0100	V	1110	0101
E	1100	0101	W	1110	0110
F	1100	0110	X	1110	0111
G	1100	0111	Y	1110	1000
H	1100	1000	Z	1110	1001
I	1100	1001	0	1111	0000
J	1101	0001	1	1111	0001
K	1101	0010	2	1111	0010
L	1101	0011	3	1111	0011
M	1101	0100	4	1111	0100
N	1101	0101	5	1111	0101
O	1101	0110	6	1111	0110
P	1101	0111	7	1111	0111
Q	1101	1000	8	1111	1000
R	1101	1001	9	1111	1001

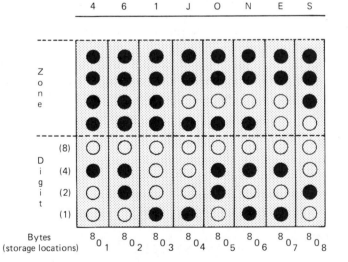

Figure 3.15. Representing the characters "461JONES" in 8 bytes of storage using the 8-bit EBCDIC code.

EBCDIC is not the only computer code, although it is used by many computers. BCD (binary-coded decimal) is an older code that uses 6 bits for internal computer representation. ASCII (for American Standard Code for Information Interchange) is another common computer code. Some computers and terminals use a 7-bit ASCII code; others use an 8-bit ASCII code similar to EBCDIC. In all cases, the code consists of the use of the binary digits 0 and 1 to represent characters.

Summary: Data Representation

1. Computers use some form of the binary numbering system:
   a. Use of 0 and 1 to represent all characters.
   b. 0 = "off" state.
   c. 1 = "on" state.
2. All decimal numbers can be converted to binary and binary numbers can be used to represent any decimal number.
3. Computers frequently use 8 binary digits, called bits, to represent all characters:
   a. Each byte consists of 8 bits: 4 bits for zone, and 4 bits for the digits 8-4-2-1.
   b. Because the 4 bits 8-4-2-1 can represent the numbers 0 through 15, this code is referred to as the hexadecimal, or base 16, code.
4. Computer codes:
   a. EBCDIC: Extended Binary Coded Decimal Interchange Code.
   b. ASCII: American Standard Code for Information Interchange (may be 7- or 8-bit code).

3.3.2   Types of CPU Memory

3.3.2.1   *Magnetic Core Memory*

Some CPUs use **magnetic cores** to represent data or instructions in memory. A magnetic core is a tiny doughnut-shaped ferrite element about the size of a grain of salt.

A magnetic core can be magnetized in one of two directions—clockwise and counterclockwise. A core that is magnetized in the clockwise direction is said to be "on" and a core magnetized in a counterclockwise direction is said to be "off." "On" cores represent the binary digit 1 and "off" cores represent the binary digit 0. Planes or groups of cores are stacked to form binary digits that represent all characters in memory, usually 8 binary digits (bits) to one storage position (byte) (see Figure 3.16).

3.3.2.2   *Integrated Circuits*

In most modern computers, core memories have been largely replaced by integrated circuits. Integrated circuits consist of hundreds of electronic components on a thin silicon wafer. Current flowing

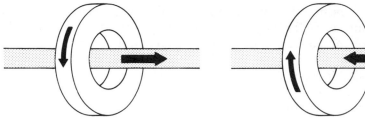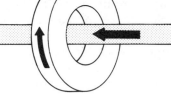

(a)   (b)

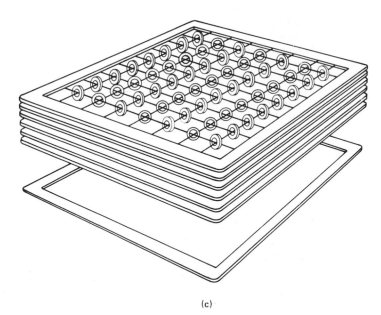

(c)

Figure 3.16. Magnetic core storage. (a) Core is magnetized; represents a 1, or the presence of a bit. (b) Current is reversed, so the core
reverses its magnetic state; represents a 0, or the absence of a bit. (c)
Cores in a plane.

through a circuit represents an "on" state used to specify the binary
digit 1; when current does not flow, this represents a binary digit of 0.

Thousands of integrated circuits can be placed on a single **chip** no
larger than a thumbnail (see Figure 3.17). This has resulted in smaller
computers with very large memories. Indeed, there are single chips
available that have the memory capacity of large-scale systems of a
decade ago. One chip can store 64,000 bytes of memory. Moreover, the
chips make servicing of computers easy and efficient. When errors

Figure 3.17. Comparison of a chip to a standard-sized paper clip.

Figure 3.18. Board containing 64,000 bytes of memory.

occur, the chips can be tested and the malfunctioning ones easily removed and replaced. In addition, the memory size of a computer can be supplemented with ease, by simply adding chips or boards where a board contains several chips. See Figure 3.18 for a board containing 64,000 bytes of memory.

Integrated circuits are made from **semiconductor** materials. There are two main types of semiconductor memories: bipolar and metal-oxide semiconductor (MOS), the latter being far more prevalent.

Integrated circuits represent the major form of memory in current computers, but there have been major innovations in memory technologies which have enhanced the capabilities of semiconductor devices.

3.3.2.3 Charge-Coupled Devices

A charge-coupled device is a variation of a metal oxide semiconductor (MOS) that includes packets of electrical charges in a small slice of silicon. Charge-coupled devices provide very high speed memories with large capacities at a relatively low cost. One million storage positions, called one **megabyte** of storage, can be represented on a CCD memory board for under $1700 (see Figure 3.19).

3.3.2.4 Magnetic Bubble Memory

Another major innovation is called magnetic bubble memory. Magnetic bubble memory consists of magnetized spots on a thin film of semiconductor material (see Figure 3.20). The speed with which it can access data is not as great as the forms of memory mentioned previously, but it has one major benefit not found in the others: data can be retained in memory even if the power is shut off. This is called **nonvolatility**. Magnetic bubble memory's nonvolatile nature is par-

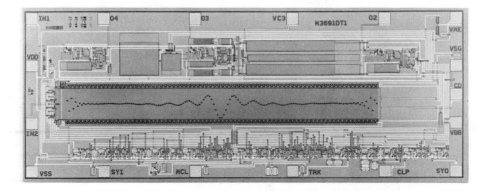

Figure 3.19.   Charge-coupled device approximately ¼ inch long.

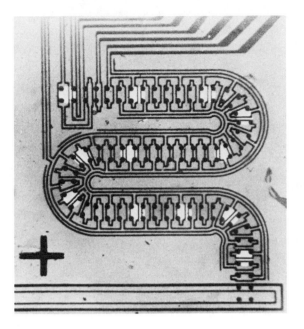

Figure 3.20. Magnetic bubble memory. The magnetic bubbles (large white dots) are four-thousandths of an inch in diameter.

ticularly important in an era when problems with energy and power supplies can mean frequent blackouts, brownouts, or power surges, all of which can have adverse effects on computer processing.

Figure 3.21 provides a historical cost comparison of core, semiconductor, and bubble memories. Note that additional experiments

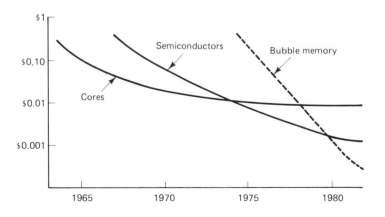

Figure 3.21. Cost comparison of core, semiconductor, and bubble memories.

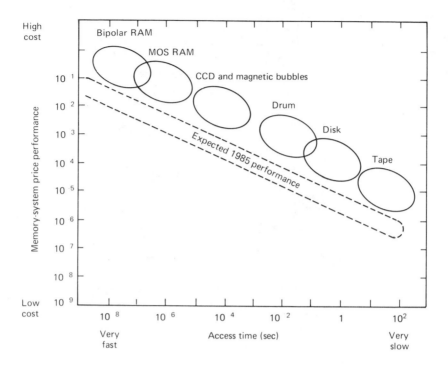

Figure 3.22. Access time versus price for various storage devices. (From *Computerworld.* Copyright by CW Communications/Inc., Framingham, MA 01701. Reprinted with permission.)

with integrated circuits as well as with optical and laser memories have resulted in even more efficient memories that will undoubtedly be of even greater significance in the future.

Previously, we indicated that auxiliary storage units, such as magnetic disk, tape, and drum, are frequently used to supplement primary storage. A comparison of these auxiliary storage devices with integrated circuit primary storage (both bipolar and MOS) and with charge-coupled devices and magnetic bubbles is illustrated in Figure 3.22.

3.3.3 Features of Primary Storage

3.3.3.1 *Random-Access Memory*

Random-access memory (RAM) is the part of memory that is used for storing programs and data. RAM is that part of memory that can be accessed or altered as needed by each program.

3.3.3.2   Read-Only Memory

Read-only memory (ROM) is the part of computer memory that contains prewired functions. This part of memory cannot be altered by programmed instructions.

ROM might contain, for example, a square-root procedure. This eliminates the need for the programmer to write a set of instructions to calculate square roots. Including such a function in the hardware is cheaper, faster, and more efficient than requiring a programmer to code it.

Functions in read-only memory are permanently stored and cannot be altered by a program. "Read-only" means that this area of storage can only be accessed; it cannot be used for storing instructions or data. ROM can only be changed by rewiring the circuits.

In short, ROM is part of the CPU hardware, which actually contains a set of instructions, or program. Thus the traditional distinction between hardware (devices) and software (programs) is slowly eroding. **Firmware** is the new term used to describe prewired hardware that has been preprogrammed to perform specific functions. More on this later when we discuss and evaluate software.

Summary: Computer Memory

I. TYPES

  A. Magnetic Core

    1. Tiny, doughnut-shaped ferrite rings.
    2. Magnetized in one direction to represent the "on" state; magnetized in the other direction to represent the "off" state.
    3. Older form of memory; still used in some computers.

  B. Integrated Circuits on a Chip

    1. Made from semiconductor material.
    2. Consists of thousands of electronic circuits on a thin silicon wafer.
    3. Two types: bipolar and metal-oxide semiconductor (MOS); the latter is more prevalent.
    4. Widely used in most computers today.
    5. Very easy to service—when a chip malfunctions, it can easily be replaced.

  C. Charge-Coupled Device

    1. Contains packets of electrical charges in a small slice of silicon.
    2. Has the ability to access data at very high speeds.
    3. Used in large computer systems where very high speed access is essential.

D. Magnetic Bubble

    1. Consists of magnetized spots on a thin semiconductor film.
    2. Relatively low access speed.
    3. Nonvolatile: data remains in storage even if the power is shut off.
    4. Used with very small computers.

E. Laser and Optical Memories

    1. Some already exist; perhaps these will be the wave of the future.

II. FEATURES OF MEMORY

A. ROM: Read-Only Memory

    1. Accessible by a program, but cannot be altered.
    2. Contains prewired functions such as square-root procedures.
    3. Because of ROM, the traditional separation between hardware and software is disappearing, being replaced by firmware—preprogrammed hardware.

B. RAM: Random-Access Memory

    1. Memory that is used for storing programs and data.

KEY TERMS

Arithmetic-logic unit
ASCII
Auxiliary storage
Batch processing
Binary number
Byte
Central processing unit (CPU)
Charge-coupled device
Chip
Computer system
Control unit
Core storage
Data transfer
EBCDIC
Firmware
Hardware
Input unit

Integrated circuit

Magnetic bubble memory

Magnetic core

Mainframe

Mass storage device

Memory size

Minicomputer

Off-line processing

On-line processing

Output unit

Primary storage

Program

RAM (random-access memory)

Real-time system

ROM (read-only memory)

Software

Supervisor

REVIEW QUESTIONS

1.   What are the main elements of a computer system?
2.   Indicate typical input and output units used with a computer system.
3.   What are the five basic operations that can be performed by the CPU?
4.   What is the difference between primary and auxiliary (or secondary) storage?
5.   What is meant by a primary storage capacity of 1 megabyte?
6.   What is the typical primary storage capacity of a small computer?
7.   What is a supervisor, and what purpose does it serve?
8.   Why is the binary numbering system or some variation of it utilized by computers to represent characters?
9.   What is 35_{10} equal to in base 2?
10.   What is 1001101_2 equal to in base 10?
11.   What is the structure of a byte?
12.   What is EBCDIC?
13.   What are the major types of CPU memory?
14.   What is meant by read-only memory?
15.   What is random-access memory?
16.   What are the main differences between batch processing and on-line processing?
17.   What is a real-time system?
18.   What type of memory is apt to be used for a small system where there is concern about the volatility of data?

APPLICATION

Consider the application below and then answer the questions that follow it.

Support Availability Buoys Bubble Applications[a]

By John Greitzer

SANTA CLARA, Calif.—National Semiconductor Corp., confident that the bubble memory market one day will take off like forecasters once predicted, said it will offer a 1M-bit bubble memory device later this year. Designated the NBM 2011, the device would bring National Semi into the company of Texas Instruments, Inc. and Intel Magnetics, Inc., an Intel Corp. subsidiary, as a supplier of 1M-bit-size bubble devices. Intel and TI introduced their 1M-bit devices in 1979.

National Semi already produces a 256K-bit bubble memory, the NBM 2256, and is a major supplier of bubble devices along with Intel, TI and Rockwell International, Inc. National Semi said its 1M-bit device will be totally compatible with its 256K-bit device.

In a related development, National Semi and a French company, Sagem S.A., said they've signed an agreement under which Sagem will second-source bubble memory devices produced by National Semi.

The market for bubble memories, by all accounts, is at least a year or two behind most predictions made several years ago. The industry has been plagued by a lack of support circuits needed to use bubble memories and by problems in production and yield.

A spokesman at National Semi said that according to earlier predictions, the market for bubble memories should be about five times larger than it is now.

He said the problems in yield and support-circuit availability soon should be straightened out. "And we're not the only ones who think so. We estimate there are at least 15 or 16 companies who are making investments in the technology to build garment wafers, which are the essential substrates for bubble memories."

His prediction may be right on the money. An Intel spokesman said Intel now is offering all the support, including the much-sought 7220 controller, for its 1M-bit bubble memory device.

"We actually started shipping all the support circuits in April. I would agree that the lack of support circuits, in general, has been a factor in holding back the bubble memory market," the Intel spokesman said.

The initial market for bubble memories appears to be companies which produce industrial control or process control systems and terminal companies.

Both National Semi and Intel said that bubble memories are well-suited for intelligent terminals to be used in harsh environments. The bubbles are much less vulnerable than magnetic tape and disk storage devices.

Bubble memories eventually could replace tape and disk products in those particular environments, the National Semi spokesman said.

As for the storage market in general, "I don't think replacement really conveys the right picture," the spokesman said. "I think bubble memory will augment tape and disk storage, not replace it. Typically, you might have a system including a bubble memory device and one floppy disk, rather than a dual-floppy system. And you'll operate out of the bubble memory, using the floppy just for backup, for archiving and that sort of thing."

The Intel spokesman said bubble memory eventually will approach the cost-per-bit of floppy disks, "but that's about five years away, I think we all agree on that."

Intel currently supplies only the 1M-bit bubble memory. There has been word of a 4M-bit bubble memory to be ready for the market sometime in 1982, but no details from Intel are available.

Under terms of the pact between National Semi and Sagem, the French company will produce bubble memory devices which are functionally compatible, and pin-for-pin compatible, with National Semi devices. Sagem plans to have the products ready for sampling by late 1980, with production quantities available in mid-1981, the companies said.

[a] *Computer Business News,* June 30, 1980, p. 1. Copyright 1980 by CW Communications/Inc., Framingham, MA 01701. Reprinted with permission.

Application Questions

1. Explain what is meant by a "1M-bit bubble memory device."
2. Why is the bubble memory market at least one or two years behind predictions made several years ago?

COMPUTER
HARDWARE
AND
SOFTWARE

Hardware

We have noted that there are two main aspects of computerization:

Hardware: actual devices used to process data
Software: actual programs used to process data

The **systems approach** adopted by computer specialists involves a determination of how software and hardware can best be utilized and integrated to satisfy the requirements of a specific application.

This chapter, which focuses on hardware, thus must also focus on the ways in which computer equipment is best utilized to meet job requirements. That is, it makes no sense to describe the vast array of computer devices that are currently in vogue if we do not adequately indicate how that equipment is best used. Our objectives, then, are as follows:

Objectives of This Chapter

1. To describe types of computer equipment or hardware
2. To focus on typical applications using that hardware
3. To specify input/output media that are utilized with various types of hardware

Overview of a Computer System

You may recall that a computer system consists of:

1. A **central processing unit** (mainframe).
2. **Input devices**: equipment that can read data and transmit it to the CPU.
3. **Output devices**: equipment that can take processed data and produce it as output. Note that some hardware, such as terminals or magnetic tape drives, are capable of both input and output functions.

In discussing hardware, we will also consider the I/O media that are processed by that hardware; that is, we will discuss features of magnetic tape as well as features of tape drives, for example.

We will subdivide our discussion of hardware and media into several categories:

I. EQUIPMENT AND MEDIA GENERALLY USED FOR FILES

    A. Punched Cards
    B. Magnetic Tapes
    C. Magnetic Disks

II. EQUIPMENT USED FOR REPORTING OR INQUIRING ABOUT THE STATUS OF A FILE

    A. Terminals
    B. Printers
    C. Computer Output Microfilm (COM)

III. SPECIALIZED EQUIPMENT AND MEDIA USED TO UPDATE FILES

    A. Cards, Tape, and Disk: used to update as well as to store files
    B. Terminals
    C. Devices That Eliminate Keying Operations or Manual Conversion of Input Data into Machine-Readable Form
        1. Magnetic ink character recognition (MICR) devices
        2. Optical character readers (OCRs)
        3. Punched paper tape devices

4.1 EQUIPMENT AND MEDIA GENERALLY USED FOR FILE PROCESSING

A file stores all the important information pertaining to a specific application. Thus an accounts receivable department in a business organization would have an accounts receivable file containing, for each customer, the amount owed, the items purchased within the last month, and so on. Files are typically stored on cards, tape, or disk.

4.1.1 Punched Card Files and Punched Card Devices

Cards tend *not* to be used very much any more for files except for very small applications. Since card devices are slow and cards themselves are fragile, this file type is not very efficient.

One main advantage of card processing, however, is that the

Figure 4.1. Standard punched card.

information stored on a card can be read by people as well as machines. We will see that this is *not* the case with tape or disk master files.

An example of a standard punched card is shown in Figure 4.1. There are 80 columns on the card and each column can store one character, that is, a letter, digit, or special symbol.[1] The characters are stored in the form of punched holes. The code used for punched data is

[1]In addition to the standard 80-column card, there is a 96-column card which can only be used with certain computer systems, such as the IBM System/3.

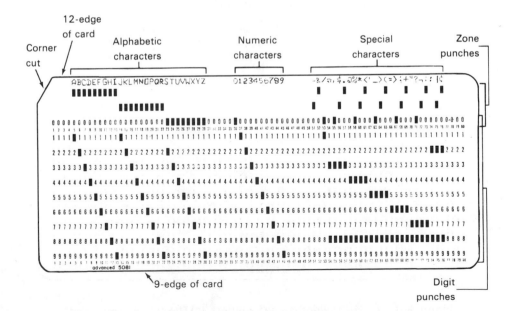

Figure 4.2. Sample punched card.

indicated in Figure 4.2 and is called the **Hollerith code**. Herman Hollerith, the inventor of the code, devised the system for his punched card tabulating equipment, which was discussed in Chapter 2.

To code a digit or integer in a specific column, a hole is punched in the corresponding **row** of that column. To represent alphabetic data, a **digit punch** is used in conjunction with a **zone punch** (see Figure 4.3).

Eighty columns of data are used to represent a record on a standard card. This record is subdivided into fields, where a **field** is a set of columns used to denote a unit of data such as a social security number, name, salary, and so on, for business applications, or the number of BTUs, ergs, ohms, and so on, for scientific applications.

At this point, we will indicate the **hierarchy** in which data is organized. We have seen that **records** are composed of related fields. For example, an employee time card is a record of data containing a NAME field, an HOURS WORKED field, and so on. A collection of related records is called a **file**. Thus a collection of all employee time cards would constitute a file (see Figure 4.4). These definitions of fields, records, and files apply to any input/output medium.

Hollerith Code

		Digit Punches								
		1	*2*	*3*	*4*	*5*	*6*	*7*	*8*	*9*
Zone Punches	*12*	A	B	C	D	E	F	G	H	I
	11	J	K	L	M	N	O	P	Q	R
	0	/	S	T	U	V	W	X	Y	Z

(a)

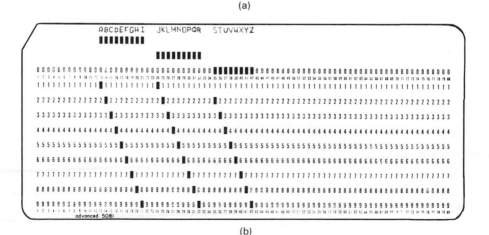

(b)

Figure 4.3. (a) The Hollerith Code for letters. (b) The alphabet punched on a card.

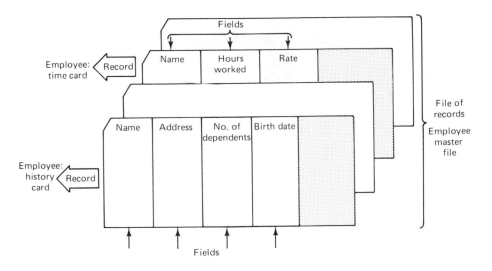

Figure 4.4. Hierarchy of data.

Data is punched into cards with the use of either:

1. *Keypunch machine* (Figure 4.5). (This is a manual device used to create the file; it is not part of a computer system.)
2. *Card punch device.* (This is a computer device used to create punched card records; see Figure 4.6.)

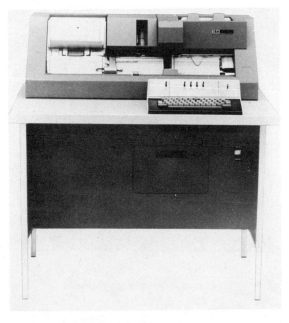

Figure 4.5. Keypunch machine.

Figure 4.6. Card punch.

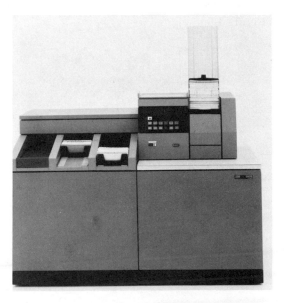

Figure 4.7. Card reader.

When a computer system reads card data it uses a card reader device (see Figure 4.7). It should be noted that some card reader devices are housed in the same cabinet as a card punch unit and are called card read/punch devices.

Following are the advantages and disadvantages of card processing.

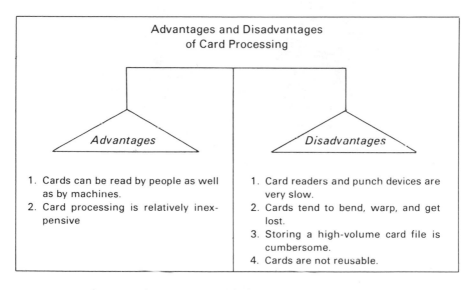

Advantages and Disadvantages
of Card Processing

Advantages

1. Cards can be read by people as well as by machines.
2. Card processing is relatively inexpensive

Disadvantages

1. Card readers and punch devices are very slow.
2. Cards tend to bend, warp, and get lost.
3. Storing a high-volume card file is cumbersome.
4. Cards are not reusable.

4.1.2   Magnetic Tape Files and Magnetic Tape Drives

A magnetic tape is a *high-speed* medium that can serve as input to, or output from, a computer. It is one of the most common file types for storing a high volume of data.

A magnetic tape drive is a device that can either read a tape or write onto a tape. Each tape drive has a **read/write head** that is accessed by the computer for either reading or writing.

Magnetic tape drives function like home tape recorders. Data can be recorded, or written, onto a tape and "played back," or read, from the same tape at a later date. If data is written on a tape, previous data is written over or destroyed. For this reason, computer centers must take precautions to protect important tapes from being inadvertently destroyed.

4.1.2.1   Features of Magnetic Tape

A typical magnetic tape (see Figure 4.8) is generally 2400 feet long but larger and smaller sizes are available. Most tapes are $\frac{1}{2}$ inch wide. The tape is made of plastic with an iron oxide coating that can be

Figure 4.8. Magnetic tape reel.

magnetized to represent data. Since the magnetized spots or *bits* are extremely small and not visible to the human eye, large volumes of data can be condensed into a relatively small area of tape. Information from an entire 80-column card, for example, can typically be stored in one-tenth of an inch of magnetic tape, or less. The average tape, which costs approximately $25, can store over 20 million characters. After a tape file has been processed and is no longer needed, the same tape may be reused repeatedly to store other information.

4.1.2.2   High-Speed Capability of Tape Drives

Because tape drives read data *electronically* by sensing magnetized areas, and write data electronically by magnetizing areas, tapes may be processed at very high speeds. Data can be read or written at speeds of from 100,000 to 300,000 characters *per second.*

Thus tape files are frequently used for large volumes of data. One tape can store hundreds of thousands of records, transmit and receive data at very high speeds, and store the data in a compact form. In many medium- or large-scale organizations, **master files** for payroll, accounts receivable, pressure levels in a fuel tank, temperature readings, and so on are stored on tape. A master file is the main data file that holds all current information for a specific department or system.

A record on a tape may be any size, as long as it is physically consistent with the size of storage. That is, it is not feasible to create 5000-position records using a 4000-position computer, since the output area (5000 positions) must be located in storage. Aside from this limitation, tape records may usually be any size. Keep in mind, however, that extremely large record sizes are more difficult to process.

4.1.2.3   Tapes for Batch Processing

Because of a tape's capacity to handle large volumes of data in a relatively short time, it is ideally suited for **batch processing**, or processing groups of data at fixed intervals.

4.1.2.4   Tapes as Input/Output

Like punched cards, tapes can be read as input to a computer and can be produced as output from a computer system. Just as a card read/punch can both read and punch card data, a tape drive can read and write tape data.

Cards can be created by a keypunch machine as well as by a card punch. Similarly, **key-to-tape encoders** can be used to create tapes.

4.1.2.5   Key-to-Tape Encoder

A key-to-tape encoder or converter is a device similar to a keypunch machine. It requires an operator to code data from a source document to a magnetic tape via a typewriter-like keyboard. The operator depresses a key for a specific character and the device converts it to the appropriate magnetized coding. Tapes encoded in this manner may be verified by the same device to ensure their accuracy. Key-to-tape encoders thus eliminate the need for punched card input by transcribing data *directly* onto magnetic tape.

4.1.2.6   Tapes for Sequential
Processing

In short, tape is a very common file medium for high-speed, voluminous processing. It does, however, have several inherent disadvantages.

Data recorded on a tape may only be processed **sequentially**. That is, to access a record with TRANSACTION NUMBER 254 from a tape file that is maintained in transaction number sequence, we must read past the first 253 records. We instruct the computer to read a record; test if it contains TRANSACTION NUMBER 254; and if it does not, to read the next record. Thus 254 records are read. There is no convenient method to instruct the tape drive to skip the first few inches of tape or to go directly to the middle of the tape.

Thus, unless all or most records from a tape file are required for processing *most of the time*, this method could become inefficient and costly.

4.1.2.7 Read/Write Feature of Tape Drives

Another disadvantage of tape processing is that a particular tape cannot usually be read from, and then written onto, during the same run. As with cards, if tape records are to be changed, a new record must be created on an output file which duplicates the old records and makes the necessary changes. In this procedure, two tape drives are needed, one to read a file as input and the other to write an output file. (See Figure 4.9 for an illustration of a tape drive).

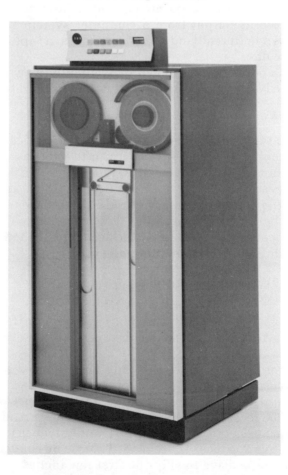

Figure 4.9. Magnetic tape drive.

4.1.2.8 Identification Problem with Tape

A third disadvantage of tape processing is the identification problem. Most medium- and large-scale computer installations have hundreds or even thousands of magnetic tapes, each utilized for a specific application. Because data recorded on these tapes is not "readable" or visible to the naked eye, it is often difficult to maintain control. If a tape is inadvertently "written over," or used as *output* for some other job, for example, the result could be an expensive re-creation process, since the writing of output would destroy the existing information. Several steps have been implemented at most installations to prevent such occurrences, or to reduce the extent of damage, should they occur.

4.1.2.9 Methods Used to Ease Tape Identification Problem

a. *External Tape Labels.* External gummed labels are placed on the face of each tape (see Figure 4.10), identifying it and indicating its **retention cycle** or how long it should be maintained. These labels are

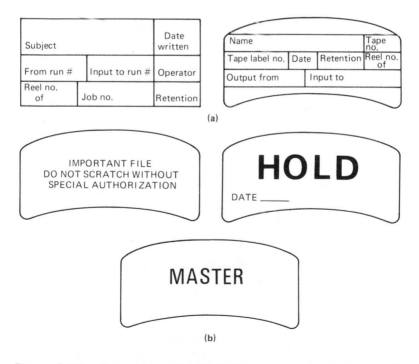

(a)

(b)

Figure 4.10. External tape labels. (a) Two commonly used external labels. (b) Three commonly used special-purpose tape labels.

clearly visible to anyone, so that chances of inadvertent misuse of a valuable tape are reduced. The problem with gummed labels, however, is that they sometimes become unglued. Their effectiveness is also directly related to the effort and training of the computer staff. If operators are negligent, the labels are sometimes ignored.

b. *Tape Librarian.* Most medium- and large-scale companies have numerous tapes that must be filed or stored and released for reuse when no longer required. Such companies employ a **tape librarian** to maintain the tape files. If he or she performs the job properly, there will be less misuse or misplacing of tapes.

c. *Internal Tape Labels.* To make the identification of tapes more reliable, most programs include a built-in routine which, for output tapes, creates a **tape label record** that is produced as any other tape record, with magnetized bits. The label is the *first* record on the tape. When the tape is used as input, at a later date, this first label record, called a **header label**, is checked as part of the program, to ascertain that the correct tape is being used.

d. *File Protection Ring* (Figure 4.11). Those available tapes that may be written on, or used as output, have a **file protection ring** inserted in the back. The tape drive is electronically sensitized so that it will *not* create an output record unless this ring is in its proper place. For those tapes that are to be maintained and not "written over," the ring has been removed. Thus if an operator erroneously uses such a tape for an output operation, the computer prints a message that states, in effect, "NO RING--NO WRITE." If the operator is cautious, he or she will examine the external label and realize that the wrong tape is being used. Sometimes, however, an operator will merely place a ring on the

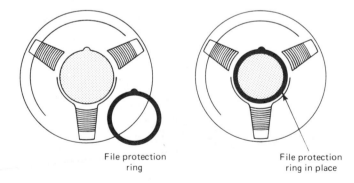

File protection
ring

File protection
ring in place

Figure 4.11. File protection ring, a plastic ring that fits into a groove in the tape reel. When the ring is in place, both reading and writing of tape records can occur. When the ring is removed, only reading can occur. In this way, the file is protected from accidental erasures.

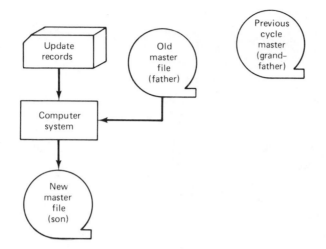

Figure 4.12. Grandfather–father–son method of file backup.

tape (any file protection ring fits all tapes) and restart the job. Thus although utilization of the ring deters the improper use of tapes, it does not totally alleviate the problem.

e. *Backup Tapes.* Since tapes can sometimes be written over or even become physically damaged, it is necessary to maintain backup tapes so that the re-creation process, should it become necessary, is not enormously costly and cumbersome.

Suppose that a new master tape is created each month. After processing, it is best to store the old master tape and update transactions *along with* the new master tape. In this way, if some mishap should befall the new master tape, it is a simple task to re-create. Normally, operators maintain *two* previous tapes as backup in addition to the present one, to prevent a serious problem. Hence the three **generations** of tapes maintained for important files are called the **grandfather–father–son** tapes (see Figure 4.12).

Note that mini- and microcomputer systems use miniaturized versions of magnetic tape called cassettes or cartridges. These are discussed in Chapter 6.

4.1.3 Magnetic Disk Files and Magnetic Disk Drives

The magnetic disk is another high-speed medium that can serve as either input to, or output from, a computer system. Like tape, it has an iron oxide coating that is used to store millions of characters of data,

Figure 4.13. Disk pack.

typically 6 to 70 million. The magnetic disk drive is used to record information onto the disk and to read information from it.

Figure 4.13 illustrates a typical disk pack. The pack resembles a series of disks similar to phonograph records that rotate on a vertical shaft.

Each surface of each disk consists of numbered concentric tracks. Each track is used to store information. A read/write head is used to read information from, and record information onto, any of the tracks.

Disk processing has many of the same advantages as tape processing. It can store large numbers of records in a condensed area. The disk drive, like the tape drive, reads and records information electronically and is thus a high-speed device. Records on a disk can essentially be any length. They are not fixed, as is the case with 80-column cards, for example.

4.1.3.1 Direct-Access Feature

Disk processing, however, has some additional features that are not available with tape processing. A disk may be used for either **direct** or **sequential** processing.

In addition to handling records in sequence, a disk has the facility to access records in some order other than the one in which they were originally recorded. The processing of records on disk is similar to the accessing of phonograph records from a jukebox. By indicating that phonograph record 106 is required, for example, the mechanism is capable of accessing 106 *directly* without first reading records 1 to 105, as is required with tape processing.

4.1.3.2 Index on a Disk

The most common method for accessing magnetic disk records directly (or randomly) is with the use of an **index**. During the creation of records, the computer uses programmed file handling routines to establish an index on the disk itself. The index essentially indicates where each record is located. This is similar in concept to the index found at the end of a book, which indicates the page where each item of information can be located.

The disk index specifies the **addresses** or locations of records that are stored on the disk. The address, in basic terms, refers to the surface number and track where a particular record can be found. A **key data field** in each record, as indicated by the programmer, is used by the computer as the basis for establishing address information in the index. As an example, if a payroll file is stored on disk, a key field would probably be SOCIAL SECURITY NUMBER or EMPLOYEE NUMBER, if this is to be used as a means of identification.

To access any disk record, then, the user need only supply a particular key data field, such as EMPLOYEE NUMBER 17537. The computer then "looks up" the corresponding disk address for this record in the index and seeks that record directly.

4.1.3.3 Input/Output Disks

In addition, disks have the advantage of permitting updates or changes to existing records *on the same disk*. In this way, a new disk need not be created to incorporate the current changes, as is usually required with tape processing. That is, the same disk may be used for *both* input and output. We can read a record from a disk and make changes to that record on the same disk; we can add records to the disk; we can delete records from the disk.

4.1.3.4 On-line Applications of Disk

This type of processing is extremely advantageous for specific applications. Suppose, for example, that a police department wishes to obtain information on three known criminals immediately. Suppose, too, that the department maintains a 100,000-record criminal file. If the criminal file were on tape (a sequential medium) each tape record would be read, in sequence, until the appropriate ones were found.

To read 100,000 data records would require considerable time. If, however, the file were on a disk pack, each of the three records could be accessed directly, in a much shorter time. We merely supply the key data field, which may be NAME or PRISON RECORD NUMBER.

Where time is critical and random processing is frequently required, disks are far more suitable than tapes. For *real-time* processing, or immediate processing of data, a disk file is usually used, since individual detail records can be used to update the disk file quickly and easily.

In recent years, more flexible disk packs have become available. Disk packs that are currently marketed range from the small **floppy disks**, also called diskettes or flexible disks, which resemble phonograph records and are used extensively with micro- and minicomputers, to much larger hard disk units (see Figure 4.14).

Figure 4.14. Floppy disks.

4.1.3.5 Disadvantages of Disk

In short, a disk is extremely advantageous for processing records directly (or randomly) as well as sequentially. Disks do, however, possess some inherent limitations:

- Disk packs are relatively expensive compared to other media, such as tape or cards. The purchase price for a typical disk pack ranges from approximately $400 to $3000, depending on the model.
- Just as with tapes, the identification of disk files often results in some problems. Since disk files, like tape files, cannot be visibly read, labels— both external (physically glued to the pack) and internal (programmed data labels)—are required.
- Tape update procedures usually result in a new master file that is created from the previous master file and a series of change records; the previous master can always be used as backup should the new master be inadvertently destroyed, lost, or even stolen, and a re-creation process deemed necessary. Since update procedures on a master disk file add to or delete from the one master, it is necessary to provide a separate backup procedure when a disk file is being processed.

4.1.3.6 Key-to-Disk Encoders

We have seen that disk files can be created as computer output. They can also be created manually with key-to-disk devices that are similar to keypunch machines and key-to-tape encoders.

4.2 DEVICES USED FOR REPORTING OR INQUIRING ABOUT THE STATUS OF A FILE

The main reason for maintaining files is to be able to provide information when required, in various forms such as reports, customer statements, and responses to inquiries. Printers, terminals, and computer output microfilm (COM) devices are typically used for providing information.

Example 1:   A payroll master file can provide information about salaries and produce payroll checks.

Example 2:   An accounts receivable master file is used for reporting to customers the status of their accounts in the form of computer-produced bills.

Example 3:   The Defense Department uses an on-line inquiry system to provide immediate information on the status of every project.

4.2.1 The Printer

A printer is one of the most common computer output devices used in business applications. It takes data that has been processed by the computer and prints it on **continuous forms**, which are sheets of paper connected by perforation marks. After an entire report has been printed, it is separated or **burst** into individual sheets.

Because the needs of companies for printers differ widely, there are numerous types with many different features available. We will consider the most common types and their associated features.

I. TYPES OF PRINTERS

  A. Serial Printer
    1. Relatively slow device
    2. Functions just like a typewriter, printing one character at a time
    3. Used primarily for interactive keyboard-print terminals (to be discussed in the next section) or minicomputers
    4. Relatively inexpensive

  B. Line Printer
    1. Moderately fast device
    2. Accumulates a total line of output and then prints, one line at a time
    3. The most common printer for moderate-speed print operations (see Figure 4.15)

  C. Page Printer
    1. Extremely fast and costly device
    2. Prints an entire page at one time
    3. Uses some electronic technique based on laser-xerographic, electrostatic, or other technology

The relative speeds of these devices are as follows:

	Speed		
Type of Printer	Low (measured in number of characters per second)	Moderate (measured in hundreds or thousands of lines per minute)	Very High (measured in tens of thousands of lines per minute)
Serial	×		
Line		×	
Page			×

Figure 4.15. Line printer.

II. FEATURES OF PRINTERS

A. Impact versus Nonimpact. An impact printer is one that generally operates by using a hammer to strike a character against an inked ribbon; the impact, then, causes an image of the character to be printed.

Impact printers function just like typewriters. Their main disadvantages are that they are relatively slow, noisy, and subject to mechanical breakdowns. Despite these disadvantages, most printers in use today are impact devices.

Nonimpact printers were recently developed to meet some of the needs that were not being satisfied by impact technology. Most high-speed page printers, for example, use some form of nonimpact device; but high speed is not the only benefit of nonimpact technology, as we will see below.

Among the nonimpact printers available are:

Types of Nonimpact Printers

Laser-xerographic ⎫
Electrosensitive ⎬ High speed
Electrophotographic ⎭
Thermal: ideal for lightweight portable terminals; quiet
Electrostatic: for plotting graphs
Ink jet: for letter-quality printing

A comparison of impact and nonimpact printers follows:

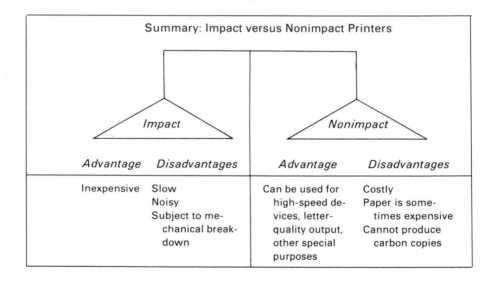

Summary: Impact versus Nonimpact Printers			
Impact		*Nonimpact*	
Advantage	*Disadvantages*	*Advantage*	*Disadvantages*
Inexpensive	Slow Noisy Subject to mechanical breakdown	Can be used for high-speed devices, letter-quality output, other special purposes	Costly Paper is sometimes expensive Cannot produce carbon copies

Table 4.1 summarizes the major features of nonimpact printers.

B. Character versus Dot Matrix: Character printers operate like typewriters. Dot matrix printers create all characters with dots that are activated within a grid (see Figure 4.16).

Figure 4.17 illustrates the average speed and cost of the various printers.

Table 4.1 *Features of Nonimpact Printers*

Type	Major Use	Technology	Advantages	Disadvantages	Typical Speed	Approx. Cost
Thermal	Low-speed terminals	Temperature sensitive; paper changes color when treated; characters are formed by selectively heating print head	Quiet; relatively inexpensive	Special-purpose paper required; cannot use preprinted form; paper fades (print quality is poor)	Several dozen to several hundred characters per second	Under $10,000
Electrosensitive	High-speed terminals	Paper has metallic coating; voltage is applied to the print mechanism, which burns away metallic coating	Low cost; high speed	Black printing on silver paper is not very attractive; print quality is poor; paper wrinkles	160–6600 characters per second	Under $5000 on the average
Ink jet	High-quality printing	Electrostatically charged drops hit the paper	High-quality printing	Relatively slow	Several hundred characters per second	Under $30,000 on the average
Electrostatic	High-speed printing and plotting	Dielectric paper moves past a stylus; voltages are applied selectively; paper then passes through a toner	Very high speed	Requires special paper; requires messy preparation	Several hundred to several thousand *lines* per minute	Tens of thousands of dollars to over $100,000

(continued on page 112.)

Table 4.1. *Cont.*

Type	Major Use	Technology	Advantages	Disadvantages	Typical Speed	Approx. Cost
Laser-xerographic	High speed	Laser beam directed onto a drum, paper then passes through a toner	Very high speed; excellent quality; the most promising high-speed print technology	High cost; requires a preparatory phase	Several hundred *pages* per minute	Several hundred thousand dollars

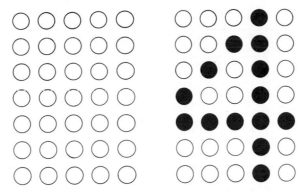

5 × 7 dot pattern

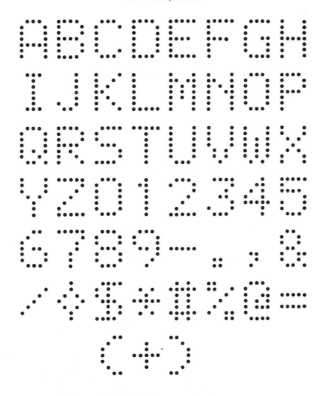

Figure 4.16. Dot matrix characters.

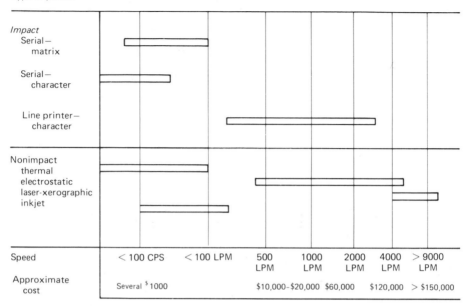

Figure 4.17. Average speed and cost of printers. CPS, characters per second; LPM, lines per minute. (Adapted from Report 705-0000-020, *Auerbach Series on Basic System Design Concepts.* Reprinted with permission of the publisher, Auerbach Publishers, Inc.)

4.2.2 The Use of Terminals as an Alternative to Punched Card Processing and Printer-Generated Reports

4.2.2.1 Some Advantages of Terminals

We have already discussed card readers, card punch machines, and printers. Although many computer systems continue to use these devices to process much of their I/O, the trend has been to utilize other input and output devices that provide a faster, more efficient, and more flexible type of communication with the CPU. In this section we consider the use of terminals as an alternative to batch-oriented cards and print devices.

One important feature of a terminal is that it can access a computer from a remote location. That is, with the use of a communication link such as a telephone line, a terminal can be linked to a CPU located anywhere in the country, or indeed the world.

These terminals enable the user to:

Enter data from remote locations.

Enter jobs—programs and data—from remote locations.

Make inquiries about the current status of central files from remote locations and obtain responses immediately.

The types of systems that make use of terminal processing are diverse. An airline reservation system is a common illustration of an application where terminals located throughout the country access a central CPU.

Some Advantages of Terminals over Card and Print Devices

1. Data entry can be made locally at the point of transaction.
   a. With card processing, a source document, such as a purchase order, must be transmitted to the computer center and keypunched onto cards before it can be processed.
   b. With terminals, data can be entered directly into the computer from some remote location.
2. Data can be processed on-line.
   a. With card processing, cards of data are usually accumulated and processed as a group in a batch-processing mode.
   b. With terminals, data can be entered directly into the computer, as the need arises.
3. Data can be processed interactively.
   a. With card and print processing, output reports are usually obtained as a result of a batch-processing operation.
   b. With terminals, a request can be made directly on the terminal and the computer response printed immediately on that same terminal. This enables a user to interact directly with the CPU.

4.2.2.2 Sample Terminal Equipment

There is quite a variety of terminals available, as will be seen. Most terminals have the capability of both transmitting and receiving computer messages. Even when the terminal is used primarily for entering data, some facility for receiving computer messages is usually necessary (control messages, error messages, and so on, from computer to operator). In this section we discuss two of the commonly used types of terminals—the typewriter terminal and the display terminal.

a. *The Typewriter Terminal.* This is one of the most widely used terminals. It can receive and transmit messages using a device like a typewriter. An operator enters input data by depressing the various keys in much the same way as data is typed on a typewriter. The terminal generally has a standard alphanumeric keyboard. There is a typed **hard-copy** printout of all data entered. A hard-copy printout is one that may be maintained for future reference, as opposed to data displayed on a screen, which is not available in tangible form after being viewed. When the computer communicates with the user, the typewriter is activated by the CPU, and the required information is printed on the typed sheet automatically.

As indicated, this is one of the most widely used I/O terminals. Operators may key in input consisting of stock receipts, purchase orders, payroll changes, and so on. In addition, these operators can make requests of the computer via the terminal and receive immediate responses.

Typewriter or hard-copy terminals are serial devices that print relatively slowly, as compared to line and page printers.

b. *The Cathode Ray Tube (CRT) or Visual Display Terminal* (see Figure 4.18). The CRT usually includes a keyboard as the standard input medium. An operator keys in data or makes inquiries using this typewriter-like unit.

The cathode ray tube (CRT) is a visual display device similar to a television screen. This output unit instantaneously displays information from the computer on the screen. It is a high-speed device, since data is *not* transmitted to a typed page using a relatively slow print mechanism. Instead, large amounts of information can be displayed instantly.

Figure 4.18. Cathode ray tube (CRT).

CRT devices are extremely beneficial where output from a computer is desired at remote locations very quickly. Airline terminals, for example, use cathode ray tubes to display flight information. Changes to the data displayed on the screen are made instantaneously. Similarly, stock brokerage firms use CRTs in conjunction with a keyboard for requesting the latest stock quotations. The computer responses are displayed on the screen. Such CRT output provides **soft copy**, a visual display with no permanent record.

For high-speed output, CRT devices are extremely beneficial. If hard-copy versions of the output are necessary, CRT devices must be equipped with additional features such as a printer or a display copier.

There are numerous types of terminals in addition to the typewriter terminal and the CRT. Many of these, such as the plotter and the point-of-sale terminal, are considered in subsequent chapters.

4.2.3 Computer Output Microfilm: An Alternative to Printed Output

There are several inherent disadvantages in producing printed output:

1. Print devices are relatively slow.
2. Printed output is very bulky and very difficult to store.

Large volumes of printed output can be stored instead on microfilm using computer output microfilm (COM) devices (see Figure 4.19). These devices can convert output from a CPU into microfilm form at speeds in excess of 120,000 characters per second. Typically, since the output is in miniaturized form, the user can save 98% of the storage space required to store the output. Figure 4.20 illustrates different types of microforms that are commonly used. It should be noted that a special reader is required to access or read the information, which is one disadvantage of COM devices. Another disadvantage is the cost of equipment, which is usually much higher than for printers.

4.3 SPECIALIZED EQUIPMENT AND MEDIA USED TO UPDATE A FILE

We have thus far discussed the media used for storing files—cards, tape, and disk. We have also considered the equipment used for obtaining output from a file—printers, terminals, and COM devices. But files must be altered to keep them current. This process of keeping a

(a)

(b)

(c)

(d)

(e)

Figure 4.19. Computer output microfilm (COM) device. (a) Loading point image tape. (b) Loading film cartridge, if required. (c) Inserting form slide, if required. (d) Pushing start button. (e) Examining finished fiche.

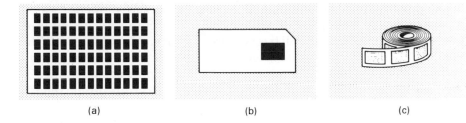

(a)　　　　　　　　　　　(b)　　　　　　　　　　(c)

Figure 4.20. Examples of microforms. (a) Microfiche card. Each microfiche card contains dozens of microfilm images. To access an individual record, a microfiche viewer must be used. (b) Aperture card. Each aperture card contains punched card data with an individual microfilm image. (c) Roll microfilm. Up to 2000 pages of information can be stored in 100 feet of 16-mm microfilm.

file current is called **updating**. There are two basic ways of ensuring that a master file is current:

1. *On-line Updating.* This is performed when the file is stored on a direct-access medium such as disk and the computer has the ability to update that file at the point of data entry *immediately*. To perform this type of updating, terminals are usually used for entering the data, and disks are used for the master file.

2. *Batch Updating.* Sometimes it is *not* necessary to have the file entirely current; that is, updating once or twice a week or even less frequently is sufficient. For example, a payroll master file that is used primarily to produce payroll checks once a week can be updated once a week as well. That is, it would not be necessary to have this file *always* current. A periodic update would suffice. This is referred to as **batch updating**. For this type of processing, the master file is usually stored on tape and change records entered on cards or cassette tapes.

The records used to store the changes are also stored on a file called a **transaction file**. This file can be a set of punched cards, a magnetic tape, or even data entered on a terminal. This transaction file can even use a medium that can be read by specialized equipment. For example, a handwritten report can serve as a transaction file if a computer has an **optical character recognition** (OCR) device that is capable of reading printed data. Similarly, bank checks can be used to update a master bank file by having specially encoded ink at the bottom of each check read by a **magnetic ink character recognition** (MICR) device. These devices eliminate the need for rekeying the data into a form suitable for input.

A punched card or magnetic tape transaction file would be created by a **data-entry operator** using a keypunch machine or a key-to-tape device. For example, a payroll transaction file on cards or tape would be created by an operator who produced one record for each payroll change. The data-entry operator would need to produce a computer-readable form from a source document such as a payroll change report, a customer bill, or a purchase order.

Devices that eliminate the need for this source-document conversion would save considerable time and labor. Terminals can do this in an on-line environment. MICR devices, OCR readers, and punched paper tape devices can do this in a batch environment.

We will consider MICR, OCR, and punched paper tape devices in this section. These are best suited for applications that utilize large volumes of data, processed in a group at fixed intervals. For batch-processing procedures, conversion from a source document is relatively costly. Since these devices are capable of reading a source document and converting it *directly* to a machine-readable form, they can save an organization both time and money.

4.3.1 Magnetic Ink Character Recognition

The banking industry is the largest user of magnetic ink character recognition (MICR) equipment which is capable of reading bank checks. The checks have account numbers, recorded in special type characters of magnetic ink, imprinted on the bottom. When a check is cashed, the amount is also imprinted by a special device. A MICR reader-sorter can interpret the data on checks, sort them into account number or branch number sequence, and transfer the data to a CPU of a computer system or to an off-line device (see Figure 4.21).

4.3.2 Optical Character Recognition

An optical character recognition (OCR) device, commonly referred to as an **optical scanner**, reads characters from printed documents (see Figure 4.22). No special ink or typing is required. Some devices can read handwritten as well as typed data.

The optical scanner senses data with the use of a photoelectric device. The data is read by a light source, which converts the characters into electrical impulses. On many devices, the input document must have characters or marks in designated positions for them to be properly sensed. The computer, then, must be instructed as to which positions will contain the data.

Figure 4.21. MICR reader/sorter.

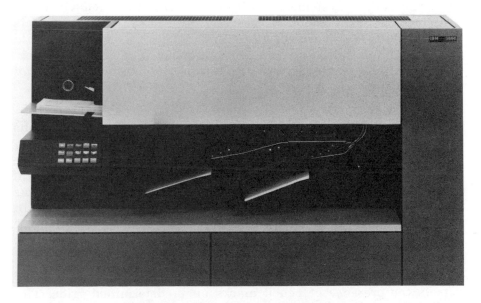

Figure 4.22. Optical character reader.

1. *Uses of OCR Equipment.*   A major use of optical scanners is in conjunction with gasoline company credit card receipts. Credit card identification from a plastic plate is imprinted on the receipt together with the amount of the purchase. These receipts are then read into a computer with the use of an optical scanner that senses the amount and customer account number. Other major users include department stores which batch-process handwritten receipts that are read by OCR equipment. Consider the tremendous advantage of reducing the need for a large and costly operations staff by using the source document as machine-readable input.

2. *Speed.*   OCR equipment varies in speed from approximately 50 characters per second, for devices that can read handwritten letters, to 3000 characters per second, and from 200 to 1200 documents per minute. Most page readers are very costly, however, ranging in price from $100,000 to $300,000 on the average, with monthly rentals from $1500 to $4500. For many applications, it is still cheaper to utilize the traditional conversion process. In one company, a systems analyst performed a cost study to determine the feasibility of acquiring an OCR device for a billing system. It was determined that an OCR device could be monetarily justified only if the system processed 10,000 documents per day. With fewer documents, the standard conversion process would be more economical. Thus we can see that such a device is relatively costly and is justifiable only when processing a voluminous quantity of input.

3. *Reliability Problem.*   In addition to cost, OCR equipment has one other disadvantage, one that results in limited reliability. Characters that are sensed by this device often must conform *rigidly* to the standard. Problems such as erasures and overlapping of positions can cause the erroneous transmission of data. In some applications, as much as 10% of the input data is unreadable because of such errors. In short, the promise of increased reliability and decreased cost in future years will make OCR equipment more widespread than it is today.

4. *Mark-Sense Devices as Optical Readers.*   A mark-sense reader detects the presence of pencil marks on predetermined grids. The typical documents to be mark-sensed are computer-scored test papers, where students are required to indicate the correct answer by penciling in grid A, B, C, D, or E. Although mark-sense devices are optical readers, they have limited facility and therefore limited use. Their capability is much less than optical scanners, where actual hand-

written or typed data can be read. But their reliability and cost are less problematic than those of more versatile optical readers.

4.3.3   Punched Paper Tape Read/Punch

A punched paper tape (Figure 4.23) is a paper tape that, like a card, is punched with holes in specified rows and columns. A paper tape read/punch (Figure 4.24) is, like a card read/punch, two separate units that can read from a paper tape or punch data into paper tape.

Punched paper tape may be produced by special adding machines, accounting machines, teletypes, and cash registers. With the aid of the read/punch it can then be used by the computer system as a source document.

Figure 4.23.   Punched paper tape.

Figure 4.24.   Punched paper tape read/punch.

Summary

In short, there are several computer devices that can read source documents directly without requiring conversion to another medium such as cards, tape, or disk. Although terminals also require a conversion process, these devices are far more versatile because they are utilized in an on-line environment.

KEY TERMS

Batch processing
Card punch
Card read/punch
Card reader
Cathode ray tube (CRT)
Computer output microfilm (COM)
Conversion of source documents
Direct access
Field
File
Floppy disk
Hard copy
Hollerith code
Index
Keypunch machine
Key-to-disk encoder
Key-to-tape encoder
Line printer
Magnetic disk
Magnetic ink character recognition (MICR)
Magnetic tape
Mark-sense reader
Master file
On-line processing
Optical character recognition (OCR)
Page printer
Punched card
Punched paper tape
Read/write head
Record

Sequential processing
Serial printer
Source document
Tape labels
Tape librarian
Terminal
Transaction file

REVIEW QUESTIONS

1. What media are commonly used for storing files?
2. What equipment can be used to eliminate the manual conversion of input data into machine-readable form?
3. What are two devices that can be used to punch data into cards?
4. What are the definitions of the following terms?
   a. Field
   b. Record
   c. File
   d. Master file
   e. Transaction file
5. What are major advantages and disadvantages of punched cards, magnetic tape, and magnetic disk?
6. Why is magnetic tape ideally suited for batch processing?
7. What identification problem arises when magnetic tape or magnetic disk files are used? How can this problem be avoided?
8. How can records in a magnetic disk file be accessed directly?
9. What are the major distinctions between impact and nonimpact printers?
10. What are the major advantages of terminals over:
    a. Punched card processing?
    b. Printer-generated reports?
11. What are the advantages and disadvantages of computer output microfilm (COM) devices?
12. What are the advantages and disadvantages of OCR devices?
13. For what applications might punched paper tape be employed?

DISCUSSION QUESTIONS

1. The use of terminals at remote locations has resulted in widespread fear among businesspeople as well as some consumer groups. Can you explain why?
2. Voice recognition equipment has been utilized with some success in recent years. What do you think might be some of the problems associated with a computer interpreting voice messages?

3. Give some examples of applications where hard-copy terminals would be more suitable than CRTs.
4. Give some examples of applications where CRTs would be more suitable than hard-copy terminals.

APPLICATION

Consider the application below and then answer the questions that follow it.

COM Takes Care of Sales for Hospital Supplier[a]

When a health care products sales representative is dealing with a busy professional, fast, accurate information on products is vital.

For 1,800 salespersons servicing the medical field for American Hospital Supply Corp. (AHSC) a single envelope containing five 4 × 6 in. cards is the next best thing to having a portable computer terminal in their attaché case.

Microfiche cards that can be viewed on a compact reader each contain the equivalent of more than 200 pages of computer reports, listing the latest price and availability of AHSC's various product lines. These can range from bedsheets to valves for open heart surgery and include precision dental equipment as well as complex, state-of-the-art respiratory therapy monitors.

"The price and availability report which often has more than 1000 pages, couldn't be printed and mailed on the weekly schedule that makes it most useful," James R. Johnson, micrographics supervisor, pointed out.

"Mailing costs, and the handling required by such a report, made it too costly to distribute on a less frequent basis."

Instead, he said, the report is output to microfiche off-line, and the required number of duplicates made quickly by automated machinery. The reports can be mailed first class for a few cents' postage each.

Backup, Archival Use

The net result for AHSC is the availability of low-cost, compact microfilm computer reports for both backup and archival purposes and enhanced information distribution capabilities in applications where paper reports had been too bulky or costly and time-consuming to distribute in the past.

[a] *Computerworld*, Feb. 25, 1980, p. SR/20. Copyright 1980 by CW Communications/Inc., Framingham, MA 01701. Reprinted with permission.

Application Questions

1. Indicate some of the advantages of COM as stated in the article.
2. Before acquiring a system like the one described in the application, what questions would you ask of a COM supplier?

A guide to software

There are two main aspects of computer processing that must be effectively correlated and tailored to meet each organization's specific needs. These are:

1. *Computer Hardware.* The input and output devices, which combined with the central processing unit, read data into the system, process the data, and produce the required output information. The ability of computer hardware to meet an organization's needs is measured by, among other things:

a. Cost
b. Speed
c. User satisfaction
d. Ease of operation
e. Type of processing required
f. Number and type of I/O devices that can be supported by the CPU

2. *Computer Software.* The computer hardware cannot be utilized effectively unless the system has been properly programmed. Computer software is the program support designed to maximize the efficient and effective use of the equipment. The ability of computer software to meet an organization's needs is measured by, among other things:

a. Cost of programs
b. Speed of processing
c. User satisfaction
d. Error rates
e. Flexibility and Modularity—the ability to easily make changes

Later we will see that the distinction between hardware and software is becoming less and less clear. That is, increasingly, a user can purchase a computer with system software, or program support, that is *built into* the hardware. This is referred to as **firmware** and is discussed in more detail at the end of the chapter.

There are basically two major types of software that an organization can acquire. In each case we are referring to a set of programs that consist of instructions designed to accomplish a specific task as efficiently and effectively as possible.

Types of Software: An Overview

1. *Application Programs.*   These are programs designed to meet the needs of each individual user. Application programs may consist of payroll programs, forecasting programs, inquiries to a data base, and so on. These programs may be written by:

Who Writes Application Programs?

1. Programmers within the user organization.
2. Consultants hired by the user organization to write a series of programs.
3. Facilities management organizations and computer manufacturers who sell packaged application programs that can (hopefully) meet the needs of many users. These tend to be less expensive but also less flexible than the other types of application support.

Note that an organization with an in-house computer is likely to have a programming staff that is called upon to write application programs. Thus consultants or facilities management organizations tend to be utilized primarily by small organizations with a limited programming staff.

2. *Operating System Software.*   These are programs that are usually supplied by the computer manufacturer or the third-party leasing agent that rents or leases the equipment to the user. These programs optimize efficient use of the computer system as a whole. The operating system consists of a **supervisor** or control program that controls all the computer's operations. The operating system also consists of a library of functions that can be called upon by the supervisor, as needed.

The objectives of this chapter are:

1. To provide an understanding of the two major types of software that an organization can acquire: application programs and operating system software
2. To examine the steps involved in writing application programs
3. To provide a survey of major high-level programming languages

We begin with a discussion of application programming, which is the main task of programmers hired by user organizations.

5.1   APPLICATION PROGRAMS

One main problem with computerized operations today is that the end product, the program, frequently does not meet the needs or expectations of the user. There are three main reasons for this:

1. Communication gap
   a. Users are often unfamiliar with the information that the computer specialist requires. Thus they cannot properly communicate their own needs.
   b. The computer specialist is often unfamiliar with the application and cannot fully understand the needs of the user.
2. Lack of adequate standards for programmers
3. Lack of proper controls

To be effective, application programs must be written to ensure that this communication gap is minimized, that standards are adhered to, and that proper controls exist. For this, the computer specialist must know precisely what is required of a program *prior to* programming. This means that the steps involved in *preparing a program*, prior to actual coding, are among the most important. We will divide our discussion into several units and each will be discussed in some detail. Note that we focus on programs that are written "in house" but that the same concepts might be employed by consulting organizations.

Steps Involved in Application Programming

1. Planning the system that incorporates the program
2. Program preparation
3. Coding the program
4. Getting the program to work
5. Implementing the program
6. Documenting the program

If a program is not part of a larger system, step 1 can be omitted.

5.1.1   Planning the System That Incorporates the Program

Application programs or software packages are not written haphazardly to satisfy each isolated user need. To do so would result in a significant duplication of effort. Moreover, many programs would be incompatible with one another.

Instead, most often a user department or division within an organization sets out to computerize an entire **system** or set of procedures. That is, in a business organization an accounts receivable system may be computerized; in an aerospace plant, the design of a new aircraft system may be computerized.

Each system consists of a set of interrelated tasks and procedures. A **systems analyst** is called upon to study all the procedures as they currently exist and to make recommendations for a computerized system that will be more efficient.

The analyst studies the existing system and determines:

Systems Analysis

1. What procedures should be computerized
2. What inputs and outputs should be redesigned for more effective processing
3. What controls should be implemented to reduce errors

After the analyst has worked out a design plan, he or she must establish:

Systems Design

1. *Program specifications*: precise descriptions of inputs, processing tasks, and outputs for each program required (Typically, a system may include numerous programs.)
2. *A plan for completion*: schedules, dates, etc.
3. A *retraining schedule* for the current user staff
4. An *implementation schedule*
5. A *cost analysis*: comparing current system costs to projected costs for the new system

---

Once these factors have been established, one or more programmers are called upon to write the required programs. For each program the analyst provides the programmer with the requirements or specifications and descriptions of what the input and output layouts should look like (see Figure 5.1).

If, however, the program is not part of a larger system, the system preparation stage can be omitted.

5.1.2. Program Preparation

The primary responsibility of the programmer is to understand fully the basic requirements of the system *as a whole*, and to ascertain

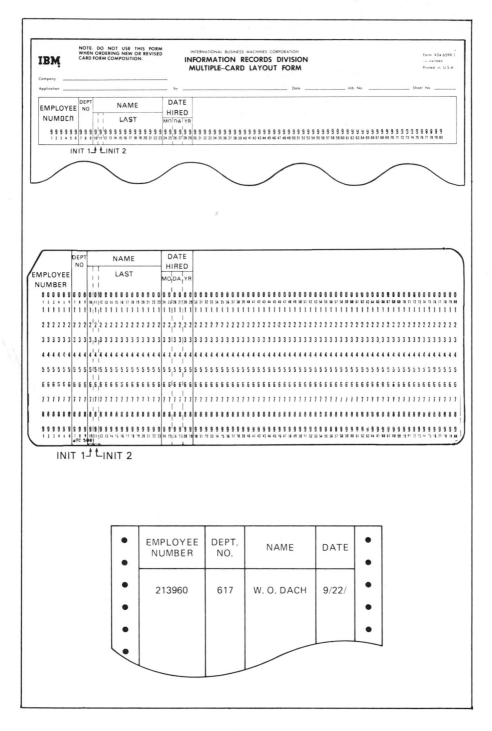

Figure 5.1. Sample data layouts.

precisely how the program will be integrated into that system. Many programming errors result because:

Reasons for Program Errors

1. The analyst did not provide the programmer with precise specifications
2. The programmer did not make every effort to fully understand all the program requirements

---

Frequently, it is useful for the programmer to communicate with the user to ensure full and proper understanding of all aspects of the program. The analyst, the programmer, and the user must agree on the following program specifications:

Specifications Required before a Program is Undertaken

1. Field descriptions for input data
2. Frequency of run
3. Arithmetic operations to be performed
4. Edit and control procedures to be performed
5. How errors are to be handled
6. Field descriptions for output
7. Frequency, control, and scheduling of output

Note that it is essential that these and all other program specifications be determined and agreed on *before* a program is written. To modify an existing program is not only sloppy and laborious, but frequently produces many errors.

Once all specifications have been determined, there are several planning tools that may be used to map out or plan the logic to be incorporated in the program. These planning tools or techniques are typically performed prior to writing the program, to minimize the possibility of logic errors.

In many instances, programmers are so eager to begin the actual coding that they skip this planning stage. To do so, however, significantly increases the risk of errors. It is as if an architect were to begin constructing a building without first preparing a blueprint.

There are two standard forms that can be used for planning program logic:

Tools for Planning Program Logic

1. Program flowcharts
2. Pseudocode

5.1.2.1 The Program Flowchart

A **program flowchart** is a pictorial representation of the logic to be used in a program. It indicates, in block diagram form, the major program elements and how they will logically integrate.

A flowchart is drawn with the use of a template (see Figure 5.2). Each flowchart contains symbols that represent a specific operation. See Figure 5.3 for a description.

Figures 5.4 and 5.5 illustrate sample program flowcharts and provide descriptions of what they mean.

Note that these flowcharts are written prior to the program to ensure that the programmer understands what tasks are specifically required and in what sequence.

5.1.2.2 Pseudocode

This planning tool utilizes a code similar to a program code for depicting logic. Pseudocode is widely used for applications that have complex logical control procedures, where a *structured* approach is most useful. The structured approach is considered in Chapter 16.

5.1.3 Coding the Program

Once the logic flow of a program has been mapped out using either a flowchart or pseudocode, the set of instructions in a program may be written. The writing of these instructions is called **coding the program**.

Programs may be coded on sheets of paper called **coding** or **program sheets**. See Figure 5.6 for a sample coding sheet.

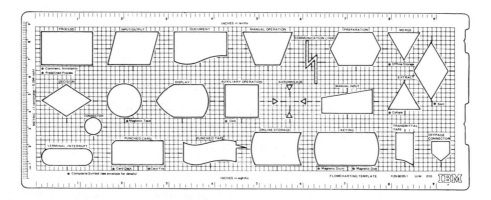

Figure 5.2. Flowcharting template.

	Symbol	Explanation
1.		**Input/output (I/O) symbol** This symbol represents any input or output operation such as READ A CARD, READ A TAPE, WRITE A LINE, etc. The specific operation at a particular point is indicated by a note inside the symbol.
2.	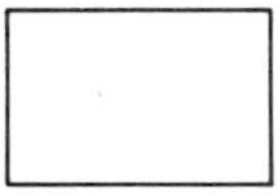	**Processing** This symbol indicates any internal computer processing, that is, any series of data transfer or arithmetic operations. We may have, for example, Add amount to total or Compute tax = 0.05 $\times$ sales or Total = X + Y + Z or Move input to output
3.	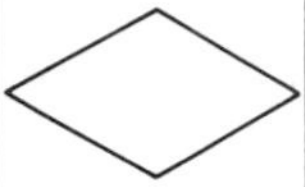	**Decision** This symbol is used to test for a logical comparison. Basically, it is used when we want the computer to ask a question. Examples of decision tests include: (a) IS AMOUNT OF SALES GREATER THAN 100.00? (b) IS AMOUNT OF SALES LESS THAN AMOUNT OF CREDIT? (c) DOES SEX FIELD = 'M'? (d) IS TOTAL = ZEROS?
4.	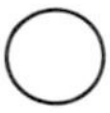	**Connector** This symbol denotes a cross-reference point indicating where the flowchart should continue. It is used to indicate a change in the normal flow of data.
5.		**Terminal** This symbol is used to denote the starting or ending point of a program.

Figure 5.3.   Major flowcharting symbols.

When the program has been completely coded on coding sheets, it must be entered into the computer. This can be performed, for example, by:

Methods for Entering Computer Programs

1. Typing the program onto a terminal that is linked on-line to a CPU
2. Typing the program into a microcomputer and then saving the program on cassette tape or floppy disk
3. Keypunching the program onto cards and entering it in batch mode

---

In each case, one line of coding is keyed onto one program line or one punched card.

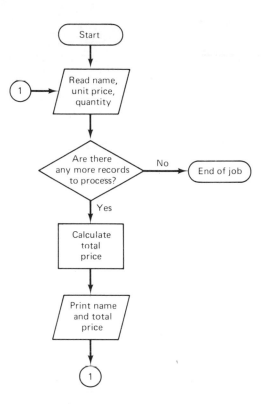

Figure 5.4. First sample flowchart.

5.1.3.1 The Machine's Own Code: Machine Language

In order to be executed, a computer program must be in **machine language**. This is a highly complex internal code that is rarely learned by programmers because:

Difficulties Associated with Machine Language Programming

1. *Machine language uses complex operation codes.* An ADD instruction, for example, may be a 58 code in machine language; a MULTIPLY may be a 4J. For programmers to code a program in machine language, they would have to know how to use such complex codes. In addition, users would find it difficult to examine a program in this language and determine what it is trying to accomplish.
2. Machine language uses actual machine addresses. An ADD instruction, for example, which adds two input fields, can place the result or sum in a third field. In machine language, all three fields must be stored in actual machine locations. To program in this language thus requires the programmer to keep track of actual machine locations. This is a cumbersome and difficult task, since addresses or storage positions can be numbered from 1 to well over 100,000, depending on the storage capacity of the computer.

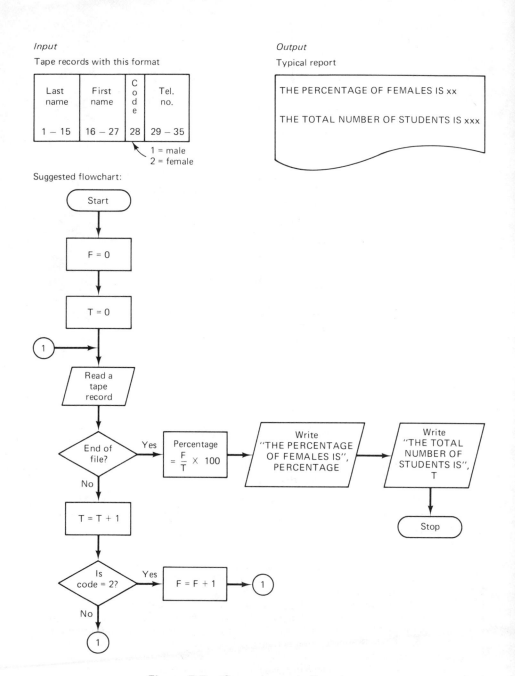

Input

Tape records with this format

Last name	First name	Code	Tel. no.
1 — 15	16 — 27	28	29 — 35

1 = male
2 = female

Output

Typical report

THE PERCENTAGE OF FEMALES IS xx

THE TOTAL NUMBER OF STUDENTS IS xxx

Suggested flowchart:

Start

F = 0

T = 0

1

Read a tape record

End of file?   Yes   Percentage $= \dfrac{F}{T} \times 100$ Write "THE PERCENTAGE OF FEMALES IS", PERCENTAGE   Write "THE TOTAL NUMBER OF STUDENTS IS", T   Stop

No

T = T + 1

Is code = 2?   Yes   F = F + 1   1

No

1

Figure 5.5. Second sample flowchart.

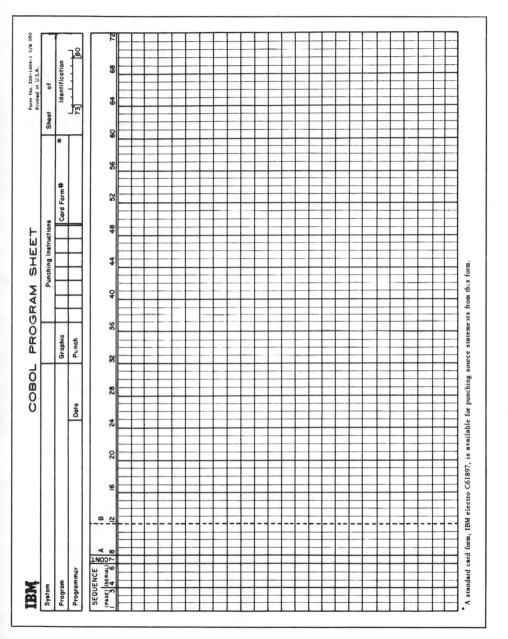

Figure 5.6. Sample coding sheet.

137

Because programming in machine language is complex and cumbersome, few programmers actually code in the machine's own language. An alternative to machine language coding is **symbolic programming**.

A symbolic programming language is far easier for the programmer to code. It uses **symbolic operation codes**, such as ADD or +, and **symbolic addresses**, such as HOLD, RESULT, and SUM, to represent actual storage positions. Thus to add two amounts to a total, we can say LET T1 = A1 + A2 rather than something like 2R 406803. The overwhelming majority of programs are coded in symbolic language rather than machine language.

5.1.3.2   Symbolic Programming

Note that a symbolic program, although easier for the programmer to code, is *not* executable. That is, it cannot be run or executed by the computer. It must first be *converted* or translated into machine language code so that the computer can understand the instructions.

A computer program can translate symbolic code into machine language. Thus a program in symbolic language requires two phases:

Two Phases Required for Symbolic Programs
1. **Translation phase:** The computer translates the symbolic code into machine code.
2. **Execution phase:** After the program is translated, the computer runs or executes it.

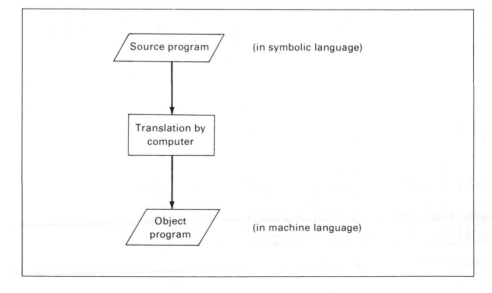

Figure 5.7.   Symbolic programming.

The symbolic program written by the programmer is called a **source program** (see Figure 5.7). Source programs are nonexecutable—they must be translated into machine language before they can be run. The translated or executable progam is called the **object program**.

5.1.4 Getting the Program to Work

5.1.4.1 The Translation Phase

The main symbolic programming languages that we will be considering are listed in Table 5.1. Each of these languages, discussed in Section 5.1.7, requires a translation process.

Regardless of the translation process used, there are three forms of output from a translation process (see Figure 5.8):

Results of a Translation

1. **Source program listing:** This is a computer-generated printout of all instructions.
2. **List of rule violations called syntax errors:** A translation process does not detect logic errors; these errors can be discovered only by testing or executing the program. But any rules that have been violated will cause the computer to print an error message during the translation phase. If the words are misspelled or improperly defined, for example, a syntax error will be denoted.
3. **Object program:** This is the machine-language equivalent of the source program.

There are two types of translator programs used to translate source programs. We will discuss them in detail:

Types of Translator Programs

1. **Compiler:** Source programs are **compiled**.
2. **Assembler:** Source programs are **assembled**.

---

a. *The Compiler: Compiling a Source Program.* High-level symbolic programming languages such as FORTRAN and COBOL are relatively easy to code. They require, however, complex translation processes called **compilations**. That is, the easier it is to code a program, the more difficult it is for the machine to translate it into its own machine language.

A special program called a **compiler**, usually supplied by the computer manufacturer, reads the source program written in a symbolic language and translates it into a machine-language equivalent called an object program.

Table 5.1. *Principal Symbolic Programming Languages.*

Languages	Features
High-level	1. Easy to program
Ada	2. More difficult for the machine to translate
APL	3. Can be run on many different computers
BASIC	
COBOL	
FORTRAN	
Pascal	
PL/1	
RPG	
Low-level	1. Similar to machine language
Assembler languages	2. More difficult to program
	3. Easier for the machine to translate
	4. Computer dependent

Each high-level language has its own compiler. Thus there is a FORTRAN compiler, a COBOL compiler, a PL/1 compiler, and so on.

Each computer has its own unique machine language. Hence compilers are designed to be run on individual computers. Thus a FORTRAN compiler that translates FORTRAN programs for the IBM S/370 would not be the same as a FORTRAN compiler used for the UNIVAC 90/60, even though the FORTRAN source program would be the same. Each compiler is capable of reading the same source program; but the translation process depends on the computer's own internal code.

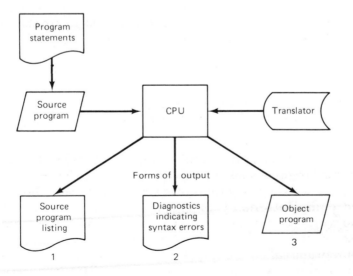

Figure 5.8. The translation process. The translator may be a compiler or an assembler.

When a program is compiled, the entire source program is entered initially; then the translation process is executed. At the end of the compilation, a listing of the program and any rule violations or syntax errors are printed.

Some translators, called **interpreters**, can translate programs interactively as each line of coding is entered.

b. *The Assembler: Assembling a Source Program.*   Low-level programming languages, or assembler languages, are similar to machine language and do *not* require complex translations. Assembler languages are very efficient and are used when it is important to optimize computer performance. Thus operating systems or complex control procedures are likely to be programmed in an assembler language.

The translator in this case is called an **assembler**. The translation process, called an **assembly**, is a high-speed operation. Since assembler language is similar to machine language, the programming is more complex, but the translation process is relatively simple.

Assembler languages tend to be machine dependent. Thus an assembler language for the IBM S/370 is different from the assembler language for a PDP 11.

Each computer supports a variety of programming languages. The large systems are likely to support all or most of the languages mentioned, whereas small or minicomputers may support only two or three.

In most cases, the translators are part of the operating system and are called in as needed. For interactive programming, the interpreter is always on-line; that is, it is in main memory always available for use.

5.1.4.2   The Execution Phase

The translation phase produces an object or machine language program, a source listing, and a listing of rule violations or syntax errors. Any syntax errors that have occurred must be corrected and the source program translated again.

When the program is free from syntax errors, it must be tested to ensure that there are no logic errors. During the execution or test phase, we determine if the program is properly performing all required operations and if it is producing the desired output.

The execution phase is used to "debug" a program, that is, to eliminate all errors or "bugs."

a. *Test Data.*   We run or execute the program with **test** or **sample data**. The output produced is then compared against the output that has been manually prepared from the same data. If everything checks, the program is considered debugged, or free of errors. It is then ready to be run on a scheduled basis.

Note that test data must be carefully prepared to incorporate *all possible conditions*. Any condition that is feasible must be included. In this way, the program tests for all possibilities and it is then unlikely that future scheduled runs of the program will result in errors. When programming errors are detected as a result of the test, the source program must be corrected, retranslated, and the test performed again.

   b. *Example of a Logic Error.*   Any condition that is inadvertently omitted from the test data can produce major errors later. Suppose, for example, that a program allows for up to 10 transaction cards for each account within an accounts receivable file. The programmer should include test data that has accounts with 1 card, 2 cards, and so on, up to 10 cards. In this way, every condition possible would be included within the test data. To assume that because the program works properly for 2 cards in an account it will therefore work for 10 cards in an account may be fallacious.

   Suppose, for example, that the program provides only one position for the NUMBER OF CARDS field. Then when there are *10* (two digits) cards for an account, erroneous processing will occur. Unless the test data includes an account with 10 cards, this erroneous condition will not be discovered until the program is run on a scheduled basis. At that time, the necessity for corrections would result in a disruption of the normal computer schedule and would waste valuable computer time.

   It is also imperative that the programmer incorporate procedures for handling errors in input. The program should contain error procedures for invalid cards, and test data should include invalid cards to ensure their proper treatment. There is an adage in computer processing that because of the large volume of data, anything that could *possibly* go wrong with input data *will* eventually go wrong. Thus error tests must be built into the program to protect its integrity.

5.1.5   Implementing the Program

Once all the programs for a specific system have been written and completely debugged, the systems analyst, together with the programmer, must arrange for converting from the old system to the new, computerized one.

   The process of conversion is a very important one and must be carefully implemented to minimize errors and to ensure a smooth transition. The programmer works closely with all operating staff to achieve the following:

Implementation Requirements
1. The conversion must be performed smoothly.
2. The operating staff must know precisely what to do.
3. The programs must run without errors.

Sometimes a program that is thought to be fully debugged produces errors during this conversion process. This may mean that the programmer did not fully provide for every contingency in the program. More critically, it may mean that the programmer did not fully understand the job requirements. In either case, the program would require modification.

Because some errors during a conversion process are likely to occur, it would be unwise, in most instances, for an organization to simply abandon the old system one day and then rely completely on the new system the next day. Instead, conversion procedures are usually performed in parallel with the old system.

5.1.6   Documenting the Program

After a program has been fully tested and implemented, the programmer must write up the full specifications for all users. This is referred to as documenting the program.

Documentation typically consists of:

Documentation Package Contains:
1. A final source listing
2. A list of control procedures incorporated
3. A list of error tests that are included in the program, together with the disposition of these errors
4. Input/output specifications
5. Flowcharts or pseudocode
6. Test data used
7. Schedules to be maintained

These and all other items are maintained by the computer facility as well as the user organization. If all pertinent data is contained within the documentation package, the program can be run and modified without requiring the original programmer's assistance. This is beneficial to the programmer, who otherwise would be called upon later, as the need arises, to make whatever adjustments are required. This is also beneficial to the organization since the programmer may leave or be unavailable when problems arise. With a complete documentation package, all important aspects of the program have been specified and there should be no need to consult the programmer.

5.1.7 Major High-Level Programming Languages

You will recall that source programs, written by the programmer, must be translated into machine language before they can be executed. There are many programming languages that can be used on many different computers that serve a wide variety of needs. In this section we describe some of the major languages in use today. They have been listed alphabetically.

5.1.7.1 APL

APL is an acronym for A Programming Language, not a very exciting name for a high-powered interactive programming language. APL was first developed in 1962 by Kenneth Iverson, who began his work at Harvard and continued at IBM.

APL is best used for interactive programming using a terminal. It can be used in the **execution mode**, where the instructions are executed as they are entered. APL can also be used in the **definition mode**, where the entire program is entered before execution begins.

An APL keyboard with numerous special symbols is required for programming in this language. The need for these special symbols for programming makes APL a difficult language to read and, for some, a difficult language to code.

Despite these disadvantages, APL is ideally suited for handling complex problems in a free-form style of coding. IBM makes APL available to many of its minicomputer users as an alternative to the more commonly used BASIC. In addition, many large and medium-sized computers support APL, particularly for time-sharing operations.

5.1.7.2 BASIC

BASIC is one of the most widely used programming languages for mini- and microcomputer use as well as for time-sharing applications. Like APL, it is an interactive language, which makes it easy to debug and correct syntax errors.

BASIC is an acronym for Beginner's All-purpose Symbolic Instruction Code. The term "Beginner's" means that it is ideally suited for teaching people who have no previous programming background. In addition to being the main programming language for mini and micro systems, it is the programming language most frequently taught, particularly for entry-level courses. You will see in Chapter 7 that BASIC is a very flexible language and is easy to learn as well.

BASIC enables the beginner to write a simple code that uses mathematically based instructions. For example,

$$F = 9/5*C + 32$$

is equivalent to setting F (Fahrenheit) equal to $\frac{9}{5}C + 32$, where C denotes Celsius. Because of its mathematical notation and its free-form style, BASIC is a popular language for engineers and scientists as well.

5.1.7.3 COBOL

COBOL, an acronym for Common Business Oriented Language is, as the name implies, a business language that can be run on many computer makes and models. It was created to satisfy normal business needs. It is an English-like language. For example, we can say:

ADD SALES-TAX TO PRICE.

Since most business-oriented problems operate on vast amounts of data, requiring high-speed processing, a business language must be capable of easily and effectively handling high-speed storage media, such as magnetic tape and disk. COBOL uses instructions that make programming for these high-level devices a simple task. That is, we can perform header label routines, blocking functions, indexing of disk records, and so on, with relative ease in COBOL.

Since most business problems do not require complex mathematical routines, a business language would not usually include high-level mathematics. Hence simple arithmetic operations are easily performed in COBOL, whereas mathematical functions such as square-root and trigonometric routines that can easily be coded in BASIC or APL are difficult to code in COBOL.

The Nature of Business-Oriented Problems

In short, business-oriented problems that generally require the processing of large amounts of high-level input and output, but do not require very complex arithmetic, are ideally suited for COBOL programming.

5.1.7.4 FORTRAN

The symbolic programming language FORTRAN is an abbreviation for Formula Translator. FORTRAN is a mathematical language that is particularly suited to setting down formulas. To add two fields A and B, for example, and place the answer in a field called C, we use the FORTRAN expression:

$$C = A + B$$

Note that this is equivalent to a mathematical formula and is very similar to BASIC.

FORTRAN is most often used for scientific or engineering applications because of its mathematical nature. It includes features for determining logarithms, trigonometric functions, and so on. Like the other languages, it has been standardized so that it can be used on many different computers.

Although FORTRAN can easily handle complex mathematical problems, it is not as well suited for high-level input/output operations as COBOL is, for example.

The Nature of Scientific Problems

Most scientific applications utilize numerous high-level mathematical operations with little input/output. That is, several numbers fed into a computer pinpointing a rocket's trajectory can result in hours of computer calculations.

For mathematical problems, we generally use many calculations and comparatively little input/output. FORTRAN, as a mathematical language, was created for handling complex calculations but sacrifices some of the ease with which high-level input/output, such as disk, can be handled.

Note that FORTRAN is used predominantly in business applications where mathematics is required. Sales forecasting and inventory control are operations that most often use FORTRAN. In short, COBOL is a more effective language when dealing with business-oriented problems that include large amounts of input/output with relatively simple calculations. FORTRAN is a more effective language when dealing with scientific or business-oriented problems that include complex calculating routines with relatively simplified input/output.

5.1.7.5 Pascal

This is one of the more recently developed and more promising programming languages, having been devised by Niklaus Wirth during the years 1968-1971.

The term "Pascal" is not an acronym or an abbreviation as are most names for programming languages. Rather, Pascal was named for the mathematician and inventor Blaise Pascal (1623-1662), who developed one of the earliest calculating machines.

The Pascal programming language is considered to have a great deal of potential for computer users because it facilitates the use of **structured programming** techniques, which will be discussed in Chapter 16. Structured programming is a technique designed to standardize programming and make debugging easier. Pascal makes use of IF-THEN-ELSE and DO-WHILE control structures, which are the very basis of structured programming techniques.

Pascal has been adopted as a primary programming language for many microcomputers. It promises to be one of the most important languages of the 1980s.

5.1.7.6   PL/1

PL/1, an abbreviation for Programming Language/1, is a symbolic language that is designed to meet the needs of both scientific and commercial computer users. That is, it is designed to combine the major advantages and features of COBOL and FORTRAN so that a user can employ it for both scientific and commercial problems. There are other versions of PL/1, such as PL/C and PL/M, that are used on some systems.

PL/1 is a most effective tool in organizations that require both scientific and commercial applications. An engineering firm, for example, that has one large computer that processes engineering and business (payroll, accounts receivable, and accounts payable) applications might best utilize PL/1 as its prime programming language. In this way, the company need not hire two types of programmers, those with knowledge of FORTRAN and those with knowledge of COBOL. Similarly, employee transfers between the scientific programming staff and the commercial programming staff can easily be made.

There are, then, many advantages to adopting a single programming language for companies that possess both scientific and commercial applications. In this way *both* high-level mathematics and high-level input/output can be effectively handled using one language and even one program. The main disadvantage of PL/1 is that it is more complex than most other languages.

5.1.7.7   RPG

Many business organizations, particularly small ones or those that rely on minicomputers, do not need the extensive options available with COBOL or PL/1. Their needs could be satisfied with a simplified language that is most often used to print output from cards or tape or disk. There is usually very little complex programming involved to produce printed output.

RPG, an abbreviation for Report Program Generator, is a symbolic language ideally suited for creating printed reports from input media. There is a minimum of programming effort required with RPG. That is, it is a very simple language. Page numbers, page headings, edited results, and final totals are printed in RPG with minimal programming effort.

5.1.7.8 Ada: The Making of a New Language

The Department of Defense has recently developed a programming language that is ideally suited for coding programs using the structured approach. This language is called Ada, named for the Countess of Lovelace, who, as we saw in Chapter 2, is considered the world's first programmer. You will recall that she worked with Charles Babbage and wrote a demonstration program for his Analytical Engine.

The language was specifically designed for large applications, particularly those that operate in a real-time environment. Although intended to be a required language for any supplier dealing with the Department of Defense, it remains to be seen whether Ada will become a standard language in the business world as well.

Table 5.2 provides a summary of the high-level programming languages discussed. Note that there are many other languages available, but these are the most common.

Summary

The symbolic languages utilized at a computer facility will depend on the type of applications or jobs generally required. That is, an organization that usually requires business-oriented programs and that has several different computers would probably utilize COBOL as a main language. A company that utilizes scientific applications or business functions with high-level mathematics would probably use FORTRAN. A company that relies on minicomputers would use BASIC, RPG, or perhaps APL. Most organizations have computers that support more than one language. Table 5.3 provides a summary of language characteristics. Table 5.4 lists the major features of the languages discussed.

A relative comparison of the major types of programming languages is shown in the following chart:

Level of User Orientation (ease of coding)	Type of Language	Level of Computer Orientation (ease of translation)
Low ↓ High	Machine language Assembler language High-level language Interactive Compiler-oriented	High ↓ Low

Table 5.2   *High-level Programming Languages*

Name	Meaning	Main Uses	Features
APL	A Programming Language	Used on minis Used with time-sharing facilities	Interactive Requires special graphics keyboard Relatively complex Scientifically oriented
BASIC	Beginner's All-Purpose Instruction Code	Used on minis for production runs Used on all systems for teaching purposes	Interactive Easy to learn Uses mathematical notation Can be used for business and scientific problems
COBOL	Common Business Oriented Language	Used on small-, medium-, and large-scale systems Not available yet for most minis or micros (compiler too complex)	Ideal for business applications Easily handles disk and tape features English-like
FORTRAN	Formula Translator	Used on small-, medium-, and large-scale systems	Ideal for scientific applications Uses mathematical notation
Pascal	Named for the mathematician Blaise Pascal	Used on all types of computers	Scientifically oriented Focuses on structured programming techniques
PL/1	Programming Language/1	Used on medium- and large-scale systems	Combines the features of COBOL and FORTRAN Somewhat complex to code
RPG	Report Program Generator	Used primarily on minicomputers but can be used on larger systems as well	Very simple language Ideally suited for printing reports

Table 5.3 *Summary of Language Characteristics*

Language Type	Characteristics
Machine language	Machine dependent Involves the use of special codes and the assignment of storage addresses
Assembler language	Machine dependent Uses symbolic operation codes (called mnemonics) and symbolic storage addresses (called operands) For every assembler language instruction, *one* machine-language instruction is generated (one-to-one language)
High-level language	Machine independent Uses English-like instructions One instruction may result in several machine-language statements (one-to-many language)

5.1.8 Evaluating Application Software

As previously noted, there are three main methods for acquiring application software:

1. In-house or internal programmers
2. Consultants or "third-party" software suppliers
3. Prepackaged applications sold by manufacturers or facilities management organizations

Table 5.5 summarizes the advantages and disadvantages of each.

Software: An Analysis

The cost of hardware is decreasing over time while the salaries that are paid to computer professionals continue to rise. Because salaries constitute such a large part of a computer facility's budget, many organizations find themselves in need of external software support even though they have a staff of programmers and systems analysts. For a breakdown of data processing costs in industry, education, and government, see Figure 5.9. The software percentages in this illustration represent third-party programs and packaged applications. It should be noted that many organizations rely on internal programmers as well as third-party programmers or packaged applications for their software support.

In short, many organizations are beginning to rely heavily on external software—third-party programs or packaged applications.

Table 5.4 *Summary of Features of Programming Languages.*

	Assembler Language	APL	BASIC	COBOL	FORTRAN	Pascal	PL/1	RPG
Interactive capability		X	X					
Standardized			X	X	X		X	
Minicomputer orientation (requires minimum storage for translators)	X	X	X		X	X		X
Machine dependent (but most efficient)	X							
Scientifically oriented	X	X	X		X	X	X	
Business oriented	X		X	X			X	X

151

Table 5.5 *Acquisition of Software*

Method of Acquisition	Advantages	Disadvantages
Internal programmer	Programmer possesses a more thorough knowledge of user's needs Maintenance and modifications are easily performed	Cost of design and debugging is relatively expensive Programmer may not be very well informed of specific application
Third-party software supplier	Supplier can provide an objective evaluation of user's needs	Less expensive than in-house programming (do not need to pay fringe benefits, etc.), but still expensive After program is complete, difficult to obtain support for maintenance and modification
Packaged applications	Lowest cost—the actual cost of the package is absorbed by a *number* of users rather than one Programmers have a great deal of knowledge of the specific applications	No flexibility Modifications are extremely costly The user organization has no control of procedures that are to be included

The federal government, however, has recently undertaken a study that indicates that external software contracts sometimes result in completely unusable products and are very costly to the user as well (see Figure 5.10). Thus the control and flexibility of internal software, although more expensive, may be more reliable, in some instances.

In any case, the programming field is an ever-expanding one (see Figure 5.11). Note, however, that with an increasing number of packaged applications and increasing reliance on firmware, the ratio of programmers to total number of computers has decreased sharply.

5.2 OPERATING SYSTEM FEATURES

Thus far, we have considered that aspect of software which relates to application programming. We have discussed the steps involved in writing application programs and the various languages used. The computer system itself operates on application programs under the control of an **operating system**. The specific characteristics of operating systems are beyond the scope of this text, but there are several features of these systems which are important to understand.

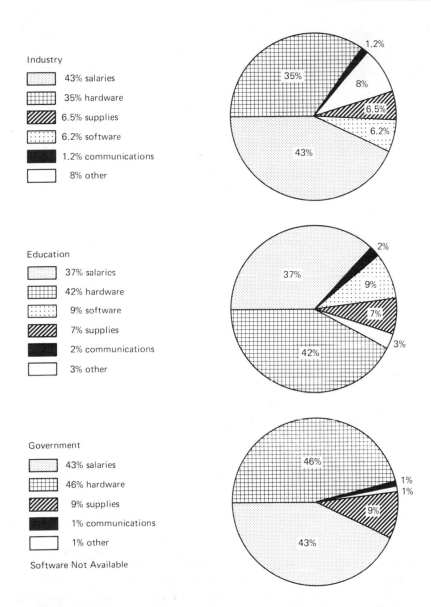

Figure 5.9. A breakdown of data processing costs in industry, education, and government. Salaries and hardware still consume the largest slices of the budget pie, but the portion devoted to software is growing. (From Louise C. Shaw, "Budgeting in 1980," *Datamation*, Jan. 1980, p. 129. Reprinted with permission of *Datamation*® magazine, © copyright by Technical Publishing Company, a Dun & Bradstreet Company, 1980. All rights reserved.)

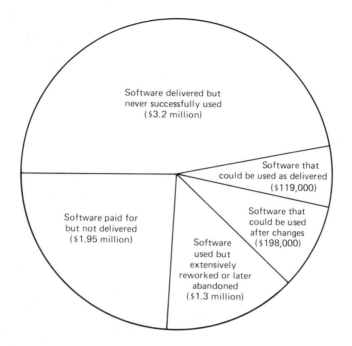

Figure 5.10 Where the money went: an analysis of federal govern-ment expenditures for software. In fiscal year 1979, federal agencies squandered $6.8 million on nine software development contracts. (From *Information Systems News*. Copyright by CMP Publications Inc., 333 East Short Road, Manhasset, N.Y. Reprinted with permission.)

5.2.1 The Supervisor

The **supervisor** is the control program of the operating system. It coordinates, interrelates, and monitors all aspects of the operating system. It is a main element of software.

Typically, the entire operating system consists of a library of compilers, assemblers, interpreters, and other programs in addition to the supervisor. The operating system is stored on an auxiliary storage device such as a disk or a drum, called the **system resident device**.

The supervisor is loaded into the main memory before any processing can begin. The supervisor is always resident in main memory when the computer is operational.

In summary, the supervisor is a control program designed to minimize the need for computer operators to constantly monitor the machine's activities. In first-, second-, and even some third-generation computers, without operating systems, several computer operators

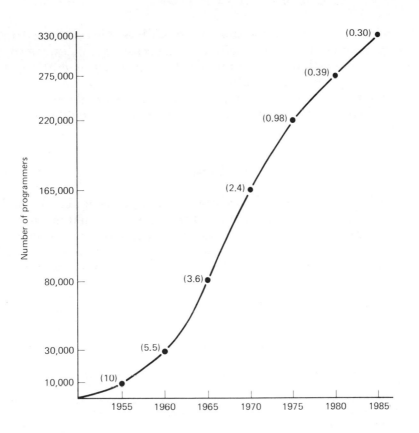

Figure 5.11. Growth of the programming profession. Numbers in parentheses indicate the ratio of programmers to the total number of computers.

Functions of the Supervisor

1. Controls the processing of data by each application program
2. Controls the calling of compilers, assemblers, and interpreters, needed for translation of source programs
3. Controls the processing of inquiry–response requests from numerous terminals in a time-sharing or on-line environment
4. Communicates the requirements of each run to the computer operator via a console typewriter
5. Maintains data on cost, time, date, and scheduling of each run

---

were required to restart jobs when errors occurred, to maintain a log of computer activities, and so on. Moreover, with such systems, the ability to process several requests automatically from remote terminals was not feasible. An operating system, then, with a supervisor or control program results in (1) more efficient processing, (2) less need for operator intervention, and (3) the ability to process several requests from different terminals simultaneously.

Changes to the operating system can be made to meet an individual company's specific needs. These changes would be made by a *systems programmer*.

5.2.2   Communicating with the Supervisor

There is a special machine-oriented language designed to enable operators, users, and programmers to communicate their needs to the supervisor and through it, to the operating system. This language is frequently called **job control language** (JCL). JCL is used to initially access data, programs, or other features of the computer system.

Computer Users Who Communicate with the Computer Using JCL

1. Terminal operator
   a. JCL is necessary for indicating which files need to be accessed for inquiry-response purposes.
   b. JCL is keyed on the terminal by the operator.
2. Programmer
   a. JCL is necessary for indicating which translator the supervisor should call in for processing, what devices the program will use, what options the program requires, and so on.
   b. JCL is entered prior to the program on a terminal, on cards, or on whatever medium the program uses.
3. Computer operator
   a. JCL is used to determine how long a specific job has been running, what tapes or disks need to be mounted for specific runs, how many terminals are being used at a specific time, and so on.

The computer operator uses a special **console terminal** linked directly to the CPU to communicate with the supervisor. This console is similarly used by the supervisor program to indicate the computer's specific requirements for each run.

5.2.3   Input/Output Control through Multiprogramming

Most modern computer systems, even many minis, usually have the control capability to process more than one program at any time. That is, several terminals can access the computer concurrently and perform the following:

I/O Capabilities of Many Systems

1. Some terminals can be used for entering data.
2. Other terminals can be used for making inquiries at the same time.
3. Still other terminals and/or local I/O units can be used for entering, debugging, and running programs at the same time.

All of these operations can be performed concurrently if the computer contains a sophisticated supervisor and a full-scale operating system.

The ability of a computer to run more than one program simultaneously is referred to as **multiprogramming**. Multiprogramming is an essential and integral feature of time-sharing and data communications applications.

To perform multiprogramming operations, the supervisor partitions the CPU into numerous sectors, each capable of storing a given program:

Main Storage	
Supervisor	
Partition 1	Partition 2
Partition 3	Partition 4

Note that although several programs may reside in memory at a given time, the CPU is capable of executing only *one* instruction at *one* time. But the supervisor enables the CPU to execute one instruction from one program, then another instruction from a second program, and so on, so that several programs can be run concurrently. Thus a slow I/O operation from one program can be executed at the same time that arithmetic operations are executed from another. Because instructions can be executed in billionths of a second, this has the effect of appearing to execute numerous instructions simultaneously.

In essence, then, when operating in a multiprogramming environment, a program is not usually run continuously from beginning to end. The net effect, however, is to run numerous programs in far less time than it would take to run them consecutively.

The supervisor can also establish priorities for each of these programs so that the instructions from a priority run are always executed first, where feasible.

5.2.4 Virtual Storage

Virtual storage is a concept in computer technology which permits a computer system to operate as if it had more primary storage capacity than it actually has. This increases the multiprogramming capability of a system.

This technique is accomplished by segmenting a program into a series of sections or modules that are stored outside the CPU, typically on a direct-access device such as magnetic disk. Instead of calling the entire program into the CPU at one time to be executed, the control system causes sections of the program to be read in and executed, one at a time. After one section has been executed, another section is brought into the CPU and uses the storage positions occupied by the previous section (see Figure 5.12). In this manner, there is an effective storage capacity far in excess of the actual storage capacity. Several large programs which, individually or collectively, might otherwise occupy too much CPU memory to be executed at the same time can thus be run simultaneously.

The computer itself handles the segmentation of programs and the swapping of program sections into and out of primary storage.

Many large and medium-sized computer systems have virtual storage (VS) operating systems.

5.2.5 Multiprocessing

Multiprocessing is the use of two or more central processing units linked together to optimize the processing of data. In a multiprocessing environment, more than one instruction can be executed by the CPUs *at the same time*. This is in contrast to multiprogramming, where one

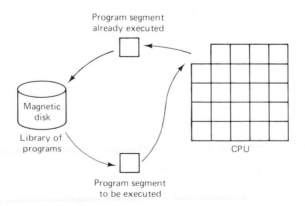

Figure 5.12. The virtual storage concept.

CPU can process different instructions from one or more programs concurrently by interleaving them. With multiprocessing, there is actually more than one CPU; hence more than one instruction can be executed *simultaneously*.

A typical application of multiprocessing is the use of a minicomputer to handle scheduling, formatting of data, editing, and summary totals so that the main CPU or mainframe can be used for high-priority or more complex tasks.

Sometimes a smaller CPU such as a minicomputer handles input/output operations from a variety of terminals. In this way, the main CPU needs to access only one unit—the minicomputer—rather than each of the numerous terminals. For such applications, the minicomputer is referred to as a **front-end processor**. The front-end processor can establish priorities for each of the terminals, queue the terminal inquiries if the mainframe is "busy," and maintain controls.

Minicomputers are used with increasing frequency in a multiprocessing environment to relieve some of the load of a mainframe and to handle input/output scheduling and data entry from remote terminals.

5.3   FIRMWARE: WHERE HARDWARE AND SOFTWARE MERGE

As already noted, it is possible to acquire as part of a computer system integrated logic circuits on a miniaturized chip which already contains a software package. Such chips are referred to as ROM (read-only memory).

In small systems where main memory is limited, the use of ROM is very popular. Whereas programs occupy bytes of main memory, ROM can be built into the system and thus not utilize *any* user memory.

There are several types of ROM:

Types of ROM

ROM: read-only memory (standard). A BASIC compiler, for example, may exist as ROM in micro and mini systems.

PROM: programmable read-only memory. This is where a chip (or chips) is ordered by the user to contain a programmed set of functions. Either the user or the manufacturer writes the code for the PROM chip.

EPROM: erasable programmable read-only memory. This is where a chip is not only programmable to include a set of functions but the program can be "erased" or overlaid with another program through a microcode procedure.

Summary: Features of Systems Software

I.   SYSTEMS SOFTWARE INCLUDES:
   A. The operating system
   B. Compilers and assemblers
   C. Input/output control routines
   D. Diagnostic routines
   E. Job control and accounting routines
   F. Report generators
II. THE SUPERVISOR
   A. This is the control program of the operating system.
   B. It is loaded into the CPU from the operating system, which is in auxiliary storage.
   C. It controls the processing of each program.
   D. The supervisor minimizes the need for operator intervention.
III. COMMUNICATING WITH THE SUPERVISOR
   A. Job control language (JCL) is the special language devised for programmers and computer operators to communicate with the CPU.
   B. Each computer's job control language is different.
IV. ADDITIONAL FEATURES OF COMPUTERS
   A. Multiprogramming
     1. This is the ability to execute more than one program concurrently.
     2. This enables systems to function in a real-time mode using numerous terminals.
   B. Multiprocessing
     1. This is the use of two or more CPUs linked together to optimize the processing of data.
     2. Minis used as front-end processors in conjunction with large mainframes are operating in a multiprocessing environment.
   C. Virtual Storage
     1. This permits a computer system to operate as if it had more primary storage capacity than it actually has.
     2. Programs are segmented and sections are swapped into and out of primary storage.
V.   FIRMWARE
   A. Software is hardwired.
   B. There are standard firmware units as well as programmable firmware units.

KEY TERMS

Ada
APL
Assembler language
BASIC
COBOL
Coding a program
Compilation (compiler)

Debugging
Erasable programmable read-only memory (EPROM)
Execution
Firmware
Flowchart
FORTRAN
High-level languages
Job control language (JCL)
Low-level languages
Machine-language program
Multiprocessing
Multiprogramming
Object program
Operating system
Pascal
PL/1
Program documentation
Programmable read-only memory (PROM)
Pseudocode
Read-only memory (ROM)
RPG
Software
Source program
Supervisor
Symbolic program
Syntax error
System resident device
Systems programmer
Template
Translation
Virtual storage

REVIEW QUESTIONS

1. Indicate the most appropriate language to be used and explain your answer.
   a. The program is to be entered on a terminal; the programmer is not extremely well versed in computer processing.
   b. There is one programming group in the company responsible for both scientific and business-oriented programs.

    c. The program requires the use of randomly accessed disk files in a business environment.

    d. The program is a fairly straightforward disk-to-printer summary report.

2. Explain the main differences between a scientific problem to be programmed and a business problem to be programmed.

3. What are the main differences between application software and system software?

4. What is the purpose of job control language? How is it used?

5. Computer systems are enhanced by the use of the following features:
    a. Multiprocessing
    b. Multiprogramming
    c. Virtual storage
    Explain these features. Indicate how on-line processing makes use of these features.

6. Under what conditions would an organization use an outside consultant to program an application?

7. What are some of the reasons why programs fail to meet their objectives adequately?

8. What are the main differences between machine language and a high-level programming language?

9. How are flowcharts used by the programmer?

10. Why is documentation of a program so important?

DISCUSSION QUESTIONS

1. Many programmers are reluctant to document their programs. Why is this so? What are some of the problems associated with improper or incomplete documentation?

2. Suppose that a program is translated and there are no syntax errors. Does that mean it is correct? Explain your answer.

3. Do you think it is easier to debug a program interactively or in a batch mode? Explain.

4. Your organization needs sales forecasting programs. What criteria would you use for determining whether you would recommend purchase of an application package or programming by an in-house programmer?

5. Compare and contrast the features of COBOL, FORTRAN, and PL/1.

6. You are a programming manager. A member of your staff writes first-rate programs but cannot communicate well with users. How would you handle the situation?

7. Do you think it would be useful for programming to be a required part of either a high school or college curriculum? Explain your answer.

8. Some colleges that require a foreign-language competency will accept knowledge of a programming language to satisfy this requirement. Do you regard this as appropriate? Explain your answer.

APPLICATION

Consider the application below and then answer the questions that follow it.

Software Production Still a Problem[a]

by Werner L. Frank

A recent report to Congress by the Comptroller General General Accounting Office (GAO) report FGMSD-80-4, Nov. 9, 1979 cited the continuing problem of developing software within the federal government. The report title summarizes the issue: "Contracting for Computer Software Development—Serious Problems Require Management Attention to Avoid Wasting Additional Millions."

The report reflected the views of 163 software contracting firms and 113 federal government project officers, as well as experience with specific contracts for software development. The indictment, as summarized herein was severe:

- Dollar overruns are fairly common in more than 50% of cases.
- Calendar overruns occur in more than 60% of cases.
- Of the nine contracts examined (admittedly eight of which were in trouble), of $6.8 million expended, the results yielded:

1. Software delivered, but never used: $3.2 million.
2. Software paid for, but never delivered: $1.95 million.
3. Software extensively reworked before use: $1.3 million.
4. Software used after changes: $198,000.
5. Software used as delivered: $119,000.

As the report concluded, "The government got for its money less than 2% of the total value of the contracts."

Can software development still be that unpredictable and troublesome in this age of enlightened practitioners who have access to higher order languages, sophisticated operating systems, a variety of implementation tools and various structured procedures and disciplines?

The report went on to cite some causes for the problems identified above:

- Lack of specific contracting skills for soliciting and subsequently administering software efforts.
- Premature rush to develop systems before adequate requirements analysis is completed.
- Tendency to commit to the entire project without proper planning or defining check points.
- Tendency to ignore final inspection and test conditions and related acceptance procedures.

The report also identified some popular observations of the software process including:

- Projects cost more and run larger than expected.
- The production system usually ends up as a "prototype" system.
- The ultimate operational system is often achieved after fixing the prototype at a cost equal to or greater than the initial development itself.

The GAO called for action by the federal government to remedy the situation by suggesting that specific guidelines be generated which would assist agencies in custom software development. In this regard, the report provided a provisional checklist of items that can serve as a basis for a more comprehensive attack on the problem.

Is Organization Enough?

But can better organization in itself, by the federal customer or any other software purchaser, really impact the fundamentals that operate in software construction?

We regretfully conclude that the customer's organization and procurement process has little influence on these factors.

So what can be done? I submit that the single most important and influencing step that can be taken when contracting for software is to require a "break-in" phase by the contractor in which he is asked to review and feed back his full understanding of the requirements and the development, as a prerequisite to the start of the actual implementation.

This activity is best carried out within the disciplines of structured analysis. It doesn't really matter which methodology is used, as long as one performs the process under a well-defined discipline.

This procedural step—while possibly retracing earlier in-house activities which may have established the user requirements in the first place—will:

- Reconfirm and authenticate the operational requirements.
- Provide expected performance parameters.
- Establish test and acceptance procedures.
- Validate the vendor's understanding and commitment.

After this step is satisfactorily completed, schedules and prices can be established and the customer can then organize to monitor and manage the software development.

In fact, the serious buyer may well wish to purchase this initial phase of the project from two qualified sources in order to provide a check and balance. It has been clearly established that most of the serious defects in software occurring during the operation of a system can be traced back to initial design flaws and oversights. Hence, extra dollars spent early in the game are the best investment that can be made to minimize postcontract problems. And yet, it is this step which is too often expected as a "freebie" in the government procurement process.

Even More . . .

But that isn't all that matters. The report overlooked two other important points.

The first is concerned with the apparent belief that "correct" specifications at the outset, and maintaining adherence to those requirements, eliminate problems in developing software.

Unfortunately there are not many systems that can be prescribed at the outset and for which changes do not abound as development progresses.

But even more important, the client or end user often does not really know what is being sought in detail until pieces of the development become visible.

This understanding of the software construction process suggests the early need for completion of basic functions of a system in order to provide a means for the user to track both progress and direction. This step becomes, therefore, an important and measurable contractual milestone.

Finally, we caution the software buyer about another overlooked aspect. This is the postcontract, operational phase during which the maintenance activity begins. The referenced GAO report emphasized the construction and delivery phase of government contracting for software, but ignored the operational impact of the delivered software.

In other words, the problems with custom-developed software in the federal government may have been found to be even worse than reported if the maintenance experience had also been studied and evaluated.

---

[a] *Computerworld*, Sept. 29, 1980, p. 41. Copyright by Werner L. Frank, Executive Vice President, Informatics Inc., Woodland Hills, CA 91364. Reprinted with permission.

Application Questions

1. What are the major problems in developing software for the federal government?
2. What does the author suggest to solve these problems?

Computer systems: with a focus on minis and micros

As previously mentioned, understanding the principles of electronic data processing means familiarization with two basic concepts:

1. **Computer hardware**: the devices that comprise a computer system
2. **Computer software:** the instructions to the computer system that enable it to function accurately and efficiently

Note that the cost of hardware relative to software has been decreasing overall, and this trend will undoubtedly continue (see Figure 6.1).

You will recall that a computer system consists of:

```
Elements of a Computer System

Input devices
Central processing unit (CPU) or mainframe
Output devices
Auxiliary or secondary storage
```

Objectives

We have already discussed each element in some detail. This chapter integrates and summarizes these elements to provide an understanding of the total computer system. Because of the growth of minicomputers and microcomputers for many applications (see Figure 6.2), a large part of this chapter focuses on these systems as either alternatives or supplements to larger systems.

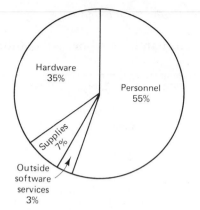

Figure 6.1. Elements of average computer installation budgets. Terminals account for 35 to 45% of hardware costs. Over time, hardware costs have been decreasing, software costs have been increasing.

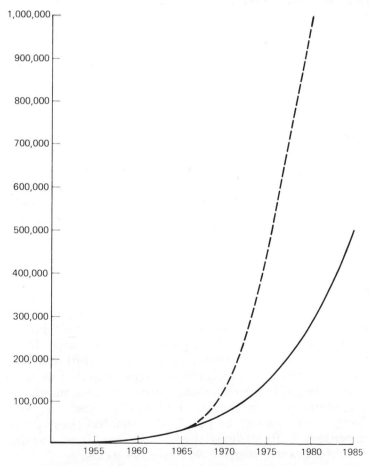

Figure 6.2. Growth of computer installations. Dashed line, number of computers, including minicomputers; solid line, number of computers, excluding minicomputers.

Computer systems can be categorized as follows:

Categories of Computer Systems
Traditional
Super
Large
Medium
Small
Recent Trends
Minis
Micros

6.1   EVALUATING COMPUTER SYSTEMS

The following elements determine the category that applies to a specific computer system.

6.1.1   Memory Size

You will recall that the number of storage positions that can be accessed in a computer system is referred to as its **memory size**. Memory sizes vary widely depending on the category of computer. Smaller-sized computers have a storage capacity or memory size that generally ranges from 32,000 to 512,000 positions, referred to as 32,000 to 512,000 (32K to 512K) **bytes** of memory. Larger systems have memory sizes in excess of several million positions or **megabytes** (MB) of storage.

6.1.2   Cost

As one would expect, larger computer systems are significantly more expensive than smaller ones. Mini- and microcomputers tend to be acquired by purchase only, because the cost is relatively low. It is possible, for example, to purchase a microcomputer with limited capability for several hundred dollars, although most micro- or mini-computer systems with numerous I/O devices cost thousands of dollars. Larger systems can be purchased, too, but they can also be leased or rented; rental prices themselves could be hundreds of thousands of dollars per year for very large systems.

6.1.3 Available Hardware

Each computer system is capable of utilizing a maximum number of hardware devices. Some smaller systems, for example, can provide access to only a handful of terminals, whereas larger systems can be linked to dozens of terminals. Similarly, some minicomputers usually cannot utilize disk drives but utilize instead floppy disks, which are miniaturized versions of the larger fixed magnetic disks that we have already discussed. Thus the size and type of hardware is itself dependent on the computer system. Moreover, the number of devices that can be linked to a CPU depends on the category of the computer system.

6.1.4 Speed

Most current large and medium-sized computer systems perform operations in speeds that are measured in **nanoseconds**, or billionths of a second. Some supercomputers, however, operate at speeds measured in **picoseconds** or trillionths of a second.

In general, the larger systems have faster access and faster processing speeds than the smaller ones.

6.1.5 Available Software

The size, type, and number of applications or user programs that can be processed by a computer system depends on its specific category. Moreover, the size and efficiency of the control programs are also computer dependent.

6.1.6 Compatibility

If software prepared for one computer can be utilized by another, without a rigorous conversion, the two systems are said to be **compatible**. The IBM S/370, for example, can be obtained in one of numerous models; the models are said to be **upwardly compatible**. That is, an organization that acquires an IBM S/370 model 138 can, if the need arises, "trade it in" for a more sophisticated model, such as the model 148, and still use the same programs. Thus manufacturers are providing users with the ability to acquire more sophisticated systems without having to redesign all the software.

In addition to reliance on upward compatibility, there are ways to enhance a given computer system by acquiring **plug-compatible**

Table 6.1. *The Big Four Computer Manufacturers*

Name	Percent of Total Large-Scale-System Market
IBM	59
Honeywell	7
Sperry-Univac	6½
Burroughs	5

machines (PCMs), which are devices that add storage capability or additional input/output as needed. These PCMs can be obtained from the computer manufacturer or from some company that specializes only in a specific type of plug-compatible device. Thus a UNIVAC computer system can be enhanced with the use of Control Data card readers, Hazeltine terminals, and so on, since all these peripheral devices can be made plug compatible to the overall computer system.

First we discuss the traditional types of computer systems and then focus on the mini- and microcomputer revolution. For a list of the major manufacturers in each category, see Tables 6.1 and 6.2.

6.2 TRADITIONAL COMPUTER SYSTEMS: SMALL-, MEDIUM-, LARGE-SCALE AND SUPERCOMPUTERS

Computer systems are manufactured by the traditional leaders in the computer field, such as Burroughs, Honeywell, IBM, NCR, and Sperry-Univac. IBM has maintained its position of leadership in the small-, medium-, and large-scale categories. Some leading minicomputer manufacturers, such as the Digital Equipment Corporation, Data General, and Hewlett-Packard, have, however, gained an edge in the small-scale-system category.

These computers are based on a **total system concept**. That is,

Table 6.2. *Top 10 U.S. Companies Overall in the Data Processing Industry*

1. IBM
2. Burroughs
3. NCR
4. Control Data
5. Sperry-Univac
6. Digital Equipment
7. Honeywell
8. Hewlett-Packard
9. Memorex
10. Data General

users acquire the CPU size and specific input/output devices that will satisfy their own needs.

Some of the smaller systems are card oriented. Most, however, have the following elements:

Elements of Traditional Computer Systems
CPU
Auxiliary storage
Line or page printer
Card reader
Card punch
Several magnetic tape drives
Several magnetic disk drives
Numerous terminals

Most of these systems can process data at speeds of several million instructions per second (frequently abbreviated MIPS).

6.2.1   Small-Scale Computers

The IBM series 34 and 38, Data General CS 30, Hewlett-Packard L50, UNIVAC BC/7, and Burroughs B-80, as examples, fall into the category of small computers (see Figure 6.3). They frequently utilize punched card input and, although they have the capability of producing high-level output, they are basically used to produce printed

Figure 6.3.   Small business computer.

output. The IBM System/3 uses a 96-column card designed with 20% more capacity than the 80-column card. The disadvantage of the 96-column card is that it cannot be used with other data processing equipment. Thus an organization that rents such equipment and uses this type of card cannot use it with most tabulating devices or other computers that employ the standard 80-column card.

6.2.2   Medium-Scale Computers

Medium-scale computers (see Figure 6.4) are more widely used and far more capable machines than small computers. These include the IBM S/370 models 138 and 148, IBM 4331, Burroughs 5500 series, and so on. These devices are most often employed at typical business and industrial organizations throughout the country. Their average rental is typically $10,000 per month or more and they are capable of high-speed, complex operations. They can also use a large number of sophisticated I/O devices. They do, however, require some operator intervention, even though they utilize complex software to handle most typical control procedures.

6.2.3   Large-Scale Computers

Large-scale computers (Figure 6.5) are the really high-level machines that have storage capacities in the megabyte (million-byte) range and typically rent for more than $100,000 per month. They usually contain

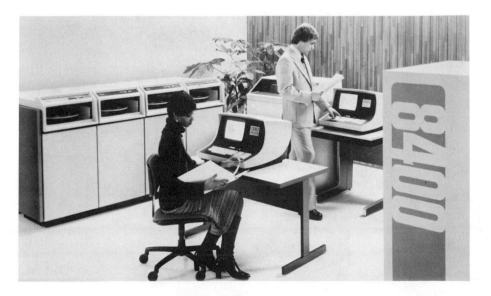

Figure 6.4.   Medium-scale computer.

Figure 6.5. Large-scale computer.

full control systems with minimal operator intervention. They are capable of linking up with dozens of sophisticated I/O devices, have high-level data communications capability, and can perform operations at very high speeds. Such large-scale computers include the IBM 303X, IBM S/370 model 168, Burroughs model 165, Honeywell 66/80, and others. For a typical breakdown of the cost for a large-scale system, see Figure 6.6. For an evaluation of trends in the medium- to large-scale systems market, see Table 6.3.

Table 6.4 provides a comparison of the various categories of computers.

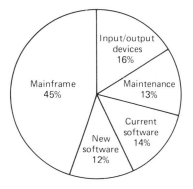

Figure 6.6. Typical breakdown of the cost for a large-scale system. (From *Computerworld*, Jan. 7, 1980, p. 65. Copyright by CW Communications/Inc., Framingham, MA 01701. Reprinted with permission.)

Table 6.3. *Estimated Worldwide Market Shares (Percent): Medium- to Large-Scale General-Purpose Mainframes.*

	1973	1978	1983
IBM	65.8	64.2	60.0
Honeywell	12.6	11.0	9.3
Burroughs	6.6	7.6	6.8
Sperry-Univac	7.1	7.1	6.0
NCR	3.8	3.9	3.4
Control Data	3.0	2.4	1.7

6.2.4 Supercomputers

Supercomputers are machines that have capabilities far beyond even the traditional large-scale systems. Their speed is in the 100 million instructions per second range.

For commercial use, supercomputers serve as **host** processors for local computer and time-sharing **networks**. For scientific use, super-computers have been applied to problems in weather forecasting, aircraft design, nuclear research, and seismic analysis. In total, there are no more than several hundred such machines in use worldwide.

Several computer manufacturers that specialize in large and medium-sized computers also build supercomputers. IBM, Control Data (Star and Cyber 7600), Amdahl, and Burroughs all market supercomputers. Cray Research specializes in supercomputers and has recently announced some extremely sophisticated hardware. See Figure 6.7 for an illustration of the Cray-1 supercomputer, which operates at about 10 times the speed of typical large-scale systems. The cost of such supercomputers is in the $12 million range.

6.3 MINIS: THE COMPUTER REVOLUTION IN MINIATURE

The trend in the computing field is currently to "think small." Many organizations have traded in their large or medium-sized central computer systems for a series of minicomputers that collectively process data more efficiently and effectively and at a lower cost. Still more organizations have augmented their existing computer facilities with minis, which are very effective in accommodating growing computational needs.

6.3.1 Defining a Mini

But just what is a minicomputer? As is the case with many attempts to categorize, there is no real consensus. We will define a minicomputer to be a system that sells for under $50,000 in its basic form and has a basic

Table 6.4. *Characteristics of the Various Computer Sizes.*

Characteristics	Large Computer Systems	Medium-Sized Computer Systems	Small Computer Systems	Minicomputer Systems	Microcomputer Systems
Purchase price	$1,000,000+	$250,000–1,000,000	$50,000–250,000	$2000–50,000	$1000–10,000
Main storage capacity	Extremely large	Large	Medium	Medium	Limited
Processing speed	Extremely fast	Fast	Moderate	Moderate	Slow
Number of I/O devices that can be supported	Extremely large	Large	Moderate	Moderate	Limited
Programming languages that can be supported and available software	Extremely high	High	Moderate	Moderate	Limited

Figure 6.7. Supercomputer.

Figure 6.8. PDP 11 minicomputer.

Table 6.5 *Top 10 Minicomputer Manufacturers.*
Digital Equipment
Hewlett-Packard
Data General
Wang Laboratories
Datapoint
Four Phase Systems
General Automation
Prime Computer
Microdata
Modular Computer Systems

memory size of 32K to 512K. Minicomputers will be distinguished from microcomputers, which will be discussed next. Microcomputers will be categorized as stand-alone units that sell for several hundred dollars in their basic form and have limited capability.

Note that this definition is only a means to identify minis broadly. This is an era in which it is not unusual for one manufacturer to market a machine as a small-scale system and another to market a machine with similar features as a mini.

Although we defined the basic memory size of minis as 32K to 512K, add-on capability can be purchased in the form of **integrated circuit chips** that provide increased flexibility. Minis also range from desktop models to the high-powered PDP 11, which is an interactive and highly powerful computer system (see Figure 6.8).

The Digital Equipment Corporation (DEC), which manufactures the PDP and VAX computers, was the pioneer in the minicomputer field in the mid-1960s; DEC still retains the largest share of this market (see Table 6.5).

6.3.2 Applications of Minis

Among the many uses of minicomputers, we will consider the following:

6.3.2.1 *Stand-Alone General-Purpose Systems*

Minicomputers may be used to perform a wide range of typical business functions, such as payroll, billing, and inventory control, for small business users.

6.3.2.2 *Dedicated, Turnkey, or Special-Purpose Systems*

A minicomputer may be used as a special-purpose device designed to satisfy the needs of a specific user and in a very specific way. For example, a mini may be preprogrammed to serve as a word-processing system. In this case, the user organization does not need to write any programs or possess any computer expertise at all. One simply "turns on" the system and it will indicate what an operator should do to achieve the desired results. This is referred to as a **turnkey system**—no programming or computer expertise is required to utilize the system, which has been preprogrammed for a specific application.

Many large organizations use **dedicated** minis for a single application. For example, minicomputers may be placed in individual warehouses to handle inventory control for that warehouse. Or, a minicomputer can be used to store, edit, and verify all transactions at a given branch office.

6.3.2.3 *Modules in a Distributed or Hierarchical Data Processing (DDP) System*

Minicomputers can be used by large organizations for two integrated purposes: to process data at a specific location and to feed into a large-scale mainframe.

A mini can, for example, organize, control, and process data from a series of terminals. The output is then transmitted at high speeds to a large-scale system which integrates the data from a network of minis. In this way the mini serves as a **front-end processor**. This is a main application of minis in large organizations today. The network of minis relieves the main computer system of edit and control procedures and also facilitates the communication system.

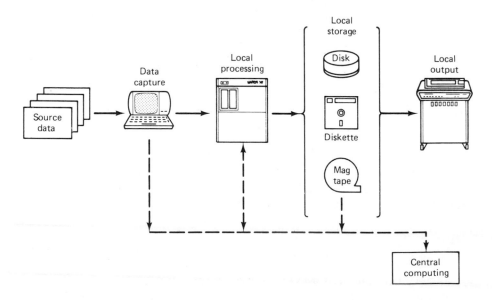

Figure 6.9. Elements of distributed processing.

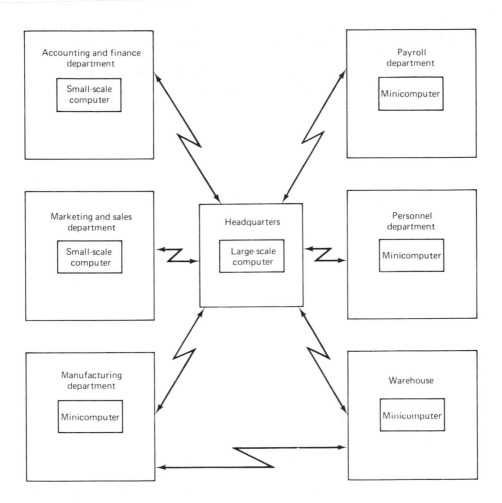

Figure 6.10. Minicomputers linked to a large mainframe in a distributed network. Arrows indicate communication links.

In addition, a mini that is linked to a large mainframe in a distributed or hierarchical network (see Figure 6.9) can alleviate some of the burdens of the main CPU, which may already be operating at or near capacity. Such use of minis can be significantly less expensive and often far more efficient than upgrading the mainframe itself (see Figure 6.10).

It has been estimated that the number of minicomputer installations now exceeds 1 million. This constitutes approximately one-fifth of the total computer market. Of the 1 million installations, about 60% are used as stand-alone general-purpose or turnkey systems in small businesses. The rest are used either in decentralized data processing organizations or as part of a distributed system.

6.3.3 Input/Output Devices Used with Minis

Minicomputer systems consist of standard I/O devices, as well as some units that are miniaturized versions of those used in larger systems. Many minis consist of the following devices:

1. Central processing unit.
2. Standard terminals, for inquiry-response (keyboard/CRT or typewriter terminal).
3. Tape cassette or cartridge device, for storing and retrieving from a cassette or cartridge; these operate like miniature magnetic tapes.
4. Floppy disk device, for storing or retrieving information from a floppy disk, which is a miniaturized magnetic disk.
5. Serial printer, for reporting purposes.

The two units that require some additional discussion are (1) tape cassette or cartridge devices and (2) floppy disk devices.

6.3.3.1 Tape Cassette or Cartridge Device

Tape cassettes and cartridges are similar to mini magnetic tapes. They are used to store data and programs that are processed sequentially in a batch mode.

Typically, the tape in a cassette is 285 feet long, as compared to the standard magnetic tape, which is usually 2400 to 3600 feet long. The **density**, or number of characters stored per inch of tape, tends to be less than that of larger tapes, averaging 200 to 800 characters per inch.

Standard cassette recorders that are used to play music may be employed to record data for a minicomputer system. But these were not really designed to provide high-quality data transmission; many minicomputer systems, therefore, utilize specially developed cassette devices.

The rate at which the tape cassette device transmits data or receives data from the CPU, called the **transfer rate**, is usually very

Table 6.6 *Comparison of Physical Characteristics of Magnetic Tapes and Tape Cassettes.*

Characteristic	Magnetic Tapes	Tape Cassettes
Record length	Unlimited	80–720 characters
Total capacity	1–45 million characters	23,000–720,000 characters
Density	800–6000 characters per inch	200–800 characters per inch

Mode of access, method or creation, and handling features are similar.

slow compared to standard magnetic tape drives. A typical range is from several hundred to several thousand characters per second. For a comparison of the physical characteristics of magnetic tapes and tape cassettes, see Table 6.6.

A tape cartridge device has features similar to that of a cassette recorder, except that it has been developed specifically for computer use and thus tends to be more reliable.

6.3.3.2   Floppy Disk Device

A floppy disk (see Figure 6.11), like a standard magnetic disk, stores data and programs using direct-access methods of processing. Hence the access time of floppy disk drives is significantly faster than that of cassette or cartridge drives.

A floppy disk is usually the size of a 45-rpm record, although there are other sizes as well. It can store the equivalent of approximately 500,000 to 1 million characters on its plastic surface, which has a magnetic oxide coating. A floppy disk has a much greater density than cartridges or cassettes, typically storing 3200 characters per inch. Some floppy disks can store data on *both* sides, thereby doubling the capacity.

The transfer rate for floppy disks is much slower than for traditional magnetic disks but is significantly faster than for cassettes

Figure 6.11.   Floppy disk device.

Table 6.7. *Comparison of Physical Characteristics of Magnetic and Floppy Disks.*

Characteristic	Magnetic Disks	Floppy Disks
Record length	Unlimited	1–1000 characters
Total capacity	1–100 million characters	256,000–1.2 million characters
Density	800–6250 characters per inch	1600–6250 characters per inch

Mode of access, method of creation, and handling features are similar.

or cartridges. Following are some facts about floppy disks.

Typical Facts about Floppy Disks

There are concentric circular tracks per surface (77+).
Each track has sectors (26+).
Each sector can store 128 or more bytes.
Each surface can store 256K to approximately 1 million bytes.
Diskette: (1) a term frequently used to describe two-sided floppies (150 tracks); (2) used
  with drives that have two read/write heads.

For a comparison of floppy disks to conventional magnetic disks, see Table 6.7.

For a comparison of cassettes, cartridges, floppies, and disks, see Figure 6.12.

6.4 MICROS: THE PERSONAL COMPUTERS

Microcomputers, sometimes called personal computers, home computers, or hobby computers, are currently available at a basic cost of several hundred to several thousand dollars. For that price, the user can obtain:

1. *A microprocessor:* This has 16K to 256K basic capacity depending on the unit.
2. *A keyboard,* for entering data and instructions.
3. *A CRT screen,* for displaying computer information.
4. *A tape cassette unit,* for storing programs and data.

See Figure 6.13 for an illustration of a microcomputer.

Sometimes a microcomputer uses a standard television as the input/output device attached to a microprocessor. This arrangement eliminates the need for a CRT screen and reduces the cost of the entire system.

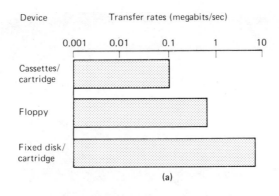

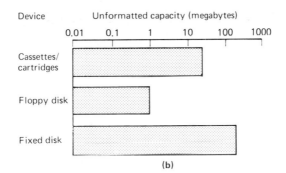

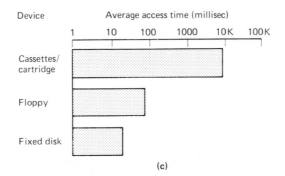

Figure 6.12. Comparison of cassettes, cartridges, floppies, and disks. (a) Device transfer rate comparison. (b) Device capacity comparison. (c) Device access time comparison. (From George Sollman, "The Coexistence of Floppies and Bubbles," *Mini-Microsystems*. Copyright by Cahners Publishing Company, Division of Reed Publishing Corporation. Reprinted with permission.)

Figure 6.13. Microcomputer.

There are many options available to augment the basic microcomputer system, but these augment the price as well. Available options include:

1. A floppy disk unit
2. A hard-copy printer
3. A voice and music synthesizer, for audio output
4. A light pen, wand, or joy stick, for making contact with the screen
5. Additional memory (RAM)

Most of these machines are programmable in a fundamental programming language such as BASIC. Table 6.8 lists the major manufacturers of these micros.

The availability of these machines at such low cost has resulted in an entirely new market for computers: the consumer. There were over 250,000 microcomputers sold in 1980 and the predictions are that by

Table 6.8. *Analysis of the Microcomputer Market.*

Manufacturer	Percent of Market
Radio Shack (TRS 80)	40
Apple	25
Commodore PET	15
IBM	10
Other	10
	100

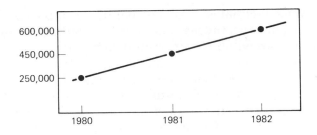

Figure 6.14. Growth of personal computers.

1985, 3.8 million personal computers will have been sold at a total cost of $4.9 billion dollars (see Figure 6.14).

The home computer is typically used for:

Applications of Personal Computers

1. *Entertainment:* Personal computers can play bridge, chess, backgammon, and thousands of other games. The user simply purchases a prepackaged program on a tape cassette or floppy disk.
2. *Computer-assisted instruction:* There are a wide variety of subjects that can be taught using a personal computer. Programs that drill students in multiplication, spelling, geography, and so on, are all available. Many of these include animated graphic displays designed to hold the attention of small children as well as adult users. There are even music synthesizers that enable people to learn to play and experiment with music.
3. *Personal and financial application:* There are programs available for balancing one's checkbook, preparing income tax returns, maintaining recipes and diet guides, and so on. The list is virtually limitless.
4. *Communications link to a time-shared service:* Numerous organizations offer up-to-the-minute stock quotations, airline information, news, literature search, and so on. The micro serves as a kind of terminal accessing a major data base.
5. *Word Processing:* Personal computers can be used for word processing, or computer–aided preparation of documents.

In short, personal computing has become a big business. There are currently over 1000 retail stores that sell computers, peripherals, and software to consumers. There are more than 400 clubs in the United States for personal computer users. There are more than 20 magazines, some with a circulation greater than 100,000, which focus on home computer uses. As the cost of technology decreases and as more and more software is made available, home computers will become increasingly popular. When microcomputers can offer word-processing capability that can replace the electric typewriter (a $250 savings) and can offer an encyclopedia of information on a disk (a $400 to $600 savings), all for $700 to $900, they become a feasible alternative to existing home technology. At that point, virtually no home could afford to be without one. Indeed, some experts predict that by 1990, one of every four homes will have a personal computer.

It should be noted that some microcomputers, with add-on components that make them viable for small business users and professional people, approach minicomputers in both cost and capability. Indeed, it is almost impossible to distinguish between a microcomputer with a 64K memory and floppy disk drives, and some

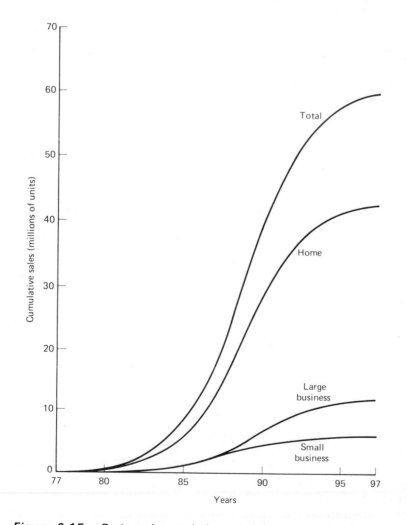

Figure 6.15. Projected cumulative sales for personal computers. [From Paul Gray, "Analyzing the Future Impacts of Personal Computers," *NCC Personal Computing Proceedings* (Montvale, NJ: AFIPS Press) p. 253. Reprinted with permission of the publisher.]

minicomputers with the same features. The cost and capability tend to be similar. Of course, at the upper end, minis have far more capability, but cost more as well.

Television as a Personal Computer

Many of the manufacturers that have specialized in electronic games have begun to offer cartridges and keyboard components to be used in conjunction with a television set as a home computer.

The TV set can be used for playing a wide variety of computer games, but it can also be used for computer-assisted instruction and various home applications as well. The use of the TV as a CRT significantly decreases the cost of the microcomputer that can be made available by Atari, Mattel, Zenith, or other manufacturers.

Anticipated cumulative sales for personal computers are indicated in Figure 6.15. Table 6.9 also provides a breakdown of the market for personal computers.

Summary: Minis and Micros

1. "Think small": The current trend in the EDP industry is on development of minis and micros for large and small business use and for the home market as well.
2. Distinction between mini and micro
   a. There is no clear distinction between a mini and a micro. Different manufacturers use different terms.
   b. Definition used in this chapter: A minicomputer is a system that sells for under $50,000 in its basic form and has a memory size of 32K to 512K. Micros sell for several hundred dollars in their basic form and have limited capability.
3. Applications of minis
   a. Stand-alone units
   b. Special-purpose "turnkey" units
   c. Modules in a distributed data processing system
4. Applications of micros
   a. Home entertainment
   b. Education
   c. Personal and financial applications
   d. Communications link to a time-shared service
   e. Word processing
5. I/O units used with minis and micros
   a. CPU, desk top, usually
   b. Terminal, with keyboard and printer or CRT, or both
   c. Tape cassette or cartridge units, similar to tape drives
   d. Floppy disk unit, similar to disk drive
6. Problems with minis and micros: Devices are not yet compatible with larger units or standardized within the industry.

Table 6.9. *U.S. Market for Personal Computers (Thousands of Units) from 1977 to 1982.*[a]

	1977	1978	1979	1980	1981	1982
For Home Use						
Hobbyists	25.1	35.1	45.0	50.0	45.0	30.0
Home programmers	6.5	80.2	145.0	210.0	260.0	290.0
Consumers	—	24.0	75.0	140.0	220.0	310.0
For Nonhome Use						
Industry	1.2	5.2	10.0	16.0	24.0	35.0
Schools	3.5	23.4	35.0	46.0	63.0	105.0
Scientists	2.2	17.8	37.0	60.0	100.0	140.0
Professionals	0.2	5.0	9.5	15.0	30.0	50.0
Low-end business	2.3	35.2	142.0	190.0	190.0	140.0
Very small business	2.0	17.0	26.5	39.0	85.0	143.0

[a] Adapted with permission from Daniel P. McGlynn, *Personal Computing*, (New York: Wiley). Original source: Creative Strategies.

KEY TERMS

Central processing unit (CPU)
Compatibility
Computer system
Dedicated computer
Distributed data processing (DDP)
Floppy disk
Front-end processor
Hardware
Host processor
Input
Large-scale computers
Mainframe
Medium-scale computers
Megabyte
Memory size
Microcomputers
Minicomputers
Nanosecond
Output
Picosecond
Plug-compatible machine (PCM)
Small-scale computers

Software
Supercomputers
Tape cartridges
Tape cassettes
Turnkey system

REVIEW QUESTIONS

1. (T or F) Minicomputers have become very popular as alternatives or supplements to larger systems.
2. (T or F) There exists no real standardized source that can be used to determine computer categories. That is, what one manufacturer calls a mini, another might call a micro.
3. (T or F) DEC's PDP 11 is classified as a minicomputer system, as are some desktop computers.
4. The largest manufacturer of minis is _____ .
5. (T or F) Minis do not have data communication capability.
6. (T or F) Minis are commonly used in distributed data processing systems.
7. A mini used to edit, format, and control data from a series of terminals before it is transmitted to the mainframe is called a _____ .
8. Explain the basic similarities and differences between floppy disks and standard magnetic disks.
9. Explain the basic similarities and differences between cassette tapes and standard magnetic tapes.
10. Explain the basic similarities and differences between cassettes and floppy disks.
11. Is the lack of standardization in the minicomputer market atypical for the computer industry? Explain your answer.
12. Indicate some of the ways in which small businesses might use minis. Indicate some of the ways in which larger businesses might use minis.
13. Do you think microcomputers will have a strong home market? Explain your answer.
14. State some of the elements you would use to determine the size of computer that Company ABC should acquire.
15. Indicate the meaning of distributed data processing and explain why it has become so popular in recent years.
16. Does the emergence of plug-compatible machines increase or decrease the problems normally associated with standardization issues and the lack of compatibility? Explain your answer.
17. Indicate the interrelationships among the three main elements of computerization: hardware, software, information systems.
18. How are turnkey minicomputer systems used by small businesses?
19. Explain how microcomputers are currently used. Are they applicable for small businesses? Explain your answer.
20. Should cost be an overriding factor when deciding on a computer system? Explain your answer.

DISCUSSION QUESTIONS

1. The president of a small company is interested in acquiring a computer system. What criteria would you use for determining whether the company would benefit most from a smaller system or a time-sharing facility?
2. Why have computer manufacturers resisted the request of many of their clients to standardize their product line? What has resulted from this resistance?
3. Why do so many computer systems need to be replaced with alternative systems?
4. Why are distributed data processing systems so popular? Why do they need even more controls than other types of systems?
5. The Computer Revolution has sometimes been called an Information Revolution. Can you explain why?
6. Can you think of potential uses for personal computers beyond those discussed in the text?

APPLICATION

Consider the application below and then answer the questions that follow it.

Personal Computers in Business: An Emerging Competitive Edge[a]

By Bill Langenes

Being competitive in business means getting important data quickly, when you need it. And this is what the personal computer does best of all.

Take, for example, a traveling insurance salesman who takes his personal computer in the car with him to keep customer and inventory information at his fingertips.

Or the senior partner in a Los Angeles law firm who calls his personal computer "my equalizer." His three-man operation uses the data and word processing capabilities of the computer to compete successfully in court with firms many times it size.

The chairman of the board of one of America's major industrial corporations has three personal computers that help him keep abreast of his company's diverse operations, while a financial analyst for a leading Wall Street investment firm uses his personal computer to keep his clients' portfolios.

These businessmen are the vanguard of a growing revolution being created by personal computers, which are bringing the power and efficiency of rapid data processing to small businesses and giving managers of larger firms "hands-on" access to business data when they need it.

Frankly, it is a revolution that is taking place faster than many of us in the personal computer industry really expected. Nearly three-quarters of a million business people are currently using small computers. They came into computer stores and made their purchases, all of which were originally identified in the "hobby" category. But, in truth, a large percentage of those hobbyists were business people learning to "do it themselves" so they could adapt the personal computer to their business needs.

As they did, they gained an advantage over their competitors who were still spending many man-hours on bookkeeping, record-keeping and report-making functions for which computers are so ideally suited.

Sharpening the Edge

Small computers are making new contributions to competitiveness by both increasing internal efficiency and improving customer service. A New Jersey industrial equipment distributor, Don Truesdell, discovered both benefits after installing his computer.

"For the first time in three or four years we were able to get each day's work done within a normal working day," he said. "Our computer has turned out to be an important sales tool as well. We can use the computer-generated product sales analysis reports to give our customers a comprehensive report on all the products they have purchased from us, which shows them we pay close attention to their requirements.

"The system also helps in our dealings with suppliers," Truesdell continued. "It gives us a good image, and they respect our operation. In fact, two of our leading suppliers have told us we are their most highly automated distributor."

Immediate results can often be seen from the use of a computer. An automotive parts warehouse installed a business system to handle inventory. In six months the inventory was reduced by $30,000 with no loss in effectiveness. Says the owner: "The computer more than paid for itself."

A South Carolina manufacturer's representative, Larry Kidd of CV Sales, Inc., found that his personal computer gave him more control of his managerial responsibilities, both financial and personnel.

"I feel that I know much more about the week-to-week progress of my business," Kidd says. He also wrote his own software programs—common among personal computer users—to produce semimonthly sales summaries for his salesmen. "Now they know exactly what their customers are ordering . . . and so do I." Impressed with the possibilities of his computer, he says "I haven't yet begun to do what I can."

Personal Computer Characteristics

Business people have really just begun to discover the wide variety of uses for personal computers. And that is what makes these small computers so unique, especially in contrast with their larger cousins, the mainframes and minicomputers.

Unlike the larger business computers, which require a specially designed room environment and a data processing staff, a personal computer is designed to be used at an individual level. It is relatively inexpensive, can be as portable as a typewriter, fits on a desk or table with no special electrical or environmental control requirements, and doesn't need a data processing professional to operate it.

But, most important, a personal computer is easy to use. Nearly any person can purchase, install and operate his own. The only demand a small computer places on its owner is that he become involved, which isn't a problem judging from the thousands of business users.

The owner of a marine construction company had no computer or programming background when he bought a microcomputer. His first program handles cash disbursements, doing a week of clerical work in a day. His next program will standardize the bidding procedure to take out the guesswork.

An editor and freelance writer who exchanged his typewriter for a personal computer says: "At the risk of sounding overly enthusiastic, I honestly feel the use of a good word processing computer system will open up a whole new dimension for any writer."

A California psychologist, using his computer to administer and score personality tests, says: "No other group has as great a potential for microcomputer application as the private practitioners, most of all clinical psychologists."

Retailers are highly recommending personal computers too. Beverly Stereo and Electronics, a Los Angeles stereo store, has tightened up its operation with programs for payroll, general ledger, sales entry and inventory. To boost sales, it uses the word processing and mailing list capabilities for producing direct mail advertising. "At the price these things sell for," owner Harry Margulies says, "any retail store with more than three or four employees could use a computer. Maybe 40 percent of them could really profit from one."

Small Computers in Big Business

For the small businessman, personal computers mean that he can economically have access to the same kind of operating and accounting information previously available only to his larger competitors. Within large companies the small computer has opened up new capabilities for department heads and for managers at their individual locations.

It is within big business that computers are truly earning their "personal" distinction. There are no programmers and no operators to go through to obtain computer-stored information. Managers themselves can get the information they need when they need it.

Deere & Company is finding that line managers want their own computers. At Ford Motor Company the treasurer's office uses three small computers. The marketing manager of a multi-million dollar California corporation keeps a personal computer beside his desk to help him analyze market data and develop plans.

Sometimes it is competitive pressure that motivates business people to computerize, as was the case of a printer. When he found that a competitor was using a programmable calculator to estimate printing bids, he went out to buy his own calculator. But he discovered wisely, that he could buy a microcomputer for not much more money and have an enormously more versatile machine capable of producing bids as well as handling general accounting.

Dollars and Sense

Obviously it doesn't take an accountant to figure out the benefits of a small computer in terms of dollars, but accountants have been some of the first effective users to enjoy the benefits.

One accountant who prepares about 1,500 tax returns annually switched from a computer service bureau costing $18,000 annually to his own microcomputer for a total one-time cost of about $11,000. It paid for itself in one tax season and is helping him prepare general ledgers for his clients all year long.

A recent analysis of the economics of small business computer implementation projected that an investment in a personal computer could, in some cases, cut manpower requirements in half and increase gross profits from 2 to 10 percent. Another way of looking at return-on-investment is to say that a personal computer would pay for itself if all it did was save 20 percent of the time of one employee for a year, which is a modest expectation indeed.

Before you go running, checkbook in hand, to your computer store, make sure you realize that no $600 computer is going to do all these things for you. In fact, some $6,000 systems might not do all of them efficiently. You should become a knowledgeable buyer and make certain you understand the system you look at. Its computing power shouldn't be too limited for your needs, and either software should exist for your purposes or you should find out how to get the assistance you need in programming the system.

The Business User's Needs

What are the special needs of the business user?

Software is certainly at the top of the list, and both manufacturers and independent software houses have reacted quickly with many new "canned" application packages.

There are also hardware considerations, some of which are discussed in this issue of APPLE.

Hardware expandability is a must. The business system should accept peripheral equipment, such as printers and disks, which are essential. The same system in other applications may require speech recognition capabilities, greater memory capacity, interfacing with a computer network, and so on.

Business system shoppers

should also carefully check out the computer retailer to be certain the dealer can provide the training and after-sale service that are necessary for full utilization of the system.

Can you benefit from the use of a personal computer system? Only you can determine that for sure. Certainly current users provide a broad sample. The availability of low-cost computer power has led International Data Corporation, a leading computer industry market research firm, to predict that virtually any organization having $500,000 in annual sales will require a computer or computer services during the next few years if it is to improve its efficiency and remain competitive in the marketplace. That's why the personal computer can truly be called "An emerging competitive edge."

[a] Courtesy of Apple Computer, Inc.

Application Questions

1. Explain the use of the term "hands on" in the application.
2. State some of the advantages of personal computers indicated in the application.
3. Indicate why personal computers are better than larger systems for some organizations.

7

Programming in BASIC

7.1 AN OVERVIEW

7.1.1 Why Learn to Program at All?

Thus far, we have focused on computer concepts and how these concepts are applied to meet specific user needs. But learning *about* computers is significantly different from actually learning how to use them. There are numerous analogies that come to mind:

1. Learning about the automobile is vastly different from learning how to drive.
2. Learning about musicians and their compositions is vastly different from learning how to play a musical instrument.

There are many people who argue that knowledge of a programming language is not essential for an appreciation of how computers are actually used. We would agree. But learning the fundamentals of a programming language would add a dimension to one's appreciation of computer processing that could simply not be obtained in any other way. It is our belief, then, that learning how to write programs will be extremely useful in understanding how computers read data, process it and produce the required output.

But there is another equally important reason for learning how to program. As already noted, the expectation is that computers will be even more prevalent in the coming years than they are now. Moreover, with the decreasing cost of hardware, many more people will have access to these machines. An ability to write programs could be an important asset to people, regardless of their perspective or occupation. Programming could serve a useful purpose for home use as well as for on-the-job applications.

7.1.2   Why BASIC?

In Chapter 5 we focused on the various major programming languages that are available and the features of each. The BASIC language is considered the most suitable for a first-level introduction to programming because:

Features of BASIC

1. It is relatively easy to learn.
2. It is relatively easy to code.
3. It can be programmed on a terminal; that is, it provides the student with the ability to directly interact with a computer.
4. It is the most commonly used programming language for mini and micro systems.

7.1.3   The Two Facets to Programming in BASIC

Because a BASIC program is most frequently entered into a computer system via a terminal, there are two aspects to learning how to program in this language:

1. Interacting with the terminal
2. Programming in BASIC

Note that neither of these facets are as standardized as one would like. Here again, the lack of overall standards in the computing field results in some difficulties for potential programmers:

1. Each computer system has its own **protocol** or method used to access the system. This protocol depends on the type of security required at the specific installation, the access modes available, the programming languages used, and so on.
2. Although there are several versions, the BASIC programming language is relatively standard. That is, a program written in BASIC for one system can usually be run on any other system that has a BASIC interpreter or compiler. Many minis and micros, however, have developed numerous additions to the standard. These are called **enhancements**. There are various versions of this *extended* BASIC, depending on the mini or micro system used. Although the versions are not 100% standardized, they are very similar. We will, however, confine ourselves to the standard version of BASIC.

Summary: General Facts about BASIC

1. BASIC has been especially developed for use in a time-sharing environment.
2. BASIC is usually entered into a computer system on a terminal (or on a micro or mini system) in an interactive mode.
3. BASIC is an acronym for Beginner's All-purpose Symbolic Instruction Code.
4. BASIC is a relatively simple language to learn and code.
5. Although a BASIC program is most often keyed into a computer on a terminal, it can be entered on punched cards in a batch mode and then compiled, if desired.
6. All programs must first be coded and then translated. These programs must then be tested with sample data to ensure their accuracy.
7. In BASIC, test data, like instructions, is usually entered on a terminal.

7.2   INTERACTING WITH A COMPUTER SYSTEM USING A TERMINAL

Actually accessing the computer system via the terminal is usually the most awesome aspect for beginners. Note, however, that although it may take some practice to understand the log-on procedures, it is virtually impossible for you to foul up the system (a fear expressed by many novices).

7.2.1   Log-On Procedures

Since the log-on procedures vary depending on the system, your computer center will provide you with the precise specifications for your system. This unit will focus on typical methods for logging on.

7.2.1.1   *Gaining Access to the Computer System*

The following are typical methods used for accessing the CPU:

a. *Dialing up the CPU Using a Telephone.*   Some terminals use telephone lines for "calling up" the CPU. Along with the terminal, there is a telephone and an acoustic coupler or modem for digital-to-analog transmission. If your system requires a dial-up, you will be given the appropriate telephone number.

b. *Turning on Hard-Wired Terminals That Are Linked Directly to the CPU.*   If each terminal is linked by cable to a CPU, the terminal can simply be turned on to gain access to the CPU.

c. *Micros Need Only Be Turned On.*   If you are running a BASIC program on a micro, you need only turn on the computer. In many instances, you can begin to code the BASIC program at this point with no further need for log-on procedures.

7.2.1.2   Steps for Logging On

Once you have gained access via a terminal, you must indicate:

1. Your authorization code
2. Your intention to write a BASIC program

These procedures are part of **job control** and depend on the protocol established at your installation.

The following are samples of typical log-on procedures:

```
%E222 PLEASE LOGON
/LOGON CSA010,A2129
% E223 LOGON ACCEPTED FOR TEN 2202, ON 04/11/81 AT 1434, LINE #050.
***HOFSTRA UNIVERSITY COMPUTING FACILITY***
  ***UNIVAC 90/60 MOD 2 ---VS/9 VER3.5***
/EXEC BASIC
% P500 LOADING VER# 009 OF BASIC.
BASIC 09, NEW OR OLD
*NEW
NEW PROGRAM NAME--STERN
READY
```

Note: Boxed entries are user supplied.

```
HELLO
RSTS V7.0-07 18-NOV-81 13:51
# 147.1
PASSWORD: STERN2
PLEASE ENTER YOUR ID CODE: S1563
YOUR ID CODE HAS BEEN VALIDATED. WELCOME TO RSTS/E V7.0!
WOULD YOU LIKE TO CREATE A NEW FILE (TYPE NEW), OR
        RETRIEVE AN OLD FILE (TYPE OLD) ---> NEW
NEW FILE NAME -- NEW PROG1 BASIC
READY
```

7.2.1.3   Transmitting a Log-On
                Message or an Instruction to
                the CPU

Most terminals have a standard keyboard for typing instructions. The printing of these instructions and the computer's responses vary; in some cases it is a visual display, in other cases it is a typewritten printout.

The programmer types any message or any BASIC instruction and then depresses a control key to indicate the end of the line; usually this is a RETURN key. On some systems, however, the user must hold down both the CONTROL key and a character such as the letter C, for example, to indicate the end of the line.

Only after the control key has been depressed will the line be transmitted to the CPU.

7.2.2 Correcting Typographical Errors

Typographical errors can easily occur during log-on procedures or during the coding of the BASIC program itself. In either case, the same rules apply:

7.2.2.1 Backspacing

Before a line has been transmitted. If a key has been depressed incorrectly, it is possible to backspace or override the specific character before the line is transmitted to the CPU.

How Backspacing Is Performed on Some Systems

Examples

1. @ key: Each @ backspaces one character.
   Example: LOGG @ON is transmitted as LOGON.
2. ← key: Each ← backspaces one character.
3. DEL: Depressing the DEL key on a CRT deletes the character entirely.

7.2.2.2 Correcting or Deleting a Line

Suppose you notice that you made a mistake *after* you transmitted the line to the CPU. That is, you already depressed the control key.

If you made a mistake in your log-on procedure, the computer will respond by asking you to retype your response. Hence you simply retype the line.

If you made a mistake in a BASIC instruction, you do the same thing: retype the line.

Example:

Coding	Explanation
10 FPRINT "HI THERE"	[note: PRINT spelled incorrectly]
10 PRINT "HI THERE"	[simply retype]

The last instruction numbered 10 will override the previous one in which PRINT was spelled incorrectly. Typing a line number by itself will eliminate that line from the program. Thus typing 10 by itself will delete line number 10.

7.2.2.3 Inserting a Line in a BASIC Program

You will discover that all BASIC instructions require **line numbers**. If you inadvertently omitted an instruction, you can enter it, even out of sequence.

Suppose that while entering a program, you typed:

```
20 LET D = A + B - C
30 PRINT D
```

Line 10, which was to read values for A, B, and C, was inadvertently omitted. The omitted line (line 10) can be typed directly *after* line 30, but it must contain its appropriate line number indicating where it belongs in the sequence of instructions. Thus the following sequence is valid:

```
20 LET D = A + B - C
30 PRINT D
10 INPUT A,B,C
```

The computer automatically executes BASIC statements in *sequence* by their line numbers, regardless of the order in which they are typed.

Numbering instructions by 10's (10, 20, 30, etc.) allows us to make insertions if the need arises.

7.2.3 Running a Program

Once the program has been entered, it must be tested or debugged. Sample data is used to determine if the program's logic produces the correct results.

To run or execute a program, type in:

```
RUN
```

Example:

```
10 INPUT A,B,C
20 LET D=A+B-C
30 PRINT D
40 END
RUN
?1,2,3
0
```

7.2.4 Listing a Program

It often becomes difficult to "proofread" a program before entering RUN if there have been many errors that have been corrected as the instructions have been entered. Consequently, before we type RUN, we often type LIST first to have the computer print out a "clean" copy of the program with all typing errors omitted. (It should be noted that LIST has no line number since it is a **system command**.) It is thus easier to check the program before having it executed. For example, we might have the following sequence (we have assigned the name SQR to the program):

```
EDIT SQR BASIC
10 PRRN@@INT SQR(18)
20 NND@@@END
LIST
*
10 PRINT SQR(18)
20 END
RUN
*
4.24264
```

It should be noted that there is also another use for LIST. If a BASIC program has been stored in the computer and a user wants to run it, he or she may want it to be listed out first. With this listing, users can refresh their memory as to the logic involved. He or she can then make any modifications that may be deemed necessary. If, as an example, the program above has been previously stored and a listing is now required, the following entries would be used:

```
EDIT SQR BASIC
LIST
```

The stored program would then be listed.

7.2.5 Saving a Program

After a program has been entered and executed, the programmer may wish to save it for future processing. To do so, you must usually type in SAVE with the name of the program:

Example:

```
SAVE TEST1
```

In this way you can call for this program whenever you need to by typing in, at a later date, a system command, such as

```
LOAD TEST1
```

It should be noted once again that many of these principles will vary slightly from one system to the next.

7.3 ESSENTIAL ELEMENTS OF A BASIC PROGRAM

7.3.1 An Overview

As noted in Chapter 5, programming in any language consists of three basic types of instructions:

Types of Instructions

1. *Input*: reads data into the computer. The data is considered *variable* because its contents are not known when we are writing the program.
2. *Processing*: operates on data by performing arithmetic or some logical test on the data.
3. *Output*: produces information that results from the processed data.

Let us begin by examining some simple instructions in BASIC, as shown in Table 7.1. In the table, we read into the computer three numbers called A, B, C. We add them and print the sum, called D. A, B, C, and D are **variable field names**. Using the steps above, we can enter any numbers for A, B, and C, and obtain the correct results in D. The variable field names can be used for integer or decimal values. Thus 10, 3.6, and even -5.2 are valid entries. The variables cannot, however, contain a comma. Thus 1000 is valid, but 1,000 is not.

Note, however, that a computer program is rarely written for operating on only one set of data. Computers are usually employed for processing large volumes of data.

Thus we would normally want to repeat the foregoing sequence of steps for not one group of three numbers, but numerous groups of numbers. To do this, we must give each instruction a **line number**. Then after printing we simply instruct the computer to repeat or GO TO the line number associated with the first instruction:

```
1 INPUT A,B,C
2 LET D=A+B+C
3 PRINT D
4 GOTO 1
```

On most computers, BASIC programs must end with an END

Table 7.1. *Simple Instruction Set in BASIC*

Type of Instruction	Basic Format	Example
Input	INPUT [field names]	INPUT A,B,C
Processing	LET [field name] = arithmetic expression	LET D = A+B+C
Output	PRINT [field name]	PRINT D

statement to signal the computer that there are no more instructions. Thus our first complete BASIC program is as follows:

```
1 INPUT A,B,C
2 LET D=A+B+C
3 PRINT D
4 GOTO 1
5 END
```

To run this program on your computer, you type in RUN. Here is a sample of the results you might get:

```
1   INPUT A,B,C
2   LET D = A+B+C
3   PRINT D
4   GO TO 1
5   END
RUN
?1,2,3
6
?2,2,2
6
   .
   .
   .
```

7.3.2   Fundamental Rules for BASIC Programs

Rules

1. Every instruction must begin with a line number. [Typically, line numbers are coded in multiples of 10 (i.e., 10, 20, 30, etc.) to allow insertions in case an instruction was inadvertently omitted.]
2. Instructions are executed in line number sequence unless a GO TO is encountered.
3. All programs end with an END statement.
4. Numeric variable names are represented by a letter or a letter followed by a digit (e.g., A, A1, B6, etc.).
5. Arithmetic operations are coded with the following symbols in a LET statement:

Symbol Used	*Operation*
+	Addition
−	Subtraction
*	Multiplication
/	Division
** (or ↑)	Exponentiation

6. Numeric constants can be used in arithmetic statements. For example:

```
10 LET D = .05 * C
```

7. Unconditional branches are coded with GO TO statements.

Using the seven basic rules described above, we can code a wide variety of programs.

Example 1: For a series of input data that indicate Celsius temperatures, write a program to calculate Fahrenheit temperatures. (Note that Fahrenheit = $\frac{9}{5}$ Celsius + 32°.)

The following is a listing of the program and an actual display of a run.

```
10 INPUT C
20 LET F=9/5*C+32
30 PRINT F
40 GOTO 10
50 END

*RUN
?32
  89.6
?STOP
*
```

Well-designed BASIC programs include a test for the end of data. That is, it is not generally desirable to force an end of run by typing STOP as we do above, although it usually works. Later, when you become more familiar with the BASIC language, we will include appropriate tests for end of data.

The fraction $\frac{9}{5}$ and the number 32 are considered numeric constants. Since the fraction $\frac{9}{5}$ could be written as 1.8, line 20 above could also be coded as:

```
20 LET F = 1.8 * C + 32
```

Example 2: For each input field representing a TOTAL, calculate a PRICE that allows a 3% discount.

```
10 INPUT T
20 LET F=T-.03*T
30 PRINT F
40 GOTO 10
50 END

            *


          RUN


        ?67
         64.99
        ?STOP
        *
```

Note again that typing STOP to force an end of run is used here for the sake of simplicity. Later, we will include appropriate end-of-data tests.

Note that any quantity T minus 0.03 of T = 0.97T. Thus line 20 could be coded as:

```
20 LET F = .97*T
```

Example 3:   Two input fields are to be entered, representing HOURS WORKED and HOURLY RATE. Calculate TOTAL WAGES for each group of input fields.

```
10 INPUT H,R
20 LET W=H*R
30 PRINT W
40 GOTO 10
50 END

      *




      RUN




      ?56,9.00
       504
      ?STOP
      *
```

Note that BASIC is a free-style language, which means that any spacing between words and expressions is permissible. This is one primary advantage of BASIC over languages like COBOL.

7.3.3   Variations on a Theme

Before adding additional instructions to our examples, let us first consider ways in which we can supplement or vary existing instructions.

7.3.3.1   Print Options

a. *Printing Alphanumeric Constants.*   You will note that in the illustrations above, we read data and printed the computed results. Usually, data that is processed is variable—it depends totally on the numbers being entered at the time.

Suppose, however, that we wish to print an alphanumeric message describing what the output field actually contains. Since we know what message we want to print beforehand, we call it a **constant**. That is, it is not dependent on input, but is always the same for a given program.

We code alphanumeric constants in BASIC by enclosing them in quotation marks. For example:

```
10 PRINT "HI THERE--I'M YOUR FRIENDLY COMPUTER"
```

will cause the computer to print the following, when statement 10 is executed:

```
HI THERE--I'M YOUR FRIENDLY COMPUTER
```

A print statement can print variables, constants, or a combination of both using a comma to separate the items:

```
10 PRINT "THE TOTAL IS ",T
```

This will print the constant together with the value of T. Thus we can augment our previous programs as follows.

Example: Print Fahrenheit temperature for Celsius temperatures read in as input:

```
10 INPUT C
20 LET F = 9/5 * C + 32
30 PRINT "FAHRENHEIT TEMPERATURE IS ",F
40 GO TO 10
50 END
```

This will result in the following after typing RUN:

```
?0
FAHRENHEIT TEMPERATURE IS           32
?25
FAHRENHEIT TEMPERATURE IS           77
?31
FAHRENHEIT TEMPERATURE IS           87.8
?STOP
```

If we really want to be specific, we can substitute the following for line 30:

```
30 PRINT "FAHRENHEIT TEMPERATURE FOR ",C," IS ",F
```

Note again that on many systems, STOP as an input field will cause the program to terminate the run.

Printing alphanumeric constants makes the output more meaningful. It can also be used for explaining to the user of the program what input should be supplied.

```
10 PRINT "ENTER A CELSIUS TEMPERATURE"
20 PRINT "I WILL THEN COMPUTE FAHRENHEIT TEMPERATURE"
30 INPUT C
40 LET F = 9/5 * C + 32
50 PRINT "FAHRENHEIT TEMPERATURE IS ",F
60 GO TO 10
70 END
```

This will result in the following dialogue between user and computer when the program is run. The data entered by the user appears after the ?.

```
ENTER A CELSIUS TEMPERATURE
I WILL THEN COMPUTE FAHRENHEIT TEMPERATURE
?15
FAHRENHEIT TEMPERATURE IS              59
ENTER A CELSIUS TEMPERATURE
I WILL THEN COMPUTE FAHRENHEIT TEMPERATURE
?22
FAHRENHEIT TEMPERATURE IS              71.6
ENTER A CELSIUS TEMPERATURE
I WILL THEN COMPUTE FAHRENHEIT TEMPERATURE
?STOP
```

If we want to print the instructions only once at the beginning, line 60 should be changed to:

```
60   GO TO 30
```

With the change in instruction 60, we would have:

```
ENTER A CELSIUS TEMPERATURE
I WILL THEN COMPUTE FAHRENHEIT TEMPERATURE
?0
FAHRENHEIT TEMPERATURE IS              32
?9
FAHRENHEIT TEMPERATURE IS              48.2
?STOP
```

b. *Printing Blank Lines.*   The following will print a blank line:

```
10 PRINT
```

7.3.3.2 Hierarchy of Arithmetic Operations

Consider the following:

```
10 INPUT B,C,D
20 LET A = B-C*D
30 PRINT A
40 GO TO 10
50 END
```

Suppose that B=10, C=5, and D=2. Will the computer perform

$$B-C*D = 10-5\times2$$

as

$$(10-5)\times2 = 10$$

or as

$$10-(5\times2) = 0$$

Clearly, if the computer performs the subtraction operation *first* and then the multiplication, the result will be different from performing the multiplication first.

The following represents the hierarchy rules used by computers:

Order of Operations
1. Exponentiation
2. Multiplication and division
3. Addition and subtraction
If an instruction has two or more operations on the same level, they are executed in sequence from left to right.

Thus, in

```
20 LET A = B-C*D
```

the multiplication is performed first, then the subtraction. That is, we have

$$10 - 5 \times 2 = 10 - 10 = 0$$

The traditional hierarchy rules can be superseded by the use of parentheses. Thus to obtain B − C multiplied by D, we code

20 LET A = (B-C)*D

Example 1:   Find the value of the hypotenuse of a right triangle, where the other two sides are entered as input:

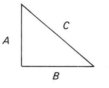

You will recall that $C = \sqrt{A^2 + B^2}$. Square roots can be calculated in BASIC by raising an expression to the 0.5 power or by using the special function SQR:

```
10 PRINT "ENTER TWO SIDES OF A TRIANGLE"
20 PRINT "I WILL COMPUTE THE HYPOTENUSE"
30 PRINT
40 INPUT A,B
50 LET C = (A**2+B**2)**.5
60 PRINT "THE HYPOTENUSE IS ",C
70 PRINT
80 GO TO 40
90 END
```

After typing RUN, the results will print as

```
ENTER TWO SIDES OF A TRIANGLE
I WILL COMPUTE THE HYPOTENUSE

?3,4
THE HYPOTENUSE IS          5

?5,6
THE HYPOTENUSE IS          7.81024968

?STOP
```

The use of the parentheses is necessary to obtain the appropriate order of operations. Line 50 could also be replaced by

50 LET C=SQR(A**2+B**2)

Example 2:   Read in three exam grades for every student in a class, and calculate the average grade:

```
10 PRINT "ENTER THREE EXAM GRADES"
20 PRINT
30 INPUT E1,E2,E3
40 LET A=(E1+E2+E3)/3
50 PRINT "THE AVERAGE IS ",A
60 GOTO 20
70 END
```

The results will be

```
ENTER THREE EXAM GRADES

?75,85,80
THE AVERAGE IS                    80

?82,89,93
THE AVERAGE IS                    88
```

Here, again, the parentheses are required for proper order of evaluation. The following is incorrect:

```
40 LET A = E1+E2+E3/3
```

Only E3 would be divided by 3 if the parentheses were omitted.

In summary, when we want an operation or a series of operations to be performed first, we enclose it in parentheses.

Example 3: Read in a principal amount, a rate of interest, and the number of periods of investment.

Compute the principal and interest earned after N periods of investment using the formula

$$P(1 + R)^N = \text{principal} + \text{interest earned}$$

```
10 INPUT P1,N,R
20 LET P = P1*(1+R)**N
30 PRINT P
40 GO TO 10
50 END
```

7.3.3.3   *Entering Alphanumeric Data Called String Variables*

Thus far, we have used an INPUT statement to enter numeric variables. You will recall that the rule for entering numeric variables is as follows:

```
                    Rule

           Numeric Variable Name:

              A single letter
                    or
         A letter followed by a digit
             (A, A1, A9, etc.)
```

E1, T, and N are all valid numeric variable names. But suppose that we want to enter alphanumeric data, such as a person's name, address, and sex. We must use a **string variable**. The rule for a string variable name is as follows:

```
                              Rule

                     String Variable Name:

Variable name followed by a $ (i.e., letter, or letter and digit, and $: A$, N$, A1$, etc.)
```

Example: Read as input a student name and three exam scores. Print the student's name and the average:

```
10 PRINT "ENTER STUDENT NAME AND 3 EXAM SCORES"
20 PRINT
30 INPUT N$,E1,E2,E3
40 LET A=(E1+E2+E3)/3
50 PRINT N$,"HAS AN AVERAGE OF ",A
60 GOTO 20
70 END
```

7.3.3.4   Other Uses of the LET Statement

A LET statement can be used, as noted, to perform an arithmetic operation and place the result in the variable field indicated. For example:

$$20 \ \text{LET} \ E=F-G$$

results in G being subtracted from F and the result placed in E.

Note, however, that the LET statement does two things:

```
                  LET Statement Functions

1. Performs the calculation indicated on the right of the = sign
2. Moves the result into the variable name specified to the left of
   the = sign
```

Consider the following:

```
10 INPUT E
20 LET E = E + 1
```

Line 20 *is* a valid statement:

1. 1 is added to E.
2. The result is placed in E.

Thus if E were read in as 16, one would be added and 17 would be placed back into E. That is, the effect of the statement

$$\boxed{\text{LET E = E + 1}}$$

is to add one to E.

Example 1:   For all salaries read in as input, provide for a $100 raise:

```
10 INPUT S
20 LET S=S+100
30 PRINT S
40 GOTO 10
50 END
```

Note that the following would produce the same results:

```
10 INPUT S
20 LET T=S+100
30 PRINT T
40 GOTO 10
50 END
```

The LET statement can also be used to move a value into a field. For example:

```
10 LET A=10.3
```

results in A containing 10.3.

Example 2:   Our Celsius-Fahrenheit problem could be coded slightly differently:

```
10 INPUT C
20 LET A=1.8
30 LET B=32
40 LET F=A*C-B
50 PRINT F
60 GOTO 10
70 END
```

Since A and B are always to contain 1.8 and 32, respectively, the following would serve just as well:

```
10 LET A=1.8
20 LET B=32
30 INPUT C
40 LET F=A*C-B
50 PRINT F
60 GOTO 30
70 END
```

In fact, the latter is more efficient since A and B are computed only *once* at the beginning, instead of each time a value of C is processed. Until the contents of A and B are altered by another LET statement, they remain as 1.8 and 32, respectively.

7.3.4   Conditional Statements

Thus far we have considered the following:

Summary of Operations
1. Reading numeric and string variables as input
2. Performing arithmetic operations using the LET statement
3. Printing numeric and string variables, as well as constants
4. Unconditionally transferring control in a program to some other point using a GO TO statement

But a major aspect of programming relates to selectively processing data depending on the contents of certain fields. That is, we may wish to calculate a commission for salespeople with total sales in excess of $1000.00. Similarly, we may want to grant discounts selectively to customers with solid credit ratings.

To do this, we need to perform a **logical test**. The IF-THEN statement is used to perform such a test. The format of the statement is as follows:

Format of IF–THEN Statement
IF [a condition exists] THEN [statement number to be branched to]

Example 1:

```
IF A = 15 THEN 60
```

means "IF A IS EQUAL TO 15, GO TO line number 60."

The conditions that can be specified in an IF-THEN statement are as follows:

Symbols used in IF –THEN Statements	
Symbol	*Meaning*
=	Equal to
<	Less than
>	Greater than
<=	Less than or equal to
>=	Greater than or equal to
<>	Not equal (less than or greater than)

Example 2: Suppose that we wish to read in a patient's name and print the message "PATIENT HAS A FEVER" for patients with temperatures in excess of 98.6. If the temperature is 98.6 or less, we print nothing.

The flowchart and program for this are as follows:

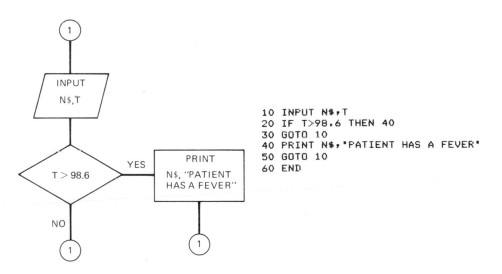

```
10 INPUT N$,T
20 IF T>98.6 THEN 40
30 GOTO 10
40 PRINT N$,"PATIENT HAS A FEVER"
50 GOTO 10
60 END
```

Note that there are two possible sequences that will be performed. For patients with temperatures of 98.6° or less, we have

```
10 INPUT N$,T
20 IF T>98.6 THEN 40
30 GOTO 10
40 PRINT N$,"PATIENT HAS A FEVER"
50 GOTO 10
60 END
```

For patients with temperatures greater than 98.6°, we have

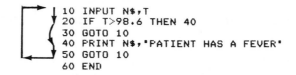

```
    10 INPUT N$,T
    20 IF T>98.6 THEN 40
    30 GOTO 10
    40 PRINT N$,"PATIENT HAS A FEVER"
    50 GOTO 10
    60 END
```

We could have coded the above as follows, without affecting the results:

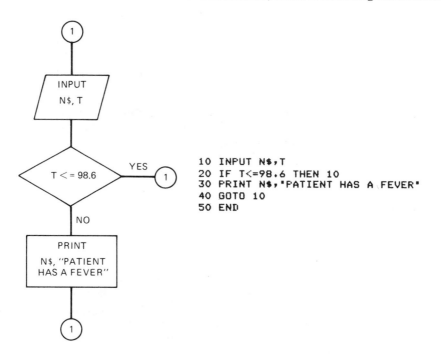

```
10 INPUT N$,T
20 IF T<=98.6 THEN 10
30 PRINT N$,"PATIENT HAS A FEVER"
40 GOTO 10
50 END
```

IF-THEN statements provide the programmer with a significant amount of flexibility and logical control capability. One such capability is **looping**, where we perform a given set of operations until a specific condition is reached.

Example 3: Calculate the sum of all integers from 1 to 100. No INPUT statement is required here, because we already know the variables to be processed.

On first glance, it may seem that the following would be appropriate:

```
10 LET T = 1+2+3+...+100
20 PRINT T
30 END
```

Note, however, that the dots ($\cdots$) would need to be replaced with the actual integers and, at best, this would be a tedious task. Logically, the following would be more appropriate:

Statement	Meaning
10 LET N=1	Initialize N at 1
20 LET S=S+N	Add N to S
30 LET N=N+1	Increment N by 1
40 IF N<=100 THEN 20	If N is less than or equal to 100, repeat
50 PRINT S	Print S (when N exceeds 100)
60 END	

In the program above, N varies from 1 to 100 and S is the variable name for the accumulator, which will hold the sum of the N integers.

Thus we have

Number of Times through the Sequence	Value of N	Value of S
0	1	0 (all variables are initialized at 0)
1	1	1
2	2	1 + 2
3	3	1 + 2 + 3
.	.	.
.	.	.
100	100	1 + 2 + 3 + · · · + 100

We could have coded our summation loop in other ways:

```
10 LET N=1
20 LET S=S+N
30 LET N=N+1
40 IF N>100 THEN 60
50 GOTO 20
60 PRINT S
70 END
```

This loop procedure enables us to do a wide variety of similar operations, with only minor modifications.

Example 4: Sum all the integers from 1 to 1000.

```
10 LET N = 1
20 LET S = S+N
30 LET N = N+1
40 IF N <= 1000 THEN 20
50 PRINT S
60 END
```

Example 5: Sum all the integers from 100 to 2000.

```
10 LET N=100
20 LET S=S+N
30 LET N=N+1
40 IF N<=2000 THEN 20
50 PRINT S
60 END
```

Example 6: Sum all the *odd* numbers from 1 to 1001. In this case our integer, N, begins at 1 and is incremented by 2 each time:

```
10 LET N=1
20 LET S=S+N
30 LET N=N+2
40 IF N<1001 THEN 20
50 PRINT S
60 END
```

Loops can be used for many different types of operations. Let us examine some additional ones.

Example 7:

Read in a value for N.
Compute N!, where $N! = N \times (N - 1) \times (N - 2) \cdots 1$.
N! is called *N factorial*.

Example 8:

$$5! = 5 \times 4 \times 3 \times 2 \times 1 = 120.$$

```
10 LET F=1
20 INPUT N
30 LET F=F*N
40 LET N=N-1
50 IF N>=1 THEN 30
60 PRINT F
70 END
```

If N = 4, the processing sequence would be as follows:

Number of Times through Statement 30	F	N
1	1	4
2	4	3
3	4×3	2
4	$4 \times 3 \times 2$	1
5	$4 \times 3 \times 2 \times 1$	
	$F = 4 \times 3 \times 2 \times 1 = 24$ when printed	

Looping operations include the following elements:

Example: Sum Odd Numbers 1 to 101	Elements in a Loop
10 N=1	1. Initialize the field.
20 S=S+N	2. Perform the required operations.
30 N=N+2	3. Modify the field each time through.
40 IF N<=101 THEN 20	4. Test the field:
50 PRINT S	a. If the operation has been
60 END	performed the required number of
	times, you are done.
	b. If not, repeat.

7.3.5 Other Uses of IF–THEN Statements

Example 1: Calculate weekly wages based on input of HOURLY RATE and HOURS WORKED. For employees who have worked more than 40 hours, pay them time-and-a-half for overtime:

```
10  INPUT  H,R
20  IF  H>40  THEN  60
30  LET  W=H*R
40  PRINT  W
50  GOTO  10
60  LET  H=H-40
70  LET  W=40*R+(H*R*1.5)
80  PRINT  W
90  GOTO  10
100  END
```

We could save a step by coding line 80 as

80 GO TO 40

and omit line 90. Since 80 and 90 in the preceding illustration duplicate 40 and 50, we can simply GO TO 40 and save a step.

Another main use of IF–THEN statements is for performing a summary function *after* all data has been read and processed. To do this, we must read all data and *determine* when the data has been completely read; then we would proceed to a separate routine. To do this, we end our data items with a "dummy" or trailer entry.

That is, suppose that we wish to compute WEEKLY WAGES based on HOURS WORKED and HOURLY RATE; ignore OVERTIME PAY in this example. In addition, we want to print the TOTAL WAGES paid for *all* employees at the end.

To do this, we indicate to the computer that if an HOURS WORKED field is entered as 99, this is a trailer entry and means that we are out of data. Thus we have

```
10 INPUT N$,H,R
20 IF H = 99 THEN 70
30 LET W = H*R
40 LET T = T+W
50 PRINT "WEEKLY WAGES FOR",N$,"IS", W
60 GO TO 10
70 PRINT "TOTAL WAGES PAID IS",T
80 END
```

Line 20 will cause a branch to 70 only when we enter 99 for HOURS WORKED. We would do so only at the end of the job. That is, the last record would contain 99 for HOURS WORKED.

Line 40 computes TOTAL WAGES by adding WEEKLY WAGES, W, each time it is computed.

Example 2:   Read three grades for each student. Print an average for each student and a class average.

To print a class average, we must determine the number of student records processed. To determine the number of records processed in any procedure, we code

```
10 INPUT E1,E2,E3
20 LET C=C+1
```

Each time an INPUT statement is executed, C is incremented by 1. C will always indicate the number of input records processed.

An exam grade of 0 will denote an end-of-data condition. Thus we have

```
10 INPUT E1,E2,E3
20 IF E1 = 0 THEN 80
30 LET C = C+1
40 LET A = (E1+E2+E3)/3
50 PRINT "THE STUDENT AVERAGE IS ",A
60 LET T = T+A
70 GOTO 10
80 LET T1 = T/C
90 PRINT "THE CLASS AVERAGE IS ",T1
100 END
```

All IF-THEN statements thus far coded compare numeric variables to numeric constants. Suppose, however, that we wish to read in names, birth dates (month and year), and sex (M for male, F for female). In this instance we want to print the birth dates of people who are female; that is, we need to compare a string variable, sex, against an alphanumeric literal "F." Note that the literal is enclosed in quotes:

```
10 INPUT N$,M,Y,S$
20 IF S$ = "F" THEN 40
30 GO TO 10
40 PRINT "THE BIRTH DATE IS ",M,"/",Y
50 GO TO 10
60 END
```

Modifying the program above, suppose, instead, that we want to print the total number of females born in April. The end of the run will be denoted by LAST in the NAME field:

```
10 INPUT N$,M,Y,S$
20 IF N$="LAST" THEN 80
30 IF M<>04 THEN 10
40 IF S$="F" THEN 60
50 GOTO 10
60 LET C=C+1
70 GOTO 10
80 PRINT "THE TOTAL NO. OF FEMALES BORN IN APRIL IS",C
90 END
```

7.3.6 REM Statement

Note that a line number, followed by REM, followed by anything else will be treated as a remark or comment in the program. That is,

5 REM THIS PROGRAM CALCULATES TOTAL FEMALES

7 REM BORN IN APRIL

could be added to the preceding program for clarification or commentary purposes.

REM statements may be coded anywhere within the program. The computer ignores REM statements during execution but prints them as part of the program listing.

7.3.7 Summary

The following program will sum up all the concepts thus far considered.

Example: Data records for an insurance company are read in with the following items:

> NAME
> SEX (M = Male, F = Female)
> BIRTH DATE (MO, YR)
> STATE (1 for NY)
> Print: % DRIVERS FROM NY
>   % DRIVERS UNDER 25
>   % DRIVERS WHO ARE FEMALE

Hint: Assume the current year to be 1983; thus anyone born after 1958 is considered to be under 25. A value of Q in the SEX field will denote the end of the data.

```
10 INPUT N$,S$,M,Y,S
20 IF S$="Q" THEN 130
30 REM Q IN SEX FIELD WILL DENOTE EOJ
40 LET T=T+1
50 REM ABOVE INSTRUCTION COUNTS NO. OF RECORDS
60 IF S<>1 THEN 80
70 LET T1=T1+1
80 IF Y<=58 THEN 100
90 LET T2=T2+1
100 IF S$<>"F" THEN 10
110 LET T3=T3+1
120 GOTO 10
130 LET T1=T1/T*100
140 PRINT "% DRIVERS FROM NY IS ",T1
150 LET T2=T2/T*100
160 PRINT "% DRIVERS UNDER 25 IS ",T2
170 LET T3=T3/T*100
180 PRINT "% DRIVERS WHO ARE FEMALE IS ",T3
190 END
```

7.3.8 READ and DATA Statements

Thus far we have considered the INPUT statement as a data entry command. This is used when we do not know what input will need to be processed at any given time.

Sometimes, however, we have some complex processing to perform where we know *precisely* what data we want to operate on. In such a case, we use READ and DATA statements in place of the INPUT command. Note that with READ and DATA statements, the data is actually part of the program; there is no need to enter additional data when RUN is typed.

Example: Suppose that for every set of values of X and Y, we would like to calculate the square root of $X^2 + Y^2$. Consider the following program:

```
10 READ X,Y
20 LET A = SQR(X ** 2 + Y ** 2)
30 PRINT A
40 GO TO 10
50 DATA 3,4
60 DATA 5,7
70 END
```

The READ statement directs the computer to get a value for X and a value for Y from a DATA statement. The first time the READ instruction is executed, the computer will get the values from the *first* DATA statement (3 and 4). After the desired calculations are performed and the answer is printed out, the computer goes back to statement 10 again. The computer is told to get *another* set of values—one for X and one for Y. Since the values in the first DATA statement have already been used, the computer knows automatically that it must get the data from statement 60, the next DATA statement. When the computer goes back to statement 10 for the third time, it finds no data to read in. A message, such as "OUT OF DATA" will then usually be printed by the computer.

It would have been equally valid to have DATA statements such as the following:

```
50 DATA 3, 4, 5, 7
```

Here, only *one* DATA statement is used. The first READ causes only the first two values in statement 50 to be used since only two variables are to be read. The second time the READ is executed, the next two values in the DATA statement are used. As many items of data as can fit on one line may be used in this form of the DATA statement.

It should be noted that DATA statements are typically located at the end of a program just before the END statement. However, since DATA statements are not instructions as such, but merely serve to provide data for the READ statements, they can be located anywhere within a BASIC program. This is true because of the fact that they do not affect the logic of the program at all. The following sequence of instructions is therefore valid:

```
10 READ X, Y
20 DATA 3, 4
30 DATA 5, 7
40 LET A = SQR(X ** 2 + Y ** 2)
50 PRINT A
60 GO TO 10
70 END
```

Thus we see that DATA statements can appear anywhere throughout the program and that they can have any one of a number of formats.

The example just discussed illustrates how *numeric* data can be included within a program. Alphanumeric data can also be included in DATA statements, although the rules vary slightly, depending on the computer on which the program is run. Some BASIC compilers require alphanumeric data to be enclosed in quotes, as illustrated in the following program excerpt:

```
10 READ N$, S
     .
     .
     .
180 DATA "JAMES PARKS",10250
190 DATA "ANNE STONE",13175
200 END
```

Statement 10 instructs the computer to get the values from a DATA statement for two fields—N$, a string variable representing name, and S, a numeric field representing salary. You will recall that when forming a string variable name, we use a letter followed by a dollar sign. The rule for forming numeric field names or variables is to use a letter or a letter followed by a digit.

The same program run on a computer where the BASIC compiler does *not* ordinarily require quotes around string variable data would appear as follows:

```
10 READ N$, S
     .
     .
     .
180 DATA JAMES PARKS,10250
190 DATA ANNE STONE,13175
200 END
```

Notice that the comma in a DATA statement is used only to separate fields of data. It may *not* be included within numeric data. That is, the number 10,250 must be entered as 10250. The following DATA statement is therefore interpreted by the computer as having four numeric values:

```
145 DATA 723, 12735, 123, 128.17
```

The four values in this statement are (1) 723, (2) 12735, (3) 123, and (4) 128.17.

7.4   ADVANCED CONCEPTS IN BASIC

7.4.1   Loops and ON–GO TO Statement

7.4.1.1   Loops and For . . . Next Statements

You will recall that a **loop** is a sequence of instructions that is to be repeated a certain number of times. Let us consider a problem that will illustrate how a loop is performed. Suppose that we wish to compute the amount of money we will accumulate at the end of one, two, and three years if we bank a specified amount at a given rate of interest. Assume that all money (principal and interest) remains in the bank. The following general formula is useful for solving problems involving compound interest:

$$P_n = P_0(1 + r)^n$$

P_n is equal to the total amount of money after n years of investment of an initial amount (P_0) at a given rate of interest (r).

We will now write a program to evaluate this formula, where values of P (principal) and R (rate of interest) are to be entered as input. We are interested in the results when n equals 1, 2, and 3.

Method 1-Without Loops

```
10 INPUT P, R
20 PRINT "          COMPOUND INTEREST RESULTS"
30 PRINT
40 PRINT "RATE OF INTEREST =", R, "INITIAL AMOUNT =", P
50 PRINT
60 LET A = P * (1 + R) ** 1
70 PRINT "AMOUNT AFTER YEAR 1 EQUALS",A
80 LET B = P * (1 + R) ** 2
90 PRINT "AMOUNT AFTER YEAR 2 EQUALS",B
100 LET C = P * (1 + R) ** 3
110 PRINT "AMOUNT AFTER YEAR 3 EQUALS",C
120 END
```

Notice that lines 60 through 110 have many similarities. Lines 60, 80, and 100 utilize the same basic formula with only one modification each time the calculation is performed—the value of the exponent is either 1, 2, or 3. Lines 70, 90, and 110, which print the output, are also very similar, except that each message indicates a different year— either 1, 2, or 3.

Notice that one routine could be established, instead of three separate routines, to compute the three values. This one routine could establish a variable exponent N, for example, which begins as 1 and is incremented by 1 each time until it exceeds 3. That is, a *loop* can be established to be executed three times, varying N from 1 to 3.

Method 2—Using a Loop

```
10 INPUT P, R
20 PRINT "          COMPOUND INTEREST RESULTS"
30 PRINT
40 PRINT "RATE OF INTEREST =", R, "INITIAL AMOUNT =",P
50 PRINT
60 LET N = 1
70 LET A = P * (1 + R) ** N
80 PRINT "AMOUNT AFTER YEAR",N,"EQUALS",A
90 IF N = 3 THEN 120
100 LET N = N + 1
110 GO TO 70
120 END
```

Notice that this program utilizes a loop. The sequence of instructions that is to be repeated begins with line 70. Lines 70 and 80 are executed for the *first* time with a value of N equal to 1. At line 90, the computer performs a test to see if the sequence should be repeated. Since N is not equal to 3 the first time the statement is executed, the computer proceeds automatically to the next line, where 1 is added to N, so that it now equals 2. With N equal to 2, the computer is then instructed at line 110 to go back to line 70 and process the sequence of instructions again.

Method 3—Using the FOR *and* NEXT *Instructions*

We have seen from the previous solutions that we wish to perform a series of operations using a variable N which begins as 1 and is incremented until it reaches 3. The FOR and NEXT statements provide some flexibility in dealing with this type of problem.

The FOR statement establishes a variable and specifies the range in which it is to vary. Thus for our problem we would have

FOR N = 1 TO 3

with an appropriate line number.

The statements to follow will be executed, for the first time, with N = 1. The NEXT statement essentially instructs the computer to repeat these steps with N at the next value (N = 2). Our NEXT statement would be coded at the end of the series of steps to be performed and would read:

NEXT N

with an appropriate line number.

This procedure would be repeated until N were equal to 3 and all the instructions performed for that value. Then the program would continue with the statement directly *following* the NEXT statement.

Let us now consider this most effective method for handling loops:

```
 10 INPUT P, R
 20 PRINT "            COMPOUND INTEREST RESULTS"
 30 PRINT
 40 PRINT "RATE OF INTEREST = ",R,"INITIAL AMOUNT = ",P
 50 PRINT
 60 FOR N = 1 TO 3
 70 LET A = P * (1 + R) ** N
 80 PRINT "AMOUNT AFTER YEAR",N,"EQUALS",A
 90 NEXT N
100 END
```

The FOR statement in line 60 indicates that the sequence of instructions *up to the* NEXT *statement* (line 90) is to be repeated three times, with N = 1 the first time, N = 2 the second time, and N = 3 the last time through the statements.

The NEXT statement (line 90) causes the field N, specified in the FOR statement (line 60), to be automatically incremented to the next value each time the sequence has been executed.

The FOR statement used in the program above will initialize N at 1 and result in N being incremented by 1 until it equals 3.

Suppose, however, that we wish to initialize N at 10 and increment N by 10 each time rather than by 1. That is, we wish N to assume the values 10, 20, 30, and so on, until N equals 100. The FOR statement is specified as

```
FOR N = 10 TO 100 STEP 10
```

The omission of the STEP option in the FOR statement implies that the variable is to be incremented by 1. In the above, we initialize N at 10 and "step" it or increment it by 10 each time the succeeding operations are performed until N is equal to 100.

Examples of FOR . . . NEXT Instructions

1. Sum the odd numbers from 101 to 1001 using a FOR . . . NEXT loop.

```
10 FOR N=101 TO 1001 STEP 2
20 LET T=T+N
30 NEXT N
40 PRINT "THE SUM OF ODD NUMBERS FROM 101-1001 IS ",T
50 END
```

2. Read a value for M. Find M!, where M! = M × (M − 1) × (M − 2) . . . × 1.

```
10 LET T=1
20 INPUT M
30 FOR N=1 TO M
40 LET T=T*N
50 NEXT N
60 PRINT "M IS",M
70 PRINT "M!=",T
80 GOTO 10
90 END
```

Note that line 30 could have been coded as

```
30  FOR N = M TO 1  STEP - 1
```

It is possible to code FOR . . . NEXT loops within FOR . . . NEXT loops. Consider the following:

Example: There are 10 math classes in College ABC. Each class has 25 students. Each line of input has a student's average. Write a BASIC program using FOR . . . NEXT loops to print 10 class averages.

```
10 FOR I=1 TO 10
20 LET T=0
30 FOR J=1 TO 25
40 INPUT G1
50 LET T=T+G1
60 NEXT J
70 PRINT "CLASS AVERAGE FOR CLASS",I,"=",T/25
80 NEXT I
90 END
```

7.4.1.2 *ON-GO TO* **Statement**

Many BASIC compilers allow the programmer to use the ON-GO TO statement, which is also known as the *computed GO TO*. The computed GO TO can be used to replace several IF statements. Consider the following program excerpt:

```
10 INPUT A, C, F
20 IF A = 1 THEN 110
30 IF A = 2 THEN 145
40 IF A = 3 THEN 65
        .
        .
        .
```

Lines 20 through 40 could be replaced with an ON-GO TO statement:

```
20 ON A GO TO 110, 145, 65
```

If A is equal to 1, a branch or transfer is made to the *first* line number indicated (110). If A is equal to 2, a branch is made to the *second* line number (145). If A is equal to 3, a branch is made to the *third* line number (65). It should be noted that if A is not equal to 1, 2, or 3, the program will ordinarily stop.

The general form of the ON-GO TO statement is

```
ON (expression) GO TO (line number) . . ., (line number)
```

It should be noted that if the value of the expression is not an integer, it will automatically be truncated to an integer. Thus if we have the statement

```
ON A + B GO TO 115, 117, 23
```

and A equals 1.3 and B equals 0.8, a branch to line 117 will be made, since A plus B equals 2.1, which is truncated to 2.

7.4.2 Arrays

There are many types of problems where it is convenient, and sometimes necessary, to store all the input data with **subscripted variables** before further processing is performed. A subscripted variable refers to either a list or a table of data stored in the computer. A **subscript** or number is necessary to indicate the position of a particular value in the list or table. Consider the following program, where each student in a particular course has taken six exams which are to be averaged by the computer.

```
10 INPUT E1, E2, E3, E4, E5, E6
20 LET A = (E1+E2+E3+E4+E5+E6)/6
30 PRINT A
40 GO TO 10
50 END
```

This oversimplified program allows the instructor to sit at the terminal, enter one student's grades at a time, and then get the average printed out before proceeding to the next student.

Notice that six different variable names were used in lines 10 and 20: E1, E2, E3, E4, E5, and E6. Suppose that the instructor had given 12 exams. We may run into several problems when writing the program. First, we cannot use variable names such as E10, E11, and E12, since a variable name can only consist of a letter, or a letter and *one* digit after it. Even if we can choose meaningful variable names, the instructions become rather cumbersome to type:

```
10 INPUT E1, E2, E3, E4, E5, E6, E7, E8, E9, T1, T2, T3
20 LET A = (E1+E2+E3+E4+E5+E6+E7+E8+E9+T1+T2+T3)/12
```

One way around such a problem is to use a subscripted variable for the exam scores. Consider again the problem where six exam scores are to be entered for each student. Suppose that we want the computer to set up a **list**, or **one-dimensional array**.[1] The term "one-dimensional array" simply means that the data can be visualized as being stored in *one* column within the computer. The name of the list will be E. It will have six slots or cells into which the numbers can be placed. After the data is stored in the list, we can refer to any specific item by indicating the appropriate *position* in the list with the use of a subscript. The values in the list can then be referred to as E(1), E(2), E(3), E(4), E(5), and E(6). E(1) refers to the first number in the list called E, E(2) refers to the second number, and so on. Figure 7.1 illustrates how the list just described can be visualized inside the computer.

Our instructions to read in the scores and average them *might* then be as follows:

```
10 INPUT E(1), E(2), E(3), E(4), E(5), E(6)
20 LET A = (E(1)+E(2)+E(3)+E(4)+E(5)+E(6))/6
```

Although these instructions illustrate the use of a subscripted variable, we have not saved anything by doing it this way. However, it may have occurred to you that we might use the FOR and NEXT statements to facilitate our programming. The following instructions simplify the coding:

---

[1] A table, or two-dimensional array, refers to data that is stored in columns and rows within the computer.

```
 5 LET T = 0
10 FOR I = 1 TO 6
20 INPUT E(I)
30 LET T = T + E(I)
40 NEXT I
50 PRINT T/6
60 GO TO 5
70 END
```

Line 5 sets up a variable T to accumulate the total of each student's grades. Line 10 indicates that the following lines (20 and 30) are to be repeated six times, with I varying from 1 to 6, in increments of 1. Lines 20 and 30 process the Ith value of E; that is, the first time through the loop, the first value of E, or the first exam grade, is entered as input and stored in the first slot of the list—E(1). This value is then added to the current value of T, which is zero. Line 40 increments I by 1 and the loop is repeated. The second time through, the second exam grade is entered and stored as E(2), and so on. After all six grades have been entered and accumulated, the computer goes to line 50 automatically, where the accumulated total for the student just processed is divided by 6, and the answer is printed out. The process is then repeated for the other students.

It should now be apparent why subscripted variables are so useful. Regardless of how many values are to be read into a particular list, essentially the same simple instructions can be used. There is one

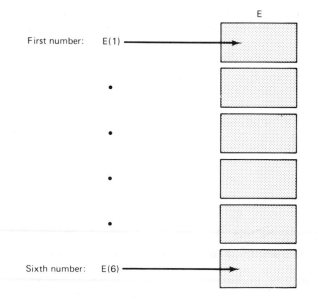

Figure 7.1.

additional instruction, however, that is necessary *if the subscript will exceed 10*. The instruction that is required is the **dimension statement** (DIM). Its purpose is to explicitly tell the computer how much room to reserve for a subscripted variable when it is known that there will be subscripts greater than 10. The BASIC compiler automatically reserves enough room to allow for a subscript up to 10 whenever a subscripted variable is encountered during compilation. If we know, for example, that there will be 12 grades entered for each student, we will need a dimension statement such as

```
10 DIM E(12)
```

at the beginning of the program. This statement explicitly tells the computer to reserve enough room for a list called E to allow for a subscript up to 12.

7.5 VERSIONS OF BASIC

Note that we have considered the standard form of BASIC that can be run on most types and sizes of computers. Usually, the BASIC program is *interpreted*, rather than compiled, so that any errors made will be indicated right after each line that contains one or more syntax errors:

```
10 INPUT A,B,C
20 LET D = A+B+C
30 PRINT D(
SYNTAX ERROR D(
```

BASIC is the major language on most minis and micros. Because of this, the manufacturers of these small computers usually provide an extended version of BASIC that permits more efficient operations and more powerful input/output commands.

In Extended BASIC, for example, an IF-THEN need not cause a branch; rather a command could be executed:

```
10 IF C=0 THEN T = T+1
```

Moreover, statements can be strung together on a single line, separated only by a semicolon or other delineator, depending on the particular version of Extended BASIC:

```
10 INPUT A,B,C; LET D = (A+B+C)/3; PRINT D
```

The version of BASIC you have learned will work on almost all computers. If you check your user manual, however, you may find that there are numerous extensions available to you.

7.6 A SUMMARY OF THE BASIC LANGUAGE

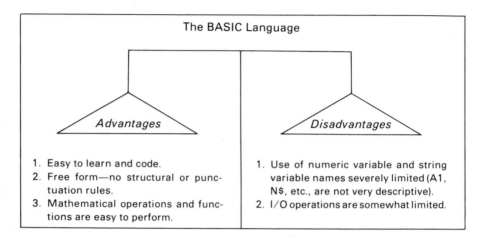

The BASIC Language

Advantages

1. Easy to learn and code.
2. Free form—no structural or punctuation rules.
3. Mathematical operations and functions are easy to perform.

Disadvantages

1. Use of numeric variable and string variable names severely limited (A1, N$, etc., are not very descriptive).
2. I/O operations are somewhat limited.

KEY TERMS

Array
Authorization code
DATA statement
DIM statement
GO TO statement
Hierarchy of operations
IF statement
INPUT
Line number
LIST
Log-on procedures
Loop
Numeric variable
ON statement
Protocol
READ statement
REM statement
RUN
STOP

String variable
Table
Trailer record

REVIEW QUESTIONS

1. Write and run a program to read in five amounts from a terminal, calculate and print their average, and then repeat the process.
2. Write a program to read in a SALES AMOUNT on a terminal. If the SALES AMOUNT is greater than $500.00, the COMMISSION is computed as 5% of the SALES AMOUNT. If the SALES AMOUNT is not greater than $500.00 but is greater than $200.00, the COMMISSION is 3% of the SALES AMOUNT. If the SALES AMOUNT is $200.00 or less, the COMMISSION is zero. Print the COMMISSION.
3. Write a program to calculate and print F.I.C.A. tax on salary to be read in on a terminal.

F.I.C.A. = 6.70% of the salary up to $32,400

(No tax is computed beyond the first $32,400.)
4. Write and run a program to read in accident data as indicated below and produce a report with the information shown. Use READ and DATA statements for the input. Supply appropriate identification on the report.
   Input: Information for each driver involved in an accident in the past year:
   a. Driver's name
   b. State code (1 for New York)
   c. Sex (M for male, F for female)
   d. Birth date (month, year)
   Output: A report that shows the following results:
   a. The percentage of drivers who were male and over 30
   b. The percentage of drivers from New York who are female
5. Change the output in the preceding problem as follows. Produce a report that lists the names of all females from New York who were involved in an accident. Indicate the total number of New York drivers involved in accidents at the end of the report. Assume that a field is added with a 1 for accident, and a 0 for no accident.
6. Write and run a program to determine the most economical quantity of each product for a manufacturing company to produce. The economic order quantity Q may be determined from the formula

$$Q = \sqrt{\frac{2RS}{I}}$$

The input for each product will consist of:

a. Product name
b. Total yearly production requirement (R)
c. Inventory carrying cost per unit (I)
d. Setup cost per order (S)

The output should be a report that lists the data for each product together with the value of Q that has been determined. Include appropriate identifying information.

7. Code a program to read in a value for A and to print the absolute value of A. The absolute value of any number is its displacement from 0. Thus the absolute value of $-3 = 3$; the absolute value of $25 = 25$. Let an input value of 999 signal an end-of-data condition.

8. Each set of input consists of a student's name and four grades for that person. Determine each student's average and print a grade based on the average as follows:

Average	Grade
90+	A
80–89	B
70–79	C
60–69	D
<60	F

The name "LAST" signals the end of the data.

9. Write a program to print the largest of three numbers A, B, and C that are read in and then repeat the process.

10. Write a program, using READ and DATA statements, to read in a code field and an amount. If the code is "A," calculate and print T, tax, as 4.5% of the amount. If the code is "B," calculate and print T, tax, as 3.7% of the amount. If code is "C," calculate and print T, tax, as 2.2% of the amount. Use this procedure for the following values:

Code	Amount
C	5200
A	463
B	8211
B	3372
A	495
B	625
C	42

11. Code a program to read the names and weights for each of several individuals and print only the names of those people who weigh less than 120 pounds or more than 250 pounds. Use READ and DATA statements.

12. Revise the preceding program to read in for each person his or her weight and height (in inches). Print the name of any person whose weight is less than 120 pounds and height is less than 64 inches or whose weight is greater than 250 pounds and height is greater than 74 inches. Print the total number of names on the report at the end.

13. Code a program to read in amount fields and to print the average amount after all input has been read. Assume that an amount of 999.99 signals an end-of-data condition. Use an INPUT statement.

14. Write a program using FOR-NEXT statements to read in the weights of 11 students and print the average. The weights will be supplied in one DATA statement. Store all the data in a list before proceeding with the calculations.

COMPUTERS
IN
SOCIETY

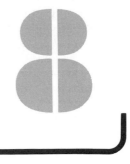

Computers in business and industry

This chapter focuses on two commercial areas of computerization: (1) *business applications,* those designed to maximize the overall profits and to minimize the overall costs of an organization; and (2) *industrial applications*, those relating specifically to manufacturing or production functions.

8.1 COMPUTERS IN BUSINESS

There are numerous ways in which computers can be used to maximize profits and minimize costs. Some basic objectives of such computerization in a business environment include the following:

> Basic Objectives of Computerized Business Functions
>
> 1. To reduce the need for human record keeping by automating clerical functions
> 2. To reduce the number of errors produced in record-keeping operations
> 3. To store data efficiently and to make that data available quickly and efficiently
> 4. To assist management by providing up-to-date information that can be used for decision-making purposes
> 5. To provide government with some of the detailed reports it requires

Typical business procedures that utilize computers include the following:

1. Accounts receivable

    Objective: to maintain and process records on money owed to a company by customers or clients

    Typical EDP functions: to maintain files, to send bills, to record and process payments
2. Accounts payable

    Objective: to maintain and process records on money owed by the company to vendors.

    Typical EDP functions: to maintain files, to process statements, to remit payments
3. Payroll

    Objective: to maintain employee payroll records and to process payroll checks

    Typical EDP functions: to maintain a payroll file, to process the file and produce paychecks, to prepare government reports on employee earnings
4. Inventory control

    Objective: to maintain records on items or goods on hand, on quantities ordered, and, in general, to control inventory

    Typical EDP functions: to maintain an inventory file, to produce purchase orders on out-of-stock items, to determine economic order quantities
5. Marketing and sales

    Objective: to determine the best combination of products to merchandise in order to maximize profits

    Typical EDP functions: to maintain sales and marketing records, to report on sales performance, to perform sales forecasts

Perhaps of most importance is the ability of computers to provide Profit-and-loss analysis as well as other status reports. That is, a computer can integrate data from the company as a whole to produce a comprehensive report.

8.1.1   Types of Computers Used in Business

The size of the business and the degree of computerization required will determine the type of computer used. Small companies can utilize mini-, micro- or small-scale computers quite effectively, whereas larger organizations need to use a network of minis and/or a large-scale computer system.

Organizations can rent, lease, or purchase a computer system. The advantages and disadvantages of each method of acquisition are indicated in Table 8.1. Companies that require computers but cannot justify the acquisition of an entire system can rent time on a large system from a *time-sharing* facility. Time-sharing enables a user to pay only for the computer time used each month.

Table 8.1. *Methods of Computer Acquisition.*

Method	Advantages	Disadvantages
Purchase	Tends to be the cheapest method of acquisition Provides the user with a sizable tax credit	Possibility that equipment obsolescence could leave the user with outdated hardware Large capital investment Maintenance is not included
Lease	Tends to be cheaper than rental Obligation of the manufacturer or its agent to support the system for a fixed period of time Purchase options available Includes maintenance	Even if dissatisfied, obligates the user to retain the equipment for the life of the lease
Rental	Provides the user with the most flexibility Provides the best protection against equipment obsolescence	Tends to be expensive Provides little protection for the user against increases in cost Usually leaves servicing of the equipment as an additional cost

8.1.2 How Business Operations Are Computerized

The impetus for a management decision to computerize a business operation is usually one or more of the following:

Reasons for Computerizing a Manual Business Operation

1. Inability to process data in the time provided
2. Costly and inefficient manual procedures
3. High error rate
4. Inability of the manual system to accommodate growth
5. Inability of management to obtain the information necessary to make decisions

---

When the manager of a business department or an executive of the company decides that a business function needs to be computerized, he or she calls upon a **systems analyst** to determine the best course of action. The systems analyst is responsible for:

Tasks of Systems Analyst

1. Analyzing the existing business procedures to determine the basic problem areas
2. Designing a new, computerized system that will operate more efficiently and effectively than the manual system
3. Implementing the new business system so that it operates smoothly

---

The systems analyst may be:

1. A staff employee in the organization
2. An outside consultant who makes recommendations to management

In either case, the systems analyst is a computer professional who normally has the following credentials:

Job Requirements for Systems Analysts

1. An undergraduate degree in business, computer science, or a computer-related discipline. (Often the analyst has some graduate training as well.)
2. A thorough understanding of how computers are used in a business environment.
3. A thorough understanding of the needs of businesspeople.
4. An ability to communicate with the users—that is, the people who currently operate the manual business system and who will need to be trained in using the new design.

See Table 8.2 for a listing of the skills typically required of a systems analyst.

The analyst, then, receives a request from management to review an existing set of procedures called a **business system** and to make recommendations for a new design. The analyst is an employee or consultant who serves as an advisor—he or she can only recommend; the decision to proceed with a new systems design for the business procedure rests with management. The analyst, then,

1. Analyzes an existing business system
2. Designs a new computerized business system

That is, the analyst who is trained in using computer systems—hardware and software technology—attempts to apply that knowledge to the design of business systems—the procedures necessary for performing a business function.

Table 8.2.   *Skills of the Systems Analyst.*[a]

1. Strong user orientation
2. Self-starter: ability to work with poorly defined objectives
3. Keen understanding of organizational flow, and company goals and objectives
4. Ability to determine in advance the impact of a system on user departments
5. Planning and control (project management) skills
6. Behavioral sensitivity to the impact of a system on individuals
7. In-depth knowledge of user departments (operations)
8. Cost consciousness and ability to estimate and adhere to costs and schedules
9. Leadership ability, administrative experience, political sensitivity
10. Technical skills (programming, systems, data base design, telecommunications, etc)

[a] Adapted from a description supplied in *Datamation*, Apr. 1980, p. 124. Reprinted with Permission of *Datamation®* magazine, ©copyright by Technical Publishing Company, a Dun & Bradstreet Company, 1980. All rights reserved.

A brief overview of the tasks involved in analyzing an existing system and designing and implementing a new one will illustrate the multifaceted nature of the analyst's job:

	Steps Involved in Systems Analysis and Design
Analysis Phase	1. *Initial request:* The analyst receives a request from management to study an existing system. 2. *Isolate objectives and constraints:* The analyst studies the objectives of the business operation and any constraints or limitations imposed on it. 3. *Data collection:* The analyst studies existing procedure manuals and forms. Then he or she interviews and observes key personnel to obtain a better understanding of how the system actually functions. 4. *Problem definition:* The analyst reports to management on the problem areas in the existing system and makes recommendations for a computerized procedure.

Design Phase	5. *New design:* If approval to proceed is obtained, the analyst designs:
	  a. New output forms.
	  b. New input forms.
	  c. Revised processing specifications—these are transmitted to the programmer, who then codes and debugs each required program.
	  d. Controls needed (e.g., audit trails).
	6. *Test the new system.*
	7. *Implement the new system.*
	8. *Prepare documentation that describes the new system in depth.*

8.1.3 Facets of Computerized Business Applications

Business operations vary depending on the tasks to be performed. But regardless of whether we are dealing with an accounting, inventory, payroll, or another business function, there are several features that are common to all of them.

8.1.3.1 Types of Files

a. *Master File.* Each business application requires a **master file**, which contains records with all pertinent data necessary for processing. A payroll master file, for example, contains all payroll data for each employee which is necessary for producing paychecks and for providing management and the government with required payroll reports.

A master file would usually be stored on tape or disk depending on:

1. The number of records in the file

2. The size of each record
3. Whether the records need to be processed on-line or in batch mode

b. *Transaction or Detail File.*   A master file that contains all the pertinent information necessary for the specific business application will fast become obsolete or dated unless it is kept current. That is, a master file needs to be revised or *updated* periodically so that it incorporates all changes. A payroll master file will need to be updated so that it reflects:

1. New employee records
2. Salary changes
3. Promotions
4. Employees who have been terminated

Change records are placed on a **transaction** or **detail file**. This file is then used to update or revise the master file.

Like the master file, a transaction file can be stored on various computer media. For example, a transaction file can be:

1. Keypunched onto cards from documents such as purchase orders, sales receipts, and payroll change forms
2. Created on a cassette, tape, disk, or diskette file by an operator at a terminal or a keyboard device

The transaction file must be *edited* before it is used to update the master file. Editing is performed to minimize the risk of errors.

8.1.3.2   Types of Processing

Each of the following procedures is usually performed by an individual program for each business function:

a. *Editing of Transaction Data.*   An **edit procedure** is the process of validating a file of data to ensure that records do not contain obvious omissions, inconsistencies, or errors. Errors in files are relatively common because of (1) source document errors made by departmental employees, and (2) conversion errors made by operations personnel in keypunching data onto cards, keying data onto tape, keying data into a terminal, and so on.

Common edit procedures are performed during updating as well.

b. *Updating a Master File.*   An **update** or **file maintenance procedure** is the process of making a master file of data current (see Table 8.3).

File maintenance procedures can be performed either on-line or in a batch-processing environment.

Table 8.3. *Files Used in Update Routines.*

Inputs

Master file: contains *all* pertinent data for a specific system and serves as a frame of reference and a source for compiling output data

Detail or transaction file: contains all current activity that is not yet part of the master file—changes to existing master records, new entries to the master file, and so on

Outputs

Updated master file: contains all previous master data that has been changed to reflect the current activity

Error list: contains any errors that have appeared during processing—unmatched records, inconsistent records, and so on

Total or control lists: contains totals of all updated records, all errors, and all new entries; such totals are used mainly for control purposes

For *on-line processing*, data that is used to update a file is usually entered on a terminal. The data is then used to immediately access the master record and make it current.

File maintenance routines are performed on-line only when the master file *must* be current at all times, to optimize the answering of customer inquiries or to optimize management's decision-making process. For example, systems that utilize a master reservation file to answer customer inquiries or to make flight reservations require the master file to be updated on-line. To wait for a periodic update cycle would invalidate much of the data on the file, since it would not be current.

Figure 8.1 illustrates a sample update procedure in an on-line environment.

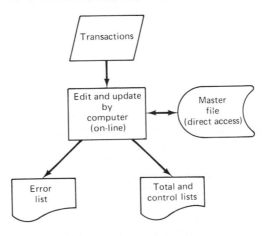

Figure 8.1. Updating in an on-line environment.

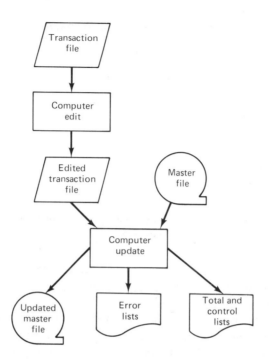

Figure 8.2. Updating in a batch-processing environment.

When data on a file need not be current or timely at any given moment, it is far more economical to batch or group all changes to the file and thus perform updates at periodic intervals. In this way, the computer is processing data more efficiently than it would on-line, where data is entered sporadically from terminals as the changes occur.

Figure 8.2 illustrates a sample update procedure in a *batch-processing environment*.

8.1.3.3 Types of Output Reporting

The types of reports typically produced in business are as follows:

1. *Detail reports:* A current or updated master file is used to produce reports on individual records. For payroll applications, producing paychecks is an illustration of detail reporting; for accounts receivable applications, producing individual bills is an example of detail reporting.
2. *Summary reports:* Where individual data is not required, but summary or total information is needed either for control or decision-making purposes, a summary report is produced.
3. *Exception reports:* Sometimes all that is needed is a list of records that do not fall within established criteria. That is, producing a list of customers

who have not paid their bills in 90 days is an example of an exception report. Such "exception reporting" is considerably cheaper than a detail or summary report.

Frequently, master files must be sorted into a specific sequence, merged with other files for summary purposes, or purged of invalid or unused records, prior to any reporting. Each of these procedures frequently requires a separate program.

The computerized procedures required for file maintenance and for reporting must be designed by a systems analyst. The analyst can:

1. Assign a programmer the job of coding, testing, and debugging the computerized procedures
2. Purchase a prepackaged or "canned" application program to perform the required procedures

Prepackaged software is available for file processing, but it tends to be somewhat inflexible and usually provides users with something less than what they actually want. However, such software is relatively inexpensive and easy to implement. The analyst usually decides whether to acquire such a package or to have programmers perform the required programming.

8.1.4 Systems Analysis: Science or Art?

Computers are considered to be rational tools that are best used when applied objectively. The analyst's job is similar to the scientist's in the following ways:

1. Analyzing a system should be approached scientifically—the analyst should have no preconceived notions, should be objective when interviewing users, and so on.
2. The tools and techniques used by the analyst are scientific in nature. The analyst functions as a scientist, rationally and without bias. He or she uses scientific methodology in determining problem areas and in designing more efficient systems.

But there is a danger of being *too* objective and too scientific when analyzing a system. That is, an experienced analyst will want to:

1. Weigh the *subjective* viewpoints of users
2. Be viewed as an individual who understands, in a humanistic sense, the needs, constraints, and limitations of users
3. Be careful to apply the tools of analysis and design in ways that will minimize disruptions

In short, if they are to be effective, systems analysts must combine a scientific approach with an appreciation for individual feelings and beliefs.

8.1.5   Traditional Systems Approach versus Management Information Systems Approach

There are two basic techniques which may be used for designing business systems:

8.1.5.1   *Traditional Systems Approach*

This approach treats each business system as an independent unit. The analyst attempts to redesign each system separately. Thus each unit is viewed as a stand-alone organizational element within the company. Its interrelationship with other units of the organization is not a major consideration for the analyst. Rather, the premise is that if each system can be made to function efficiently and effectively, the entire organization will, correspondingly, function better. The organization is viewed as the sum of all its business systems.

More recently, management has become somewhat dissatisfied with this traditional systems approach, for two major reasons.

1. It is not easy to perform cross-sectional or comprehensive analyses of the company's overall operations. Each system remains separate when the traditional approach is applied. That is, it is possible for each system to be very efficient, but management may not be able to obtain appropriate company-wide data, because each system was designed independently and, as a result, integrated information cannot be provided.
2. When each unit is designed independently, there is considerable duplication of effort. A sales system and a marketing system, for example, would include many similar elements, but if each is designed independently, there is no basis for coordination of interrelated data.

8.1.5.2   *Management Information Systems Approach*

Management information systems (MIS) are designed to eliminate the problems inherent in the traditional systems approach.

MIS systems include:

1. *One centralized data base with all information relevant to the company's business:* Instead of each department maintaining separate files, one **data base** contains all pertinent information. This eliminates duplication of effort (see Figure 8.3).

2. *Interrelationship of data:* To minimize the difficulties associated with processing a central data base, methods must be developed for easy retrieval and updating of data records.
3. *Inquiry ability:* With an MIS system that has a centralized data base, management can obtain any information it needs at any time. MIS systems usually provide management with its own terminals for inquiry about the status of any single function or of any functional units.

Software packages are used to facilitate the processing of a centralized data base and for making interrelated data available. This means that management can obtain company-wide information much more easily. Using this approach, the entire organization is viewed from the "top down" and each business system becomes a subset of this top-down approach.

MIS systems, then, are less fragmented and more integrated than

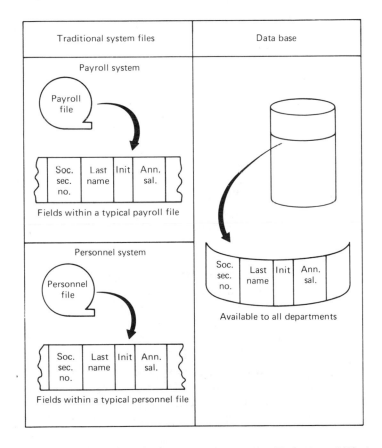

Figure 8.3. Comparison of traditional system files to an MIS data base.

traditional systems. There are, however, several inherent disadvantages to the MIS approach.

Failures of MIS Systems

1. MIS systems are very costly.
2. MIS systems require advanced data communication systems and the most modern hardware.
3. MIS systems require several years before they can be implemented.
4. MIS requires sophisticated software support.
5. In general, it is very difficult to provide a totally integrated output that can serve the operating staff of each business system as well as high-level management.
6. Lack of proper communication between users and computer professionals make many MIS systems infeasible. The users have difficulty defining their needs and the computer professionals have difficulty providing management with its desired output.

Thus most organizations view an integrated approach toward systems design as an appropriate technique, but few have succeeded in providing a totally effective design. The concepts for such designs are still being developed, but there are many obstacles yet to be overcome.

8.1.6 Centralized versus Decentralized Computer: Types of Computer Facilities

Traditionally, a computer installation and the various computer professionals who help to operate it and maximize its utility are under the direction of a central staff. When one group of employees reports to an executive who is responsible for the overall operations of the company's computer facility, this is referred to as a **centralized data processing** organization.

The alternatives to centralized data processing are: (1) decentralized data processing or (2) distributed data processing (DDP) (see Figure 8.4). Decentralized data processing means that each business system, such as accounting, payroll, and inventory, has its *own* computer facility and limited staff. There may or may not be a large central computer directing, monitoring, or controlling the activities of each computer facility in a decentralized environment.

In a **decentralized data processing** environment, each business area is responsible for its own data processing needs. This makes it easier to assess the value of computers for each individual user and to monitor the efficiency and effectiveness of computers in the specific areas.

Each department may hire its own computing staff that is competent not only in the computer field but in the particular appli-

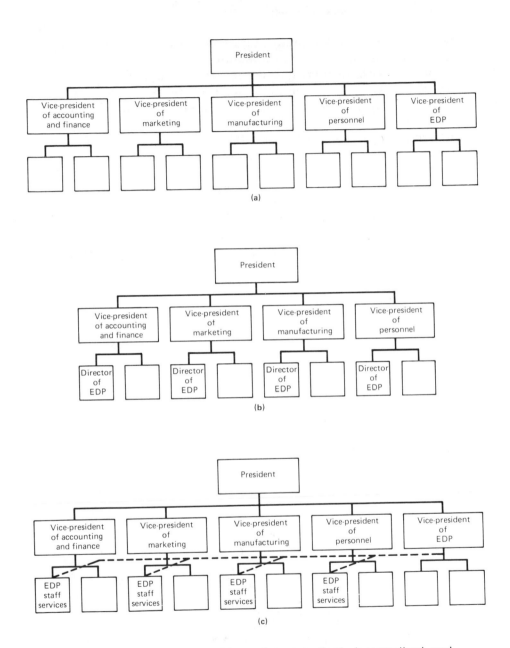

Figure 8.4. Organization charts for centralized, decentralized, and distributed computer facilities. (a) Centralized computer facility. There usually exists a lack of integration from department to department. (b) Decentralized computer facilities. (c) Distributed computer facilities.

cation area as well. This approach minimizes communication problems between user and computer professional.

Finally, with the increased flexibility and capability of mini and micro computers, it is sometimes not only feasible but financially advantageous to use smaller computers for specific applications.

But with a decentralized system, a top-down or management approach is not feasible. Moreover, there is significant duplication of effort and no standardization. Distributed data processing is an effort to combine the advantages of both the centralized and the decentralized approaches. This tends to be expensive in terms of "people" costs.

In a **distributed data processing** (DDP) environment, each department has its own computer facility, but there is one central computer controlling, coordinating, and integrating the data proces-

Table 8.4. *Advantages and Disadvantages of the Three Types of Computer Organization.*

Type of Organization	Advantages	Disadvantages
Centralized DP	Standardized equipment and procedures DP specialists work as a group; DP procedures become more professional; better supervision of activities Reduces duplication of effort	Difficult to assess each user's DP needs, costs, and the effectiveness of DP for that user Difficult to determine priorities for computer use Management-level resistance to DP exists because control of activities is in the hands of the DP manager
Decentralized DP	Direct control by users minimizes the traditional communication gap: computer professionals better understand department's needs More direct response to user needs; no pressure from other departments Easier to assess the effectiveness of each DP facility	Duplication in files, processing, and reporting Lack of standardization May or may not cost more
Distributed DP	Combines the advantages of both the centralized and decentralized approach and minimizes the disadvantages Facilitates the processing of management information systems	Requires tighter control and security Requires integration of data

sing activities of all departments. This enables users to satisfy their own specific needs and it also enables top-level management to obtain information about the company as a whole.

In a DDP environment, an organization has a centralized facility with a network of distributed computer systems at key locations. In this way, the distributed system can provide operations staff and managers with their informational needs. In addition, the central computer can be used to filter and compile management information from each individual area. In fact, management information systems utilize a distributed network for satisfying the specific needs of operations staff and middle management of each department.

One main difficulty with the distributed approach is that security and control procedures must be carefully implemented. When increasing numbers of users have access to both departmental data and centralized data, as they might in an MIS-distributed environment, it becomes easier, either inadvertently or consciously, to violate the system, producing errors or frauds.

Table 8.4 provides a summary of the advantages and disadvantages of the centralized, decentralized, and distributed approaches.

8.1.7 Automating the Office

There are several innovations in computerization that have resulted in automated office techniques. These include word processing, source data automation, and electronic mail.

8.1.7.1 Word Processing

A computer system, usually a mini, can be linked to several terminals, with each terminal used by a typist or operator. The terminals have CRTs with keyboards for text entry. The typist keys the data which is printed on the screen and makes corrections as necessary. When the screen contains completely error-free data, the operator obtains a hard-copy printout. A tape or disk record of the printout is also created (see Figure 8.5).

The report can later be corrected, amended, or appended by simply reentering the tape or disk and making the necessary changes.

The advantages of such a system include:

Advantages of Word-Processing Systems

1. Minimizing the need to manually retype pages of text
2. Facilitating the creation of standardized output or "form letters"
3. Maintaining a memory file of correspondence

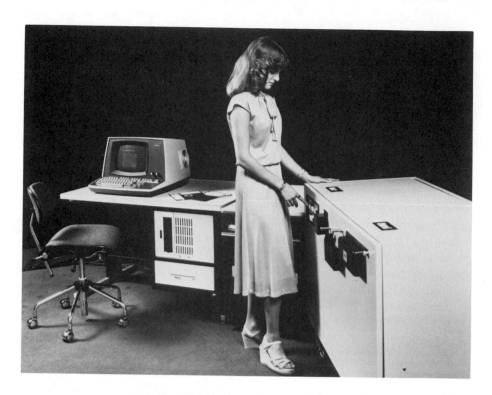

Figure 8.5. Example of a word-processing system.

Sometimes several terminals are linked to one minicomputer that provides each with word-processing capability. Sometimes an **intelligent terminal** with edit and formatting capability functions as a stand-alone word-processing unit.

8.1.7.2 Source Data Automation

In numerous offices, terminals may be used:

1. For creating traditional output—purchase requisitions, invoices, time cards, sales receipts, and so on, and, at the same time,
2. For storing information in some machine-readable form for future batch processing or for on-line processing. That is, the terminal can produce a computerized record along with the traditional output.

Source data automation has revolutionized many office procedures by performing the above two functions simultaneously. This eliminates the need for future conversion of purchase requisitions, invoices, and so on, into machine-readable form.

8.1.7.3   *Facsimile Devices or*
Electronic Mail

With the use of data communications equipment, main offices can transmit hard-copy documents to branch offices without having to use postal services. A printed report can be duplicated at various remote locations with the use of **facsimile** devices in a matter of seconds or minutes. Figure 8.6 illustrates typical facsimile devices.

These units make it possible for offices to receive reports from remote locations without having to mail the documents. Whereas postal services can take several days, facsimile devices can reproduce the documents in minutes.

8.2   COMPUTERS IN INDUSTRY

In this chapter we have thus far considered the use of computers for business applications. This section focuses on computers in an industrial environment. We will consider computers as manufacturing, production, and industrial research tools.

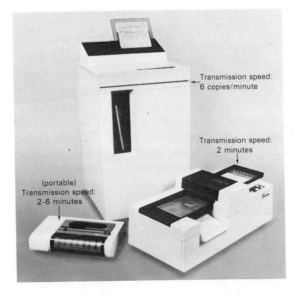

Figure 8.6.   Facsimile devices.

8.2.1 Computers in Manufacturing

The use of computers in the manufacturing sector represents the largest single market for computers in the United States, even larger than in the business sector. Approximately 20% of all installed computers are used for manufacturing purposes. It has been estimated that $20 billion per year is spent on computers in manufacturing.

The primary objective of computers used in a manufacturing environment is to *automate* a given set of production activities or tasks. Automation also requires the control or monitoring of these activities. The ultimate goal of automated functions is to maximize efficiency and to minimize the need for operator intervention. There are three automated functions performed in a manufacturing environment that depend on computerization:

Automated Activities in a Manufacturing Environment

1. *Process control:* the use of computers to process continuous-flow materials such as chemicals, petroleum, energy, etc.
2. *Production control:* the use of computers to monitor, control, and schedule assembly-line functions
3. *Numerical control:* the use of computers to automatically produce machine tools to required specifications

---

We will discuss each of these computerized manufacturing activities in detail.

8.2.1.1 Process Control

The production of chemicals in a chemical plant, of oil in an oil refinery, and of electricity in a generating station are complex industrial activities.

Computer equipment is used in these industries to measure continuously the key variables such as flow of fluid, pressure, and temperature. If the measured quantities deviate from a prescribed standard, the computer will perform one of two functions, depending on how it has been programmed:

1. It will notify the supervisor via a terminal about the discrepancy.
2. It will automatically make the necessary adjustments.

Thus far, the main user of computerized process control is the petroleum industry. That is, computers are used, in increasing numbers, to monitor and control the operations in major oil refineries.

There are several major reasons why computers are ideally suited for process control activities:

254

1. *Data gathering:* Industries that utilize a continuous flow of liquid and gaseous materials require constant monitoring. The ability of computers to operate at the same level of efficiency for an indefinite period of time makes them ideally suited for monitoring activities.
2. *Data analysis:* Some industries utilize a continuous flow of materials that are frequently volatile and very dangerous. Chemical and gas explosions, fires, and leakages pose a constant and serious threat. Computers can maximize safety by continually monitoring the levels of material.
3. *Data control and reporting:* In such industries, when a discrepancy is detected, the necessary correction must be made very quickly in order to reduce the risks of explosion and fire. Computers that automatically make the necessary adjustments can minimize such dangers by decreasing response time.

The use of computers in process control activities is an important example of a **feedback mechanism**. A feedback mechanism is a technique that, in effect, enables a machine to correct itself. Machines that perform a given activity can also monitor the effectiveness of that performance; in addition, they can contain mechanisms that will automatically adjust the operations performed if they do not meet preestablished criteria (see Figure 8.7).

Feedback mechanisms in computerized process control, then:

Figure 8.7. New fuel processes are investigated by computer in Thagard Oil research program. A research analyst uses a computer system for graphical display of data acquired from a thermal reactor. Processes being investigated include coal gasification, conversion of municipal refuse to fuel, and oil shale extraction. The program is being conducted for Southern California Edison, which hopes to reduce its reliance on costly imported low-sulfur oil fuels.

1. Monitor the effectiveness of the computer operation
2. Adjust the operation itself—through program modification—if desired standards are not met

The concept is similar to that of a thermostat, which not only monitors the temperature but turns the burner on and off depending on whether the desired temperature has been reached or exceeded.

Example—Computers in the Paper Industry:[1]   A computer in the paper industry:

1. Controls the basic weight of the paper by regulating the amount of pulp fiber per unit of area. Controlling the weight results in a more even distribution of fiber per area of paper. This increases the uniformity of a roll of paper.
2. Controls the moisture content of paper. The higher the moisture content, the tougher the paper and the better it is for newsprint. But because of certain limits in the manufacturing process, there is a maximum moisture level that can be tolerated by a paper machine. Also, an increase in moisture content increases the weight of paper, which, in turn, would need to be controlled for uniformity.
3. Automatically adjusts the machine for different grades of paper during a changeover in production.
4. Automatically controls the chemicals used to treat the paper.

[1]This example was excerpted from "Computer Control in Manufacturing Industries," ed. Jacob Sonny, *Hofstra University Yearbook of Business*, Series 14, Vol. 4.

Computer Talk: It's a Here and Now Technology[a]

People will respond more rapidly to "alert and alarm voice messages over a public address system than to visual systems" said Leonard Magnuson, Director, Marketing and Sales, Votrax. He cited one process control line within a chemical plant that uses the Votrax voice synthesizer to alert supervisors via computerized voice on a public address system of problems in the process and how to correct the problems. Previously the firm used a central control room with 1300 lights and a loud buzzer, he said.

Critical voice messages—including those in a pilot's cockpit will replace buzzers, gongs, and bells in "alert and alarm systems" Magnuson predicted. "And the microwave oven in your kitchen will talk back to you in a friendly voice," he said. "Voice as output will become as important to the CRT and printer as the CRT and printer have become in the past."

Another small but growing area for voice responses is telephone companies that provide specialized call-in services such as sports scores, stock quotations, ski and weather conditions and commodity and livestock prices.

[a]Frederick W. Miller, *Infosystems*. Copyright, Hitchcock Publishing Company. Reprinted with permission.

Figure 8.8.

The functions listed above are performed with the use of special sensors that are connected to the computer.

The ability of some computers to provide **voice messages** has greatly increased the potential of automated process control systems (see Figure 8.8).

8.2.1.2 Production Control

Assembly-line activities that result in the production of manu-factured items can be monitored and controlled by computers. This is referred to as **production control**. The computer is used to (1) monitor time spent on each activity by the workers at given stations, (2) specify the status of the product and the tools used to produce it, (3) indicate faulty parts of machinery which can cause breakdowns or delays, and (4) alert supervisors to queues that form as a result of timing problems.

When a computer is used for production control, terminals are located at key stations. These terminals provide foremen with informa-

Figure 8.9. An operator of automated distribution system at Gallo Sales Co., the largest wine distributor in Northern California, monitors the flow of thousands of orders each evening into the trucks for delivery next day. The system selects the wine cases and then controls their flow through an intricate maze more than 2 miles long over both gravity and powered conveyors. The automated system has speeded the order-filling process and reduced errors considerably.

tion necessary to correct any problems or to adjust the assembly-line activities (see Figure 8.9).

Terminals can also be used in factories for data collection purposes to coordinate shipping and inventory data.

Example 1: Computerized production control is used to manufacture computer parts. The Digital Equipment Corporation has instituted a production control system that uses bar-coded labels to monitor the production of integrated circuit boards. The bar codes can be used to track and test all phases of the assembly and testing process.

The bar-coded labels on each product can be read with a manual light pen to indicate the status of the product.

Example 2: Robots are used in the automobile industry. The Ford Motor Company and General Motors have been experimenting with the use of computer-controlled robots as production tools. These robots have been used successfully for die casting, spray painting, and body welding. There are approximately 4000 such robots used in production facilities in the United States. The Japanese, however, have invested considerably more effort in robots and have in use more than 30,000 robots.

See Figure 8.10 for an illustration of an industrial robot. Figure 8.11 describes the use of such a robot in an assembly plant. Note that experiments are currently being performed to make robots more flexible for industrial applications (see Figure 8.12).

8.2.1.3   Numerical Control

You may recall that in 1801 Jacquard developed an automated weaving loom. With the use of a punched tape, the weaving loom was automatically instructed as to the size, type, and color of each stitch.

Figure 8.10.   An industrial robot drills, routs, and trims F-16 fighter fuselage panels.

Programmable Universal Machine for Assembly[a]

GM's "PUMA" (Programmable Universal Machine for Assembly) robot is said to be the latest and probably the most advanced robot in the world today. PUMA is capable of "seeing" although its first job will be sightless work at a Delco plant in Rochester, NY—assisting in the assembly of small electric motors by picking up a hot part—about 450 degrees—positioning it, adding a component, then placing the part on a conveyor belt for further work.

"What comes out is consistent quality," said Al Williams, midwest regional manager, Unimation Inc., Danbury, CT, the nation's largest maker of industrial robots. "If a guy leaves out a couple of welds, someone gets in a car with rattles. With the robot, you get an improved product."

[a] *Infosystems*. Copyright, Hitchcock Publishing Company. Reprinted with permission.

Figure 8.11.

Numerical control machines operate in exactly the same way except that they are used to control the production of machine tools. Numerical control devices can automatically drill, grind, and shape metal according to required specifications.

These machines have typically been controlled by a punched paper tape. The tape serves as a kind of program indicating the functions to be performed and the sequence of functions as well. It transmits signals to the motors, which then perform the required tasks. Numerical control machines are used to produce machine tools that must have a very high precision, such as hydraulic presses and milling

NBS Industrial Robot Keeps an Eye on Its Work[a]

Researchers at the National Bureau of Standards have demonstrated a new system to give industrial robots simple powers of vision.

The NBS roboticists hope that their "eye"—built with a microprocessor, solid-state TV camera, and strobe light source—can be developed into a low-cost system allowing robots to locate objects anywhere in their range of operation and to adjust themselves to grasp the object from the proper angle.

Although robot systems can greatly improve efficiency and quality control, they have limited use outside of large, mass-produced operations because of their inflexibility.

NBS is now working on refining the robot's ability to distinguish between different kinds of objects and making the system more easily programmable for different tasks.

[a] "New Applications," ed. Demetrios Michalopolos, *Computer*. © IEEE. Reprinted with permission.

Figure 8.12.

Figure 8.13. Automated numerical control facility. This machine is being used to manufacture aluminum warhead sections for torpedoes. The computer control for this machine is at the right and the circular tool bank is at the left. Thirty-two different tools are mounted in the toolholder and are changed by the machine automatically as needed. The table on which the material is machined can be rotated to any one of 360,000 settings.

machines. Since computers can be adjusted to produce very finely tuned or precise output, they are ideal for numerical control purposes.

In recent years, the use of punched paper tape to control machine operations has come to be very inefficient. Paper tape itself has been phased out of large-scale computer facilities because it is bulky, damages easily, and requires significant maintenance.

Newer systems utilize more durable computer media, such as magnetic tape or disk to drive a numerical control machine. A system recently installed by the McDonnell Douglas Corporation saved the company over $100,000 in paper tape costs alone. This saving may seem extraordinary, but a company like McDonnell Douglas has a high-level numerical control facility that typically utilizes millions of feet of tape.

See Figure 8.13 for an illustration of an automated numerical control facility.

8.2.1.4 Benefits of Computers in Manufacturing

There are both tangible and intangible benefits to be derived from computers used in a manufacturing environment. The tangible benefits include:

Tangible Benefits of Computers in Manufacturing

1. Faster processing (see Figure 8.14)
2. Greater degree of accuracy
3. Flexibility—ability to alter specifications automatically
4. Machines can run unattended for short periods of time
5. Reduced cost per unit of output
6. Increased uniformity

The intangible benefits include:

Intangible Benefits of Computers in Manufacturing

1. Better quality control
2. More effective scheduling
3. Simplified planning requirements
4. Need for reduced inventory
5. Increased job satisfaction—machines perform all the mundane tasks

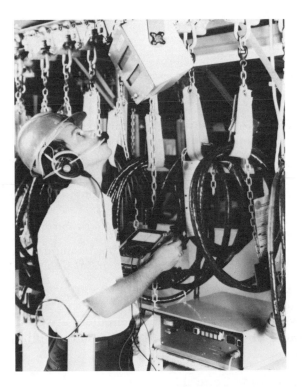

Figure 8.14. An intelligent voice terminal allows increased productivity of assembly-line workers while providing data into a central computer without keyboards or punched cards.

The ultimate goal of computers in manufacturing is the **auto-mated factory**, where computing devices would handle every facet of the production process. Thus far, there has been no complete application of the automated factory, but there has been progress in this area.

Case Study: Computer-Managed Parts Manufacturing

This is a system in which a computer handles the operation of several machines. A conveyor moves the product from one machine to another. The system functions like an automated assembly line, where the computer performs each of several tasks in sequence and monitors the progress as well.

8.2.1.5 Types of Computers Used in Manufacturing

There are many types of systems that can be used in manufacturing, two of which are:

1. **Turnkey system:** A turnkey system is a complete hardware and software package designed by the manufacturer to perform a given set of tasks. The user virtually "turns the key" and the system operates automatically.

   Advantage: No computer expertise is needed to operate or use this system.

   Disadvantage: The system has no flexibility—it can perform only the specified tasks.

2. **Special-purpose computers:** These are devices designed for a manufacturing environment, which can be programmed to perform a variety of tasks. Either the user or special software houses can program these machines.

   Advantage: Flexibility—they can be programmed to perform the precise tasks required.

   Disadvantage: They require computer expertise to operate.

   The main programming language used for manufacturing applications is called APT, an acronym for A Programming Tool.

Turnkey and special-purpose computers are available in a variety of sizes. Minicomputers are very popular for this application, as are large-scale systems. In general, minicomputers are used for a smaller set of operations where fewer output stations are required.

8.2.2 Transportation Control

Computers are used by the air traffic controllers to monitor and regulate airplanes in the vicinity of an airport. Since airplanes take off and land every few seconds at major airports, it would simply not be feasible for people alone to monitor traffic. Computers automatically provide the data necessary to maintain an appropriate traffic pattern.

Computers have also been used with increasing frequency to control vehicle and pedestrian traffic.

1. A computer can be programmed on an hourly basis to adjust the traffic lights automatically at fixed intervals of time when traffic patterns are known to shift—that is, during rush hours, certain lights will be green for shorter intervals, no left turn will be permitted, and so on.
2. A computer can be programmed to compile actual data on traffic patterns and to adjust the lights accordingly. There are sensors in the street which indicate the number of cars that pass. If this number exceeds a predetermined amount, the light will adjust to allow traffic to move faster.

8.2.3 Computer-Aided Design

Computer-aided design, sometimes abbreviated CAD, is a technique used in industry for the design, development, and testing of any kind of equipment. Its objective is to make use of a computer's capability to maximize the efficiency of any design. Using a computer to simulate an actual design, a program can be written to perform:

> Applications of CAD
>
> Stress analysis
> Model building
> Weight analysis
> Structural analysis
> Alternative design test

The most suitable hardware for computer-aided design systems includes a CPU and a **graphics display terminal**.

The graphics display terminal is a cathode ray tube (CRT) which has the ability to display forms and figures as well as characters (see Figure 8.15). The user can create or adjust any design with the use of:

> Data Entry Devices Used with CRT
>
> 1. *A keyboard:* Depressing the appropriate keys causes specific changes to the picture.
> 2. *A light pen or wand:* Using a pen or wand, as an artist might use a brush, causes changes to the design.
> 3. *Voice data entry:* Speaking into a microphone causes specified changes to the picture. The computer has a fixed vocabulary.

Computer-aided design is used extensively in the automotive and aerospace industries to design cars and airplanes. Various structural

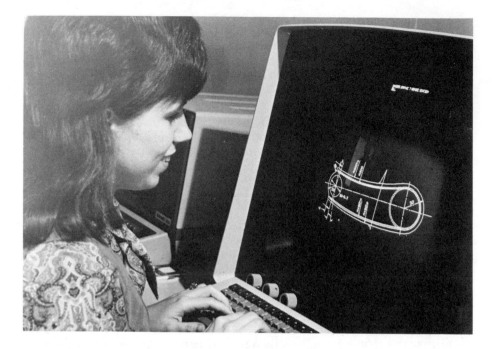

Figure 8.15. Use of a graphics display terminal for computer-aided design.

tests can be performed using the computer without actually having to build an expensive prototype. Indeed, the space industry depends on computer-aided design—it is not possible, for example, to simulate mechanically the behavior of a space shuttle in space—computers must be used to simulate the environment and test the equipment. Surgical devices have also been devised using computer-aided design.

With the cost of graphics display terminals decreasing and the introduction of even more versatile, color systems, it is possible to purchase a minicomputer turnkey computer-aided design system for as little as $100,000.

For a summary of the uses of computers in industry, consider the following excerpt from an *Infosystems* article on computer-aided design:

> There is no doubt that the managers of manufacturing operations are on the front side of the learning curve in the use of computers. Engineering, manufacturing and inventory managers have seen the power of the computer move out of the central computer room and put to uses they never would have dreamed possible a few years ago. Possibly, the microprocessor has opened their eyes. Certainly, the computer control of machine tools and numerical control devices are some examples. And the strides made in computer-aided

CADAM: Interactive Graphics for Design Engineers[1]

Producing a modern aircraft can require more mechanical drawings than rivets.

Traditionally, engineers sketch, then draftsmen draft. Then engineers discover needed changes or improvements, and draftsmen draft some more. A lot more. Move a stiffener or bracket, say, two inches to the left, and a chain reaction of changes riffles through the entire set of drawings.

But now the computer has opened up a new way to meet design engineering needs with speed and reliability for a broad range of products, from high performance aircraft to complex integrated circuits. Computer-Graphics Augmented Design and Manufacturing (CADAM), a set of interactive programs available from IBM, allows the designer to sketch directly on the screen of a graphic terminal. He defines lines and contours by pressing keys and positioning a light pen, and the computer displays what he has expressed.

Curve fitting, or reducing the design to a set of control equations, is completed interactively at the terminal, eliminating coding, card punching, and repeated computer batch runs. Then CADAM converts the preliminary design to a dimensioned drawing with auxiliary views.

If something needs fixing—if, for example, the dimensional drawing reveals a problem of component or subassembly compatibility—the pieces can be moved around with the light pen and CADAM will revise all of the affected drawings. And do it automatically.

CADAM encourages doodling, an important source of design inspiration. The user can translate or rotate any graphic element. Or change its scale. Or stack parts, separate them, or watch moving parts move.

CADAM stores the design as it is developed, displays any element on demand, then generates the final detailed drawings. It supports complete design of the part, including structural members and such elements as ribs, stiffeners, lightening holes and fasteners. Once a design is stored in the system, CADAM analysis programs can calculate its weight or determine its structural properties. Any frequently used design element or drawing symbol can be stored and reproduced automatically whenever it is needed.

As its name implies, CADAM includes a direct link to manufacturing. It can generate a "part program" (path of travel) for the cutter of an automatic machine tool.

CADAM has cut drafting manhours drastically for engineering departments—by as much as 90 percent or more on a few special tasks. It helps prevent and correct errors and improves the quality of the engineering product. One user's experience is described below.

Computer-Aided Design

The complex shape of a supersonic aircraft fuselage appears in crisp white lines on a CRT screen. The design engineer seated at the terminal presses a few keys and the image of the craft's landing gear unfolds into the extended position.

But the engineer observes some interference between the landing gear and the fuselage. Swiftly he touches the keys and moves a light pen across the surface of the screen. As he works, the shape of the fuselage alters slightly and when the landing gear descends again, it is clear of all obstructions.

[1]DP Engineering Dialogue, IBM, appearing in *Automotive Engineering*. Courtesy of IBM.

Figure 8.16.

design (CAD) would make believers even of the most ardent "doubting Thomas."[1]

Figure 8.16 describes how graphics terminals can be used by engineers for design work.

8.3   Computers and Automation: Effects on Workers

8.3.1   Automation: A Brief Background

The Industrial Revolution of the eighteenth and nineteenth centuries resulted in many changes in living conditions, goods and products available, and in our very concept of progress and civilization. But one area that caused considerable concern then and continues to be a potential source of problems is the effects of automation on the work force. One way in which the term **alienation** is used is to describe the feelings of people who are directly affected by automation in their jobs and even in their everyday lives. Alienation has come to mean the feeling of displacement or dissatisfaction which results from the widespread use of machines that take the place of human activities.

A recent public survey attempted to determine the level of alienation that people feel in our society. A total of 1513 adult Americans were interviewed, and approximately half of them said that they felt a moderate or high degree of alienation in our society.[2]

Degree of Alienation	
High	21%
Moderate	28
Low	34
Not alienated	17

Many individuals feel alienated because of the power of bureaucracies that affect our lives. Many others are alienated because they have lost a sense of pride in their work and feel that their jobs are menial and unskilled. In both cases, computerization has added to this alienation by contributing to the depersonalization that exists.

---

[1]*Infosystems*. Copyright, Hitchcock Publishing Company. Reprinted with permission.

[2]Alan F. Westin, "The Impact of Computers on Privacy," *Datamation*.

8.3.2 The Hawthorne Experiments

This century has been marked by an increasing movement toward mechanization, automation, and depersonalization, all of which have been fostered by the Computer Revolution.

"Scientific management" is a concept that has evolved largely as a result of this increased industrialization. The underlying assumption of this "scientific management" approach is that the way to achieve the best performance of workers and the highest degree of productivity is to consider "scientifically" all modes of operation and select the most efficient set of procedures. This scientific approach implies, to some, that to consider human factors, such as job satisfaction and attitude toward company policies, is unnecessary and counterproductive.

About 50 years ago, two sociologists demonstrated, quite by accident, problems inherent in the scientific management approach. Some organizations have learned the lessons demonstrated by the sociologists; many have not.

In the years 1927-1932, Elton Mayo and Fritz J. Roethlisberger conducted some industrial management experiments at the Western Electric Company in Hawthorne, New Jersey. The experiments have since been known as the "Hawthorne Experiments."

Mayo and Roethlisberger, using the scientific methodology employed by many sociologists, attempted to determine an appropriate balance of physical conditions in the plant, one that would result in the highest level of productivity. The two men addressed themselves to questions relating to how much lighting would maximize productivity, the optimum number of coffee breaks that should be taken to maximize efficiency, the best times for those breaks, the best temperature level at which employees should work, and so on.

The sociologists selected a random sample of employees who were to serve as subjects. A wide variety of physical conditions were imposed on this sample in an effort to determine the most efficacious conditions.

To the surprise of the researchers, productivity rose steadily during the course of the experiments, *regardless* of the physical conditions imposed. Utterly frustrated in attempting to explain this phenomenon, the experimenters decided to question the subjects. They found that the employees were so flattered to be taking part in the study and so pleased that a study was being undertaken to determine the most comfortable physical environment for them that they felt compelled to do their very best for the organization. Thus their productivity continued to rise.

The two researchers utilizing the scientific management approach demonstrated that human relations and human factors are of considerable importance in increasing productivity and in obtaining cooperation.

8.3.3 Computers and Automation

The Hawthorne Experiments provide a lesson that computer professionals and management would do well to remember. Dealing with employees on a human level, and soliciting their assistance and support, could have very positive effects. In general, computerization and automation require the cooperation of the work force if success is to be achieved. See Figure 8.17 for a more recent example.

In business automation, a principal reason why computerization fails to meet expectations in many instances is because computer professionals have not solicited the advice and assistance of the employees who are performing the tasks manually. These employees

---

Editorial[a]

Regard for the Worker

Hardly a day passes that a reader of general-interest newspapers and magazines does not see a story about a computer foul-up or about computerization's dehumanizing effect on the work environment.

Unfortunately, many of these stories are true. Often systems are installed with little regard for the worker—especially if a project ends up exceeding budget.

Each of us probably knows of an installation whose order entry operation was converted to CRTs and everything was changed but the lighting. Even more chilling to the employee is the highly regarded feature of many of these installations that allows the system to track and report the number of each employee's hourly keystrokes.

Much has also been written about installations using electronic editing, where copy editors who began working on CRTs for the first time reported eyestrain, backaches and other symptoms resulting from changes in the work environment.

This is all unfortunate and gives automation a bad name. It was therefore uplifting to read the results of a study of 12,000 white-collar municipal employees in 42 cities conducted by the Public Policy Research Organization (PPRO) at the University of California at Irvine [CW, March 17]. The individuals surveyed were end users who work with computer-generated data.

The PPRO found that rather than dehumanizing the white-collar work environment, computer-generated information enlarged the scope of workers' jobs and did not increase supervisory control over an employee's work.

There were some negative findings, however: Respondents reported greater job pressure arising from time constraints. Apparently their input is on a tighter schedule while output is often slow.

The PPRO also found that one problem we have been talking about for years—communication with end-user departments—has not improved much. These municipal employees complained of difficulties in their interaction with computer specialists and slow response to their information requests. Let's hope the next time we read the results of such a study that this area is improved.

[a]*Computerworld*, May 24, 1980, p. 20. Copyright 1980 by CW Communications/Inc., Framingham, MA 01701. Reprinted with permission.

Figure 8.17.

understand the current system best; they can indicate its flaws and can frequently make concrete suggestions for improvement. But many computer professionals believe that their own expertise is far more important for effective computerization and that the advice of existing personnel is unnecessary. This leads to a critical communication gap, which is perhaps the single most important reason why business systems fail to meet objectives.

Similarly, many manufacturing facilities automate one or more aspects of their operations without soliciting the support and cooperation of the work force. Without this support, the chance that an automated system will succeed is greatly reduced.

If management takes the time to assure employees that

1. Jobs are not in jeopardy
2. Machines will perform some of the more laborious and boring tasks
3. Workers will be free to perform more skilled and interesting jobs
4. Workers skills will be upgraded as necessary through retraining

the effects of automation would be far more satisfactory.

To quote two leading experts in the field of "people-oriented computer systems":

> Because the computer, one of the foremost technological developments of our time, has often been used with little sensitivity to its impact on people, it has repelled many who could have helped add significantly to the benefits computerization offers.[1]

The most critical concern of workers with regard to computerization and automation is the threat of unemployment.

There is considerable controversy over the actual effect of computerization on the work force:

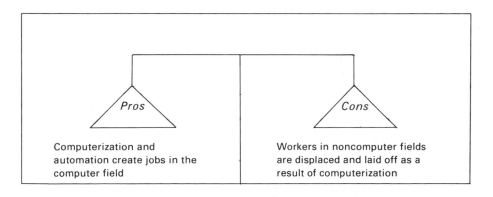

Pros

Computerization and automation create jobs in the computer field

Cons

Workers in noncomputer fields are displaced and laid off as a result of computerization

[1] Edward A. Tomeski and Harold Lazarus, "A Humanized Approach to Computers," *Computers and Automation*.

Thus there is no clear answer as to whether the net effect of computerization and automation is to increase or decrease the number of jobs.

You may be wondering why studies have not been conducted to resolve this controversy. Indeed, many studies have been made and the results published; but once a computerized or automated procedure has been implemented, it is not easy to compare it to a manual system. Computerized systems have several results that cannot be directly compared to manual systems:

Results of Computerization

1. Increased accuracy
2. A greater volume of output
3. The ability to perform operations that were not, or could not be, performed before
4. Increased sales and growth

It must also be kept in mind that the cost of computerization is initially very high; indeed, the true costs cannot be determined for several years, until the system has been completely debugged, the staff retrained, and the work force stabilized.

Thus the problems encountered in attempting to evaluate both the benefits derived from computerization and automation, and the costs associated with the conversion, make any comparisons very difficult. Moreover, the net effect of computerization and automation on employment levels is also hard to evaluate. If the work force increases 10% or even remains the same, for example, but the gross sales of a company increase by 20%, what is the effect of computerization on the employment level? There are many ways of explaining that effect, but none that would be definitive.

In summary, alienation and disaffection that result from computerization and automation can be significantly reduced if organizations make the effort necessary to solicit the support of workers. Unemployment problems resulting from automation can sometimes be dissipated if employees are willing to be retrained to perform computer-related tasks.

KEY TERMS

Batch processing
Centralized data processing
Collection of data
Computer-aided design (CAD)

Decentralized data processing
Detail file
Distributed data processing (DDP)
Edit procedure
Electronic data processing (EDP)
Electronic mail
Exception report
Facsimile device
File maintenance
Graphics display terminal
Hawthorne Experiments
Intelligent terminal
Management information system (MIS)
Master file
Numerical control
On-line processing
Problem definition
Process control
Production control
Source data automation
Special-purpose computer
Systems analyst
Time-sharing
Transaction file
Turnkey system
Update procedure
Word processing

REVIEW QUESTIONS

1. What are the major ways in which an organization can acquire a computer system? What are the advantages and disadvantages of each method of acquisition?
2. What are the major responsibilities of a systems analyst?
3. What are the differences between a master file and a detail file?
4. What is an edit procedure?
5. Under what circumstances would a file maintenance procedure be performed on-line? In a batch-processing environment?
6. Can you identify the various files used in update routines?
7. What is meant by each of the following?
   a. Detail reports
   b. Summary reports
   c. Exception reports

8. How does the traditional systems approach used for designing business systems differ from the management information systems approach?
9. What are the major features of each of the following types of computer facilities?
    a. Centralized
    b. Decentralized
    c. Distributed data processing
10. How does a typical word-processing system function?
11. How can computers be used in each of the following manufacturing applications?
    a. Process control
    b. Production control
    c. Numerical control
12. What are some of the intangible benefits of using computers in manufacturing?
13. What is meant by computer-aided design, and how is it typically accomplished?
14. What is the significance of the Hawthorne Experiments?
15. Is systems analysis considered a science or an art?

DISCUSSION QUESTIONS

1. Do you think it is essential for top management at a company to have some expertise in the computer area? Explain your answer.
2. Do you think computers will continue to be viewed as a threat to employees in the future?
3. Suppose that you are a worker in a factory. An aspect of your job that you enjoy performing is being automated. To compensate for this, you are permitted to leave work $\frac{1}{2}$ hour earlier each day. On the whole, would you be satisfied or dissatisfied?
4. To avoid the unemployment that might result from newly automated procedures, employees are given incentives to retire earlier. Is this an equitable way of resolving the problem?
5. How may electronic mail and word processing revolutionize the business office?
6. Is the user in any way responsible for the failure of business systems? Explain.
7. Why is it so difficult to define the impact of computers on employment?
8. Do you think computers will be able to replace managers or administrators in the future?

APPLICATION

Consider the application below and then answer the questions that follow it.

Automation Viewed Threat to Workers[a]

By Bruce Hoard

ANAHEIM, Calif.—Unrestrained automation is an insidious juggernaut that threatens to undermine employment and strip workers of their identity, panelists said at the National Computer Conference here recently.

Judith McCullough, a former clerk now associated with Working Women-Los Angeles, said office workers are wondering if word processing and other office automation machinery will replace them by 1990.

"That could be reality if present trends continue," she said. She citied instances in which banks and insurance companies have eliminated or changed secretarial positions with the end result being either the loss of jobs or the creation of undiversified, one-task positions.

One office worker who enjoyed using word processors was distraught because she was expected to perform more work and instruct trainees, but without a raise in pay, McCullough claimed.

High Stakes for Women

Women have a particularly high stake in the battle against unchecked office automation because 90% of the jobs to be changed by it are currently filled by women, she said.

"It is important that we, as the women doing the work, evaluate automated offices," she said.

The advent of automated offices means harassment for office workers in the form of rigid guidelines in areas such as output speed and error rate, she said, adding, "the overall main thrust of automation is to centralize and control office workers like they have never been controlled before."

Although women will protest unwarranted changes in the office structure during the '80s, the battle will be a difficult one, McCullough said, quoting an IBM executive as saying, "They will respond when we break their arms, and we're in the twisting stage now."

Productivity Crisis

Harley Shaiken, a machinist and author who advised the United Auto Workers (UAW) in their negotiations with the Ford Motor Co., said the productivity crisis will be "on center stage" in the '80s.

In order to combat that crisis, industry will turn to powerful forms of automation in the shape of computers in general and microprocessors in particular, he said.

If that happens, "We could lose sight of central social problems and consequences" and end up with high "structured" unemployment and a low quality of working life, Shaiken warned.

Technology has held out a promise to provide economic growth, he said, but he questioned the expense in terms of jobs, adding "DP" may soon take on a new meaning—displaced person.

Robotics poses a particularly dangerous threat to workers, the author of *Technology as Politics* said. One out of every five jobs on automobile assembly lines will be replaceable by robots in 1985, he quoted from a 1977 report.

General Motors' Programmable Universal Machines for Assembly (Puma) plan will "treat people as cogs, and worse yet, they will be cogs," Shaiken said. With Puma, one worker will labor alongside several robots and follow a mechanically set pace.

"The problem is power masquerading as technology," he said. "A democratic society requires a democratic technology plus the input of people shaping it and their own futures."

Loss of Control

Michael Cooley, a mechanical engineer with Lucas Aerospace in the UK and author of *Architect or Bee? The Human/Technology Relationship*, attacked the loss of human control in the workplace. "We relate to society and other people by the work we do and now we are denying people that," he said.

The capital-intensive nature of automated production processes is largely responsible for the dehumanization of industry, the Briton said, giving as an example the case of a spray painter on a production line. Previously the worker was responsible for turning the spray on and off, but now he merely acts as a guide for it, Cooley said. While the change may seem negligible to some, the psychological effect can be disastrous, he added.

In one automobile manufacturing plant, workers are subject to an agreement on the makeup of their rest allowance, he said. For trips to the lavatory (placed strategically near the assembly line), they are allowed 1.62 minutes, for fatigue, 1.3 minutes, for sitting down after standing too long, 65 seconds.

White-collar workers are beginning to feel the effects of automation just as blue-collar workers did before them, the mechanical engineer explained.

High-speed design systems have put tremendous strain on designers to the point where one study revealed designers working with an interactive graphics system lost 30% of their ability to deal with new problems during the first hour of operation, 80% in the second "and thereafter were completely shattered," Cooley claimed.

Such systems could be designed to depend more on their human operators, but to do so would put more power on the shop floor—an occurence management is dead set against, he said.

Cooley cited another study performed on scientific workers who were given some simple but original problems to solve. Based on the results, it was determined that a pure mathematician reaches his peak performance at about age 24 or 25 and a theoretical physicist at around 26.

The study went on to suggest these workers should follow a career pattern that pays them the most during peak performance age and increasingly less as they go \through \"career\ deescalation," he added.

[a] *Computerworld*, June 2, 1980, p. 1. Copyright 1980 by CW Communications/Inc., Framingham, MA 01701. Reprinted with permission.

Application Questions

1. Do word-processing systems pose a threat to employment opportunities? Explain your answer.
2. Is there any way to minimize the possibility of job displacement that may result from the use of word-processing systems?

Computers in education

There are two broad meanings for the term "computers in education." One refers to the *teaching about computers*; the other refers to the use of computers *within the educational process*.

Teaching about computers is what this book is designed to accomplish—it serves as a "computer literacy" text. The term "computers in education," however, almost always refers to the latter meaning. In this chapter, then, we consider the ways in which computer technology has been employed to enhance the educational process. We focus on the current uses of computers within the educational process, some stumbling blocks to these uses, and some predictions for the future.

9.1 COMPUTER-ASSISTED INSTRUCTION: HARDWARE CONSIDERATIONS

Computer-assisted instruction (CAI) is one major use of computers in education. The term implies that the computer is used for instructional purposes; that is, it serves as a teaching machine. CAI is used for a wide variety of subjects and for virtually all ages and achievements levels.

Figure 9.1 provides a schematic of computer devices used for CAI. Note that there is one CPU or mainframe which stores the instructional material, makes it available to the user, and controls the flow of data.

Terminals can be placed (1) locally—near the computer—or (2) remotely—not within the same physical location. If terminals are located near the CPU, they can be "hardwired," or linked to the computer by cables. Thus if a school or university has a mainframe on

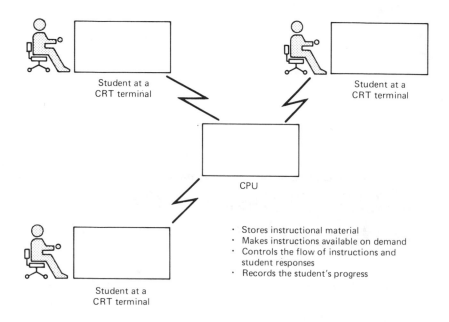

Student at a
CRT terminal

Student at a
CRT terminal

CPU

- Stores instructional material
- Makes instructions available on demand
- Controls the flow of instructions and
  student responses
- Records the student's progress

Student at a
CRT terminal

Figure 9.1. Schematic of computer devices used for CAI.

campus used for CAI purposes, the student terminals can be hooked directly to the CPU with cables.

In other instances, it is not feasible to hardwire all student terminals to the CPU. The University of Illinois at Urbana-Champaign, for example, has a large data base of CAI material called PLATO IV (more on this later). If schools throughout the United States and Canada wish to access the data base, they can link their student terminals to the PLATO IV mainframe in Illinois or purchase a PLATO system of their own. To use the system at Urbana, terminals must transmit and receive signals over *telephone lines*. When terminals and a CPU communicate over telephone lines, we call this **data communications** (see Figure 9.2).

Computer-assisted instructional systems may have one CPU and any number of terminals. These terminals can access the CPU at any time; moreover, many terminals have simultaneous access to the CPU, so that different lessons can be taught at the same time. To do this, a CPU must have a *time-sharing* facility—it must be able to partition itself and run several different requests at the same time.

A student with access to a terminal can use any instructional material stored by the CPU. The CAI system is programmed in such a way that students converse with the computer in English—no programming knowledge is necessary.

The terminals used for CAI purposes can receive and transmit

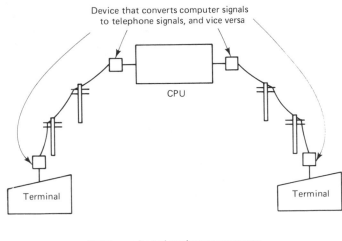

Device that converts computer signals
to telephone signals, and vice versa

CPU

Terminal

Terminal

· CPU transmits and receives messages over
  telephone lines.
· Student must "dial up" computer before
  receiving any messages.
· Computer operates in a time-sharing mode.

Figure 9.2. Illustration of data communications.

messages in a variety of ways, the most common being the typewriter and the CRT (see Figure 9.3).

There are, of course, many variations of these types of terminals. Some terminals, for example, can transmit messages to the CPU with a "light pen" that the student uses to touch a CRT screen. This is particularly useful for young children and others who find it difficult to type. (See Figure 9.4 for an illustration of a light pen used with a CRT.)

Similarly, some CPUs can transmit audio messages to a student. The messages are stored on a tape and the CPU accesses what is needed. This is particularly useful for conversing with young children or people with visual problems.

The cathode ray tube (CRT) is ideally suited for CAI use for several important reasons:

1. *Speed:* A CRT *displays* instructional material rather than printing it. That is, this material can appear on the screen instantaneously. If the computer had to transmit this material over a typewriter terminal, it would take many seconds—and the seconds do add up!!

2. *Paper savings:* Since information is displayed on a screen rather than being printed, the CRT does not require the use of volumes of paper. Of course, if the student wanted to *save* some of the computer's output, the CRT alone would *not* be sufficient and some *hard-copy* printout device would be required.

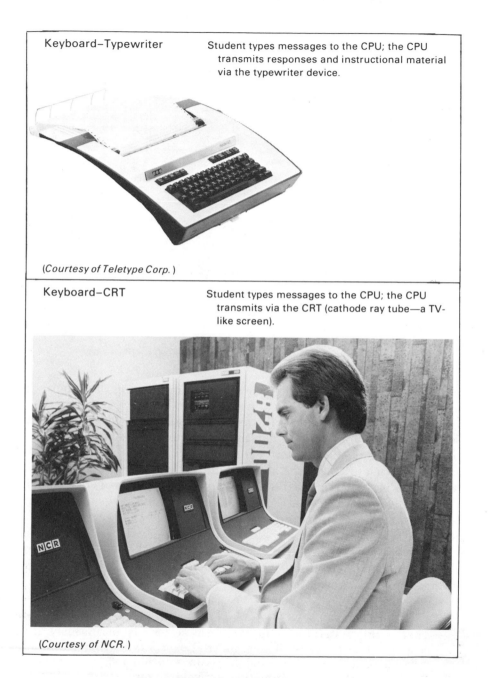

Keyboard–Typewriter Student types messages to the CPU; the CPU transmits responses and instructional material via the typewriter device.

(Courtesy of Teletype Corp.)

Keyboard–CRT Student types messages to the CPU; the CPU transmits via the CRT (cathode ray tube—a TV-like screen).

(Courtesy of NCR.)

Figure 9.3. Most common terminals.

Figure 9.4. Example of a CRT with a light pen.

Figure 9.5. Microcomputer used for CAI.

3. *Graphics:* Unlike typewriter devices, the CRT can have the ability to display graphs, pictures, and even animated figures on the screen, often in color. For some instructional purposes, such as the teaching of statistics, the use of a CRT with graphics display ability is essential. For other instructional purposes, the use of graphics displays makes the lessons more interesting and dynamic.

Most CAI applications use a main CPU linked to several student terminals for providing instructional material. Note, however, that microcomputers can also be an effective CAI tool. For several hundred dollars, a school can acquire a microcomputer that displays data on a CRT; users can respond via a keyboard. In this case each microcomputer can function as a "stand-alone" CAI device. That is, there is no need for a large mainframe, for data communications, or for time-sharing. Each microcomputer functions independently (see Figure 9.5).

A main advantage to using microcomputers for CAI purposes is cost. A main disadvantage, however, is that microcomputers have only limited storage and limited capability; hence they cannot do as much as a mainframe—more on this later. Combining all methods that may be used, approximately 75% of all public schools provide some form of CAI. This is a significant increase over a decade ago, where only 10% of public schools utilized CAI.

9.2 CAI: SOFTWARE CONSIDERATIONS

9.2.1 Elements of a CAI Sequence

A typical CAI sequence consists of the following elements:

1. *Text material:* A short module or section is prepared which includes explanatory material in the form of lessons. These modules must be written clearly and they usually include diagrams, displays, or graphics, as necessary.
2. *Test questions requiring student responses:* After reading the text module, the student is required to answer questions on that lesson or material. The computer analyzes the responses. Correct answers are reinforced with expressions of approval. The computer also indicates any problem areas that may become evident as a result of the student's responses.
3. *Additional, backup instructional material:* If the student has difficulty with the original text, alternative texts *on the same subject* are displayed. These are typically written by different instructors—in this way, the student has the opportunity to learn from alternative teaching techniques.
4. *Analysis of progress:* Typically, at the end of a CAI session, students are provided with a progress report, indicating subjects mastered, the percentage of correct responses, and subjects requiring further attention. This analysis can be stored for the instructor's use as well.

See Figure 9.6 for a typical dialogue between a computer and a user in a CAI environment.

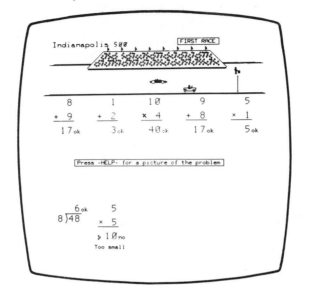

An elementary game of arithmetic drill and practice.
The student makes a mistake and must correct it.

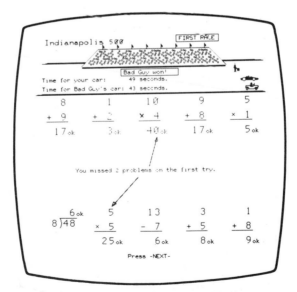

At the end of the race, the lesson points out the student's
mistakes and the length of time the student took to finish
the race.

Figure 9.6. Mathematics lesson.

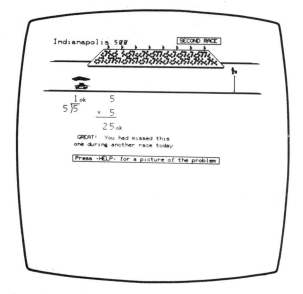

During the second race, the student races against the previous best time. The lesson repeats problems that the student missed during the first race.

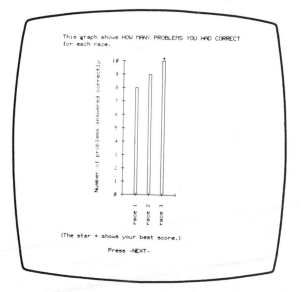

After the races, a graph shows the student's improvement.

Figure 9.6. (Continued)

The typical CAI sequence with the four elements listed above makes use of a technique referred to as the **programmed-instruction** format. Note that programmed instruction is not exclusively a computer concept. That is, other media, such as textbooks, can also make use of these four steps. Books that include short modules of text, followed by questions and supplemental text, utilize this same technique.

The computer is ideally suited for CAI using the programmed-instruction format for several reasons:

1. *Interactive ability:* The computer can interact directly with the student, analyze student problems, skip to alternative texts, "reward" correct answers with approving responses, and so on. The ability of a computer to interact with students and have a dialogue is a critical feature of CAI.
2. *Storage capability, flexibility, and logical control:* The computer can store instructional material and branch to various modules much quicker and more conveniently than can students using books.
3. *Display features:* The computer provides an electronic flexibility that transcends the typical text approach. Animated characters can dance across the screen, making a text much more interesting; graphic displays in color can be produced; and slide projection is possible as well as verbal instructions. See Figure 9.7 for an illustration of the use of animation for CAI.

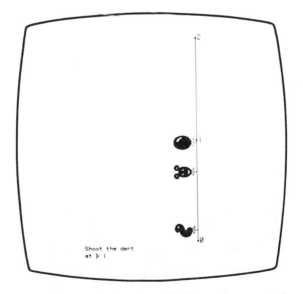

A lesson that teaches fractions. The student must shoot a dart at a balloon by typing a fraction.

Figure 9.7. Use of animation for CAI.

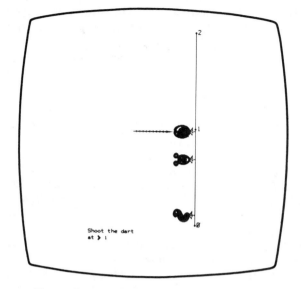

Photo shows dart during animated sequence.

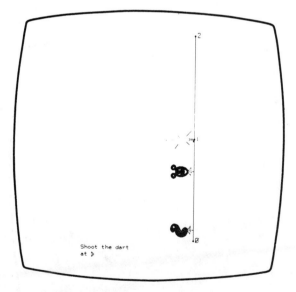

Balloon explodes when hit by dart.

Figure 9.7. (Continued)

9.2.2 Types of CAI Lessons

Thus far, we have focused only on the actual hardware and some of the software used for CAI purposes. Note that the devices are used in much the same way as they are used for other applications.

By now, you must be wondering about how computer-assisted instruction actually functions. You will recall that CAI can be used for a wide variety of subjects and for all age and achievement levels. We now discuss three main types of CAI instructional formats—drill-and-practice, tutorial, and simulation.

9.2.2.1 Drill-and-Practice

One major use of CAI is for drill-and-practice. That is, students use the computer to "bone-up" on or practice certain drills. The CAI sequence in Figure 9.8 will serve as an illustration.

Figure 9.8. A young student is conversing with the computer. Here is a sample of the dialogue:

TIMOTHY:	HI.
COMPUTER:	HI. PLEASE TELL ME YOUR NAME.
TIMOTHY:	TIM STONE.
COMPUTER:	IT'S NICE TO MEET YOU, TIM. LET'S BEGIN WITH SOME ARITHMETIC. WHAT IS THE SUM OF 23 AND 28?
TIMOTHY:	41.
COMPUTER:	I THINK YOU FORGOT TO CARRY. TRY IT AGAIN.
TIMOTHY:	51.
COMPUTER:	VERY GOOD!! NOW TRY ADDING 58 AND 27.
	:
COMPUTER:	VERY NICE. YOUR SCORE IS 92%—YOU GOT 23 OF 25 CORRECT. NOW LET'S DO SOME SPELLING. PLEASE PUT ON YOUR EARPHONES.
COMPUTER-EARPHONES:	PLEASE SPELL FAMILY.
TIMOTHY:	FAMLY
COMPUTER-CRT:	YOU LEFT OUT ONE LETTER. FAM_LY. TRY IT AGAIN.
TIMOTHY:	FAMILY
COMPUTER-EARPHONES:	VERY GOOD!
	:
	IT WAS VERY NICE WORKING WITH YOU, TIM—HOPE YOU HAD FUN.

Figure 9.8. Conversational CAI.

There are many electronic games on the market today that can serve the same CAI purposes. That is, such electronic games function as miniature CAI computers. Texas Instrument's "Dataman" can be used for drill-and-practice arithmetic in much the same way that our illustration indicated. Similarly, Texas Instrument's "Speak 'n Spell" helps children practice their spelling and other skills. These devices have built-in microprocessors that make them highly effective teaching tools.

Note, however, that computers (as well as electronic games) used for simple drill-and-practice serve an important function, but this application makes use of only a very small range of a computer's capability.

In summary, where students need to simply memorize certain facts rather than to understand complex concepts, CAI for drill-and-practice is ideal. This use of CAI tends to be popular because:

CAI for Drill-and-Practice

1. Students can take as long as necessary to master the subject.
2. Instructors generally do not enjoy teaching drill-and-practice concepts.
3. This application is relatively inexpensive to automate.

9.2.2.2   *Tutorial*

The more conceptual subjects require, in contrast to drill-and-practice, a *tutorial* approach. That is, the subject must be explained clearly, problem areas anticipated, and conceptual understanding achieved. These subjects are of course more difficult to computerize effectively. For these subjects, the text material must be clearly presented and be very well organized; in addition, student responses must be carefully evaluated so that specific difficulties with the subject can be discerned. The program must be written so that the responses are analyzed and a proper review is provided. The program must be able to determine which subject area is giving a student problems. Alternative tutorial modules must then be displayed.

Computers are used for tutorial CAI in almost all subjects, ranging from statistics to algebra, from chemistry to foreign languages, from grammar to psychology. These tutorials usually make use of the programmed-instruction format described in Section 9.2.2.1:

1. Main text
2. Test questions: analyzed by the computer; correct answers are reinforced
3. Alternate text: for students having difficulty
4. Analysis of student progress

In general, computers are ideally suited for tutorial work. Instructors can indicate a specific track for each student based on the student's abilities. A lesson plan can be mapped out and the computer can then proceed to provide instruction at the student's own pace.

Note, then, that the areas for CAI are virtually limitless. Any subject that can be taught using a text can be taught using a computer. Note, too, that some subjects are better suited than others to this approach. In general, subjects that require conceptual knowledge, such as calculus or physics, are harder to adapt to the typical CAI format than are other subjects.

9.2.2.3 Simulation

Thus far, we have considered two of the main formats for CAI instruction: drill-and-practice and tutorial, using the programmed-instruction approach. The third major format, one that accounts for a good deal of the success of CAI and for its future potential, is simulation. A simulation, in this context, is a model or an approximation of a real-life situation. Computers are used, for example, to simulate flight conditions so that student pilots and student air traffic controllers can make decisions and have those decisions analyzed without affecting the lives of people. The computer displays a specific situation, the student must make adjustments, and the computer displays the results. Of course, such students must have actual, real-world experience as well, but these simulations are an extremely effective tool for enhancing the educational process.

When is Simulation Most Beneficial?

1. When the necessary equipment is not available because it is too expensive, too dangerous, or too complex for student use
2. When the sample size available in the real world is not large enough to allow generalizations (e.g., medical students need numerous cases to generalize about diagnosis)
3. When experiments require an extended time period (e.g., genetics)
4. When experimentation is not directly available (in subjects such as politics, sociology, ecology)
5. When exploring alternative management decision strategies in the commercial or manufacturing sectors is not feasible

---

Here, again, there are scores of subjects that can benefit from simulation techniques. The Harvard Business School Management Game, for example, uses the computer to simulate conditions at a large corporation. Through various decisions, students must increase the profit and decrease the losses for the company. Each decision is recorded and appropriately entered, the results are displayed, and additional decisions must be made.

Since it is sometimes impractical to enable students to perform chemical or other scientific experiments themselves, particularly when explosive materials are needed, the computer can be used to simulate laboratory conditions.

Medical students use simulations to suggest treatment for patients, the computer then responds to this treatment, and so on.

9.2.3   Who Writes the CAI Lessons?

In short, the computer is used for CAI purposes in three general ways: drill-and-practice, tutorial, and simulation. Note, however, that the key component to any effective CAI sequence is the instructional material. Writing the text, asking key questions, evaluating responses, and anticipating problem areas require a sound pedagogic approach that only experienced educators possess. There is nothing more tedious than a poorly constructed text module, particularly if it uses the programmed-instruction format in a boring manner.

A well-prepared CAI text, the very crux of any application, is, therefore, difficult to write. Ideally, teams of teachers collaborate in this effort to produce the text material. The programming effort, which includes the appropriate branching and logical control and maximizes the visual display features, such as graphics, requires a computer professional.

There are three ways that the CAI sequence can be prepared:

1. The combined effort of educators and computer professionals
2. Educators who learn enough programming to write their own CAI sequences
3. Computer professionals who learn enough about the educational process to write their own CAI sequences

The use of a combined staff of educators and computer professionals has the best chance of success but is also the most costly effort. There is also the possibility of a communication gap, similar to the one described in Chapter 1. On the one hand, we have educators who know precisely what pedagogic techniques to use but do not know how to utilize a computer effectively; and, on the other hand, we have computer professionals who understand about machines but have difficulty determining the educator's actual requirements.

For educators who wish to write their own CAI sequences, there are English-like programming languages, such as TUTOR and COURSEWRITER, which make it relatively easy to prepare a CAI program. But since many teachers are not well versed in the computer's capability and versatility, their efforts are sometimes a little disappointing.

Computer professionals who attempt to write CAI sequences without the assistance of professional educators usually restrict themselves to very simple lessons.

Note that there are two methods for obtaining CAI sequences:

1. Schools may elect to have their own teaching and computing staff write the packages.
2. Schools may select from thousands of prepackaged CAI programs on many subjects at various educational levels. These packages may be leased or purchased from CAI suppliers.

The advantage of the former method is that the package is written for a specific student population, whereas prepackaged CAI programs are more general in nature. The disadvantage of this first method, however, is that the staff writing the CAI sequence is frequently not expert in the required techniques. In the end, each organization must decide the most suitable method of acquisition to fill its needs.

CAI Requirements

1. A sound, pedagogic approach to the subject matter.
2. A knowledge of computer concepts and techniques that can enhance the learning process.
3. Writing CAI modules:
   a. Educators and programmers must work closely.
   b. Schools can obtain prepackaged CAI sequences or have their own teachers write the CAI sequences.

Regardless of who actually writes the CAI program, it should contain the following:

Features of CAI Programs

1. *A complete set of instructions that students can easily follow.*
2. *An ability to anticipate student responses:* On the simplest level, this means that the program should be able to accept "Y" for "yes." "T" for "true," and so on. On a more sophisticated level, it should test for alternative responses in a quiz, be able to interpret key responses (even wrong ones), and so on.
3. *An interesting and challenging student–machine dialogue:* The program should enable students to ask questions, ask for additional help, skip sections of text, and even express their opinions on the subject matter and the pedagogic approach.
4. *A sophisticated logical control sequence:* Branching instructions are the cornerstone to CAI programs. These programs must be flexible enough to skip to various modules, review previous sections as necessary, skip to question–answer sequences when the student feels ready, and so on.

9.3 CONTROVERSIES AND DEBATES OVER CAI

9.3.1 CAI: A Supplement to Classroom Teaching or a Replacement for It?

It has been the philosophy of this text that computers can be used as effective tools for most applications under the proper conditions. The phrase "under the proper conditions" includes, among other things, the fact that the computer must be continually monitored and that human control and recovery procedures must be effectively utilized.

With respect to CAI, it is important to note that this application is most effective *as a supplement to traditional teaching*. That is, the computer can be used for various lessons that take advantage of its capability. At the same time, the computer can free experienced educators to deal with specific problems and to teach subjects for which CAI would not be as useful.

To utilize a computer as a replacement for a teacher has many intrinsic problems and we believe is not a feasible alternative. There is simply no substitute for the intuition, experience, and judgment of the professional educator.

9.3.2 Advantages of CAI

Thus far, we have considered the basic format of CAI and its three main applications: drill-and-practice, tutorial, and simulation. From our discussion you probably became aware of some of the advantages of CAI, as well as some of the disadvantages. Let us first consider the potential advantages of this type of instruction.

9.3.2.1 *Availability*

The computer can provide virtually unlimited availability. That is, the typical constraints on a teacher's time are not factors that limit a computer's ability. Whereas a teacher is available only during specific hours, and usually for group lessons, a computer can be ready to use all the time and on an individual basis.

9.3.2.2 *Individualized Instruction*

Students at CAI terminals can proceed through lessons at their own rate. Each terminal can access specific lessons, independently of the others (see Figure 9.9).

Individualized instruction benefits the slower student who may not learn well in a classroom situation. Peer pressure frequently inhibits the progress of such students.

Figure 9.9. CAI system.

Individualized instruction also benefits the more advanced student, who is frequently prevented from moving ahead in a traditional group situation.

9.3.2.3 Student–Machine Interaction

The student-machine interaction tends to be challenging and stimulating for students, at least at the beginning. In addition, it is a particularly useful approach where there exist great cultural differences between the traditional teacher and the student. CAI has had, for example, notable success in teaching American Indians. Since a machine is not considered a cultural force in the same way as a teacher would be, there is frequently less resistance and less hostility than might be involved with a teacher-student interaction, where students and teacher have different ethnic backgrounds. Of course, to be particularly effective, instructional material can be prepared so that it is relatively culture-free or can be designed specifically to appeal to particular cultures or socioeconomic groups.

9.3.2.4 Instructional Effectiveness

Using a typical CAI sequence, students who cannot understand the main text are given access to alternative explanations. In this way, numerous instructional formats are available. Students then have a greater chance of grasping the material than if they were in a traditional classroom setting.

Moreover, interaction at a terminal provides the student with immediate feedback. The student responds to questions relating to the text and in this way problem areas are quickly discerned.

Studies have indicated that CAI lessons require less student time than when the same lesson is presented in a classroom. Thus a typical one-hour classroom arithmetic lesson may only require one-half or two-thirds of an hour of the student's time at a terminal.

Finally, the computer can employ numerous teaching techniques that may be otherwise difficult to use in a traditional setting. A graphics display terminal using animated characters on a screen is a stimulating tool that instructors may not be able to introduce in a classroom situation. Slides, movies, and drawings can all be presented right on a screen. A map can be displayed on a screen and at the touch of a key, various demographic data can be superimposed on that map. There are even music synthesizers which can be used for CAI purposes.

9.3.2.5 Where Student–Teacher Ratio Is High

Where experienced teachers are in short supply, even those who are not impressed with CAI techniques would agree that a computer is better than having classes with insufficient teacher coverage. Here, again, it is the disadvantaged and culturally alienated groups that tend to suffer from a lack of teachers.

9.3.2.6 For Handicapped Students

Handicapped or confined students frequently benefit from CAI in the home or hospital, since private tutors are difficult to find and expensive as well. There are, for example, CAI devices which are capable of providing audio responses and accepting, as input, verbal messages. These have been enormously helpful in teaching visually impaired people.

On-the-job training for business, industrial, and military applications may also require individualized and expensive instruction. Where such requirements exist, CAI is an effective solution.

But what about the actual success of CAI techniques? There have been numerous studies undertaken which shed light on the effectiveness of CAI. Based on these, there is evidence to suggest that CAI techniques work at least as well as conventional classroom methods. More important, perhaps, the evidence indicates that CAI usually results in faster learning.

9.3.3 Disadvantages of CAI

There are three main difficulties connected with the widespread utilization of CAI. They relate to cost, pedagogy, and socialization. We will discuss each in detail.

9.3.3.1 Cost

There are four basic costs associated with CAI:

1. *Terminals:* Typically, these vary in price from several hundred dollars to $2000.
2. *Telephone costs:* These costs are incurred when accessing large-scale computer systems in a time-sharing environment. Telephone costs are generally high, and are dependent on such factors as the distance of the remote terminals from the mainframe and the amount of connect time involved.
3. *CPU cost:* This, of course, depends on the size of the CPU. Rental costs for a large CPU with time-sharing capability can run thousands of dollars per month. A minicomputer with somewhat less versatility but with the ability to interact with numerous terminals can be obtained for a purchase price of less than $50,000. A microcomputer that can function as an independent terminal with more limited capability can be obtained for several hundred dollars.
4. *Software and lesson preparation:* Although the cost of hardware (1 through 3 above) is decreasing each year, the cost of lesson preparation is heavily dependent on human factors and hence is increasing in cost.

It has been estimated that in order for a CAI sequence to be cost-effective, it should be obtainable at approximately $0.35 per hour of student use. At that price, it can begin to compete with traditional classroom costs. The cost for an average CAI sequence is typically over $1.00. If, however, we accept the evidence indicating that CAI lessons require less time and that one hour of CAI use is really equivalent to several hours of classroom instruction, the cost figure becomes more reasonable.

Assuming that progress in this area will continue at the predicted rates, we can expect CAI to become more cost-effective in the future. It has been determined that traditional instructional costs have been increasing at the rate of 8% a year, while CAI costs have been decreasing at the rate of 5% a year. Although such cost figures will need to be viewed in conjunction with the supply of educators, CAI is clearly becoming more feasible.

Costs: A Past, Present, and Future Assessment

When CAI first took shape in the 1960s, there was a serious shortage of trained and experienced educators. Hence the CAI teaching technique, one that would require fewer teachers in the classroom, was seen as a progressive and workable supplement to traditional education.

Now, however, there no longer is a shortage of teachers. In fact, there are many trained and experienced teachers who are currently unemployed. In this context, the costs associated with CAI are seen as excessive by some and its use as a supplement to traditional education is no longer universally lauded as a progressive step.

In short, it is not realistic to view the future of CAI only in terms of its current cost components. That is, the cost factors themselves, as well as the way people view these factors, tend to change over time.

In the future, we can anticipate the following changes:

1. The cost of hardware will continue to fall.
2. The cost of CAI lesson preparation will also fall.
3. The availability and capability of computers will increase.
4. The overabundance of educators will lessen.

If there are no dramatic social changes within the next few years, we can expect CAI to become increasingly attractive as a cost-effective educational tool.

9.3.3.2 Pedagogy

Some criticism of CAI comes from within the educational community itself. First, there is no consensus among educators as to the best educational techniques. Thus there is considerable reluctance on the part of educational administrators to use a computer to automate traditional teaching techniques. This is often the case because they are not at all sure that traditional techniques are always worthwhile or effective. Many educators are reluctant to propagate these traditional techniques with the use of automation.

For example, is drill-and-practice itself an effective pedagogic technique? Does it really foster learning? Will simulating a real-world situation actually facilitate the decision-making process? Is the programmed-instruction format adequate for most subjects? Until these and other questions are adequately answered, programming a computer to use these techniques may be inappropriate.

With 75% of all public schools currently making use of computers for educational purposes, the effectiveness of CAI as well as of the teaching methods considered will be easier to assess in the future.

There is also some concern among educators about the use of computers to compensate for existing educational problems. That is, it is relatively easy to use a computer to teach new topics such as the "new" math, space-age concepts, and so on, to compensate for teachers who are not making an effort to learn new skills. This sort of compensation may not be in the best interest of the overall educational process.

It would be extremely inadvisable to use a computer to teach subjects because experienced teachers cannot be found. This would mean that society is avoiding or postponing a real solution to a social problem—the fact that fewer people are skilled enough and interested enough to teach that subject. All users of computers, as well as computer specialists, should work to discourage such use or at least to recognize it as a convenience rather than as a solution.

9.3.3.3   *Socialization*

The third major controversy regarding the effectiveness of CAI also relates to pedagogy. Many people argue that using a computer for instructional purposes will have negative social and educational consequences.

A teacher's role is a good deal more than providing facts and concepts. To many youngsters and even to many more mature students, a teacher is a social force, an authority figure who imparts the traditional values, attitudes, and customs of our society. To utilize a computer for learning purposes means that a student's interaction with the teacher is reduced. This is particularly problematic in situations where the teacher represents the only stable force in a child's environment.

To carry this argument a bit further, the time that youngsters spend with the computer is time they might otherwise spend in a social environment, learning to communicate in a group situation with their peers and teachers.

Another social problem to which CAI contributes is the loss of motivation resulting from standardization. In general, with the use of CAI, students are required to answer specific questions in a specific way before they can move on to more advanced topics; the expectation, then, is for standardized responses. Since large groups of students will be provided with exactly the same material, they will begin to respond to educational stimuli in the same way. This can easily stifle individuality, creativity, and even motivation and may also be a decidedly negative effect of overuse of CAI.

9.4   COMPUTER-MANAGED INSTRUCTION (CMI)

Using a computer for educational purposes means more than programming it to function as a teaching machine. To be truly effective, the computer must also help to "manage" the educational process. That is, the computer must store the results of each CAI sequence so that instructors can determine the reliability and validity of each specific method of instruction.

The term that describes the use of computers to maintain records

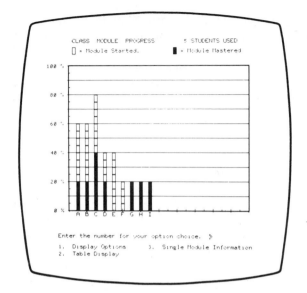

The class progress report shows how students are doing in the course.

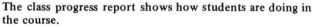

The individual student record shows the student progress in each module: scores, attempts, and mastered or unmastered. Modules A and B are optional for this student.

Figure 9.10. CMI instructor options.

on the effectiveness of CAI is called computer-managed instruction (CMI). CMI is used to assist the educator as follows:

CMI Elements
1. Provide an initial test of students to determine their level of preparation and to assign the appropriate level of instruction
2. Determine the most effective learning techniques for each individual student, based on the initial test results
3. Maintain records on the progress of students
4. Determine the reliability of the test questions themselves
5. Determine the effectiveness of each learning module itself

With CMI, the teacher can be given reports on students' successes and problem areas (see Figure 9.10).

Note that all properly designed systems contain **feedback mechanisms**—techniques used to enable the system to correct errors. In a sense, computer-managed instruction provides the CAI sequences with a method of evaluation and can also be used for eliminating poorly designed questions and/or sequences. Thus CMI functions as a kind of feedback mechanism.

For some systems, CMI takes on an even broader significance. Since "managing" instruction can be construed as encompassing all of the administrative and decision-making functions relating to education, CMI sometimes includes computerized registration procedures, class scheduling, and staffing as well.

9.5   MAJOR CAI SYSTEMS

As previously noted, most schools make use of CAI in some form or another. Such utilization ranges from microcomputers with tapes or disks that contain simple instructional or game-playing sequences, to sophisticated large-scale systems with a wide variety of CAI modules.

Let us consider two widely used, large-scale CAI systems that can be made available to schools on limited budgets through time-sharing. These two systems are called PLATO and TICCIT.

9.5.1   PLATO

PLATO is the largest available CAI system. The term PLATO is an abbreviation for Programmed Logic for Automatic Teaching Operations. (You will discover, if you have not already, that computer professionals are very fond of using catchy acronyms.) PLATO was developed at the University of Illinois at Urbana, Illinois. It utilized equipment manufactured by the Control Data Corporation and cost about $6 million to develop. The first PLATO system was completed in 1960; subsequent versions have since been developed.

The primary objectives of the PLATO system are to provide a high quality of instruction for all educational levels and to make the cost of CAI competitive with classroom techniques.

The University of Illinois maintains a large-scale Control Data computer system with thousands of CAI lessons in hundreds of subjects. The university makes instructional material available to users (public and private schools, colleges and universities) all over the United States and Canada. The users pay for the PLATO terminals, communication costs (usually to the telephone company) for access to the University's CPU, and for use of the system itself. The following chart provides some additional facts about PLATO.

Facts about PLATO

PLATO IV system supports more than 1000 terminals controlled by a central CPU in Urbana, Illinois.

These terminals operate from 167 locations.

Over 600 terminals can be utilized simultaneously.

There are more than 7000 hours of instruction available in 150 subject areas.

Urbana is not the only center of PLATO in the United States. There are other universities that support this system.

In addition, the Control Data Corporation sells PLATO services to individual users.

Because PLATO is run on such a large CPU, users have easy access and the "wait time" is usually negligible.

The PLATO terminal is a heat-sensitive plasma panel costing about twice the typical terminal price. The benefit of this terminal, however, is that it has a **touch panel**. Thus students do not need to key in responses—they can simply touch the screen at select locations to indicate their answers. When light beams on the screen are interrupted by a student's finger, the position of interruption is transmitted to the computer. This is particuarly useful for small children and handicapped people with a coordination problem. Touching a screen, as opposed to typing responses, is significantly easier for such students.

See Figure 9.11 for an illustration of how PLATO, with its plasma-panel terminals, can be used to teach youngsters how to read.

TOUCH PANEL

In addition to using the keyboard, users can enter information into the computer with the touch panel. The touch panel is a transparent plastic film on the CRT, containing a 16 by 16 grid of electrodes which defines 256 touch-sensitive areas. When a lesson acti-vates the touch panel, the user can respond to a question by touching a particular area of the screen instead of typing the answer on the keyboard. The touch panel detects the location, sends that information to the computer, and sounds a tone to acknowledge the touch.

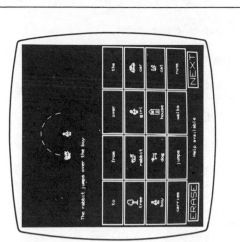

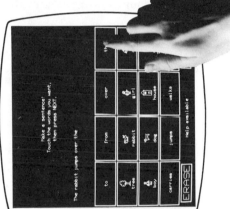

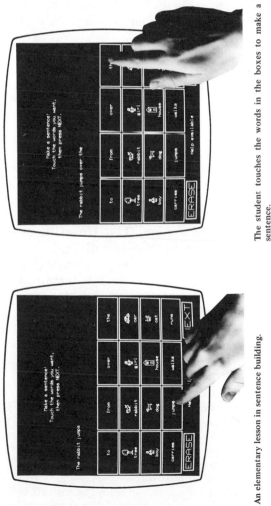

An elementary lesson in sentence building.

The student touches the words in the boxes to make a sentence.

A grammatically correct sentence results in an animation of the sentence.

Figure 9.11. Touch panel lesson.

With the PLATO system students can request:

1. Reference material
2. Additional information
3. Review of a topic
4. A test
5. A more difficult topic

PLATO makes available the standard programmed-instruction format, simulations, and many lessons with a heavy use of graphics. In addition, there are many peripherals available, such as:

1. *Slide projection:* for displaying images of color photos
2. *Audio responses:* to play back prerecorded messages
3. *Music synthesizer:* to reproduce music

In addition to using the system's instructional material, educators can program their own lessons using a simplified language called COURSEWRITER.

The current cost of the PLATO system is approximately $2 per student per hour of terminal use. This is not yet competitive with the cost of traditional classroom education, but, with hardware coming down in price, the future cost picture for PLATO will probably be brighter.

9.5.2   TICCIT

TICCIT is an acronym for Time Shared Interactive Computer Controlled Information Television. This CAI system was begun in 1971 by the MITRE Corporation, a nonprofit research and development company. Much of the educational material has been supplied by the Brigham Young University. The Hazeltine Corporation currently makes TICCIT available commercially.

The TICCIT system cost approximately $441,000 to develop. It currently serves approximately 150 terminal users. The TICCIT system itself operates on a minicomputer. It makes use of color TV sets, headphones for audio use, and other peripheral equipment. Its goal is to make the system available for less than $1 per terminal hour. Educators can write their own lessons in a language called TUTOR.

Differences between PLATO and
TICCIT

There are some basic differences between the PLATO and TICCIT systems that are really indicative of philosophical divergences within the computing field:

1. PLATO utilizes large-scale, powerful, and extremely versatile equipment. The emphasis is on hardware.
2. TICCIT utilizes a minicomputer and terminals that are far less versatile. The emphasis is on "courseware" as opposed to hardware.

3. PLATO terminals were developed specifically for this system. As a result, they are significantly more versatile and expensive.
4. TICCIT makes use of generally available hardware—there were no hardware development costs for this system.

The premise in the PLATO system is that hardware should be the main component; the premise in the TICCIT system is that software should be the main component.

There have been recent studies undertaken to compare the effectiveness of these two approaches but, to date, there has been no definitive analysis.

Note that in addition to PLATO and TICCIT, there are many other extensive and successful CAI projects. The Minnesota Educational Computing Consortium (MECC), for example, as well as the University of Oregon and many professional societies, have done some very important work in CAI. CAI packages for microcomputers are available and have begun to provide users on a limited budget with wide-ranging educational applications. In many instances, these packages are as good as those offered by the larger systems, and the cost is far less.

With the increasing use of microcomputers, it is likely that CAI can be made available to a wide variety of students.

KEY TERMS

Computer-assisted instruction (CAI)
Computer-managed instructions (CMI)
COURSEWRITER
Light pen
Management game
PLATO
Programmed instruction
Simulation
TICCIT
TUTOR

REVIEW QUESTIONS

1. How is each of the following used in a CAI environment?
   a. Time-sharing
   b. Data communications
   c. Microcomputer
   d. Plasma screen terminal
   e. CRT

2. Why is a CRT or a plasma screen terminal generally a more appropriate device than a traditional typewriter terminal?
3. Indicate a list of criteria that you would use to decide whether a school's CAI functions should be handled by several microcomputers or by a time-shared service.
4. Provide a list of criteria you would use for determining whether prepackaged CAI software should be leased by a school or whether the school should give released time to faculty for software development.
5. Describe the programmed-instruction format.
6. Describe three basic techniques used for CAI purposes.
7. Indicate the relationship between CAI and CMI.
8. State the basic advantages and disadvantages of the CAI approach.
9. Indicate several methods that may be used by students for communicating with the computer in a CAI environment.
10. Describe the basic features of the PLATO and TICCIT systems.

DISCUSSION QUESTIONS

1. There is some concern within the educational community that computers will affect the field of education in much the same way as the automobile affected walking and television affected reading. Comment on this. Indicate whether you agree or disagree and why. State methods that can be used to avoid such negative results.
2. There are some who fear or distrust the use of computers within education because they see it leading to a computer priesthood, where only the most technically proficient computer specialists can succeed. Comment on this, indicating whether you agree or disagree.
3. One major complaint that many people have about programmed instruction is that it is tedious and long. Do you think that computers can circumvent this criticism? Explain your answer.
4. Many computer centers, particularly at educational institutions, complain that students like to play games on the computer rather than use it for instruction. To what extent do you think that this is a valid criticism?
5. There are many people who object to electronic media, in all forms, because of its standardizing effect. Comment on steps that should be taken to avoid this potential danger.
6. This chapter indicates that CAI is used in public schools as a supplement to, and not a replacement for, the teacher. On the college level, however, there are numerous introductory courses, at some of the best institutions, that utilize a computer in place of an instructor. That is, there are teaching assistants available, but no instructor. Comment on this approach, indicating what you consider to be its possible advantages as well as potential problems.
7. How would you react to a course in which you enrolled that was taught by computer?
8. What criteria would you use for evaluating a CAI package?
9. If you were using a CAI package to teach a lesson, what controls would

you build into the CMI portion to determine the effectiveness of the CAI lesson?

10. Why are graphics packages so useful for CAI?

11. Indicate some subjects, not discussed in the chapter, which are ideally suited for CAI. Indicate some subjects, not discussed in this chapter, which you believe could not be adequately taught with CAI.

APPLICATION

Based on the application below, describe the potential of computer equipment for handicapped people.

Plato-Based Plan Lets Disabled Work at Home[a]

By Bruce Hoard

MINNEAPOLIS—Just when they thought their careers had ended, many disabled people have found a computer-based program that is putting them back to work in their own homes.

The program is called Homework, and Control Data Corp. is using it to salvage experience and expertise that would have otherwise been lost.

Developed by CDC, Homework was built around the firm's computer-based education system, Plato. With Plato, participants learn programming and related skills which they use to develop new application software and educational courseware for the Plato system.

The program has two goals, according to CDC spokesman W. M. Shaffer. It allows CDC to keep its good people and allows the workers to continue to support themselves and derive the kind of job satisfaction they are accustomed to.

Terminal Capabilities

The Homework training period can last anywhere between three months and a year. Trainees proceed through the modules of lessons at their own pace as they are instructed by the terminal and text materials. Once they return to work, the Plato terminal automatically logs their active hours.

The terminals are equipped with a keyboard featuring an unlimited character set that allows the user to designate each key as a letter, word or other object best suited for his means. There is also a touch-sensitive CRT screen which receives tactile commands from users who cannot, or prefer not to type.

The terminals are linked by dial-up lines to three CDC Cyber 730 CPUs at the Plato network data service center in Arden Hills, Minn. Each Cyber system has 128K bytes of main memory and a shared two million-word extended core memory.

Communication with others is important to housebound employees. The Plato terminals enable participants to keep in touch with coworkers and supervisors and also attend staff meetings several times a month.

The psychological lift of returning to work has done wonders for people like Joan Saladin, a former administrative assistant for CDC in Dayton, Ohio, who suffered a ruptured brain aneurism and subsequent stroke in 1974. At the time, doctors gave her only a 20% chance of living and virtually no chance of resuming her career.

Saladin beat the odds, but her speech was badly slurred and she had to learn to walk again when she left the hospital. Today, speaking normally, she commented on her experience.

"I wanted to die. I was a vegetable. I didn't realize I could do anything of value again," she said.

She recently completed her Homework training and now works as a data entry clerk. Her independence from social security was a great boost for her confidence, she said.

Forty people are presently involved with the program, and one other beside Saladin has returned to work full-time with CDC. The early program emphasis on courseware development has been broadened to include other subjects such as business applications programming.

On the Horizon

Other possibilities are on the horizon, according to K.L. Anderson, program manager for Homework. "As the program becomes more sophisticated, we will be able to take persons with special skills and let each have a choice of job training alternatives."

Company officials think the concept will also eventually become useful to the able-bodied population. According to them, there are many jobs which could be performed in the home, and eliminating the need to commute would help alleviate the national energy crisis.

CDC has plans to market the Homework concept and has already had inquiries from several companies, all of which were not DP-related.

If used on a widespread basis, CDC feels the program could greatly reduce the social costs of maintaining incomes for the 4.7 million unemployed and disabled Americans between the ages of 16 and 64.

10

Computers and health

When we think in terms of computer technology as applied to specific fields, we usually think of the speed, the potential increase in accuracy, and the potential decrease in cost that could result. When using these factors as criteria for measuring a computer's effectiveness, we are really thinking in terms of quantifiable elements. Speed, cost, and error reduction, just to name a few, are measurable entities. But frequently the changes brought about by the use of computers cannot be evaluated adequately in quantitative terms. That is, the use of electronic devices results in *qualitative* changes to specific fields and the services they offer. These changes are difficult, if not impossible, to measure and become a matter of considerable controversy when evaluating the effectiveness of computers.

The potential for computers to improve the quality of services is perhaps most dramatic in the health field. In addition, the controversy surrounding the widespread use of computers is perhaps most intense in this field.

Computers can be used in the health field in many ways. They can be used, for example, as the basis of **hospital information systems**. The objective of many such information systems is to automate hospital procedures and to maintain records on employees and patients. Patient information is stored for traditional record-keeping purposes and for evaluating, diagnosing, and treating the patient as well. That is, an information system can actually assist in providing medical care to patients.

Because hospital information systems have not been implemented on a large-scale basis, it is difficult to provide a general view of their features that would be applicable to all or even most users. Some systems focus on the accounting functions at a hospital, with little attention to computers as medical tools; others have made significant inroads in the use of computers as diagnostic and evaluative tools. When computers are used primarily for record keeping, we will call this a **hospital information system**; when computers are used primarily for diagnostic and evaluative purposes, we will call this a **medical information system**. The very few systems that focus both on record keeping and medical diagnosis are called **health information systems** (see Figure 10.1).

Thus we will divide our discussion into three broad categories:

1. *The hospital information system:* as an application of the management information systems (MIS) approach. In this instance, the system focuses primarily on business applications—accounting, purchasing, inventory, and so on.
2. *The medical information system:* focusing on the use of computers for clinical research, diagnosis, treatment, and evaluation. In this case the medical information system may include medical evaluation as well as some business systems functions. Or, a medical information system may be a laboratory, research, or university-based facility that does *not* include a hospital-based financial system but focuses exclusively on the medical function.
3. *The health information system:* This would be a large MIS hospital-based system that includes medical evaluation as well as business systems functions.

10.1 HOSPITAL INFORMATION SYSTEMS

10.1.1 Basic Objectives

As the term implies, management information systems are designed to assist management, specifically by facilitating the decision-making process. But MIS systems are designed to provide information to *all* levels within an organization, not just top management. For this reason, some organizations simply use the term "information systems" to describe their centralized operations.

MIS systems were initially designed for business applications, but there are many other areas where MIS techniques are equally applicable. One such area is hospital administration.

It has been estimated that $200 billion per year is spent on health care in the United States and that the cost of hospital care has been increasing, in recent years, at almost twice the current inflation rate. Moreover, there are currently three employees for every hospital bed in the United States, a rather high employee-to-user ratio.

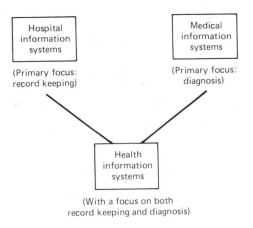

Figure 10.1. Various types of health-related systems.

With the increasing costs of operating a hospital, it becomes imperative that administrators make every effort to increase efficiency. In addition, medical services themselves are becoming more complex and more costly. As a result, the ability of hospitals to provide adequate care, to render appropriate services at a reasonable cost, and to provide information to governmental agencies for Medicare, Medicaid, and so on, has become a major concern.

By coordinating and interrelating administrative services at a hospital, the potential exists for:

1. Decreasing cost
2. Improving patient care
3. Providing administrators with up-to-date information that could lead to a more efficiently run hospital

The coordination and interrelationship of hospital administrative services is the task of a hospital information system. Its objectives and techniques are the same as those in a management information system. All of the features that make an MIS system so attractive are used in hospital information systems as well.

10.1.1.1 Centralized Data Base

A hospital's centralized data base would include the following:

1. All patient data
2. Drug utilization and inventory data
3. Laboratory data
4. General inventory
5. Accounts receivable

6. Accounts payable
7. Payroll
8. Personnel

10.1.1.2 Interrelationship of Data

The ability to interrelate the types of data listed above would decrease duplication of effort, minimize the cost of record keeping, and enhance the efficiency of a hospital's administration.

It would also enable hospitals to obtain information that was never before available. That is, hospitals could:

1. Maintain medical and accounting data on a patient from the time of admission to the time of discharge. When a lab test is ordered for a patient, his or her bill would automatically be updated; a claim would be filed with the insurance company; dietary restrictions regarding the needs of each test would be relayed to the dietician, nurses, and so on (see Figure 10.2).
2. Maintain drug records. These records could be used to monitor inventory, to determine the overall effectiveness of specific drugs in certain situations, to determine contraindications of drugs when used in conjunction with other medicines, and so on (see Figure 10.3).
3. Maintain laboratory records. These records could be used to reduce the costs of tests by automating the billing process and by reducing errors or duplication in testing caused by lack of appropriate coordination. They could also help to determine the effectiveness of specific laboratory tests in diagnosing illness.

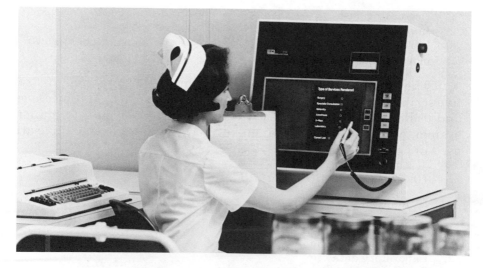

Figure 10.2. Maintaining medical and accounting data on a hospital patient.

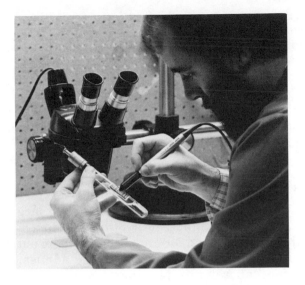

Figure 10.3. Using a bar code reader to maintain drug records.

4. Maintain statistical data on hospital patients to assist in medical research. Ultimately, this additional data can help in diagnosing, preventing, and curing specific illnesses.
5. Provide traditional operating functions, such as billing, inventory control, and payroll.
6. Maintain audit records on hospital services, facilities available, overall efficiency, and so on. When a patient is discharged, the bed would automatically be made available, the dietician would be notified, accounting would be notified, and so on. This would reduce delays and errors caused by inefficient data recording.
7. Automatically prepare the necessary medical insurance forms.

A noted physician testifying at a U.S. Senate hearing on rampant inefficiencies in hospital administration and how they could be avoided with carefully designed hospital information systems indicated the following:

> There have been studies of medication errors showing that one of six medications administered is incorrect in some respect. The study I am referring to suggests that the only reason it doesn't get worse is that the patient himself functions as a kind of quality control device. On the one hand, it is not at all unusual for a woman to be wheeled into the X-ray department in the morning and after lying there for a couple of hours waiting to have an upper GI series, the technician asks if she had breakfast and she says yes and he says he can't do this procedure unless you have an empty stomach, so we'll keep you an extra day. . . . We are talking not just about a

cost problem, but we a talking about organizational complexity and communication breakdown.

This is precisely the sort of waste that a well-designed data base would avoid.[1]

10.1.1.3 Inquiry Ability

Physicians could inquire about the status of patients; hospital pharmacists could inquire about the drug treatment being given to any patient; nurses could monitor the treatment and schedule of patients, and so on.

10.1.1.4 Hardware Support

Typical hospital information systems use a large CPU or mainframe with peripheral input/output devices for maintaining and updating the data base and for providing periodic output.

Terminals are usually available at the admissions office, each nurse's station, laboratories, pharmacy, and the accounting department (see Figure 10.4). These can be used to inquire about various aspects of hospital services and for updating the data base.

10.1.1.5 Use for Audit Procedures

As we have seen, the main purpose of a hospital information system is to provide more efficient and effective care. It can also be used to audit the *quality* of care and to assess existing hospital policies. This in turn will hopefully improve the efficiency of operations.

Moreover, hospitals that seek accreditation or federal funding are

[1]"Computers in Health Care," M. Hodge, *Hearings before the Subcommittee on Domestic and International Science Planning, Analysis and Cooperation of the Committee on Science and Technology*, U.S. House of Representatives, 95th Congress, 2nd Session.

Figure 10.4.   Terminal at a nurse's station.

required to provide an internal review of their organization. With a hospital information system, this can be performed automatically. Assistant Director Carl R. Fischer of the Yale-New Haven Hospital, which has an information system, explains how that system is used for a particular function:

> We put every patient in [the system] on the first day of his admission. We put in his diagnosis. Then we use the retrospective diagnoses to say how long the patient should stay. Daily, the computer prints out a review list. "Mr. X should be reviewed today." Then a nurse . . . goes out on the ward to find out what has happened to the patient, whether there has been a new diagnosis, when treatment has been ordered and when the patient will be discharged. At most [other] hospitals, doctors are rarely, if ever, questioned about current cases, especially about the length of time their patients remain in the hospital.[1]

Sometimes the audit procedure performed by a hospital information system can provide insight into hospital policies and procedures which could be applicable to other hospitals:

> Among the major findings of [several computerized hospital] studies is the discovery that a hospital is not so different from a business in the sense that it can experience some economies of scale. The New York Hospital learned that, as it treated more and more cases of any particular diagnosis, the hospital seemed to become more efficient in providing the treatment, and the cost per case dropped dramatically. The finding strongly supports an idea current in medical planning that hospitals can be most efficient if they specialize in treating only certain kinds of diseases.[2]

Note that the 1972 Amendment to the Social Security Act mandates that Professional Standards Review Organizations be established to review the quality of medical care provided to institutions that receive Medicaid funds. This further increases the need for appropriate audits and controls at hospitals.

Medical evaluation is frequently part of an information system, but because it can be a stand-alone effort and because of its importance, we discuss it separately in the next section.

10.1.2   Reasons Why Hospital Information Systems Are Scarce

In 1982, 93% of the hospitals with 100 beds or more reported that they were using computers or service bureaus that supplied some computing capability. But the great majority of these were using computers to automate specific aspects of their operations; that is, the use of

---

[1] As cited in Deborah Shapley, "Computers in Medicine: Hospitals Cope with Costs, Quality Review," *Science*, Vol. 187, p. 730.

[2] As cited in Deborah Shapley, "Computers in Medicine: Hospitals Cope with Costs, Quality Review," *Science*, Vol. 187, p. 730.

computers to integrate hospital activities and to provide immediate and current information is simply not that common.

The fact is that very few hospitals have full information systems. The federal government reports that there are only nine fully operational hospital information systems in the United States. The reasons for this scarcity are diverse.

10.1.2.1 Cost

The development costs range from $230,000 for small systems to $10,000,000 for large-scale systems, with the average cost in excess of $1 million. In addition to these development costs, the range of operating expenses is from $154,000 to $539,000 per year.

In short, despite the potential benefits to be derived from an information system, very few of them are actually in operation. This situation exists for management information systems, as well, and the major reason is similar: the cost.

10.1.2.2 Fear and Resistance

Another reason why hospitals have not adopted the information systems approach is because of the fear and resistance expressed by hospital personnel. Many people simply do not like to use machines, particularly in a hospital environment, where interpersonal relationships are considered important. Moreover, many people view computers as a threat to job security. Because of this resistance, the use of automated devices to achieve a specific goal is often seen as a deterrent to effective care.

The only method that could possibly counteract such forces is education. Employees should be made to understand that computers are not to be used to replace their own skills, but to augment and enhance them. Moreover, computers almost never result in a decline in employment; in fact, quite the opposite is usually true. When computers are used, more and more people are needed to provide essential services. See Chapter 8 for a discussion of the effects of automation on the work force.

10.1.2.3 Threat to Privacy

An information system stores a significant amount of data on all patients. It also makes that data available to numerous hospital employees.

Without the proper use of controls (and even sometimes *with* the proper use of controls), this data could be used in ways that would violate the confidentiality of patients. Such concerns have prompted many people to object to the use of information systems.

NY Implementing Patient System That Fueled Controversy over Privacy[a]

A medical and financial information system is finally being implemented after nearly a year of debate and compromise between civil libertarians, the state medical profession and the State of NY.

The system that sparked the controversy is the Statewide Planning and Research Cooperative System (Sparcs), which will act as a centralized management information system to provide hospitals and state and federal governments with fiscal and medical planning data.

Once the system is fully implemented, information on each patient entering any one of the state's 300 in-patient hospitals will be compiled on a standardized form.

Information to be reported will include the dates of admission and discharge, the procedure performed, insurance identification number, the patient's address and birth date, and the hospital into which the patient was admitted.

The Sparcs system is expected to be a model for the rest of the country. . . . The U.S. Department of HEW has granted the state $4 million to finance the project. Once the system is in full operation, it will allow hospital planning committees and state and federal governments to examine hospital costs, set reimbursement rates, allocate limited resources and even help in identifying illness and death patterns.

Disagreement over the project arose when it was announced last year. Privacy groups contended that the system would invade patient privacy and encourage potential information abuse. . . . Under the revisions, the patient will not be identified by name. Instead, a medical record number will be assigned; attending physicians will also be assigned a number.

[a] Ann Dooley, *Computerworld*. Copyright 1980 by CW Communications/Inc., Framingham, MA 01701. Reprinted with permission.

Figure 10.5.

With every data base, even manual ones, there is the chance that unscrupulous people may infiltrate the system or that unintentional violations might occur. This risk is far greater when computers are used, as we will see in Chapters 13 and 14.

Any hospital that implements an information system must maintain close control of its data base and monitor inquiries very closely. See Figure 10.5 for an article that considers this issue in detail.

10.1.2.4 Inadequacy of Existing Software

Traditionally, information systems packages have been made available by computer manufacturers, software houses, or other organizations that have developed them. Packages for hospital information systems, however, are not readily available.

Each hospital has its own requirements and its own unique set of procedures. Moreover, hospitals have traditionally avoided efforts, for administrative reasons, to standardize operations. Autonomy is a highly valued attribute in hospitals.

As a result, few vendors have attempted to develop or market standardized hospital information systems. This means that whatever systems are in existence require even more funds to develop for use in a particular hospital, since there are few, if any, available models.

Some computer organizations are beginning to take the initiative in this area, recognizing that health care systems can be made profitable:

> Society cannot afford the cost of today's health care systems and the main initiative to meet this major societal need for better and more affordable health care should come from business. What is needed is a fundamental change in which business takes the initiative and provides the leadership for planning and managing the implementation of programs to meet the needs of society.[1]

10.1.2.5 A Question of Priorities

Technology in general has in the past been viewed as something to be evaluated separate and apart from cost factors; that is, technology was traditionally valued as a critical force in civilization and, hence, something to be supported despite the cost. Now that our economy is no longer able to support widespread technological growth regardless of cost, we must evaluate each application and compare its value and expense to other applications.

Is it appropriate, for example, for the federal government to invest $1 million in a hospital information system that will enhance the quality of health care and which might save lives in the process rather than to invest the money in efforts to build a safer automobile, which might save even more lives? Such questions are exceedingly difficult to answer, but since not everything can be funded, they must be resolved.

When many divergent groups compete for the funding of a project, the ability of any organization to invest in a $1 million technological application such as a hospital information system decreases dramatically. Moreover, with this increased competition for financial support, even the desirability of such a system is questioned by many people.

10.2 MEDICAL INFORMATION SYSTEMS: FOCUSING ON COMPUTERS IN DIAGNOSIS, TREATMENT, CLINICAL EVALUATION, AND RESEARCH

In the preceding section we considered the use of computers in the health field as an administrative tool. For that application, the hospital is viewed as a major business organization; its records are maintained by computer in ways that are similar to MIS utilization.

[1]Control Data Corporation release, William Norris.

This not only increases efficiency but results in more effective patient care.

Another major use of computers in the health field, one that is at least as important as the one just described, is the use of computers as tools for assisting in the evaluation of patient illness, in recommending treatment, and in assessing results.

When computers are used as health care tools, assisting in diagnosis, treatment, and evaluation, the system is usually referred to as a **medical information system**. Hospital information systems usually refer primarily to an administrative use of computers, and health information systems combine both concepts.

As you might expect, medical information systems have not been universally supported by health care professionals. Many nurses, physicians, pharmacists, and technicians disapprove of this application. Most people would agree that computers as administrative tools can ease the burden of hospital employees, but their use by health care professionals has not met with similar acceptance.

Let us reiterate a point that has special meaning when applied to the medical field: there is no substitute for the experience, "know-how," intuition, and judgment of trained specialists. The computer can only be effective, not as a substitute for human input, but as a supplement to it.

10.2.1   Computers as Diagnostic Tools in Medical Information Systems

A computer can be used to assist the physician in a variety of ways. One important method is called **multiphasic screening**—a preliminary analysis of the patient's history and current medical symptoms. In this application, a computer can collect and store the data normally obtained by a doctor or nurse, or, in a hospital, by the admissions office clerk. This computerized procedure:

1. Saves staff time.
2. Facilitates communication with people who have difficulties with the English language. (The computer can ask the appropriate questions in a variety of languages.)
3. Minimizes the difficulty that many patients have in describing their symptoms. Typically, the computer provides a graphic display of the human body and asks the patient to point to the area that hurts.
4. Minimizes the tensions that some people may feel when talking to a doctor. (Of course, some people may not be favorably disposed to talking to a machine either.)
5. Stores the data and can make preliminary judgments as to tests that should be ordered, drugs to be prescribed, and contraindications to which to be alerted.

A computerized multiphasic screening operation could be a stand-alone application—that is, functioning independently of any other computerized procedure.

Usually, however, the computerized multiphasic screening procedure is part of a larger medical information system. In this way, the data obtained can be used not only by the attending physician but by the hospital pharmacy and the laboratory.

The following is a dialogue between a patient and a computer terminal, which has been used for some years at a clinic in Edinburgh concerned with stomach ailments. All new patients irrespective of age or sex are asked to use the terminal. They could reply to the computer's questions with one of three keys, labeled "YES," "NO," and "?"[1]

COMPUTER: THIS IS A COMPUTER TALKING TO YOU. I CAN ASK YOU QUESTIONS BUT I CAN ONLY UNDERSTAND SIMPLE ANSWERS, SO YOU CAN ONLY TALK TO ME BY PUSHING EITHER THE **YES**, **NO** OR **?** BUTTON. YOU SHOULD ONLY PRESS THE '?' BUTTON IF YOU DON'T UNDERSTAND THE QUESTION I AM ASKING YOU. NOW, DO YOU UNDERSTAND EVERYTHING I'VE SAID UP TO NOW? PUSH ONE OF THE BUTTONS.

PATIENT: YES

COMPUTER: THANKS. NOW I WANT TO ASK YOU ONE OR TWO QUESTIONS ABOUT WHY YOU ARE HERE. PLEASE REMEMBER THAT THIS IS ALL IN COMPLETE CONFIDENCE JUST AS WITH DOCTORS. ONLY DOCTORS AND NURSES WILL SEE YOUR ANSWERS. ARE YOU QUITE HAPPY ABOUT THIS? PUSH ONE OF THE BUTTONS.

PATIENT: YES

COMPUTER: GOOD. BY THE WAY, DON'T FEEL THAT YOU HAVE TO PRESS THE BUTTON THE VERY INSTANT THAT I HAVE FINISHED TYPING. IF YOU FEEL YOU NEED TO THINK A BIT BEFORE YOU ANSWER, OR NEED TO READ THE QUESTION OVER AGAIN THEN GO AHEAD AND DO SO. TAKE YOUR TIME IF YOU WANT TO. REMEMBER, HOWEVER, THAT I CAN'T TALK TO YOU AGAIN UNTIL YOU HAVE PUSHED ONE OF THE BUTTONS. WELL, FIRST OF ALL THEN, IS ONE OF THE REASONS YOU VISITED YOUR DOCTOR BECAUSE YOU WERE SUFFERING FROM DISCOMFORT OR PAINS IN THE STOMACH?

[1] James Martin, *The Wired Society* (Englewood Cliffs, NJ: Prentice-Hall), p. 24. Reprinted with permission.

PATIENT: YES

COMPUTER: COULD YOU TELL ME HAS THE PAIN OR DISCOM-
FORT BEEN CONTINUOUS SINCE IT STARTED?
PRESS ONE OF THE BUTTONS.

PATIENT: NO

COMPUTER: I'D JUST LIKE TO BE QUITE CERTAIN OF THIS
POINT. HAVE YOU HAD TIMES, DAYS OR WEEKS,
WHEN YOU'VE BEEN COMPLETELY FREE OF THE
PAIN?

PATIENT: YES

COMPUTER: I SEE. TELL ME IS THE DISCOMFORT RELATED TO
TAKING FOOD—DOES EATING HAVE SOMETHING
TO DO WITH IT? PUSH "YES" OR "NO."

PATIENT: ?

COMPUTER: I AM TRYING TO FIND OUT WHETHER THIS PAIN
OR DISCOMFORT OF YOURS IS IN SOME WAY
AFFECTED BY THE THINGS THAT YOU EAT OR
WHEN YOU EAT. IF IT DOES SEEM TO HAVE
SOMETHING TO DO WITH EATING PRESS "YES,"
IF NOT PRESS "NO."

PATIENT: YES

COMPUTER: WHEN YOU HAVE THE PAIN OR DISCOMFORT DO
YOU GET RELIEF FROM INDIGESTION TABLETS
OR LIQUID MEDICINES? PRESS "YES" OR "NO."

PATIENT: YES

COMPUTER: TELL ME DOES THE PAIN EVER WAKE YOU IN
THE EARLY HOURS OF THE MORNING? "YES"
OR "NO"?

PATIENT: NO

COMPUTER: ONE FINAL QUESTION, WHICH I WOULD LIKE
YOU TO THINK CAREFULLY ABOUT. HAVE ANY
MEMBERS OF YOUR FAMILY—YOUR FATHER,
MOTHER, UNCLES, AUNTS, BROTHERS OR SIS-
TERS—EVER SUFFERED FROM STOMACH OR
DUODENAL ULCERS AS FAR AS YOU KNOW? IF
ANY OF THEM HAVE HAD AN ULCER, PRESS
"YES," IF THEY HAVEN'T PRESS "NO."

PATIENT: NO

COMPUTER: WELL, THANK YOU VERY MUCH. THAT'S ALL I
WANT TO ASK YOU. THANKS FOR BEING SO HELP-
FUL. IN A SECOND THE PAPER WILL START TO
UNROLL AND WHEN IT STOPS PLEASE TEAR IT
OFF AND HAND IT TO THE NURSE OUTSIDE.
GOODBYE.

10.2.2 Examples

The Kaiser Foundation Hospital in Oakland, California, employs a 25-step physical exam by computer which is used by approximately 5000 people per year. It is generally regarded as highly effective by both patients and physicians as a preliminary screening tool.

Patients are impressed by the system because they can actively participate in the diagnostic process. Moreover, they can take all the time they need to describe symptoms and conditions, and the communication problem that commonly exists between a frightened patient and a harried physician is minimized.

The Massachusetts General Hospital has an interactive medical information system that has also met with considerable success. It took five years to develop at a cost of $2.5 million, which was provided, in part, by the federal government. In conjunction with this system, the hospital has developed a programming language called MUMPS designed for use in the health care field. MUMPS is an abbreviation for Massachusetts (General Hospital) Utility Multi Programming System. The language is so well designed that there is significant interest in using it outside the medical industry. It is currently being used in over 1000 systems.

The system uses a medium-sized computer with 30 visual display terminals and 3 print terminals.

In short, many hospitals throughout the United States have instituted multiphasic screening centers that use computers for providing a patient history, an initial screening, and even a preliminary diagnosis. Some have these screening procedures interactively linked with larger medical information systems.

One of the most ambitious projects to date is the PROMIS system developed at the University of Vermont. PROMIS, an acronym for Problem-Oriented Medical Information System, is designed to alleviate some major problems in the health care field, such as:

1. The lack of coordination among those supplying care
2. The need to rely on one's memory for diagnosis and treatment
3. The lack of recorded reasons why various observations, diagnoses, and treatment patterns are made
4. The lack of feedback—doctors do not usually check themselves to assess their diagnostic ability

This system has been used in various medical services (gynecology, internal medicine, etc.) for many years to assist physicians in diagnosing and treating patients. Terminals are used by health services staff to inquire about a patient or a specific illness at the hospital. The terminals may also be used by key staff members to update the files.

The confidentiality of patients is preserved with the use of a coded system. Each person with access to the computer is given a special code which enables him or her to access only specific aspects of the system. There have been no known violations of security with this system.

From the point of view of the hospital staff, PROMIS has been highly successful. As a relatively inexpensive computer system, it provides physicians and other staff with the ability to communicate with one another in a manner that is most effective for the patient. This system is currently being packaged and standardized so that other hospitals can use it.

Note that multiphasic screening applications have two facets:

1. They can be used for individual patient care.
2. They can be used for medical research to generate statistics which can determine on a general level the effectiveness of specific treatment, drugs, and so on.

Despite the success of the sample cases noted, many multiphasic screening and computerized medical information facilities have been eliminated. All the reasons why hospital information systems have not been widely adopted apply to medical information systems as well, but the primary reason in most instances is resistance on the part of physicians. As professionals, many medical doctors resent the use of computers because they believe that machines might be used in assessing medical techniques. Physicians believe that each case is unique and must be viewed in its entirety by the attending physician and no one else.

Many proponents of computers as diagnostic tools and as instruments for maintaining proper records believe that effective systems will reduce medical malpractice settlements. Since all the data will be documented, doctors will not be as vulnerable. Others believe that such systems will increase the risk of malpractice litigation.

10.3   THE HEALTH INFORMATION SYSTEM

10.3.1   Characteristics of a Health Information System

10.3.1.1   *Full Definition of a Health Information System*

A health information system is a computer-based system that stores data on patient history, creates and maintains a computerized medical record for every patient, and makes the data available for the following uses: patient care, administration and business management, monitoring and evaluating medical care services, clinical research, and planning of medical care resources.

10.3.1.2   Reasons for Implementing
Health Information Systems

1   Need for coordinated effort increases as the number of employees and the number of hospital beds increases
2.   Need to remember increased amounts of data about each patient, tests, procedures, and drug treatment reduces the physician's effectiveness
3.   Needs of third-party payment systems (i.e., Medicare, Medicaid, medical insurance companies) result in increased paperwork
4.   Need for quality review and assessment at hospitals is a major audit function
5.   Increase in malpractice litigation has created new pressures for careful documentation of clinical treatment

10.3.1.3   Costs Associated
with Health Information Systems

Although it is hard to evaluate, operating costs for a hospital-based medical information system range from $4 to $9 per patient per day. This is 4 to 7% of the total operating budget of most hospitals. For multiphasic screening clinics at ambulatory care sites, the costs range from $0.50 to a high of $14 per patient visit.

10.4   OTHER HEALTH-RELATED
USES OF COMPUTERS

10.4.1   Mini Medical Systems

Many physicians and drug stores have begun to acquire mini- and microcomputers for their office in an effort to expedite the handling of patient billing, drug inventories, and so on.

In addition, some doctors use these small computers to assess their own diagnostic or treatment abilities. They enter patient data, update the files as necessary, and use statistical routines to measure the effectiveness of treatment. Such systems can also be used, in the abstract, to determine the susceptibility of people with specific characteristics to certain illnesses.

As the prices of minis and micros decrease, and as the software and hardware support increases, more and more physicians will be acquiring such systems.

Corner Drug Stores Get Computers[a]

A wide variety of state and federal regulations, dealing with everything from pricing policies to maintenance patient profiles to warning customers about possible drug side effects, has forced the pharmacist to devote more and more time to accounting, legal and administrative matters. To lighten this burden, General Computer Corp., Macedonia, Ohio, has derived a stand-alone computer system, featuring Honeywell Level 6 minicomputers, capable of performing a multitude of pharmacy-related tasks. The system:

Maintains both inventory control and patient profiles consisting of complete, up-to-date medical histories on each customer for as long as the law requires

Monitors drug-to-drug interactions at the ingredient level

Ranks potential interactions by severity, but leaves the decision up to the druggist

Substitutes generic names for brand names to save patients money

Indicates whether the purchase of certain drugs is covered by the agency the patient has assigned to pay for them

Computes all price extensions

Prepares end-of-year statements by family for tax purposes

Keeps an audit trail for controlled substances as required by federal regulations

[a] *Infosystems*. Copyright, Hitchcock Publishing Company. Reprinted with permission.

Figure 10.6.

For a general review of computers used in drug stores, see Figure 10.6.

10.4.2 Computers for Treatment and Evaluation

10.4.2.1 Eye and Ear Surgery Using Microcomputers

There have been numerous scientific advances in brain, eye, and ear surgery that have relied upon computers. Tiny microprocessors can be used to assist brain surgeons in operating on patients. Similarly, a computer can be used by a deaf person to convert sounds into electrical signals that can be carried to the inner ear. Deaf people then learn to correlate certain vibrations with specific sounds (see Figure 10.7).

In addition, scientific advances have been made in helping blind people to make use of the computer. A computer can be used to "see" light patterns and, through electrical signals, to activate the cornea. Sightless people can then correlate various signals with specific images.

Research in these areas is relatively new, but significant improvements on the quality of care will no doubt be made in the future.

Computer Research May Hold Hope
for Totally Deaf[a]

WASHINGTON, D.C.—Miniaturized computers may play a key role in the future development of "artifical hearing" for tens of thousands of deaf persons who cannot be helped by conventional hearing aids, according to scientists meeting here today.

Researchers representing the University of Utah in Salt Lake City and the Ear Research Institute in Los Angeles described experimental work employing mini computers to stimulate the inner ear. They reported that a subject, deaf from infancy, was able to sense "sounds" from the computer and differentiate them from vibrations.

Their latest experiments involved implanting a series of pinhead-sized platinum electrodes within the tiny, snail-shell-like cochlea (or inner ear), connected to an array of photo-isolated stimulus drivers designed by the Utah group. These drivers are controlled by a Digital Equipment Corp. PDP-8 minicomputer. Deaf patients recognize different tones depending upon which electrode is stimulated, and further changes in sound can be achieved by changing the stimulus frequency. More complex sounds can be created by stimulating different electrodes at different frequencies under computer control; such experiments are now in progress.

[a] Courtesy of Digital Equipment Corp.

Figure 10.7.

10.4.2.2 Computers Used to Treat Stutterers

Progress has also been made in treating stutterers with the use of computers. The patient uses a microphone to respond to the computer's questions. The device analyzes these responses and prints a message that either praises the patient for his or her speech or is highly critical of the response. This sort of therapy has resulted in a fast-paced recovery process for many stutterers.

Stuttering is largely a psychological disorder that relates to a person's problem in communicating with others. Many patients prefer to communicate with a machine because they believe that they are not being evaluated or judged in their therapy. In this instance, at least, the use of an impartial or nonjudgmental device often produces better results than a therapist can.

10.4.3 Computers in Medical Research

Computers have been used in recent years to assist physicians, biologists, and biochemists in the research area. These machines have been used to develop mathematical models to describe the behavior of biological systems. When the descriptions provided by these models are relatively error-free, the model can then be used to predict how various stimuli would affect the biological system:

An investigator creates the model of a biological system to be studied in the form of a computer program. Initially the program is tested by the data that are available either from previous knowledge of the literature or from previous research results which have been achieved. If the model passes scrutiny at that point, one attempts to simulate or mimic the behavior of a real biological system using the model.[1]

Sometimes computers are used in medical research as retrieval systems, in much the same way as they are used for any data base application.

MEDLARS is an acronym for Medical Library based literature retrieval system. This system is based at the National Library of Medicine in Bethesda, Maryland. It has access to approximately 3.5 million references to articles and books in the health field, and makes this data available to over 600 universities, medical schools, hospitals, and government agencies.

Such a library retrieval system is becoming increasingly available, not just in the medical field but in many areas. The era in which literature searches had to be performed manually and updated as time permitted is fast becoming obsolete.

10.4.4   Computers for Simulation

There are numerous software packages that can be employed to simulate patient conditions. These are used by medical students to test their diagnostic abilities and to increase their knowledge about various illnesses.

The Ohio State University College of Medicine uses one such simulation package called CASE, for Computer-Aided Simulation of the Clinical Encounter. This is a type of CAI package.

The CASE package enables medical students to "practice" without risking the lives of patients. Moreover, the system provides students with an opportunity to "treat" certain diseases with which they might not otherwise come into contact because of regional or calendar considerations.

Such simulation packages are not restricted to medical students. There are similar training systems for dieticians, laboratory technicians, pharmacists, and so on. The health field makes widespread use of this aspect of computer-assisted instruction.

[1]"Computers in Health Care," A. Pratt, *Hearings before the Subcommittee on Domestic and International Science Planning, Analysis and Cooperation of the Committee on Science and Technology,* U.S. House of Representatives, 95th Congress, 2nd Session.

10.4.5 The Use of CAT Scanners

A relatively new diagnostic technique known as computed axial tomography, or the CAT scan, has provided doctors with the ability to obtain information about organs that was previously obtainable only through surgery. This revolutionary X-ray technique resulted in the 1979 Nobel Prize for Physiology and Medicine for the developers, Allan McLeod Cormack, a physicist, and Godfrey Newbold Hounsfield, an electronic engineer.

The CAT scanning technique basically involves rotating an X-ray tube around a specific area of the body, thereby producing a detailed photographic "slice" of the anatomy—that is, a cross-sectional picture or tomogram. A computer then processes this information and projects it on a display screen. CAT scans have proven particularly useful for diagnosing brain tumors, cancer of the pancreas, and other internal disorders that are extremely difficult to diagnose without surgery.

Notwithstanding its great value as a diagnostic tool, however, the CAT scanner has generated much controversy. This is not surprising when it is realized that it costs approximately $850,000 for the latest model. The cost to the patient for each CAT scan is $250 to $350. Several issues have been raised regarding its use:

1. Since the costs of acquiring and operating the machine are ultimately passed on to individuals through higher hospital and medical insurance charges, can the expense be justified? It has been charged, for example, that some hospitals deploy the scanner for routine and often unnecessary screening in order to generate profits from the charges.
2. Some companies have discarded plans to develop improved versions of the CAT scanner since the federal government has significantly decreased the funds it provides to hospitals for acquisition of these machines. This has been a direct result of the government's program to curb health costs.
3. Medical experts disagree on how and when the CAT scanners need to be used and whether they are cost-effective, because, in some instances, there exist alternative techniques that can be used to make diagnoses.

10.4.6 And Many More Possibilities

In this section we have only touched on the wide variety of diagnostic tools that use computer technology. Among those not considered in depth are:

1. Ultrasound images for abdominal, obstetric, and gynecological studies.
2. Intensive care unit and coronary care unit monitors at nurses' station (see Figure 10.8).
3. Operating room monitors.
4. Applications in nuclear medicine.

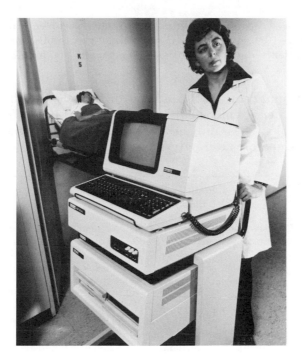

Figure 10.8. Intensive care unit and coronary care unit monitors.

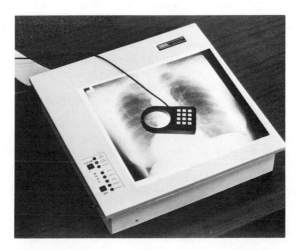

Figure 10.9. X-rays can be converted into digitized form for input into a computer for analysis.

5. Programs and equipment that analyze electrocardiograms and X-rays (see Figure 10.9). A recent EKG program, for example, was tested on 1435 heart patients and found to be 97% accurate compared to physicians' evaluations.

In addition, computers are used to provide peripheral support, such as computerized blood banks (see Figure 10.10) and computerized insurance banks. These may be tied into medical information systems and can thus operate interactively.

Computer-Readable Labels
Aid Blood Dispatch, Safety[a]

NEW YORK CITY—New York Blood Center is using minicomputers, laser scanners and bar-coded labels to make the transfer of blood from donor to recipient safer and more efficient.

The blood center project is part of a national effort to label all blood and blood products with a uniform, machine-readable label that can be used by all blood banks in the United States.

The move toward uniformity developed out of concern that incompatible labeling techniques were springing up throughout the blood banking community. Labels used in one blood center could not be read by machines in any other center, according to Dr. Eric Brodheim, chairman of the American Blood Commission's Committee for Commonality in Blood Banking Automation (CCBBA).

"Labeling practices among the country's 7,000 blood banks were well on the way to producing a Tower of Babel," said Dr. Brodheim. "Every blood center interested in electronic processing was designing its own type of label. Not only would it be impossible for one blood center or hospital to read the label of any other, it would be impossible for computer companies to produce a system that could be used by all."

If the trend continued, the result would be that individual systems would have to be developed for each center making these systems too costly for most to consider, he said. "Equipment manufacturers will build to a set of standards but are reluctant to cater to individual peculiarities."

During two years of research, the CCBBA Symbol Selection Task Force examined a variety of bar codes as well as magnetic strips such as those sometimes used on the backs of credit cards and numbers that can be read by both the human eye and by machines such as those on bank checks.

The new uniform label, assembled in several stages, will contain bar codes similar to those on grocery products, identifying the drawing center and donor, unit number, name of the blood product, relevant laboratory test results and expiration date.

When the blood reaches its destination, the crossmatching to the recipient can be automatically recorded by passing a hand-held reader across the bar code. The CCBBA is presently considering a corresponding bar code for hospital bracelets identifying the particular patient for whom the blood is intended. For blood banks and hospitals where electronic equipment is not available the new label prominently displays duplicate information in eye-readable form.

[a] Courtesy of Digital Equipment Corporation.

Figure 10.10.

With increased flexibility of hardware and software, and increased standardization in the health care field, the use of computers will no doubt be an even more effective tool for increasing efficiency and for maximizing effective health care services.

It should be noted that the United States actually lags behind countries like England, France, and Switzerland in the application of data processing to health care. These countries have, in many instances, more advanced computerized health care systems.

10.5   IS A HOSPITAL NEGLIGENT FOR FAILING TO USE A COMPUTER?

In an ordinary negligence lawsuit, the defendant must typically demonstrate that he or she acted with reasonable prudence or due care under a given set of circumstances in order to avoid liability. Traditionally, a medical malpractice suit against a hospital employs the "community practice" rule as a measure of the standard of care. That is, the hospital has been required to show that it has exercised care and skill comparable to that used by other hospitals in treating similar conditions. The "community practice" rule has traditionally taken into consideration whether the hospital is in a rural area or an urban area, since urban hospitals typically are larger and can afford more sophisticated medical equipment.

The question exists as to whether a hospital might be held liable for negligence even though it meets the "community practice" standard. For example, could liability attach for failing to use a computer despite the fact that computers are not customarily used in most hospitals for diagnostic and treatment purposes? This type of problem was addressed by Judge Learned Hand in the case of *The T. J. Hooper*, in the early 1930s. That case, although not directly related to hospital care, may have implications for the health field. In that case, the defendant-owners of *The T. J. Hooper*, a boat involved in an accident, claimed that due to fog they could not see where they were when the accident occurred. They argued that they were not negligent for failing to have radar on board, since similar boats did not, in fact, use such equipment. In deciding against the owners, Judge Hand stated the following:

> [I]n most cases reasonable prudence is in fact common prudence; but strictly it is never its measure; a whole calling may have unduly lagged in the adoption of new and available devices. It never may set its own test, however persuasive be its usages. Courts must in the end say what is required; there are precautions so imperative that even their universal disregard will not excuse their omission.

Thus, the needs of society, rather than the "community practice" rule, prevailed. It remains to be seen if this type of standard will be applied in hospital malpractice cases. That is, it may eventually be determined that hospitals are required to have the most sophisticated equipment available if failure to use such equipment results in diagnostic errors.

KEY TERMS

CAT scanner
Centralized data base
Health information systems
Hospital information systems
Management information system (MIS)
Medical information systems
Microcomputers
Mini medical systems
Multiphasic screening
MUMPS
PROMIS
Simulation

REVIEW QUESTIONS

1. Define what is meant by each of the following:
   a. Hospital information system
   b. Medical information system
   c. Health information system
2. What are the similarities between a management information system and a hospital information system?
3. What type of data is typically included in the data base of a hospital information system?
4. What are some of the major explanations as to why hospital information systems are not very prevalent?
5. What is multiphasic screening?
6. What is a major explanation as to why medical information systems have not been widely adopted?
7. Explain how computers can be used in drugstores.
8. How can computers aid those who are blind or deaf?
9. How can computers help stutterers?
10. How can computer simulation be used by medical students and researchers?
11. What are the advantages of CAT (computed axial tomography) scanners? Why have CAT scanners generated controversy?

DISCUSSION QUESTIONS

1. A hospital decides to acquire a hospital information system. What methods would you suggest for avoiding the fear and resistance so common among hospital employees currently using such systems?
2. If you were a hospital administrator thinking about acquiring a hospital information system, what questions would you ask of the agent?
3. How are computers used in medical training?
4. What benefits would a computer provide to assist the physician in making diagnoses?
5. Do you think that health information systems will become more widespread in the coming years? Explain your answer.

APPLICATION

Consider the application below and then answer the questions that follow it.

Computer-Aided Technique Diagnoses Arthritic Knees[a]

Scientists at the University of Akron have developed a computer-aided, electro-acoustical technique for monitoring and evaluating knee noises that promises to aid in the diagnosis and treatment of arthritis and other joint disorders.

While investigators have been trying since the 1880's to use noises produced by the moving knee as a noninvasive diagnostic tool, they have always given up eventually because of a lack of sophisticated equipment. "Those researchers mainly used the stethoscope," Dr. Mamerto Chu noted, "but they could never remember exactly how the joint sounded the day before or the last time they listened to it."

The noises produced by the patients' knees now generate waveforms on an oscilloscope in analog form, Chu observed. Such recorded knee data is converted from analog-to-digital (A/D) form by a Texas Instrument Inc. Model 960A minicomputer with 32K bytes of memory, at a rate of 12,000 samples per second, he noted.

Each completed cycle of the knee data contains 18 records, with each record consisting of 2,048 data samples.

A Tektronix, Inc. 4013 graphics terminal is used to monitor the minicomputer during the A/D conversion process and for editing the marking signals from the converted data. After the conversion, the digitized acoustic signals are analyzed using two Fortran programs.

While the technique could help to diagnose knee joint problems, it also would be useful in indicating the effectiveness or ineffectiveness of any drugs for the treatment of a condition.

---

[a]Marguerite Zientara, *Computerworld*. Copyright 1980 by CW Communications/Inc., Framingham, MA 01701. Reprinted with permission.

Application Questions

1. How are graphics display terminals used in the application?
2. Explain how the technique described could be useful in indicating the effectiveness of drugs for the treatment of a condition.
3. Do you think a course on computers should be offered to medical researchers, or should researchers simply rely on computer professionals to assist them in their studies? Explain your answer.

11

Computers as scientific tools: a focus on artificial intelligence

We have thus far considered numerous activities performed by computers. You have seen that the ability of machines to perform repetitive operations quickly and accurately has been universally recognized and fairly well accepted. But when that ability is applied to tasks traditionally performed by people, particularly by professionals, there is a wide disparity of opinion as to its effectiveness and its potentially dehumanizing effects. The use of computers in education and in medical information processing, just to name two areas, has been both praised and criticized by many leaders in the field.

Artificial intelligence, perhaps more than even the other fields, represents an application of computers that brings into question the virtues and disadvantages of human-machine interaction.

11.1 CONTROVERSIES OVER ARTIFICIAL INTELLIGENCE

Artificial intelligence (AI) is a scientific application of computers that has aroused considerable controversy on both a social and a philosophical level.

To begin with, there is no universally accepted definition of the term or its objectives. Definitions range from modest descriptions of scientific applications to very broad statements about its use and its potential.

Some experts describe artificial intelligence as a narrowly focused field that has as its prime objective the programming of computers in such a fashion that they appear to make "intelligent" decisions. The purpose of this application is to enable computers to make complex decisions and to perform problem-solving tasks. If a machine can be programmed to do reasonably well at some predefined task, it will be said to display "intelligence."

Other proponents of artificial intelligence believe that the value of AI goes beyond its practical ability to enable machines to function as if they had intelligence. These experts claim that AI techniques and discoveries will be of considerable value to students of psychology. The AI supporters believe that the goals of artificial intelligence and of the psychological sciences in general are the same: to understand intelligent processes. For them, AI techniques provide researchers with an understanding of the human mind and how one thinks.

Thus there are, broadly stated, two categories of AI proponents. One group focuses on the application of computers for problem-solving functions; the other focuses on the use of computers as problem-solving tools for the primary purpose of providing greater insight into human thought processes.

The direction of AI research is, of course, integrally related to the objectives of the researchers. There are scientists who focus on AI techniques and on enhancing the computer's ability to perform certain tasks. For example, chess-playing programs have been written by AI experts to demonstrate the ability of machines to make complex decisions. Similarly, other game-playing programs have been designed to demonstrate the ways in which machines can be programmed to display intelligence. These game-playing tasks can serve as entertainment, can be used to challenge a human opponent's mental acuity, or can simply demonstrate the level of complexity and sophistication that may be programmed into a machine.

Other AI tasks include language translation and general problem solving. There are even robots that have been developed by AI researchers to serve as mechanical servants.

These applications, and others, which will be discussed in more detail in the following pages, have one or both of the following goals:

1. To provide some "intelligent" assistance for problem-solving tasks
2. To provide a new dimension to our understanding of the human mind

The applications that are undertaken by both types of AI researchers are similar; the controversy surrounding AI applications is more directly related to the ultimate purpose of the application, not to the work itself.

In short, there is some degree of divergence among AI researchers as to the scope of their work and its ultimate objectives. Those who object to AI as a research field cite one or more of the following reasons:

A Critical Evaluation of Artificial Intelligence

1. The problem-solving ability of the machines has not even approached the predictions made by AI proponents 10 and 20 years ago. Hence it is poor policy to continue to support this area of research.
2. The concept that AI can provide us with insight into human thought processes is not only wrong but is unethical as well. By continued government funding for AI, we are encouraging research in an area that should not be pursued, on moral grounds. There is a dimension to human intelligence which cannot and should not be attempted by programming a machine.
3. Since psychologists themselves have not yet agreed on a definition of "intelligence," it is somewhat premature to investigate ways of producing an artificial form of that intelligence. Some psychologists use IQ (intelligence quotient) as a measure of human intelligence. Others claim that human intelligence is not quantifiable; judgment, intuition, and creativity are aspects of intelligence that are exceedingly difficult, if not impossible, to measure. Hence without an agreement among psychologists as to the definition of intelligence, attention to "artificial intelligence" may well be misguided.

In this chapter we explore the background of AI, typical applications, and some of the larger issues that surround its use.

11.2   ALAN TURING AND HIS DEFINITION OF MACHINE INTELLIGENCE

Even before electronic digital computers began to emerge as scientific and commercial tools, a British mathematician, Alan M. Turing, in the late 1940s considered the problem of determining whether machines can be viewed as displaying "intelligence." Rather than attempting to provide a definition of intelligence, which he knew would only serve to foster controversy, he rephrased the problem by attempting to determine if machines can be made to function in ways similar to the way we behave when we say we are thinking.

This attempt to sidestep the question of what intelligence is was very ingenious. It enabled Turing to propose a kind of imitation game which could then be used to characterize machine "intelligence."

Can a Machine Play This Game?[a]

The new form of the problem can be described in terms of a game which we call the "imitation game." It is played with three people, a man (A), a woman (B), and an interrogator (C) who may be of either sex. The interrogator stays in a room apart from the other two. The object of the game for the interrogator is to determine which of the other two is the man and which is the woman. He knows them by labels X and Y, and at the end of the game he says either "X is A and Y is B" or "X is B and Y is A." The interrogator is allowed to put questions to A and B thus:

C: Will X please tell me the length of his or her hair? Now suppose X is actually A, then A must answer. It is A's object in the game to try to cause C to make the wrong identification. His answer might therefore be

"My hair is shingled, and the longest strands are about nine inches long."

In order that tones of voice may not help the interrogator the answers should be written, or better still, typewritten. The ideal arrangement is to have a teleprinter communicating between the two rooms. Alternatively, the question and answers can be repeated by an intermediary. The object of the game for the third player (B) is to help the interrogator. The best strategy for her is probably to give truthful answers. She can add such things as "I am the woman, don't listen to him!" to her answers, but it will avail nothing as the man can make similar remarks.

We now ask the question, "What will happen when a machine takes the part of A in this game?" Will the interrogator decide wrongly as often when the game is played like this as he does when the game is played between a man and a woman? These questions replace our original, "Can machines think?"

[a] Alan Ross Anderson, *Minds and Machines*, (Englewood Cliffs, NJ: Prentice-Hall), p. 7. Reprinted by permission of Prentice-Hall, Inc.

Figure 11.1.

The test requires a person to ask questions, and on the basis of the answers, he or she must determine if the respondent is another human being or a machine. If the person is unable to make this determination accurately when asking questions of a machine, the device is said to possess intelligence (see Figure 11.1).

Turing's test has remained a kind of model for AI. Turing believed that by the year 2000 such a machine could be programmed to imitate human responses. Indeed, many AI researchers are attempting to demonstrate such capability, but thus far no machine or machine program has even approached this goal. We do, however, still have over a decade to determine if Turing's prediction was too optimistic or if, in fact, it will be possible to have communication between people and machines in which the human being finds it difficult to determine if the respondent is another human being or a machine.

The following lists the areas traditionally considered to be research fields in AI:

Areas of Research in Artificial Intelligence

Heuristics
   Game playing
   Theorem proving
   General problem solving
Robotics
Language and linguistics
Computer-assisted instruction
Cybernetics

We will consider each of these in some detail.

11.3   HEURISTIC PROGRAMMING: A MAJOR AI TECHNIQUE

A main area of AI research focuses on the use of machines to simulate the problem-solving techniques of human beings. Most problem-solving techniques use a dimension or a thought process which goes beyond that of a fixed set of rules or algorithms. That is, playing tic-tac-toe may be viewed as a problem-solving task, but it is one of the few that can be defined in terms of a given set of rules. Even without the use of complex formulas, most people could establish an algorithm to be used that would ensure either victory or, at worst, a tie game. Hence tic-tac-toe would be an easy problem-solving game to computerize. Most tasks, however, rely on more complex strategies, judgments, or even intuitive skills where algorithms would be insufficient to define the appropriate moves. AI researchers have been attempting to develop programs to enable machines to do reasonably well at these more complex tasks.

For such problems, **heuristic programming techniques** are used. These represent strategies or shortcut rules which may be employed to solve a problem but which do not explore every conceivable alternative. According to James Slagle, an AI proponent:

> A heuristic is a rule of thumb, strategy, method or trick used to improve the efficiency of a system which tries to discover the solutions of complex problems.[1]

Heuristic programming has met with considerable success in

[1]James Slagle, *Artificial Intelligence: The Heuristic Programming Approach* (New York: McGraw-Hill), p. 3.

game playing, theorem proving, and in general, problem solving. We will consider each in depth.

11.3.1   Game Playing Using Heuristics

One main area in which problem-solving techniques have been used is in game playing, such as chess, GO, and so on. In these games, the computer does not have the capacity to store all possible moves. In chess, for example, there are 10^{120} moves, a number far in excess of the capacity of all computers. Various strategies need to be worked out in which sets of moves are analyzed and rejected or applied as necessary.

Efforts to program computers to play chess date back to the 1950s. Claude E. Shannon, the founder of communication theory, wrote an article entitled "A Chess-Playing Machine" in which he described the techniques to be used:

> Investigating one particular line of play for 40 moves would be as bad as investigating all lines for just two moves. A suitable compromise would be to examine the important possible varia-tions—that is, forcing moves, captures and main threats—and carry out the investigation of the possible moves far enough to make the consequences of each fairly clear. It is possible to set up some rough criteria for selecting important variations, not as efficiently as a chess master, but sufficiently well to reduce the number of variations appreciably and thereby permit a deeper investigation of the moves actually considered.[1]

Chess is one game that has indeed captured the imagination of many AI pioneers. It provides a prime example of how heuristic programming can be employed. In 1957, a computer was programmed to play a passable amateur game. This success prompted the designers, two of the major AI researchers in the world, Allen Newell and Herbert A. Simon of the Carnegie Institute of Technology, to predict, in 1958,

> that within ten years a digital computer will be the world's chess champion, unless the rules bar it from competition.[2]

The rules have not barred it from competition, but the prediction was nonetheless overly optimistic. Chess-playing machines have met with

[1] Claude E. Shannon, "A Chess-Playing Machine," reprinted in *The World of Mathematics*, ed. James R. Newman (New York: Simon and Schuster), p. 2129.

[2] Herbert A. Simon and Allen Newell, "Heuristic Problem Solving: The Next Advance in Operations Research," *Operations Research*, Vol. 6, p. 6.

considerable success but they do not beat human masters. Here, again, there are two views on this:

1. Simon and Newell are correct in their predictions about the future success of chess-playing machines; they were simply too optimistic about the time it would take.
2. Although computers can play chess, they will never effectively compete against the masters.

Currently, there are numerous chess-playing machines with built-in microprocessors which are relatively inexpensive and can provide enough challenge to the average or above-average chess player. This, in itself, is a major accomplishment. In addition, machines have entered major competitions and, although they do not always win, they do reasonably well (see Figure 11.2).

In short, many critics of AI claim that Simon and Newell's predictions about chess-playing machines were not borne out and never will be. Others prefer to focus on the gains already made in this area of artificial intelligence, not only in chess but in many other games as well.

Computers vs. Chess Champions[a]

Is there a chess computer capable of defeating the world champion?

Not yet. But Edward Fredkin, a professor at the Massachusetts Institute of Technology, under the supervision of Carnegie-Mellon University in Pittsburgh, has established a $100,000 prize for a computer program that could accomplish the feat. A series of competitions—expected to last years—will begin in November to determine the computer best qualified to take on humans.

Dr. Hans Berliner, head of Carnegie-Mellon University's computer science department said he considered it a 50-50 possibility that a computer could be developed by 1990 to a point where it could be successful against a human champion. Other computer experts, however, said it may take many more years, if it could ever be done.

As of now, the computer program at Northwestern University, which is called Chess 4.9, is considered the best chess program in the world. Its chess playing skill has been estimated at about 2,000 on the international chess-rating scale, which is better than 95 per cent of U.S. tournament players.

The computer program used by Bell Laboratories is considered the second best. One of its developers, Kenneth Thompson, said last night that the notion of a computer beating a human champion within the next 20 years "was way out in fantasy land." He said that if chess computer programs improved "perfectly," it would take about 65 to 70 years to develop the computer to the point where it can beat a champion player. "That's a big 'if' ", he added.   **—Topol**

[a]*Newsday*, May 9, 1980. Copyright 1980, Newsday, Inc. Reprinted with permission.

Figure 11.2.

11.3.2 Theorem Proving Using Heuristics

Since AI uses essentially rational methods to simulate thought processes, it seems natural that one main application would be mathematics.

In 1957, Newell, Clifford Shaw, and Simon developed a program that enabled a machine to prove a series of mathematical theorems. The program, called the *Logic Theorist*, used trial-and-error methods as a heuristic tool. This trial-and-error technique was similar to the one employed by college students when proving theorems. The program was able to prove 38 of 52 theorems in the *Principia Mathematica*, a major work on mathematical theorems.

These theorems had all been proven before, but in some instances the computerized techniques resulted in novel approaches which had never been used before.

Simon has predicted that a heuristics program will someday prove a theorem not yet proven by mathematicians. Such an accomplishment would no doubt be of great importance to the mathematical community.

11.3.3 General Problem Solving Using Heuristics

Perhaps the most ambitious heuristics project undertaken by Newell, Shaw, and Simon at Carnegie was the *General Problem Solver*. This was a program begun in 1959 designed to simulate a wide range of human problem-solving techniques. The program used the following techniques:

1. Search methods to determine the best strategy
2. Evaluative methods for pattern recognition
3. Performance-improvement mechanisms based on experience
4. Plans for solution

The General Problem Solver was capable of solving the Tower of Hanoi problem. This problem begins with a fixed number of blocks of increasing size on a post. The blocks must be transferred to another post but at no time may a larger block be placed on a smaller one (see Figure 11.3).

Moreover, the General Problem Solver was used to solve brain teasers. For example, consider the brain teaser that focuses on three missionaries and three cannibals on an island with a rowboat big enough to accommodate two people. The objective is to get all six people to the other side, but at no time can a missionary and a cannibal be in

Objective—to place the blocks on another post without ever placing a larger block on a smaller one:

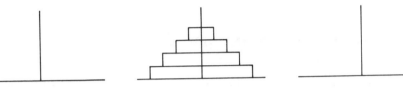

Figure 11.3. Tower of Hanoi problem.

the boat together. The computer, using this General Problem Solver, took 969 seconds to solve the problem.

This program was used on other, even more complex problems and it performed remarkably well. With the use of functional analysis of tasks and "means-end" analysis, the computer was able to handle a wide range of problems.

Despite the specific successes of the problem solver, its developers abandoned the project in 1967. They had hoped to demonstrate that the program simulated human problem solving; that is, it was their aim to demonstrate that theories in psychology would be able to draw on techniques used in the programs. When they saw that there were conceptual difficulties, they decided to pursue other areas of research.

11.4 ROBOTICS

Even before computer power existed, science fiction writers and readers fantasized about robots that would possess some degree of intelligence and could serve people. Such robots have always been depicted as machines with anthropomorphic, or human-like, qualities.

There has been significant research in the area of computerized robots at Stanford University, Stanford Research Institute, and MIT. The objective is to create an entity with human attributes such as sight, speech, perception, movement, and decision-making ability.

These machines can analyze visual patterns using a TV camera. Some have pressure-sensitized "fingers" which have a sense of touch.

Most can move about. Some can analyze speech. All use AI techniques in demonstrating understanding or intelligence.

Aside from the entertainment value of such machines, they can provide very real benefits. Experiments have demonstrated that they can be very effective as tools for handicapped people. They can also be used in military organizations to investigate hostile ground and to serve as mechanical soldiers. You will recall that Chapter 8 discussed robots used in an industrial setting.

11.5 LANGUAGE AND LINGUISTICS

The only way that intelligence can be demonstrated is with the use of some method of communication. Moreover, the ability to understand, the key ingredient of intelligence, requires one to understand language.

Hence the study of AI is integrally related to the study of language. In some colleges, linguistics departments have a course in artificial intelligence. In these colleges, it is believed that the techniques used in AI will shed light on how languages evolve and how they compare with one another. In other schools, linguistics is a subject taught in AI departments. This implies that AI scholars recognize the need to understand language development in order to program machines so that these devices could demonstrate intelligence.

In short, one area of AI research focuses on the study of languages. If a program could be written that is capable of translating from one language to another, the machine could be said to "understand" language. In this context it can be said to demonstrate "intelligence." Translation, however, requires not only mechanical lookup of words, but syntactical conversions and conceptual categorizations of phrases which are very difficult to reduce to a series of mechanical rules.

In the 1960s, researchers had considerable success in writing programs that would produce mechanical dictionaries. Anthony Oettinger at Harvard was the first to produce a Russian-English dictionary by computer.

This initial success led the federal government to invest $20 million in translation research to see if computerized translations of textual material were possible.

Such complex applications in linguistics, however, have not met with similar success. Programming a machine to understand words and idioms is possible, but understanding the syntax or context of a sentence is far more difficult. Consider the following sentence, for example:

> The man frightened the dog with the red fur.

According to the normal rules of grammar, an adjectival clause usually refers to the noun directly preceding it. Using this rule, one would assume that:

1. The man frightened the dog.
2. The dog had red fur.

Sometimes, however, the traditional rules of grammar would need to be superseded by our understanding of the context of a sentence. For example:

> The man frightened the dog with the loud bell.

The referent in this case may not be the dog. For most of us, the sentence would be understood to mean:

1. The man frightened the dog.
2. The man used a loud bell to frighten the dog.

Hence in this instance the traditional rules of grammar would not apply. Our understanding of the context of the sentence must be based on something more comprehensive and less formal than grammatical rules. See Figure 11.4 for an additional illustration.

Machine Translation[a]

In the 1960s there was a big push to use computers to do foreign-language translation. Computers were supplied with a small bilingual dictionary with the corresponding words in the two languages. It soon became apparent that word-for-word translation was virtually useless. The addition of a dictionary of phrases brought only marginal improvement.

These translators can be tested by translating English to Russian and then Russian back to English. Hopefully, one should end up with about the same as one started. Using this method, the maxim, "Out of sight, out of mind" ended up as "The person is blind, and is insane".

Another example was: "The spirit is willing but the flesh is weak." It was translated as "The wine is good but the meat is raw".

Needless to say, computer translation is presently used very little. And it is doubtful that it will be useful in the near future.

[a] Dennie van Tassel, ed., *The Compleat Computer* (*Chicago: SRA*), p. 26.

Figure 11.4.

Understanding the context or construct of a sentence frequently requires an understanding of cultural factors that are implicit in the language. Sentences that use descriptors relating to dress, politics, matters of the economy, and even personality attributes are often not directly translatable into other languages spoken by people in different cultures.

Such difficulties in evaluating a language have implications in areas other than translation. That is, the ability of a machine to communicate conversationally with human beings or to "understand" a given command is also affected by its ability to evaluate language.

Proponents of AI believe that original estimates for effecting such understanding of language were too optimistic and that more time is needed to define all the evaluative tools and rules used in such understanding. Others are not convinced that understanding language is in fact a definable process. These people believe that a machine's ability to converse with human beings and to actually "understand" the English language will always be primitive. Rules will never suffice, they claim, because the process is far too complex and too culturally dependent.

11.6 CYBERNETICS AND OTHER AREAS OF COMPUTER RESEARCH

Artificial intelligence has implications for many other areas of computer research. Cybernetics, for example, is the study of control and communication in machines and in living organisms. The study of control and communication is, of course, very closely related to artificial intelligence. The research fields of cybernetics and AI are therefore integrally related to one another.

More specifically, the field of cybernetics is concerned with the comparative study of the human nervous system, specifically the brain, and computer systems. Cyberneticists believe that biological systems and computer systems have important concepts in common.

Communication theory is another new field that has evolved as a result of the Computer Revolution. Methods used to optimize communication and to minimize noise levels are related to AI as well.

If one objective of artificial intelligence is to program computers so that they exhibit some "intelligence," then CAI, computer-assisted instruction, could certainly make use of AI techniques. That is, using such techniques a computer can be programmed to function as an idealized tutor. It can evaluate student answers, analyze student errors, and, on the basis of that analysis, provide alternative teaching techniques.

In short, any area of computer research that has as its goal the programming of a machine to make reasonable decisions could benefit from techniques used in artificial intelligence.

11.7 ARTIFICIAL INTELLIGENCE: THE LARGER ISSUES

Clearly, the controversies surrounding artificial intelligence relate to the larger issues that humanists and technocrats have been debating since the Industrial Revolution.

To many, AI techniques represent the fulfillment of the "Frankenstein" image depicted by Mary Shelley over 150 years ago. A machine that simulates human behavior or thought, like Frankenstein or R2D2 of *Star Wars*, represents a giant step toward dehumanizing human beings.

AI proponents, on the other hand, tend to believe in a *mechanistic* universe—a universe in which all matter can be explained in terms of computable, mechanical entities. For these people, the distinctions made by humanists between mind and body have no reality. The mind is just another entity that can be explained in computable terms.

To shed additional light on the controversies surrounding artificial intelligence, we will consider two hotly debated aspects of AI.

11.7.1 Do AI Techniques Provide Machines with the Capability to "Learn"?

AI techniques frequently contain routines that can modify the problem-solving ability of a machine through experience. If, for example, a given chess-playing routine causes the computer to lose the game, it "learns" from this mistake and never makes the same sequence of moves again.

In this context, machines do indeed "learn." Moreover, it is in this context that a machine can be said to respond more cleverly or "intelligently" than the persons who programmed it.

11.7.2 Can Machines Simulate Human Behavior?

To demonstrate the ability of a machine to communicate in conversational English, Joseph Weizenbaum of MIT wrote a program called ELIZA. The purpose of this program was not only to simulate human responses, but to provide some insight into language analysis.

Weizenbaum stated that, like Eliza of Pygmalion fame, a machine could be taught to speak increasingly well.

Weizenbaum describes the techniques used by ELIZA as follows:

> I gave ELIZA a script designed to permit it to play (I should really say parody) the role of a Rogerian psychotherapist engaged in an initial interview with a patient. The Rogerian psychotherapist is really easy to imitate because much of his technique consists of drawing his patient out by reflecting the patient's statements back to him.[1]

The program consists of a series of "open" questions commonly used by psychologists. These questions simply ask users to expand on various responses, then key words are selected from these responses to ask more specific questions, and so on.

> Men are all alike.
> IN WHAT WAY?
> They're always bugging us about something or other.
> CAN YOU THINK OF A SPECIFIC EXAMPLE?
> Well, my boyfriend made me come here.
> YOUR BOYFRIEND MADE YOU COME HERE?
> He says I'm depressed much of the time.
> I AM SORRY TO HEAR YOU ARE DEPRESSED.
> It's true. I am unhappy.
> DO YOU THINK COMING HERE WILL HELP YOU NOT TO BE UNHAPPY?
> I need some help, that much seems certain.
> WHAT WOULD IT MEAN TO YOU IF YOU GOT SOME HELP?
> Perhaps I could learn to get along with my mother.
> TELL ME MORE ABOUT YOUR FAMILY.
> My mother takes care of me.
> WHO ELSE IN YOUR FAMILY TAKES CARE OF YOU?[2]

Note that it was Weizenbaum's purpose to demonstrate a conversational program using techniques employed by psychotherapists. Much to his own amazement, however, many people—including practicing psychologists—regarded ELIZA as an automated psychotherapist! Students and research assistants would sit at a terminal and communicate with ELIZA on an emotional and personal level, sometimes for hours. Psychotherapists wrote journal articles suggesting ways in which the program could be improved. Moreover, many people claimed ELIZA demonstrated that a machine could indeed provide a general solution to natural language communication.

[1]Reprinted with permission from Joseph Weizenbaum, *Computer Power and Human Reason* (San Francisco: W. J. Freeman), p. 4.

[2]Reprinted with permission from Joseph Weizenbaum, *Computer Power and Human Reason* (San Francisco: W. J. Freeman), p. 4.

Rather than basking in all this glory, Weizenbaum was outraged at the ease with which people were willing to accept a machine as a surrogate human being. He wrote a book entitled *Computer Power and Human Reason* in which he expressed his indignation at this turn of events:

1. Simulated psychotherapist:

    A number of practicing psychologists seriously believed the DOCTOR [ELIZA] computer program could grow into a nearly complete automatic form of psychotherapy. . . . There are undoubtedly many techniques to facilitate the therapist's imaginative projection into the patient's inner life. But that it was possible for even one practicing psychologist to advocate that this crucial component of the therapeutic process be entirely supplanted by pure technology—that I had not imagined. . . .

    What can the psychologist's image of his patient be when he sees himself as a therapist, not as an engaged human being acting as a healer, but as an information processor following rules, etc.

2. On human interaction:

    I was startled to see how quickly and how very deeply people conversing with DOCTOR became emotionally involved with the computer and how unequivocally they anthropomorphized it.

3. On natural language:

    Another widespread, and to me surprising, reaction to the ELIZA program was the spread of a belief that it demonstrated a general solution to the problem of computer understanding of natural language. In my paper, I had tried to say that no general solution to the problem was possible, that language is understood only in contextual frameworks.

Weizenbaum concluded that even well-educated people are all too willing to accept technology without even understanding it:

> The reaction to ELIZA showed me more vividly than anything I had seen hitherto the enormously exaggerated attributes an even well-educated audience is capable of making, even striving to make, to a technology it does not understand.[1]

Weizenbaum, then, is critical of those who develop programs to simulate human behavior. He is also critical of those who accept this research and its implications without questioning. Such criticisms have even greater weight than those leveled by humanists, since

---

[1] Reprinted with permission from Joseph Weizenbaum, *Computer Power and Human Reason* (San Francisco: W. J. Freeman), p. 4.

Weizenbaum himself is an AI pioneer. He is not calling for an end to AI research, just a more realistic appraisal of its goals, objectives, and perspective.

11.7.3 Is the Human Brain a Computing Machine?

Many scientists have claimed that the computer itself operates like a human brain. John von Neumann, an extremely important figure in the early history of computing, stated the following:

> The neuron transmits an impulse . . . the nerve impulse seems in the main to be an all-or-none affair comparable to a binary digit.[1]

If, in fact, a computer functions like the human brain, then the implications of artificial intelligence and cybernetics for psychology would be so profound as to effect a revolution in its own right. Indeed, some AI pioneers make the claim that computer science, with the use of AI, will result in a new understanding of the human mind:

> Computer science has brought a flood of such ideas, well defined and experimentally implemented, for thinking about thinking, only a fraction of them have distinguishable representatives in traditional psychology. . . . But just as astronomy succeeded astrology, following Kepler's discovery of planetary regularities, the discovery of these many principles in empirical explorations of intellectual processes in machines should lead to a science eventually.[2]

Hubert Dreyfus, a philosopher, attempts to refute the claims of AI that machines can simulate human behavior:

> In playing games such as chess, in solving complex problems, and in using language metaphorically, humans do not seem to be following strict rules. On the contrary, they seem to be using global perceptual organization, making pragmatic distinctions between essential and inessential operations appealing to paradigm cases and using a shared sense of the situation to get their meanings across.[3]

But even Dreyfus, in a rare moment of uncertainty, hedges:

---

[1] John von Neumann, "The General and Logical Theory of Automata," reprinted in *The World of Mathematics*, ed. James R. Newman (New York: Simon and Schuster), p. 2077.

[2] M. Minsky, and S. Papert, *Artificial Intelligence Progress Report* (Cambridge, MA: MIT), p. 34.

[3] Hubert Dreyfus, *What Computers Can't Do: A Critique of Artificial Reason* (New York: Harper & Row), p. 5.

Of course, all this orderly but apparently nonrulelike activity might nonetheless be the result of unconsciously following rules.[1]

Weizenbaum, however, is much more emphatic in his claim that the human brain is definitely not a computer:

> Whatever else a brain may be it most certainly is *not* a digital computer. . . . We are today about as far from building a computer modelled on the human brain as Archimedes was from building an atom bomb.

But, here again, Weizenbaum does not suggest that we abandon studies in this field, just that we keep such studies in perspective. It may be that in some ways the human brain and a computer are comparable and that it will enhance our understanding of both to explore these similarities. The fault lies in assuming that the human brain is *nothing more than* a computer:

> I will . . . try to maintain the position that there is nothing wrong with viewing man as an information processor nor with attempting to understand him from that perspective, providing, however, that we never act as though any single perspective can comprehend the whole man.
>
> Seeing man as an information processing system does not in itself dehumanize him, and may well contribute to his humanity in that it may lead him to a deeper understanding of one specific aspect of his human nature.[2]

The arguments described above, when taken to their logical conclusion, really address the question of whether a human being is something separate and apart from all other entities in the universe. There are those who believe that computers can be used to understand human thought processes and that those thought processes are subject to a traditional natural law which has yet to be discovered. In a recent article, Herbert Simon took this position, indicating that his belief is really part of a larger issue surrounding the human-machine controversy:

> What the computer and progress in artificial intelligence challenge is an ethic that rests on man's apartness from the rest of nature. An alternative ethic, of course, views man as a part of nature, governed by natural law, subject to the forces of gravity and the demands of his body. The debate about AI and the simulation of man's thinking is, in considerable part, a confrontation of these two views of man's

[1] Hubert Dreyfus, *What Computers Can't Do: A Critique of Artificial Reason* (New York: Harper & Row), p. 5.

[2] Reprinted with permission from Joseph Weizenbaum, *Computer Power and Human Reason* (San Francisco: W. J. Freeman), p. 140.

place in the universe. It is a new chapter in the vitalism-mechanism controversy.[1]

Opponents of AI research, as well as those who support it but believe in some measure of control, are really speaking the language of humanists:

> Ultimately a line dividing human and machine intelligence must be drawn. If there is no such line, then advocates of computerized psychotherapy may be merely heralds of an age in which man has finally been recognized as nothing but a clockwork.[2]

In short, most people would agree that artificial intelligence has achieved a considerable degree of success in the past two decades. The disagreement that exists seems to focus on the significance of these achievements. Some supporters of AI believe that the techniques that have been developed contribute to our understanding of the human mind. Others do not believe that this is the case; for them, human intelligence is something that *cannot and should not* be simulated by machines.

11.8   COMPUTERS IN THE SCIENCES: A GENERAL OVERVIEW

Thus far, we have considered various scientific uses of computers. That is, we have focused on computers in the health and medical fields in Chapter 10 and in artificial intelligence in this chapter.

There are, of course, numerous scientific areas in which computers have been effective over the last four decades. Computers and calculators were introduced initially because they could perform intricate, repetitive arithmetic operations with a high degree of accuracy. This was required by scientists who needed astronomical tables and by the military, which needed ballistics tables.

The use of the computer in the sciences falls into two categories: (1) passive—as a scientific instrument that can be used to test a hypothesis; that is, to assist in the experimental process, or (2) active—as an integral piece of scientific equipment without which the scientific study could not be performed.

---

[1] H. A. Simon, "What Computers Mean for Man and Society," *Science*, Vol. 195, p. 986.

[2] Reprinted with permission from Joseph Weizenbaum, *Computer Power and Human Reason* (San Francisco: W. J. Freeman), p. 8.

11.8.1 Passive Role

As a scientific instrument used to test a hypothesis or to assist in the experimental process, the computer sometimes functions as a "number cruncher"—a device that can operate on numerical data quickly and accurately and produce statistical analysis as necessary (see Figure 11.5).

There are numerous scientific areas in the physical, chemical, and biological sciences in which computers are used to facilitate the experimental process.

11.8.2 Active Role

In some instances, the computer as a number cruncher enables scientists to conduct experiments and perform functions that would not otherwise be possible.

The space program, for example, would not have been conceivable without the use of computers to simulate space conditions in the experimental stage and to monitor each activity once the program was executed. It would have been too costly, labor intensive, and risky to have proceeded without computers (see Figure 11.6).

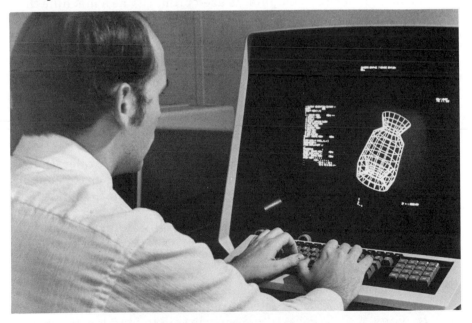

Figure 11.5. A program allows engineers to create structural analysis models, such as this rocket housing, in less than one hour, compared with up to 10 days required using manual methods.

Figure 11.6. Space shuttle launches are conducted by personnel using the consoles shown.

Thus, even when a computer is used primarily as a machine that operates on voluminous data, it can play an active role in the sciences. Quantitative results in an experiment may produce qualitative results in the sciences.

Similar achievements have been made in chemistry with the use of the computer, specifically in X-ray crystallography. Computers have been used to determine the structure of protein molecules. Here, computational power was absolutely essential to analyze crystallographic data. Recombinant DNA studies also rely heavily on computers to simulate molecular structures.

Computers have been used similarly in petroleum exploration to assist in determining the location of subterranean petroleum or natural gas. While at sea, a ship generates a series of sharp sounds. The seismic disturbances which travel down through the water are transmitted as digital signals to a computer. From this data, the computer can assist in determining the probability of a subterranean petroleum or natural gas find.

Computers have also been used to simulate various experiments where the actual testing might be dangerous. Thermonuclear fusion experiments have been conducted through simulation.

In many of these cases a computer is said to function as a **black box**, capable of performing a variety of functions. In these instances, the computer is simply fed the mathematical formulas and, with a program, used to produce the necessary results.

KEY TERMS

Artificial intelligence (AI)
Computer-assisted instruction (CAI)
Cybernetics
ELIZA
General Problem Solver
Heuristics
Linguistics
Mechanistic view
Simulation
Turing, Alan
Turing test
von Neumann, John
Weizenbaum, Joseph

REVIEW QUESTIONS

1. What is meant by artificial intelligence?
2. What are some of the major criticisms of AI research?
3. What did Alan Turing suggest to characterize machine "intelligence"?
4. What is meant by heuristic programming?
5. What are some of the applications for which heuristic programming has been used?
6. What problems have been encountered in writing programs to perform translation of one language into another?
7. What is cybernetics?
8. What is meant when it is said that AI proponents tend to believe in a mechanistic universe?
9. What is the real significance of Joseph Weizenbaum's program called ELIZA? Why was Weizenbaum outraged at the program's success?
10. What arguments can be made for and against the proposition that machines can simulate human behavior?

DISCUSSION QUESTIONS

1. What is the difference between an algorithm and a heuristic?
2. Do you think computers will be successful in the future in translating texts? Explain.
3. Do you believe that artificial intelligence research should be supported by government agencies? Explain your answer.

4. What are some of the similarities between a digital computer and the brain? What are some of the differences?
5. Do you think that Turing's test is adequate for determining whether a computer actually "thinks"?
6. Provide a definition of intelligence. Do you think a computer can be programmed to be "intelligent" according to your definition?
7. Why is a computer sometimes referred to as a "black box"?

APPLICATION

Consider the application below and then answer the questions that follow it.

Down to Earth[a]

Prospector, a computer geologist, can match exploration data against known deposits of metallic ores, find the best drilling sites advise what additional data are needed to verify its conclusions, and even explain its "reasoning," according to SRI International.

Consisting of sophisticated computer models which currently encode information concerning nine classes of ore deposits, Prospector contains in memory 400 rock and mineral terms that link information about a possible ore deposit with 900 rules for making decisions.

While more models must be developed and encoded to span the spectrum of ore deposits of economic interest, Prospector demonstrates that a field geologist, exploring a site with such a computer-based consultant, could determine such things as: which model best fits the available field data; where the most favorable deposit sites are; what additional data would be most helpful in reaching firmer conclusions; and, what are the bases for these conclusions and recommendations.

These computer models were described in a paper entitled "Rule-Based Modeling of Ore Deposits for Mineral Exploration," presented at the American Association for the Advancement of Science meeting in San Francisco by two SRI International researchers, Richard O. Duda and Peter E. Hart. The presentation was based on studies for the U.S. Geological Survey and the National Science Foundation, conducted by Duda, Hart and other scientists and engineers.

Their studies developed models which can organize information on mineralization and other geological data into coherent patterns. These models aid in the diagnosis of the existing data and employ both probabilistic and logical reasoning procedures to determine how the information and hypotheses are related.

[a] *Personal Computing*, Apr. 1980, p. 14. Reprinted with permission.

Application Questions

1. Explain the term "computer models" as used here.
2. Explain how these models are used.

Computers
and the
consumer

12.1 POINT-OF-SALE SYSTEMS

One main area of computer utilization that directly affects the consumer is **point-of-sale** (POS) **systems**. Broadly stated, this is the use of computers in retail establishments to enter data at the actual point where a sale is transacted.

There are numerous manufacturers of POS systems and a wide variety of devices, but the concepts employed are very similar. There are three main areas of applications:

Three Main POS Applications

1. *Supermarkets*: mainly for inventory control and rapid cash transaction reporting
2. *Department stores:* mainly for inventory control, transaction reporting, and charge or credit accounting
3. *Fast-food establishments:* mainly for rapid cash-transaction reporting

---

Both supermarkets and fast-food establishments depend primarily on cash transactions; hence in these systems, charge account recording is not a consideration. Rather, a POS terminal serves as an automatic cash register which can perform a variety of operations in addition to tabulating sales, such as inventory control and automatic data recording. There are currently about 17,000 users of this type of POS system (see Figure 12.1).

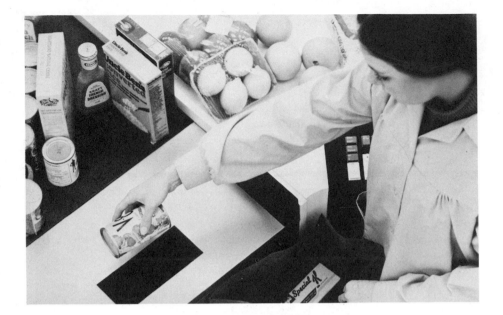

Figure 12.1. Supermarket POS system.

Figure 12.2. Department store POS system.

In department stores, POS systems have, as their main objective, charge account recording. Other point-of-sale features are, of course, also available (see Figure 12.2).

12.1.1   Types of POS Systems

There are several varieties of POS systems, each with distinct features:

12.1.1.1   On-line POS System

1. With minicomputers in a distributed data processing environment (see Figure 12.3):
    a. Automatic registers at each point of sale.
    b. Data is automatically transmitted to a minicomputer within the store for formatting, editing, and verification.
    c. Each store's mini is linked to a mainframe at a central location for master file updating, inquiry, and reporting.
    d. Traditional terminals are available for each store to obtain responses to inquiries and for reporting to management.
2. Centralized POS system (see Figure 12.4):
    a. Automatic registers at each point of sale.
    b. Data is automatically transmitted via telecommunications lines to a remote CPU.
    c. Traditional terminals are available for inquiry and reporting.

12.1.1.2   Batch POS System
(Figure 12.5)

1. Automatic registers at each point of sale.
2. Off-line storage of data from these registers in the form of tape cassettes or floppy disks.
3. Off-line storage media are processed periodically to update master files and produce required reports.

12.1.2   POS Terminals

Electronic cash registers or POS terminals are devices that function like traditional cash registers, except that they have greater capability and can perform many tasks automatically (see Figure 12.2). The functions of these POS terminals are:

Functions of an Electronic Cash Register

Perform automatic extensions (unit price × number of items)
Determine the tax for all taxable items
Determine discounts
Adjust for coupons
Void transactions
Process credits or returns

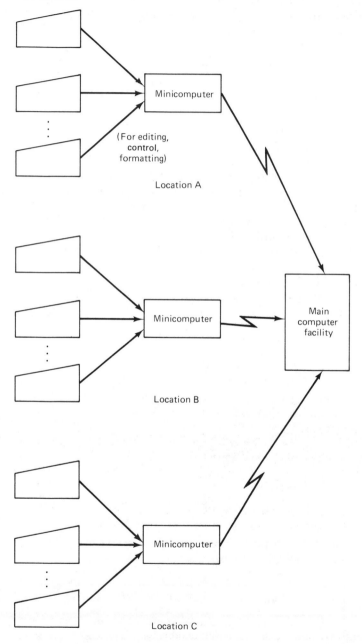

POS terminals

Minicomputer

(For editing,
control,
formatting)

Location A

Minicomputer

Location B

Minicomputer

Location C

Main
computer
facility

Figure 12.3. On-line distributed POS system.

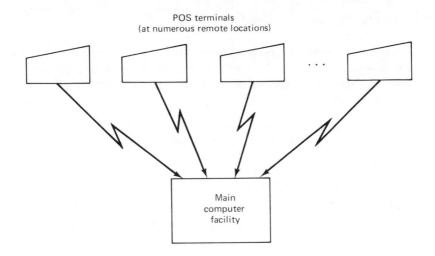

POS terminals
(at numerous remote locations)

Main
computer
facility

Figure 12.4. On-line centralized POS system.

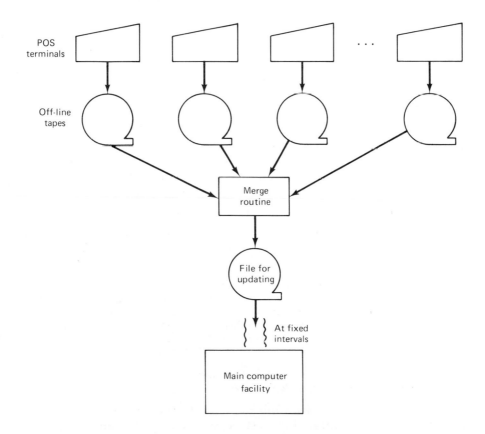

POS
terminals

Off-line
tapes

Merge
routine

File for
updating

At fixed
intervals

Main computer
facility

Figure 12.5. Batch POS system.

In addition, these POS terminals can store all the data recorded in a machine-readable form such as tape or disk, or they can immediately transmit the data to a mainframe for on-line file updating.

Each POS terminal:

1. Minimizes the risk of operator errors
2. Serves as a data-entry device for computer processing

12.1.2.1 On-line Processing with the Use of POS Terminals

When POS terminals are used with on-line systems, either in a distributed environment or in a traditional centralized organization, there are numerous benefits:

POS Terminals with On-line Systems
1. Inventory and sales data are automatically updated on the master files as items are purchased or returned.
2. Store managers and central administration can inquire about the status of inventory and make changes to stock items as necessary.
3. Bank checks can be verified through a central clearing file at the store or even at a bank, if there is a link between the store and the bank. (See the next section.)
4. Where charge accounts exist, POS terminals can perform on-line verification of each transaction to make certain that the charge card is valid and that the credit amount has not been exceeded.

As noted, an on-line system can use a distributed network with a mini at each location or simply have POS terminals at each remote location linked to a central computer. The use of minis, although incurring the cost of an additional and often expensive piece of equipment, has the following advantages:

Advantages of Minis for POS Systems
1. The store's transactions are processed through one central device; thus they can be edited, tallied, and controlled more stringently.
2. Communication costs are reduced since the mini serves in a network as the *only* device that communicates with the mainframe. Rather than having 30 or 40 POS terminals using communication lines, we have one mini that coordinates the transfer of data from all the terminals to the mainframe.

12.1.2.2 Batch Processing with the Use of POS Terminals

POS terminals use electronic devices; this does *not* mean, however, that data is being entered directly into a CPU. The terminals may simply be accumulating the transaction data on tape or disk and storing it for future processing.

Devices that perform check or credit verification may simply scan a tape that is entered once a day, for example. If this is the case, the POS terminal is operating in an off-line environment. It can perform credit checks against files that are current only through the previous updating cycle.

In an off-line system, a credit card lost today would not be registered by the system until the next updating cycle. Thus you may find that notification of loss means that *beginning the following day,* the store will no longer honor the card.

Off-line systems, then, clearly have their disadvantages—they are not updated directly. The main advantage is, of course, cost. It is much cheaper to update a master file once a day, usually during off-hours when communication costs are reduced and when a steady stream of data maximizes the efficient use of the CPU.

Each department store or supermarket must determine which system is cost-effective. If inventories can be adequately adjusted once a day, for example, without any major problems, then an off-line POS system would be preferable. If, however, out-of-stock conditions plague the store resulting in a loss of sales and customers, an on-line system might prove to be more cost-effective.

Similarly, suppose a department store loses, for example, $10,000 per day from illegal use of stolen credit cards or from people exceeding their credit limits. It may want to implement an on-line POS system that costs $50,000 per week; this may prove to be cost-effective.

12.1.3 How Supermarket Products Are Marked for POS Systems

There are two methods that can be used for entering data into a POS system: manual and automatic. The manual method requires the cashier to identify the item by depressing several keys indicating a code and to enter the price of the item. In a supermarket, this process requires the price to be stamped on each individual item.

Clearly, automatic devices that read coded item markings on the product and "look up" their prices in stored tables would increase the efficiency of operation.

In supermarkets, there has been a movement since 1973 to have product manufacturers stamp on each item a special code called a Universal Product Code (UPC) (see Figure 12.6). Currently, 90% of all manufacturers have implemented the technique of stamping a UPC on each item to be sold. There are devices that can read the UPC and look up the prices electronically. This means that the individual pricing of each product is unnecessary.

As you see from the illustration and as you can verify by examining virtually any supermarket item, the UPC consists of a

Figure 12.6. Sample Universal Product Code.

series of bars of differing widths with different spacing between them. Most items have 10 bars; the first five identify the manufacturer and the last five identify the product.

If the UPC can be read by a POS terminal, there is no need for a cashier to enter a product code. Moreover, if the terminal can "look up" the price of each item in a table, there is no necessity for the cashier to key in prices either. This reduces the risk of errors and increases efficiency. It also enables stores to run sales or increase prices without having to manually change the price of each item on the shelf.

There are devices available that can automatically read this

Figure 12.7. System that uses a bar code reader to record each order automatically as it is filled, and to update inventory and accounts receivable files.

Universal Product Code. Some are wand devices which the cashier simply passes over the UPC to record the item purchased (see Figure 12.7). There are also laser beam devices which use an electric eye mechanism for reading the Universal Product Code (see Figure 12.1).

Both types of entry devices (wand and laser beam devices) are used in many supermarkets and other retail stores. They do, however, need to be perfected. In some cases, there is a 10 to 20% rejection rate, which means that because of irregularities in the label, the automatic device will not read properly; in these instances, the cashier assumes the traditional role of entering data by depressing keys on the register.

When using automatic devices for data entry to point-of-sale terminals, the prices may be stored off-line on a cassette or floppy disk, or the system can look up prices in an on-line mode. The on-line mode enables immediate updating of prices by store managers.

Initially, there was significant consumer resistance to point-of-sale systems. Automatic data entry using UPC meant that there was no need to record individual prices on each item. Since the need to stamp each item was expensive and time consuming, the temptation for stores to eliminate individual pricing was great. Consumers objected to that rather strongly. Supermarkets and discount stores have been sensitive to this objection and have continued to mark the prices on each item. It should be noted that several states have already passed legislation requiring price stamping. But with the increasing avail-

Figure 12.8.   Portable bar code reader.

ability of bar code readers at very low costs, it will be possible for consumers to use their own individual hand-held devices to read the UPC; using a tape or disk supplied by the store they can obtain readouts of all prices without the need for individual pricing (see Figure 12.8). Stores maintain that elimination of item pricing will result in substantial savings that could then be passed on to the consumer.

To minimize consumer resistance, POS terminals have swivel displays which can be easily seen by the customer at the checkout counter. Some POS terminals have dual readouts, where one can be viewed by the customer and one by the cashier. These readouts are optional on most POS terminals. Hence you will occasionally find a thrifty retailer who is so unconcerned about consumer acceptance that he or she does not make a readout visible to the consumer.

The success of the Universal Product Code as a bar code and the availability of bar code readers has prompted other industries to adopt modified versions for their own purposes. Manufacturing plants, as well as department stores, use modified bar codes and accompanying readers to identify their products. These bar code readers can determine from the code:

Vendor
Style
Color
Size
Department
Store
Price

The use of POS systems in supermarkets, department stores, and fast-food chains has the added advantage of being able to supply management with summary and detail reports. Since data from all points of sale can be collected and processed very quickly, reports containing the following data can be supplied whenever desired:

Reports Available on Demand from POS Systems
Cash flow patterns
Salesperson totals
Inventory control
New-item tracking
Pattern on returns
Analysis of promotions and advertisements
Labor scheduling

In addition, automatic purchase ordering, billing, payroll, and other traditional business functions can be performed automatically.

The main obstacle to POS terminals and POS systems in many

retail establishments is, of course, cost. The terminal itself costs, on the average, between $3000 and $3500 and the wands for reading the Universal Product Code cost about $300. Since one terminal is required at *each* point of sale and a central computer is to be used as well, the cost is sometimes prohibitive. But if the present trend continues, with hardware costs decreasing over time and labor costs on the rise, more and more retail establishments will find POS systems cost-effective.

As for optional features, many POS systems have emergency backup batteries. If a retail establishment depends entirely on its point-of-sale terminals for data entry, a blackout or even a reduction in power might mean a virtual shutdown of operations. To eliminate the risks, many POS terminals come with a battery or generator which can operate for several hours.

Many POS terminals have also been designed so that they are compatible with the anticipated banking industry's electronic funds transfer systems, which permit automatic flow of information between store and bank. We discuss this further in the next section.

Figure 12.9 describes the success of one fast-food POS system.

12.2 ELECTRONIC FUNDS TRANSFER SYSTEMS

A second major area of computer utilization that directly affects the consumer is electronic funds transfer (EFT) systems. Broadly stated, this is the use of computers in banks to enter data from the actual point

---

Hungry? System Orders Food 37 Seconds Faster[a]

A [California] statewide fast food restaurant chain is processing orders 37 seconds faster than it did mechanically, thanks to a mini-computer-based control and communications system.

The system allows each order for food to be automatically transmitted from the cashier's terminal to the cook's printer in the kitchen, eliminating the need for handwriting orders or handcarrying those orders to the kitchen.

With each store selling about 1,000 hamburgers, 700 orders of French fries and 1,500 soft drinks to about 800 customers every day, the time saved means more customers served, fewer cashiers needed at the stations and more personnel in the kitchen.

The system . . . can also figure the price per hamburger as well as for all other items on the menu to determine production costs and profit margins. When there is a price change or additional program modification, central headquarters mails new disks to the stores.

Every morning an IBM Series/1 minicomputer with 128K of memory located at the chain's headquarters polls the store's computers for sales and inventory statistics for later processing.

[a]Marguerite Zientara, *Computerworld*. Copyright 1980 by CW Communications/Inc., Framingham, MA 01701. Reprinted with permission.

Figure 12.9.

where a transaction is made, and to update the banking records on a regular basis.

EFT systems can operate (1) within a single branch, (2) in a distributed network linking the transactions of all branch offices for a large bank, and (3) in conjunction with point-of-sale systems to automatically transfer funds from a customer's bank account when a purchase is made. We begin by focusing on EFT systems that operate within the banking industry, independent of point-of-sale interaction.

EFT systems make use of computer equipment in a manner similar to POS systems.

12.2.1 Types of EFT Systems

12.2.1.1 On-line EFT Systems

1. With minicomputers in a distributed data processing environment:
   a. Either automatic teller machines are used at each point of transaction or a teller with a touch-tone phone keys in the appropriate data
   b. Data is automatically transmitted to a minicomputer within the bank for performing the appropriate arithmetic, formatting, editing, and verification
   c. Each branch office's mini is linked to a CPU at the main office for master file updating, inquiry, and reporting
   d. Standard terminals are available for each branch to obtain responses to inquiries and for reporting to management
2. Centralized EFT system:
   a. Either automatic teller machines are used at each point of transaction or a teller with a touch-tone telephone keys in the appropriate data
   b. Data is automatically transmitted via telecommunication lines to a remote CPU
   c. Traditional terminals are available at each branch for inquiry and reporting

12.2.1.2 Batch EFT Systems

1. Automatic teller machines are used or a teller with a touch-tone phone keys in data at each point of transaction
2. Data from these registers is stored off-line on floppy disks or tape cassettes
3. Off-line storage media are processed periodically to update master files and produce required reports

Because of the delay in processing with a batch system, on-line EFT systems are far more prevalent.

12.2.2 Basic Concepts of EFT

Electronic funds transfer (EFT) is a system for electronically recording debits and credits in financial accounts. Major EFT applications that are currently being developed include:

Figure 12.10. Automatic teller machine.

1. *The Use of Automatic Teller Machines (ATMs) to Facilitate Deposits and Withdrawals from Bank Accounts* (see Figure 12.10). There are approximately 9500 of the EFT terminals in use today. They can provide 24-hour banking service. Typically, an ATM is located in the lobby of a bank. If a customer wishes to withdraw cash, for example, he or she inserts a plastic bank identification card into the terminal and keys in a personal identification code. Once the computer verifies this data, it displays a message on the terminal screen directing the customer to indicate the type of transaction (withdrawal, in this case) and the amount involved. After this data is entered, the computer ascertains if there are sufficient funds in the account. If there are, the money is automatically supplied to the customer by special money-handling equipment, together with a receipt indicating the details of the transaction (see Figure 12.11).

2. *The Use of EFT Terminals for Point-of-Sale (POS) Operations.* This typically involves the immediate electronic transfer of money at the point at which a sale occurs. To pay for merchandise in a store, for example, a customer presents his or her bank card, typically referred to as a "debit card," to the salesperson. This card is inserted into an EFT terminal that has a direct link to the customer's bank account (see Figure 12.12). The customer ordinarily keys in his or her personal identification code. If there are sufficient funds in the customer's account, they are transferred electronically at that time to the store's

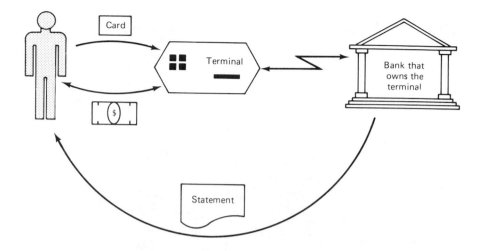

Figure 12.11.   Remote banking.

bank account. This is unlike existing bank credit cards in that the transaction results in an immediate and automatic debit to the customer's existing account and an automatic credit to the store's account.

3. *Preauthorized Banking.*   This EFT system involves deposits and payments that are made electronically. Typical applications include:

a.   The direct deposit of funds, such as salary, social security payments, and stock dividends, to an individual's bank account
b.   The direct payment by the bank of regular expenses, such as mortgage and car payments
c.   The use of a touch-tone telephone to authorize a bank to pay certain bills directly or to transfer money from one bank account to another

4. *Automated Clearinghouse Procedures.*   This application uses an electronic network to facilitate the exchange of funds among financial institutions that are involved with the check-clearing process. Typically, these procedures can take many days and result in numerous exchanges of paper.

5. *Check Guarantee Services.*   This enables a retail establishment to have direct communication with the customer's bank for check-cashing purposes. The bank guarantees the check that is used to pay for goods and services if, of course, there are sufficient funds in the account.

There are, then, numerous services that can be obtained in an EFT system.

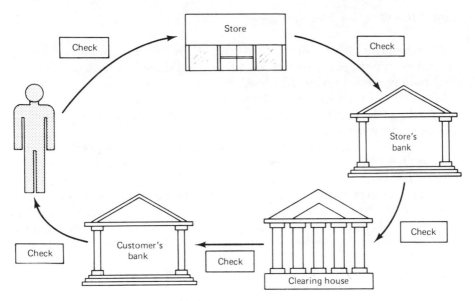

(a) Present point-of-sale check cycle

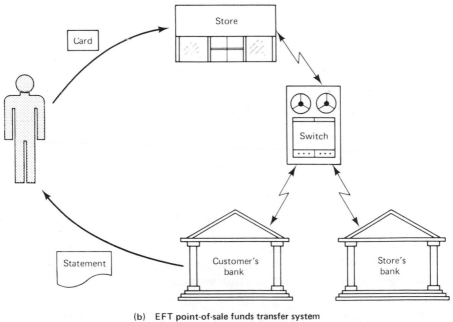

(b) EFT point-of-sale funds transfer system
using a central switch

Figure 12.12.   Payment by a consumer using (a) a check, and (b) an
EFT system with a central switch. (Courtesy of "Audit Considerations in
Electric Funds Transfer Systems," American Institute of Certified Public
Accountants. Copyright by the American Institute of Certified Public
Accountants, Inc.)

When the idea for electronic funds transfer was conceived, many financial experts, as well as computer professionals, predicted that the technology would ultimately lead to a cashless and checkless society. They believed that EFT would have even more profound effects on the economy and on an individual's purchase power than the introduction of the credit card in the 1950s.

But for many reasons which we will discuss, this prediction has not yet been borne out. There are, in fact, many who now believe that EFT will never have the profound effect on the economy once predicted.

It is interesting to note that despite the current uses of electronic banking, the financial system in this country relies more heavily today on cash and checks than in the past. Recent studies have revealed the following facts about cash and check transactions in the United States:

1. The volume of checks grows at an annual rate of approximately 7% each year.
2. Currency in circulation expands at a rate of approximately 8% each year.
3. There are approximately eight times as many cash transactions as there are check transactions.
4. There are approximately six times as many check transactions as credit card transactions.
5. Over 90% of financial transactions are currently conducted by check.

A main objective of EFT is to reduce the costs associated with cash and check transactions. In the United States alone, over 100,000,000 checks are processed daily; most of these are processed manually or with the use of MICR (magnetic ink character recognition) reader-sorters. The expectation is that the use of electronic devices together with bank cards will reduce the amount of paper that must be handled and will also reduce the need for manual intervention.

There is, however, very little data comparing the costs of the various alternative methods of payment, such as cash, checks, credit cards, and EFT transactions. Moreover, it is extremely difficult to predict the data communications cost that would be associated with the automatic transfer of funds from one account to another, not to mention the computer costs.

Thus the efforts under way to implement EFT systems have not really been accompanied by definitive cost studies; more on this later.

12.2.3 Major Social Issues Concerning EFT

Many issues have emerged in connection with the social consequences of EFT. In addition to questions about cost justification, issues such as privacy, security, and consumer acceptance have generated much debate about the efficacy of these systems. In recognition of the widespread controversy, the U.S. Congress, in 1974, created a two-year National Commission on EFT. Its task was to study and recommend appropriate legislative action and an administrative policy concerning the development of EFT systems throughout the country. The Commission, in its final report in October 1977, detailed many of the main concerns and problems that required resolution. Yet, to date, many of the policy issues that it raised have still not been resolved.

Over the years, several diverse philosophical approaches have been suggested for consideration by policymakers attempting to provide direction for EFT development:

1. The "free enterprise" approach takes the position that the most important factor in an EFT system is its profitability to the organizations that operate or utilize the system. Profitability is of more consequence to the overall success of any such system than is the social issue of privacy.
2. The "libertarian" approach takes the position that the most important criterion to be considered in the development of EFT systems is the effect on the individual. If an EFT system will interfere with the individual's right to privacy, for example, it should not be developed. The primary consideration for such policymakers is the benefit that accrues to the individual.
3. Another view takes the approach that the needs of government are paramount. The most important consideration in the development of EFT systems is how well government functions will be served. The government's need to access personal data in an EFT data base, for example, would be a major concern.
4. A fourth view suggests that *any* EFT system would involve some degree of bureaucratic control or monitoring and would by its very nature present a potential threat to privacy and liberty. Such a threat, according to this view, is totally unacceptable.

12.2.3.1   Privacy

As discussed above, there are many people who view EFT as a serious threat to privacy. An electronic system that maintains detailed records on an individual's spending patterns and activities has the potential for abuse by the government and other parties. With such a system, it is possible to maintain surveillance of any person by keeping records on where he or she shops, what is purchased, and so on.

A key issue here revolves around how the concept of privacy is actually to be defined. This problem was pointed out in a study entitled "Value Choices in Electronic Funds Transfer Policy" that was submitted to the Domestic Council Committee on the Right of Privacy. How are we, for example, to determine what records we are morally, ethically, and legally entitled to maintain and what records we should not maintain?

[T]he very notion of privacy is an evaluative concept. It is misleading to discuss the privacy afforded by a data system as an objective fact, like the core capacity of a computer or the number of records in a file. No concept of privacy is meaningful without some specification of the values which one supposes it to entail. We speak of the invasion of privacy, for example, as the *unwarranted* collection or examination of personal data, or as the *unjustified* intrusion of public scrutiny into certain *inappropriate* areas of personal life. Such terminology assumes some notion of what intrusions *are* justified or what collections of data *are* warranted—and these, of course, are value questions. It would be a mistake to assume that these questions are easy to resolve, or that all informed persons would resolve them in the same way.

Many other issues relating to privacy have been raised. For example, who will be able to legitimately gain access to EFT data? Will the Internal Revenue Service be able to review EFT records of particular individuals to check the validity of income tax returns? Will welfare agencies, for example, be able to monitor the activities of welfare recipients to ascertain if government funds are being used to purchase goods considered to be unnecessary luxuries by the agencies?

Because EFT systems will leave "data trails" where currently there may not be any records of transactions, there are numerous ways in which such systems can be used for monitoring purposes. For example, in point-of-sale transactions conducted with cash, there is no

---

EFT: A Potential Threat to Privacy
Survey Reveals Banks Release Unauthorized Data[a]

A study conducted for David F. Linowes, professor of political economy and public policy, University of Illinois, by that college's Survey Research Laboratory, and based on reports by 34 of the nation's largest banks, indicated the following:

Most banks do not inform customers of routine disclosure practices to government agencies (74% of the banks) or non-government sources (85%).

Half of the banks seek information about individuals from third parties without first obtaining written permission.

Most institutions (61%) release information to non-governmental inquirers without subpoena. Of these, all furnish information to credit grantors, and 25% supply information to landlords.

`alling for enactment of a proposed privacy statute, Linowes said that Americans ˴enerally have faith that the information they disclose to banks does not travel much further. Today, this belief is no longer valid."

[a]*Infosystems*, Feb. 1980, p. 18. Copyright, Hitchcock Publishing Company. Reprinted with permission.

Figure 12.13.

need to maintain customer records in a master file. In an EFT system, on the other hand, detailed records would be kept for every transaction. This type of data could easily lend itself to an increased surveillance capability. It should be noted that many proponents of EFT systems point to the fact that the same potential privacy problem occurs within check payment systems. Most commercial banks, for example, maintain microfilmed copies of all checks processed. It is thus possible for a bank employee or for bureaucratic agencies to glean much information from the checks of particular individuals. But check transactions do not provide a total picture of an individual's spending patterns since one could always pay for goods and services in cash; EFT systems would provide such a total picture. Figure 12.13 indicates some facts about EFT and privacy.

12.2.3.2 Security

It has been suggested that the use of EFT systems reduces the potential for frauds because fewer people are involved in the transfer of funds. The direct deposit of funds and the automatic payment to creditors, both performed electronically, reduce the opportunities for fraud that have traditionally been present in manual, paper-based systems. Indeed, a recent study was conducted by the American Bankers Association of 134 banks that use automated teller machines. Almost 80% of the banks indicated that they had fewer losses than when the banks operated previously under their manually based system. The greatest risk to an EFT system, resulting in two-thirds of all losses, was attributable to theft or loss of customer EFT cards and to the ability of an unauthorized user to determine one's personal identification number.

There are, however, several additional potential security problems with EFT systems:

1. The accessibility of EFT data by bank-employed remote terminal operators
2. The possibility of access to the data by other bank employees or outsiders
3. The illegal wiretapping of communications lines by unscrupulous computer or communications experts

There are thus several major issues relating to security that must be carefully identified and considered.

12.2.3.3 Consumer Acceptance

It must be noted that consumer acceptance of EFT is essential before it can succeed over alternative payment systems. Consumers must be convinced that sufficient benefits will be passed on to them to persuade them to accept EFT services. Banks have a great deal to gain from an EFT system, but unless the consumer realizes some benefits, there will be significant resistance.

Check-payment systems offer several distinct benefits to consumers that are not found in EFT systems.

a. *Check Float.*   A consumer can take advantage of the "float" time inherent in the processing of checks. Goods and services can be paid by check even though the money is not actually in an account when the check is drawn. Since it takes several days for a check to clear, the money can be deposited in the checking account in the interim at the customer's convenience.

There is no float in an EFT system. The funds are transferred electronically at the time the transaction takes place. If there are insufficient funds in an EFT account, either the transaction cannot be completed or an alternative payment method must be used.

b. *Stop Payment Orders.*   With a check, a consumer has the opportunity to stop payment while the check is proceeding through the clearing process. Thus if a consumer receives unsatisfactory or incomplete performance, he or she can easily notify the bank and direct them not to honor the check.

In an EFT system, since payment is made electronically at the time of the transaction, the customer does not have the same opportunity to stop payment, if necessary. The mechanism for seeking immediate redress for unsatisfactory performance is somewhat more cumbersome. The customer typically must first seek to have the establishment that was paid rectify the problem. If satisfaction is not received, the customer notifies the organization operating the EFT system of the situation to have them issue a credit.

c. *Liability for Forged Signatures.*   When checks are used, the liability for payment of forged checks has been clearly resolved by statute. Under the Uniform Commercial Code, which has been adopted in virtually every state of the United States, a party whose signature is forged on a check is *not* liable. The Code provides that the customer has a duty to use reasonable care when examining the bank statement and canceled checks and to look for a possible forgery, unauthorized signature, or any alteration, such as a raised amount. The customer must report to the bank any irregularities within a reasonable time after the statement is made available. In the event that there are discrepancies, the bank must be notified usually within 14 days after the first forgery and statement were made available to the customer. If these measures are taken, the bank must assume responsibility for any irregularities.

In an EFT system, the problem of unauthorized transactions takes on a new dimension, since electronic transfers of funds can be made without documents, such as checks. Suppose that an individual's EFT or "debit" card is used by someone who, without authority, has obtained the individual's personal identification number. There is a heavy burden on the customer to prove that this is an unauthorized use. There is no forged signature, for example, which can be used to indicate a forgery. The issue of responsibility is currently under consideration. Many banks have placed a maximum liability of $50 on the customer; others still regard liability for unauthorized use as something that must be negotiated.

d. *The Cost of Banking Services.* The check collection system is, of course, subsidized by the banking industry. Although it is difficult to be precise, the cost for the banking industry to process a check has been estimated to be at least $0.18 to $0.23 per check. The full cost is not directly passed on to check users. Some banks offer free checking, for example, if a certain balance is maintained in the checking account. Other banks charge a flat fee per check processed, typically $0.10. There has been much concern in the banking industry that if checks continue to be subsidized, it will be very difficult to persuade customers to switch to EFT services. Since there would be no direct cost benefit to customers, they would not be inclined to support such a change.

To encourage customer support of EFT systems, many retail establishments that have point-of-sale and electronic funds transfer capability offer customers a discount when they use their EFT or "debit" cards.

There is one major benefit of EFT systems for the customer: convenience. Funds can be transferred automatically into one's account; moreover, regular payments for home mortgage, car loan, and insurance can be made automatically. Whereas point-of-sale systems in retail establishments have met with consumer resistance, automatic teller machines as part of an EFT system have been much more successful. Customers like the convenience of being able to cash checks or make deposits at any time of the day without standing in line.

But the issue of cost, like the issues of privacy and security, is still a difficult one. The cost of a credit card transaction, for example, has been estimated at $0.50, which is more than twice that of a check transaction. Will use of EFT cards, then, result in increased, rather than decreased, banking costs? And if so, will the consumer be asked to share in the added cost of such services? Until these questions are resolved, there is apt to be some consumer resistance to electronic funds transfer systems.

Conclusion

We have seen that there are many pros and cons to the implementation of EFT systems. Although EFT might offer convenience, efficiency, and perhaps more protection against certain types of fraud, the potential threat to privacy, the unknown costs involved, and the need for extensive consumer education to encourage acceptance highlight just some of the major issues that must be dealt with in the future. A recent Conference on EFT Research and Public Policy brought together representatives from financial institutions, government agencies, retail establishments, consumer organizations, and the computer industry to discuss the kind of research that is still needed to guide EFT development. Thirty-seven research issues relating to EFT were ranked in the order of importance by the conference participants. The six highest-ranked issues were:

1. The costs and benefits of EFT to the consumer
2. The comparative costs of current payment systems and EFT
3. The definition of EFT regulation and what should be regulated
4. The impact of EFT on the long-range character of society
5. The need for educating consumers regarding their EFT-related rights
6. The rules for being able to access EFT data

It is clear that much research must be done to understand the impact of EFT on society and to identify the key issues that must be faced as such systems are developed. It is equally clear that Congress will need to provide more direction to develop these systems throughout the United States. There are currently over 200 fully operational EFT systems in operation and the number is expected to exceed 500 by the late 1980s. Banking laws vary from one state to another. For example, in some states, automated teller machines are subject to regulations concerning the operation of branch facilities, whereas in other states, terminals are not considered branch operations. It is therefore necessary to enact laws and regulations on a national level to facilitate the uniform development of EFT systems and to ensure that consumers are properly protected.

12.3 SECURITY: A CRITICAL PROBLEM FOR POS AND EFT APPLICATIONS

POS and EFT systems result in procedures that are predominantly automatic and that rely heavily on computer equipment.

The use of computer devices to process most or all transactions in such computer-oriented areas as POS and EFT poses potential problems for both retail establishments and banks. On-line processing of data requires very precise controls and constant monitoring of the system. Moreover, unless there are appropriate backup and emergency procedures, a system breakdown could have very serious ramifications.

System breakdowns can come in many forms and an organization must be prepared. POS, EFT, and indeed any automatic procedure can be seriously affected by:

1. Computer breakdown
2. Manual error or fraud
3. Power outage
4. Natural disaster—fire, flood, earthquake, and so on.

Every organization must implement procedures for dealing with such risks. EFT and POS systems are particularly vulnerable because transaction processing and customer services in both applications would be virtually impossible if the computer were not functioning.

Before considering specific measures used to counteract the effects of each of the four problems mentioned above, it is important to note that prevention is a far better control than recovery procedures. Insofar as is possible, POS and EFT systems should incorporate controls that will monitor the computer's activity and record any possible problems *before* a breakdown occurs. Moreover, controls and audits can minimize the risk of errors and fraud.

Every computerized system should include an emergency manual backup procedure in case of a system failure.

In addition, training seminars and practice drills are useful for emphasizing the potential risks, the ways they can be detected, and emergency methods to be used for reducing loss.

Now let us consider each risk independently.

12.3.1   Methods Used to Minimize Computer Breakdown and the Losses Resulting from Such a Breakdown

1. Service the machines periodically; maintain proper environmental conditions, such as proper humidity and temperature.
2. Use computer software and hardware monitors that report on efficiency.
3. Use integrated circuit boards to reduce the risk of computer breakdowns. When a problem is detected, a new board can be inserted and the old one fixed at leisure.
4. Duplicate master disk files in case of a breakdown or a "head crash," where the disk drive destroys the data file by inadvertently scratching the disk's surface.

12.3.2 Methods Used to Minimize Manual Errors or Fraud

1. Use authorization codes and change them periodically.
2. Implement numerous verification and control procedures.
3. Provide control listings, which should be checked manually.
4. Perform numerous audits, some of which are not scheduled in advance.

12.3.3 Dealing with Power Outages

Largely as a result of ever-increasing energy problems, blackouts and brownouts have become very frequent during peak periods. Reducing the supply of electricity to a computer center or having frequent power surges can have very serious effects. If a computer system does not have a constant supply of electricity, all data stored internally or being processed at the time will usually be lost. Because incidents of power problems have been growing in recent years, the following measures have become available:

1. The user can purchase an *uninterruptible power supply unit*, which functions as a control unit monitoring the supply of electricity and which can also function as a generator if there is a sudden loss of electricity. This will, of course, minimize the risk of losing data.
2. The user can purchase a battery for mini- or small computer systems. Batteries can function for several hours in case of a power failure.
3. Magnetic bubble memory units have the ability to retain data and instructions stored in the computer even if the power is shut off.

12.3.4 What to Do about Natural Disasters

To prevent the loss of valuable data and program files, most computer installations purchase sophisticated detection and fire suppression systems.

Quick detection of a fire, flood, or earthquake with the use of an alarm will enable trained computer specialists to implement measures designed to minimize loss.

Fire suppression systems come in many varieties. Sprinkler systems significantly reduce the risk of personal injury but they are inappropriate for protecting machinery and files.

Another type of fire suppression system which is frequently used in a computer center is a system that injects a chemical agent that will extinguish a fire. This protects machines and files better than sprinkler systems, but it has a potentially harmful effect on people who may remain on the scene.

Because of a growing dependence on POS and EFT systems by retail establishments and banks, security measures for information processing have become a grave concern. Many organizations employ a security specialist who is responsible for minimizing risks and reducing losses if a disaster occurs. These specialists are responsible for training, backup procedures, and implementation of manual means should a computer fail. In addition, they recommend the purchase and utilization of whatever devices, procedures, or techniques they deem necessary for preventing or controlling potential hazards.

KEY TERMS

Automatic teller machine (ATM)

Batch processing

Centralized data processing

Distributed data processing (DDP)

Electronic cash register

Electronic funds transfer (EFT) system

Laser beam readers

Magnetic bubble memory

Off-line processing

On-line processing

Point-of-sale (POS) system

Uninterruptible power supply

Universal Product Code (UPC)

Wand readers

REVIEW QUESTIONS

1. What are the major differences between an on-line POS system and a batch POS system?
2. What are the major benefits to be derived from using POS terminals with on-line systems?
3. What advantages are there to using minicomputers for certain POS systems?
4. Under what circumstances could a batch POS system be justified?
5. Explain how the Universal Product Code (UPC) is used. What are the advantages and disadvantages of the UPC?
6. What is an electronic funds transfer system?
7. What are the main features of the different types of EFT systems?
8. What are some of the major EFT applications?

9.   What are major social issues that have emerged in connection with EFT systems?
10.   What are some of the major philosophical approaches that have been suggested with regard to implementation of EFT systems?

DISCUSSION QUESTIONS

1.   Do you think it is feasible for citizens to use a terminal in the home for registering their opinions to legislatures or for actual voting? How might that affect the political system?
2.   What are the advantages and disadvantages of EFT systems from the consumer's point of view?
3.   Should consumer groups be permitted to participate in discussions of computer utilization that will directly affect them?
4.   Is it important for the government to pass laws pertaining to EFT use? Explain your answer.
5.   What guidelines would you establish for implementing an EFT system?

APPLICATION

Consider the application below and then answer the questions that follow it.

Perspectives on Electronic Funds Transfer[a]

A speech by William S. Anderson, Chairman, NCR Corporation

Throughout the world, banking is in a period of dramatic change. One of the most far-reaching changes is accelerated progress toward full implementation of electronic funds transfer. Despite legal and regulatory complexities, sometimes conflicting interests of the various parties, and misgivings of those who fear it, EFT is coming on a broad scale. Indeed, in many areas it is here already.

Because EFT has become a factor in the business of bankers, retailers, and suppliers of data processing systems and services, it is important that we move quickly to resolve the remaining questions blocking further progress. My purpose today is to give an overview of EFT from the perspective of a system supplier, to report on progress to date, and to discuss the major problems we must overcome in the near term.

As you well know, electronic funds transfer is not a single concept. It is a spectrum of interrelated developments that is revolutionizing the way governments, banks, businesses, and individuals handle money. All EFT services are based on the premise that it is easier, faster, and cheaper to move electrons than to move paper.

A flood of checks

The trend toward EFT started in the 1960s when the flood of checks became a monumental problem for banks. This was especially true in countries where checks are a particularly popular method of payment. In the United States the problem is further complicated by a relatively inefficient clearing mechanism. Not only are Americans the world's most prolific check-writers, but the U.S. payment mechanism itself magnifies the cost of "float" by lengthening the time required to move transactions through the payment pipeline.

To be sure, other countries have "float" problems, too. But in most cases the situation is improved by primarily cash-based economies and more direct check clearing systems than in the United States.

U.S. banking laws retard progress

The biggest obstacle to EFT in the United States has been the number of individual banks and the fact that all of them are limited to specific geographic areas. Banks with aggressive EFT programs could not offer their services beyond their home states. In some states, such as Ohio, where NCR's headquarters is located, until recently banks were actually limited to a single county. As a result some areas in the United States have a full range of EFT services, whilst banks in other parts of the country have hardly progressed beyond manual deposits and withdrawals.

The current status of EFT

Throughout the world there are in excess of 30,000 automatic teller terminals in use, and the number is growing every day. In fact, banks are installing these popular customer convenience systems as fast as the suppliers can produce them.

Another EFT service which has become popular in the United States in the limited areas where it is currently available is bill payment by telephone. Banks, savings and loan associations, and credit unions in other areas are under pressure to initiate this service. And this pressure will grow if postal rates rise and the cost of writing checks increases, as it certainly will when the Federal Reserve System begins charging banks for clearing checks. Telephone payment is the first real alternative Americans have had to checks, and they are accepting it readily when it is offered.

Future prospects for EFT

Now, exactly what EFT progress can we realistically expect in the next five and ten years? Let me list just a few likely developments; in the next five years:

- National and international networks will tie local EFT networks together. In the United States the national network will resemble a private-sector automatic clearing-house system for consumer transactions.

- Nationwide banks will become a reality in the United States as federal restrictions on areas of bank operation are eliminated.

- Worldwide there will be fewer credit cards and debit cards per person, because of system standardization.

- The banking system in the United States will begin to catch up with systems in other industrial nations, as outdated laws and regulations are replaced by new legislation on both the state and federal levels.

- Comprehensive POS networks linking a large number of financial institutions and retailers will be implemented in a limited number of areas.

In ten years we expect to see:

- A definite start toward home banking and shopping through terminals using telephone or cable television lines.

- New methods of positive personal identification to facilitate nationwide EFT and provide greater security. These new methods may include handprint identification or voiceprint analysis.

- Finally, check volume will begin to level.

And there is one other development of interest to all bankers and retailers. The price of the systems necessary to implement EFT technology will continue to decrease, relative to the results produced.

[a] Courtesy of NCR.

Application Questions

1. Do you think Mr. Anderson, the author, is in favor of EFT? Explain your answer.
2. Evaluate the "future prospects" that Anderson sees for EFT. Is he, in general, optimistic or pessimistic?

Computer crime and security

Now that computers are being used with increasing frequency for a wide variety of business and social applications, the legal issues involving these uses have, in recent years, become very critical. These issues include such concerns as (1) the invasion of an individual's privacy resulting from the improper access to computer data banks; (2) the legal rights and obligations of an individual in an electronic funds transfer (EFT) environment; and (3) the commission of fraud, or other crime, with the use of a computer.

These concerns have prompted many states, the legal departments of some commercial and academic organizations, and the federal government to examine the issues more closely.

Moreover, there are numerous computer-related lawsuits which are currently being adjudicated and which may result in serious problems for the computer professional and the computing industry, in general. Such cases include (1) programmers being sued for professional malpractice; (2) hospitals being sued for malpractice for failing to utilize computers to monitor patient's vital signs (see Chapter 10); and (3) libel by computer, where a credit agency is being sued for having issued a defamatory computer-produced report concerning someone's credit.

In this chapter we consider the following aspects of these legal issues:

1. Computer crimes and specific laws that have been enacted to prosecute or prevent them
2. Major aspects of computer security

The issues relating to the invasion of privacy and other legal concerns are considered in Chapter 14.

13.1 COMPUTER CRIMES AND SPECIFIC LAWS THAT HAVE BEEN ENACTED TO PROSECUTE OR PREVENT THEM

13.1.1 The Dearth of Precedence in Dealing with Computer Crime

Because the computing field is relatively new, efforts to deal with computer-related crimes have only begun. Indeed, 1978 was the first year in which a state enacted a specific law dealing with computer crime.

The legal profession itself is partly responsible for this delay. In general, attorneys tend to specialize in particular fields such as tax law, patent law, real estate law, and so on. There is, however, only a miniscule segment of lawyers who can be classified as computer attorneys or who would be able to handle computer-related cases.

In addition, the various government agencies as well as the private sector have not, until very recently, focused on the need to minimize the potential hazards in technologically related fields, in general, and in the computing field specifically.

13.1.2 The Prevalence of Computer-Related Crimes

One might suggest that the inattention described above is justifiable, because the occurrence of such crimes is negligible. Note, however, that the average loss from a computer crime has been estimated at $600,000. One documented computer scheme, the Equity Funding case, which will be discussed in detail, resulted in a $2 billion fraud!

Thus, when such crimes are committed, the amount of fraud is frequently staggering, and not negligible at all. Note, in addition, that many similar crimes frequently go undetected or unreported. Even if an organization learns that a computer crime has been committed and discovers the perpetrator as well, the organization frequently decides *not* to bring criminal charges against the individual. Such organizations are sometimes concerned that adverse publicity will highlight weaknesses in their operations. Customers at a specific bank, for example, might understandably take their business elsewhere if they were to learn that their bank's computer system had been violated.

Another reason why organizations fail to report such criminal action relates to their inability to provide proper protection. That is, they are deeply concerned with the lack of security and consider it, therefore, their first priority to learn how such crimes are actually committed and how they can be avoided. For this reason, it is not unusual for an organization learning of an individual's ability to commit a computer crime to *hire* that individual as a computer security consultant! In this instance the adage "crime does not pay" appears to be in serious trouble! But the other adage "it takes a thief to know a thief" takes on added significance!

Let us consider some of the more widely known and more ingenious types of computer crimes before proceeding to a discussion of various computer crime laws that have been enacted.

13.1.3   Types of Computer Crimes

13.1.3.1   *Theft of Business Funds by Computer*

One major aspect of computer crime is the use of machines to steal money from a business organization.

For most business applications where a significant amount of data needs to be processed, the computer is an exceedingly useful tool. There are, however, several aspects of computer use in these areas that make them very vulnerable:

1. Master files are stored in machine-readable form. Most main files are stored on tape or disk, media that are uniquely suited for computer processing but which cannot be directly verified by people. That is, one cannot "read" from a tape or disk without the use of a computer and a program that issues the correct instructions. Since such files are not manually usable, it is possible to make unauthorized changes that could go undetected for a long time.
2. Computer users are frequently unfamiliar with computer processing and rely extensively on the expertise of the computer professional. This makes it relatively easy for computer specialists to bilk the system.
3. Auditors frequently use computer printouts exclusively in checking for discrepancies. In this instance, a computer professional who steals funds but makes the books balance would go undetected for a relatively long time.

When money is stolen from businesses, it can be the work of an employee who understands the system or a client or customer with an ingenious scheme. Let us consider some examples.

a. *The Equity Funding Fraud.*   The largest business fraud ever undertaken was carried out at the Equity Funding Corporation with the use of a computer. Equity Funding, whose shares were traded on the stock market, was a company with headquarters in Los Angeles. It dealt in mutual funds and insurance policies. It offered customers who bought mutual funds the opportunity to buy life insurance as well.

In the early 1970s, the chairman of the board and other high-level executives of Equity Funding undertook a fraudulent scheme, with the use of a computer, to make the company appear more profitable than it actually was. A more profitable company would manifest itself in higher prices for the company's stock; the chairman and other executives were, of course, major stockholders. These individuals could then reap huge profits by selling their shares of Equity Funding at the inflated price.

The nature of the scheme was relatively simple. The computer was used to generate, as one of the company's assets, insurance policies on nonexistent people. The company would then sell these policies to other insurance companies, a practice known as reinsurance and commonly used by insurance firms to spread insurance risks among companies.

The computer maintained records on approximately 97,000 insurance policies, of which almost two-thirds were for fictitious policyholders. The face value of these bogus policies was $2.1 billion. The fictitious computerized records on magnetic tape were generated by extracting data from the valid policies (one-third of the total) that contained genuine data for real policyholders.

Computerized lists of Equity Funding's insurance policies—real and fictitious—were then sold to other insurance companies (reinsurers). The executives of Equity Funding paid the premiums to the reinsurers for the fictitious policies and routinely generated documentation, including fake medical reports, to show that some of the fictitious people who were insured had died. In addition to inflating the value of their stock, the executives were able to receive over $1 million in insurance proceeds by declaring themselves as beneficiaries!

Eventually, in March 1973, a former employee of Equity Funding revealed the fraud. Twenty-two people were eventually convicted as a result of this conspiracy, including three auditors.

There are several astounding aspects to this case. First, the insurance fraud went on for several years without being detected by the company's external auditors. At that time, auditors consistently accepted computer printouts as being beyond reproach. Second, the fraud was planned *and* executed by the top executives of the company, who themselves entered bogus data. The manager of Management Information Systems was not aware that the computer was being used to perpetrate a $2 billion fraud.

It should be noted that the perpetrators were convicted of federal charges of computer fraud and received sentences of up to eight years in prison.

b. *Use of Computer in a Fraudulent Billing Scheme.* Recently, a man from Long Island, New York, was convicted of grand larceny in connection with a fraudulent billing scheme that netted $1 to $2 million. A microcomputer in his home had been used to keep track of his billings. Approximately 60,000 entries were stored on disk. The computer had been programmed to send out second notices when outstanding bills were not paid.

The scheme essentially involved sending fraudulent bills to small municipal governments around the country for services and/or supplies that had never been delivered. Thousands of bills, averaging about $400 each, had been sent throughout the country. Municipalities paid the bills routinely without verifying whether or not they were legitimate. Finally, one municipality got suspicious when it was billed $508 under two different company names.

In this, as in most cases, the use of a computer made it much easier for a person to commit a crime. Moreover, the person committing the crime is not a lower-level employee but a technical expert, a professional.

c. *Theft of a Penny by Computer.*   A classic case of a perpetrator who took advantage of human nature is the case of a programmer who used a terminal from his home to access the payroll program at the company where he worked. He reasoned that when employees receive a computer-produced payroll check, very few add up the deductions on the stub, subtract that total from gross pay and thus verify that the net pay on the check is correct *to the penny*. Even if an employee did find a one-cent discrepancy in the net pay figure, this might easily be attributed to some sort of computer truncation. In any event, it would not be likely for someone to complain about underpayment of one cent.

The programmer modified the payroll program so that whenever a salary amount was to be rounded to a dollars and cents figure, it was, instead, truncated. That is, $286.039 was processed as $286.03, instead of $286.04, which would be the correct amount. Each cent thus improperly withheld was added to the programmer's own check. Since the company had several thousand employees for whom checks were prepared by computer, this amounted to a nice sum for the programmer each pay period.

The individual was able to proceed undetected in this manner because each audit, which compared the total salaries against the paychecks and government reports, always checked.

It should be noted, however, that the scheme was eventually discovered and the perpetrator convicted of computer fraud.

13.1.3.2   *Theft of Data and Computer Services*

In previous eras, when data important to an organization's well-being was stored in file cabinets or in desk drawers, the danger of theft was at least visible and the measures that could be used for protection were very clear. With the current use of computers to process and store such data, and the use of communication lines to transmit it over long distances, the threat of penetrating a system and improperly accessing an organization's vital files increases. Moreover, such invasion can frequently go undetected for a long time.

Simple wiretapping of telephone lines used for data communications can provide unscrupulous people with, for example, secret drug formulas being prepared by a pharmaceutical company and transmitted to its subsidiaries, confidential customer information, financial data, and so on.

Moreover, similar illegal techniques enable individuals to improperly access a time-sharing facility at no expense. That is, an individual can obtain computer services without paying for them. In addition, the theft of software could have serious ramifications for an organization. If others have illegal access to the techniques and methodologies employed by the organization, the results could be catastrophic.

Let us consider an example.

Example—Executive of Company Charged with Accessing a Rival's Computer System: The vice-president of a New York-based service bureau was indicted for having allegedly tampered with a rival company's computer-stored data. The executive gained access by use of a terminal to the other company's computer system based near Los Angeles. On 196 different occasions during a seven-month period, he:

1.   Retrieved and manipulated data on the other computer system
2.   Learned the names of the other company's customers who used that computer system
3.   Deleted 158 access codes from the other system, thereby denying subscribers assigned those codes any ability to use the computer

Four of the other company's customers include major federal agencies: the State Department, the Department of the Treasury, General Services Administration, and the Tennessee Valley Authority.

The executive could face a maximum of five year's imprisonment and a $1000 fine for each of 10 wire fraud counts. It is a felony under federal law to use a telephone to obtain unauthorized access to a computer system.

13.1.3.3   The Use of Computers for Sabotage or for Personal Gain

We have already seen how computers can be used to line one's pockets. But frequently people have other reasons for penetrating a computer system. Sometimes the results of such illegal access are more serious than if financial gain were the only motive.

Individuals sometimes feel they have personal or political reasons that justify the destruction of private property. Sabotaging an organization's computer system by destroying files or software could mean the end of that organization.

In addition, the use of computers for personal gain, in some way that is not necessarily financial, is a major problem area. Let us consider the following illustration.

Example—Computer Used to Alter Grades at College: Two former students of Queens College, New York, were indicted recently on charges of falsifying a total of 154 grades of 19 students. They were alleged to have changed the data on magnetic disk over a period of three years. One of those indicted was a former computer operator at the college's data processing center. He was indicted on:

1. One count of falsifying business records
2. One count of receiving a bribe
3. Two counts of receiving reward for official misconduct
4. One count of violating a state education law prohibiting unlawful acts wit'ı respect to examinations

He could receive up to seven years in jail. The other student, who arranged for grade changes to be made, was indicted on one count of falsifying business records. He could receive up to four years in jail.

As a result of these indictments, an audit of grades was conducted by the college with the following results:

1. Nine degrees were revoked.
2. Four students face disciplinary action.
3. The Phi Beta Kappa key of the former computer operator was revoked since 13 of his grades had also been changed.
4. The college has revised its data processing security procedures and grade-recording system.

The case came to light when an instructor noticed a discrepancy between the grades he had submitted and a computer printout of marks in his department. Note that if it were not for the chance observation on the part of the instructor, this scheme could well have continued. Moreover, one wonders how many other institutions have, unknown to them, similar problems.

13.1.3.4   Use of Computers to Commit Fraud in the Banking Industry

The banking industry is particularly vulnerable to computer crime for several reasons:

1. Unscrupulous individuals often look to banks for their illegal schemes since that is where the money is!
2. The banking industry is very dependent on computer technology.

3. Many large banks have centralized banking systems that process billions of transactions; they have many stations at which crimes may be committed.

We have seen in Chapter 12 how electronic funds transfer systems can result in increased crimes. Indeed, the widespread use of computers in the banking field, in general, has increased the risks.

Let us consider an example:

Example—Use of Falsified Magnetic Ink Characters on Checks to Steal Over $1 Million: One of the most ingenious and successful computer fraud schemes, which netted over $1 million, involved the use of false magnetic ink characters on checks. The perpetrator opened a checking account at a New York commercial bank and received preprinted checks and deposit slips from the bank. Checks contain magnetic ink characters on the bottom which indicate not only the account number, but also a three-digit code designating the bank where the account is located. A magnetic ink character recognition (MICR) reader-sorter can interpret these characters and sort the checks into bank number and/or account number sequence.

The perpetrator knew that a check that has been deposited in a checking account requires a certain number of days to clear before it can be drawn against. Under the Uniform Commercial Code, which has been adopted across the country, a bank must notify a depositor within a specific number of days if a particular check "bounces" or, in legal terms, if it is dishonored. If the specific number of days lapses without any notification of dishonor, the check is assumed valid and the depositor can draw against it.

To exploit this legal principle, the perpetrator did the following. Upon receiving blank checks when the account was opened, he had a printer illegally make up a new set of checks identical to the original, with one major modification—the magnetic characters indicating the bank code and account number were changed. The new code referred to a bank on the West Coast. The new checks thus had the name of a New York bank printed on them, together with a set of magnetic ink characters indicating a *different* bank.

The perpetrator opened an account at another bank and made deposits, using the altered checks described above. Each check deposited was routed through the Federal Reserve check-clearing system to the bank on which the check was drawn. Since the check-clearing system uses MICR sorters to route the checks, only the altered bank codes (and not the bank named on the face of the check) were picked up on these checks. Thus the checks were routed to a West Coast bank. When each check was received at the West Coast bank, a MICR reader-sorter was used to pick up the account number. Since there was no legitimate account at that bank with such a number, the checks were rejected. An operator would notice that the name of the bank printed on the check corresponded to a New York bank and would send the check there, assuming that it had been misrouted by mistake. After it was returned to the New York bank, the check was put into the computerized system for final processing. However, once again the MICR equipment caused the check to be routed to the West Coast!

The end result was that due to all these delays in transit, the checks were assumed to have cleared since no notices of dishonor had been received. Thus, in effect, the checks were honored when they should have bounced. This fraud resulted in a loss of over $1 million. The perpetrator was never discovered.

13.1.4   Computer Crime Laws

As indicated earlier, although computers have been in use for almost 40 years, it was not until 1978 that the first computer crime laws were enacted in this country—in Arizona and Florida. In 1979, other states, such as California, Colorado, Illinois, Michigan, New Mexico, North Carolina, Rhode Island, and Utah, adopted crime bills. A number of other states currently have legislation pending. Congress is considering a federal computer crime law.

The major explanations for the sudden proliferation of laws dealing explicitly with computer crime are twofold:

1. *The recent surge in computer crimes.* It has been estimated that this type of so-called "white-collar" crime conservatively costs American business over $300 million a year.
2. *The inadequacy of existing statutes to deal with computer crimes.* Until now, if caught, a computer criminal has stood only a 3% chance of going to jail.

Prosecutors have often found themselves hindered in dealing with computer offenders. Definitions in criminal statutes did not specifically relate to the unique aspects of computer crime and hence numerous loopholes existed. As an example, consider the case of personnel data stored on magnetic tape that someone erased without authorization. Previously, when a prosecutor wanted to use one of the criminal statutes, such as a theft (larceny) statute, the following type of technicality arose: the offender did not physically *take* anything of value—only data was erased. Many of the new computer crime statutes have been designed specifically to handle unique aspects of computer offenses. For example, an item of value now includes confidential information stored on computer media, such as magnetic tape, magnetic disk, and so on.

Since, as of this writing, only a handful of states have actually enacted specific computer crime statutes, it would be useful to analyze how some computer offenses have typically been dealt with in selected states. This analysis will provide some insight into the criminal aspects of computer abuse and illustrate how the same offense can be treated in an entirely different manner depending on the state in which it is committed. Many computer offenses have involved the theft of programs (software) themselves, of the intentional and unauthorized destruction or modification of someone else's programs. This type of offense can typically be committed in one of two ways—either through use of a terminal or through physical access to a computer center itself.

Let us consider, for example, the utilization of a terminal to gain unauthorized access to software in order to steal it. We will look at several different approaches which have been used in some states.

1. *Software as a "Trade Secret."*   In some states, programs that are developed and owned by a company are considered trade secrets. Consequently, when these programs are stolen, it is treated as the offense often called "misappropriation of a trade secret." States such as California, New York, New Jersey, and Texas have statutes dealing specifically with this type of offense. In New York, for example, a person convicted of this type of crime can receive up to four years in prison and a possible fine up to double the amount of the monetary gain from the commission of the crime.

2. *Software as Property.*   Some states have larceny statutes that cover this type of offense. In New York, for example, there is a larceny statute that covers the situation when property stolen (in this case a program) has value that can be ascertained. The New York statute basically defines value as "the market value of the property at the time and place of the crime, or if such cannot be satisfactorily ascertained, the cost of replacement of the property within a reasonable time after the crime." Thus, an organization could ascertain the value of software by determining the cost of replacement.

Grand larceny in the second degree, for example, applies where the value of the property stolen exceeds $1500. This can result in a prison sentence of up to seven years in addition to a fine.

3. *Theft of Services.*   In some states, the perpetrator may be guilty of the criminal charge of "theft of services." This can occur when, without authorization, access to another's computer system is obtained; in such instances, the computer can be instructed to list out various programs on the perpetrator's remote terminal. In New York, theft of services is a class A misdemeanor that can result in up to one year's imprisonment and a fine up to $1000.

4. *Software Transmitted over a Telephone.*   In some states, such as Illinois, a perpetrator who steals software by using a remote terminal connected by telephone to a computer may be guilty of sending a false telephone message with intent to defraud.

5. *Credit Card Fraud and Forgery.*   In some states, if the perpetrator gains access to a computer system by unauthorized use of an account number or authorization code, credit card fraud may have been committed. In addition, in some states, this act may be construed as forgery.

In summary, there is no consensus, among the states, as to how computer crimes should be prosecuted. Since the computer field is relatively new and the techniques employed are atypical, efforts to use existing laws or to modify them have proven somewhat problematic.

13.1.5   Computer Crime and the Federal Government

In cases where there has been unauthorized use of (1) federal computers or (2) computers used in interstate commerce, a *federal* crime has been committed. As in the case with state-regulated crimes, it has not always been clear whether a specific computer offense could be prosecuted as a crime under an existing law. As a result, federal prosecutors have often found themselves failing to win convictions.

There is legislation currently pending before Congress known as the Federal Computer Systems Protection Act. When enacted, it will become the first federal computer crime law. In the past, federal prosecutors have had to rely on some 40 different federal statutes, such as the Wire Fraud Statute of 1934. Clearly, many of these are obsolete or inapplicable. Changes are coming, but justice moves slowly.

An important point to recognize is that both federal and state statutes may apply to the same computer crime. This means that it is possible for a perpetrator to be prosecuted on the federal as well as state level for the same offense. The question of double jeopardy cannot be applied, since the federal government and any state government are separate sovereigns. Consequently, each is permitted to prosecute an offender regardless of what action, if any, the other sovereign takes.

13.2   MAJOR ASPECTS OF COMPUTER SECURITY

There are two primary methods for dealing with the threat of computer crimes. One, as noted, is to enact legislation that will punish the perpetrator of such a crime. But this, of course, has its intrinsic problems. It is useful only if the criminals are caught, if charges are brought, and if the perpetrators are prosecuted.

In this instance, an ounce of prevention may well be worth the proverbial pound of cure. That is, methods need to be implemented in organizations to ensure the integrity and security of computer systems, in an effort to *prevent* the execution of such crimes. You have already seen one common method for minimizing the unauthorized use of computers: a log-on code.

Note that the need for security of computer systems goes beyond the threat of theft. Lack of proper security in computer utilization could have very serious ramifications for society in general:

1. In May 1979, a breach of computer-controlled security occurred at the Virginia Electric and Power Company's nuclear plant. An unknown intruder was able to override a computerized, magnetic card-controlled access system to gain entry to a building where nuclear fuel elements were stored. Approximately $6 million worth of damage resulted, but consider the possibility of the intruder precipitating a nuclear accident!

2. In February 1979, the Agriculture Department admitted that its computer security was so lax that unauthorized employees used its computer system an estimated *6000* times during a one-year period! Unauthorized users had access to secret crop forecasts, census data, and trade secrets.

   Perhaps the most astounding aspect of this case is that although the computer kept logs on the *thousands* of security breaches, no one reviewed these logs, nor was any corrective action taken at the time the breaches occurred.

3. Recently, auditors for the General Services Administration in Washington, D.C., were able to trick this government agency into sending a check for $95,256 to a fictitious company for goods never ordered by the federal government. False data had been entered into the agency's computer system by the auditors to demonstrate weaknesses in the payment procedures used by the agency.

4. The General Accounting Office (G.A.O), the investigatory agency for Congress, recently discovered a serious lack of security in the Social Security Administration's computer system. The Social Security Administration maintains computerized records on over 170 million Americans and has 1300 offices throughout the country. The G.A.O.'s concern with security was prompted, in part, by reports of employees within the Social Security Administration who were improperly manipulating files and/or selling confidential information. The G.A.O. discovered several design and management problems that resulted in security weaknesses.

   a. Records can be created, as well as accessed, from most of the 3900 terminals throughout the country. These terminals should only be authorized to *access* Social Security files in Washington, D.C. One relatively simple security procedure that can be implemented is to permit "read-only" capability at such a terminal.

   b. As a rule, almost any Social Security Administration employee can access the agency's files and even create new records without being required by the computer system to provide any identification indicating appropriate authorization.

   c. In many Social Security offices throughout the country, terminals are located where *any* employee can use them.

The issue of invasion of privacy is, of course, relevant here, but we consider it in more detail in Chapter 14.

There are three main areas of computer processing which require their own respective forms of security: hardware, software, and data. For a system to be relatively secure, all three areas must be protected.

Efforts must be made to protect these areas from destruction (whether intentional or accidental), unauthorized modification, theft, and any form of illegal access.

Note that threats to computer security include not only intentional criminal acts, but also accidental acts as well as acts of God. Acts of omission—failure to perform required operations at required times— may be just as destructive as acts of commission—deliberate, criminal acts. In general, threats to security are typically categorized as:

1. Natural acts, such as fire, flood, and other acts of God
2. Unintentional acts, including human errors in data entry and pro- gramming, and malfunctions in hardware
3. Intentional acts, including the various types of computer crimes dis- cussed above, as well as sabotage and industrial espionage

The value of information to an organization must be carefully assessed by management so that an appropriate level of security is implemented:

> Two principles of information security need to be better understood. First, there is no such thing in practice as an "unbreakable code." There are theoretically unbreakable systems, but they must be used by people, and people make mistakes that can lead to lapses in security. The second principle derives in part from the first. One can get whatever degree of protection one wants (short of perfection) if one is willing to pay for it. The expectations of the thief, as well as the intrinsic value of the information to its owner, must guide the expenditure of security resources. Thus, the key to satisfactory information security is to determine the value of the information *to the potential unauthorized user*, as well as its intrinsic value to its legitimate owner, and then to design a security system that will make it more costly than the smaller of these two values to obtain information without permission during the appropriate length of time.[1]

In summary, management must strive for a security system that is (1) commensurate with the likely security risks to which the system will be exposed, and (2) economically justifiable.

13.2.1 Techniques Used to Ensure the Security of a Computer System

The methods used to protect hardware are essentially the same as methods used to protect any other equipment. Security guards, fire alarms, flood warning systems, and other detection devices are all used to protect the computer system itself. The protection of software and data, however, is somewhat more complex. That is, the unauthorized use of files can go undetected for a considerable period.

[1]T.A. Dolotta et al., *Data Processing in 1980-1985: A Study of Potential Limitations to Progress* (New York: Wiley), p. 30.

We shall divide our discussion into three sections: (1) preventing unauthorized access to a computer via terminals, (2) preventing unauthorized entry to a computer center, and (3) preventing unauthorized modifications to software.

13.2.1.1   Preventing Unauthorized Access to a Computer via Terminals

The following partial list of security precautions suggests some of the common techniques utilized to minimize unauthorized access to a data bank through use of a terminal.

1. Permit access to a file and particular records only for those with proper authorization codes. These codes should not only be changed frequently but their distribution should be limited to those users who absolutely require them.

2. When authorization codes for a particular data bank are distributed to various users, designate by means of the code whether a specific user should have the capability when accessing records to "read only," "write only," or "read and write." As an example, a policeman who is checking a license plate number to determine if a car is stolen needs read-only capability and should not be permitted to create new records. Allowing a user to change data on files can lead to more computer frauds.

3. Program the computer to "log off" automatically a terminal where the user does not precisely follow the correct procedures for entering authorization codes. In addition, a terminal should be logged off automatically if access is attempted for a specific file when the staff that controls that file is off duty. For example, if a company's payroll department does not work after 5:00 P.M., no access to the payroll file should be allowed after that time unless a special code approved by the department head has been issued.

4. Use various encryption or "scrambling" techniques which will render computer data unintelligible when a wiretap occurs.

   An example will illustrate how encryption works. Citibank, the second largest bank in the United States, uses encryption for transmitting data in its electronic funds transfer (EFT) system. There are two encryption keys or encoding procedures required—one key is used at the point of transmission to encode the data to be transmitted. The other key is used at the destination point to convert the encrypted transmission to an understandable and usable format. These keys are changed daily and are themselves divided into segments, with each segment being stored in a different vault. Thus it is extremely unlikely that a perpetrator who intercepted a transmission could readily understand or make use of the data.

The techniques discussed thus far deal with only one aspect of computer security—access to computer data through unauthorized use of terminals and/or wiretapping.

13.2.1.2 Preventing Unauthorized Entry to a Computer Center

This usually involves the use of physical controls—guards, alarms, detection devices, and so on. The following partial list suggests some additional techniques that are available and being employed in varying degrees by some computer centers to prevent unauthorized access to *both* hardware and software.

1. Sign-in logs.
2. Use of badges.
3. Use of keys to unlock on-site terminals that are hard-wired (directly connected to the computer).
4. Use of security guards.
5. Fire, smoke, and burglar alarms.
6. Use of fingerprints and voiceprints for identification.
7. Use of shredding machines to destroy verification lists that are produced by the computer. After files are created or updated and it is determined that the computer's records are accurate, verification lists need to be destroyed.
8. Use of backup files on media such as magnetic tape or disk. These can be stored in fireproof vaults in case it is necessary to recreate files that have been lost, stolen, or accidentally destroyed.

Figure 13.1. Elevator control system designed to prevent unauthorized access to the computer floor.

Figure 13.2. Use of a badge to open the door to a computer center.

Figure 13.1 illustrates an elevator control system that can be used to prevent access to the computer floor unless an appropriate identification card is used and a special code is keyed in. Similarly, Figure 13.2 illustrates a device that can be used to open the door to a computer center if an authorized badge is inserted and a code keyed in. In addition to restricting the hours of entry for a particular area, the device can record the identification of each individual and the elapsed time spent in a restricted area.

13.2.1.3   Preventing Unauthorized Modifications to Software

A major concern is to control which users get access to different files in the system. In this case, we are often dealing with users who, in fact, have authorization to get into the system through a terminal but are only authorized to access a small segment of the data stored. Obviously, the authorization should be limited to one's own programs and files. It should be noted that some perpetrators have gained unauthorized access to some programs and files in either of the following ways:

1.   By exploiting software bugs in the operating system (the program that

controls the entire computer's operations) to obtain direct access to data whenever the perpetrator wants to.

2. By modifying the operating system so that sensitive or classified information can be routinely obtained by an unauthorized user.

This last type of security problem is not only quite sophisticated, but is obviously difficult to detect, especially since the modified program works correctly as far as the intended user is concerned.

Methods used to prevent unauthorized file access include:

1. Storage protection features built into the operating system that permit only specified users access to particular data.
2. Audit procedures that include a check on the data retrieved by each user; if an employee is placed in charge of security, it is possible to maintain records on who uses which files.
3. Error detection procedures that record and print all invalid attempts to access a file and all users who have accessed a file for a time period considered to be excessive.

Some organizations implement security precautions as the need arises, in response to a crisis. Others plan ahead and implement security systems designed to minimize any potential threat. Note that there are companies that, for a fee, will analyze any organization's security needs and provide whatever measures or procedures they feel are necessary.

Figure 13.3 illustrates a computer-based security system. Following are major categories of sensing, detection, and control equip-

Figure 13.3. Computer-based security system.

ment commonly employed with the security and building management system shown. This peripheral sensing equipment is linked to remote automatic data terminals, which, in turn, are connected by cable trunk to the command console.

Intrusion, detection, perimeter: This category comprises sensing devices that react to unauthorized entry through points in the perimeter, principally doors, windows, skylights, and other access points in walls, roof, and floor. Magnetic contacts, disclosing opening of doors and windows, are one example of a perimeter protection device.

Intrusion detection, interior space: Also designated as "interior traps" and involving use of microwave, ultrasonic, and infrared motion detectors that are actuated by the motion of an intruder within the device's area of coverage.

Fire alarms, manual: Pull-box type fire stations are manually actuated by building personnel, transmitting a coded signal directly to the command console, where it is identified by zone.

Fire alarms, automatic: A wide range of sensing devices that react to conditions of a fire, including smoke, heat, and the infrared energy produced by flame. Automatic fire sensing devices include fixed-temperature and rate-of-rise heat detectors, ionization smoke detectors, spot- and beam-type photoelectric detectors, and infrared flame detectors.

Sprinkler water flow: Solid-state detection equipment reacts to the flow of water through sprinkler risers, indicating system operation and probable presence of fire.

Sprinkler supervision: Electrical sensors react to changes-of-status in key points of the sprinkler system, including closing of valves, loss of air pressure in dry pipe systems, and inadequate water level in overhead water supply tanks.

Emergency call: For high-security areas of the building, manually actuated emergency signaling devices allow silent, unobtrusive summoning of assistance in the event of a robbery or other emergency.

Industrial process supervision: Automatic sensing equipment maintains a constant check of certain important phases of industrial processes to detect and report abnormal conditions to the command console for prompt correction.

Energy management: Devices turn on and off heating, ventilating, and air conditioning equipment in line with computer programs based on building occupancy and power demand schedules on a time-of-day, day-of-week basis.

In summary, there are numerous techniques that can be used to reduce the risks. But no system is foolproof. No matter what security measures are implemented, there is always the possibility that a chance occurrence or a deliberate act could violate the system. Realistically, one can only hope to minimize such possibilities.

KEY TERMS

Authorization code

Computer crime

Computer security

Electronic funds transfer (EFT) system

Magnetic ink characters

REVIEW QUESTIONS

1. What are some of the major legal issues that have arisen in connection with the widespread use of computers?
2. Why do organizations frequently fail to prosecute perpetrators of computer crimes?
3. Why do computer crimes in business organizations frequently go undetected for long periods of time?
4. How was the Equity Funding fraud able to go undetected for several years?
5. What explanations are there for the sudden proliferation of computer crime laws?
6. How have computer offenses typically been dealt with in various states?
7. What are the major categories of threats to computer security?
8. What are some of the common techniques utilized to minimize unauthorized access to a data bank through use of a terminal?
9. What are some of the common means used to prevent unauthorized entry to a computer center?
10. How can the threat of "internal" attacks be prevented?

DISCUSSION QUESTIONS

1. Describe some of the disasters that might occur if the federal government did not incorporate proper security measures in its systems. Describe some of the disasters that have occurred.
2. Why is it so difficult to detect computer crimes?
3. Can security measures be built into the hardware? Explain.
4. What are some of the hazards that could compromise the integrity of a computer system?
5. Why have security problems become more prevalent in recent years?

APPLICATION

Consider the application below and then answer the questions that follow it.

Confidentiality and Computerized Patient Information[a]

by George J. Polli

It is 4:00 a.m. and you are just finishing your routine checks as the security director for a large metropolitan hospital. Security personnel are on duty, and the facility is locked for the night. It has been cleared except for the emergency room.

Before feeling satisfied with your efforts, think about the following potential breaches of your security: the computer repairman may actually be a thief intending to steal some of the more expensive components of your computer. The open telephone line connected to your on-line hospital information system may be draining your unsecured confidential information for unauthorized use by unscrupulous firms. That data processing employee who always stays late may be stealing computer time to sell to his own outside clients. And that gentleman in the white coat with the stethoscope who has just asked the night shift medical record clerk for a copy of the files on three patients may actually be a private investigator.

Medical records security has always been a problem. Today, however, computer technology has compounded the problem by permitting the accumulation, storage and analysis of an unlimited amount of medical information. The ability of the computer to store vast amounts of medical data has resulted in public and private scrutiny of this technology to guard against its misuse.

Many times such misuse occurs because of inadequate security policies or improper training of personnel. The harm that results from the misuse of such data may be felt by the patient, whether the misuse is accidental or intentional. The hidden results of lack of confidentiality are people not seeking medical care for fear of disclosure.

Because of recent technological innovations, the need to protect the confidentiality of information in medical records has been intensified. An added impetus to this is the increased awareness of personal privacy on the part of the general public. As people become more knowledgeable of the potential threat of personal exposure, they become more demanding with respect to their personal information.

Corporate Personnel/ Medical Record

These principles are important to a larger audience than hospital security directors. Many companies maintain employee medical records. In larger corporations, these records have been abstracted so that they can be accessed via computer.

Computerization is an asset to a corporate medical staff in that it permits them to process quickly and routinely a large data base of employee medical histories. Unfortunately, improper access to this data can result in unnecessary and embarrassing disclosure of information concerning employees.

Primary Issues

Three primary issues must be considered to ensure confidentiality of information from medical records stored in computerized data banks. They are privacy, confidentiality and security.

Privacy concerns the obligation to withhold personal information from revelation. A patient may not want certain information, such as may be kept in medical records, disclosed solely for personal reasons.

Confidentiality concerns an agreement between individuals to limit the extent of revelation of information. The patient's expectations of confidentiality arise from the obligation to protect the patient's privacy. They also result from the clinical desirability of such an agreement to allow a free flow of information between the physician and the patient.

Security concerns a responsibility to protect personal information from revelation to preserve confidentiality.

The confidentiality of physician/patient communication is desirable to insure free and open disclosure of all information needed to establish a proper diagnosis and attain a desirable clinical outcome. Protecting the confidentiality of the personal and medical information in such medical records is also necessary to prevent humiliation, embarrassment or discomfort of patients.

At the same time, patients have legitimate desires to have medical information concerning their care and treatment forwarded to others. The increasing incidence of personal injury litigation, and the expanding use of life, accident and health insurance, are major factors that have multiplied the number of persons who have a legitimate interest in the information.

It may, for example, be desirable for a patient to have certain information transmitted directly to third parties concerned with the payment of the patient's bill or to a workman's attorney, a succeeding attending physician, a law enforcement agency, military authorities or a perspective employer.

Society at large also has claims on medical information. Reports of infections, contagious or communicable diseases, wound reports, incidents of child abuse and birth and death reports are included in public reporting laws. For these and other purposes, the individual's rights are overridden by the need for information to protect the community as a whole. Most of these disclosures are codified in law, with strict limits on information to be reported and the uses and further disclosure permitted.

Types of Threats

Individuals involved in breaching security of hospital records can be categorized into three groups: current employees, ex-employees and individuals who have never been employed or affiliated with the facility.

Historically, it has been difficult for an individual who has never been an employee of an institution to gain the knowledge and tools necessary to breach the facility's security. As more people become knowledgeable of computer technology, however, this threat increases.

As hospitals move toward standardized and integrated hospital information systems, many more types of information will be included in the computer data base than just medical records. Individuals gaining access to the computer data base can use the computer itself to steal both information and materials through false checks, orders or shipping requests. To protect from external threats, on-line and even batch computer systems should include check points to ensure that a technically-sophisticated person attempting to test the security defenses of a facility will be detected.

Ex-employees are currently the greatest threat to security. They are aware of current security practices, are knowledgeable of current operating routines and, in many cases, still retain the access codes for the facility's computer. Acting out of greed or revenge, these individuals can steal, disturb, or erase large segments of information, thereby disrupting current operations with little, if any, difficulty.

Proper security measures include removing terminated employees from the computer environment and taking positive steps, such as computer access code changes, to ensure the ex-employee cannot disrupt the site.

Access to information by current employees is necessary for the facility to function effectively. Any steps to increase the security of information by making it more difficult to use by current employees has to be examined in light of its cost/benefit impact on operations.

Nevertheless, current employees represent a serious problem in controlling both inadvertent access to confidential information and deliberate attempts to access information outside the roles and responsibilities of the individuals involved.

⋮

In general, the recorded instances of theft or misuse of computerized data are few compared with instances in which information maintained in conventional, non-computerized data repositories is misused or stolen. The recorded instances of computerized data misuse, however, suggest that when such an occurrence takes place, it involves exceptionally large segments of information. Such misuse may be more extensive than realized, because it may not be reported. It also may remain cloaked because of the technical abilities of those involved.

Steps Toward Threat Containment

Three important factors will reduce the probability of misuse of medical records or hospital computer facilities. These factors are knowledge of potential threats, analysis of the potential threats and cooperation between the hospital medical staff and administrators.

Computer technology used in the medical setting is an important subset of the use of computer technology throughout the U.S. economy. Many of the problems that can occur in the hospital setting are problems that can and have occurred in other industries; therefore, hospital security directors are well advised to become familiar with data processing security practices common in other settings. This includes an awareness of basic computer technology, other installations and their security procedures and security procedures that might be easily implemented at your own site.

A detailed security audit of any specific hospital facility should incorporate measures of computer site vulnerability, a review of personnel hiring and firing practices, review of procedures that control routing access to information and facilities and an evaluation of backup facilities necessary to ensure continued operation of the facility in the event the site was disabled. . . .

Accrediting Guidelines for Computer Service Bureaus

Some hospitals in the United States do not have in-house computers for storing medical information. They use computer service bureaus to provide data processing support for physicians who wish to automate their information.

The computer service bureau maintains computerized medical data bases that include medical information used to produce reports. Because much of the data is sensitive, it is important that these organizations establish explicit confidentiality procedures to protect against intentional or inadvertent release of confidential medical information to individuals or organizations not authorized to receive it.

1. The computer service bureau should specifically identify a physical security procedure to prevent access to the computer facility by unauthorized personnel.

2. Personnel audit procedures should be developed to establish a record in the event of unauthorized disclosure of medical data. A roster of past and present service bureau personnel with specified levels of access to medical data base should be maintained.

3. Procedures should be developed to prevent the co-mingling of computerized medical records with those of other service bureau clients. In addition, procedures should be developed to protect against inadvertent mixing of the client reports.

4. Information in a computerized medical data base should under no circumstances be released without the express permission of the physician and the patient. This stipulation should appear in any agreement between the computer service bureau and the facility that addresses work to be performed.

5. Procedures should be developed to advise computer service bureau employees of the confidential nature of the med-

ical data processed. These procedures should explicitly address employees' responsibilities. Specific administrative sanctions should exist to prevent employee breaches of confidentiality and security procedures.

6. On termination of a computer service bureau contract, those computer files maintained should be turned over to the facility or destroyed. In the event of file erasure, the com-

puter service bureau should verify in writing that the erasure has taken place.

7. The computer service bureau is strongly encouraged to make available to physicians and patients a brochure or other written document, that specifically outlines the procedures the computer service bureau uses to protect the confidentiality of patient-identifiable medical data processed by the bureau.

Application Questions

1. What are the three primary issues that must be considered to ensure confidentiality of medical records stored in a computerized data bank?
2. What is the greatest threat to the security of hospital records stored in a computerized data bank?
3. For those hospitals that use service bureaus instead of in-house computers for storing medical information, what guidelines should be established to maintain the confidentiality of medical records?

14

The privacy question and other legal issues

14.1 THE ISSUE OF PRIVACY

We have seen that computers have added a new dimension to our lives—one that, for the most part, has had many positive effects. Numerous strides have been made in fields such as medicine, science, and business that simply would not have been attainable from a cost and time standpoint without the utilization of computers. Nevertheless, the growing concern for an individual's right to privacy has raised serious philosophical and legal questions about the limits that should be imposed on computerization from a societal point of view. It is feared by some that the "Big Brother" image characterized in George Orwell's *1984* may become more of a reality than computer specialists would care to admit. As the late Senator Hubert Humphrey said:

> We act differently if we believe we are being observed. If we can never be sure whether or not we are being watched and listened to, all our actions will be altered and our very character will change.

The balance between an individual's right to privacy, on the one hand, and the public's "need to know" is indeed a very delicate one.

It is interesting to note that according to a recent poll, 54% of the American public considers the present use of computers to be a threat to personal privacy. The poll also showed that 63% of the public agrees with the philosophy that if privacy is to be preserved, the use of computers must be monitored more closely in the future.

The Congressional findings that led to the Privacy Act of 1974 can best sum up the concern for privacy. Section 2(a) of the Act reads as follows:

The Congress finds that

1. The privacy of an individual is directly affected by the collection, maintenance, use, and dissemination of personal information by Federal agencies.
2. The increasing use of computers and sophisticated information technology, while essential to the efficient operations of the Government, has greatly magnified the harm to individual privacy that can occur from any collection, maintenance, use, or dissemination of personal information.
3. The opportunities for an individual to secure employment, insurance, and credit, and his/her right to due process, and other legal protections are endangered by the misuse of certain information systems.
4. The right to privacy is a personal and fundamental right protected by the Constitution of the United States.
5. In order to protect the privacy of individuals identified in information systems maintained by Federal agencies, it is necessary and proper for the Congress to regulate the collection, maintenance, use, and dissemination of information by such agencies.

In recent years, as the capability of computers has increased, their use has spread to many fields; in some instances, computer applications have raised serious philosophical issues as to the efficacy, legality, and even morality of such use.

14.1.1   The National Crime Information Center

The Federal Bureau of Investigation (FBI), for example, maintains a computerized National Crime Information Center (NCIC) in Washington, D.C. There are over 7 million active records in the NCIC, covering data such as wanted persons, missing persons, criminal histories, stolen vehicles and parts, stolen or missing guns, and stolen, embezzled, counterfeit, or missing securities. Data in the NCIC is exchanged with and for the official use of federal criminal justice agencies as well as criminal justice agencies throughout the United States. There are currently over 6000 terminals in the NCIC network serving agencies in the 50 states, the District of Columbia, and the Commonwealth of Puerto Rico. The present annual budget for operating NCIC is $5 million.

The FBI has sought permission and funds from Congress to operate a central message-switching center between state and local police agencies through the National Crime Information Center. To date, Congress has blocked the FBI's attempts, fearing that it might lead to a national police data bank. The fear is that the FBI's proposal might lead to FBI dominance over state and local law enforcement agencies and thus transform the FBI into a national police force. In connection with the criminal history file, the Office of Technology Assessment, a congressional agency, has raised the following key question: To what extent, if any, might the maintenance and use of the file contribute to the growth of federal social control and become an instrument for undermining the democratic foundation upon which this nation is based?

14.1.2   The National Security Agency and Computers

It is now known that over the last 25 years, one of the Federal Government's most secret agencies, the National Security Agency (NSA), has played an important role in shaping this country's privately owned communications network of computers. The purpose of the agency is twofold: (1) to protect sensitive United States communications from intrusion by foreign powers, and (2) to collect intelligence data to be disseminated to other agencies, such as the Central Intelligence Agency, for their use. The NSA has, for many years, been a major source of research funds for the computer industry. Notwithstanding the positive work performed by the agency, a report issued by the Senate Select Committee on Intelligence has raised serious questions about the consequences of some of the agency's activities.

1.   The committee concluded that as a result of the agency's ability to monitor electronic transmissions, its potential to violate the privacy of individuals is unmatched by any other intelligence agency.
2.   The committee found instances involving international communication when the agency had intercepted and disseminated messages that the American sender or receiver had hoped would be private.

With the proliferation of data banks in existence, there are several potential threats to an individual's privacy that must be (1) recognized, (2) assessed, and (3) prevented, when establishing computer systems and networks:

1.   There is the possibility that those who have authorization to access the data banks will misuse or abuse their authority.
2.   Another potential threat is that outsiders who have no authorization to access the information will find a way to penetrate a particular system in order to retrieve, modify, delete, or add information.
3.   There is always the possibility that one or more weaknesses in the design of a particular system will result in the unintentional disclosure of information.

14.1.3 Federal Computer Matching Programs

To increase personal privacy protection, guidelines have been established by the Office of Management and Budget in connection with what is called **federal computer matching programs**. The matching programs are used, for example, to compare personnel lists of federal agencies with computer files of people receiving welfare benefits. The objective is to uncover cases of welfare fraud. The risk of invasion of privacy, however, is very great.

Some of the key procedures for which the guidelines provide include the following:

1. Any agency that is using a matching program must submit a complete description of the program to the Office of Management and Budget and to Congress.
2. Generally, it must be shown that some financial benefit will be realized as a result of running the matching program. This benefit must significantly outweigh (a) the cost of performing the match and (b) any potential harm to the parties involved, such as public disclosure of information about an individual or improper termination of welfare benefits.
3. Records or "hits" of people identified by the program should be destroyed within six months after the match unless they are needed for further investigation or prosecution. The Office of Management and Budget must be notified in writing of the disposition of this type of record.

14.1.4 Financial Data Banks

You will recall that when we discussed electronic funds transfer (EFT) systems, we indicated that EFT is viewed by some as a serious threat to privacy. A system that maintains records on an individual's spending patterns and on the time and place of each transaction is considered objectionable by many people. With such a system, it would be possible to monitor an individual's behavioral pattern, which is obviously undesirable and a threat to a free society.

Similarly, the large number of computer banks of credit information in this country has given rise to concern about the possible invasion of an individual's privacy—a concern that is quite warranted. A debt-collection agency, for example, was charged with illegally tapping computer banks of credit information and using the data to harass debtors. The company had improperly obtained authorization codes and was thus able to gain access to confidential information in the data banks. The information thus obtained was used to intimidate individuals into paying their debts, since the people realized that their activities were being monitored.

It should be noted that a recent legislative proposal being considered by Congress would permit disclosure of EFT transactions to a government agency only *after* the agency had first obtained a court order.

14.1.5 The Social Security Number Controversy

We are all aware of the prevalent use of the social security number by various governmental agencies, employers, banks, and other institutions. There are several key factors that make the social security number extremely attractive as a universal means of identification.

1. It is a unique number. Although there are very rare exceptions that have occurred by accident, no two people in the United States are assigned the same number by the Social Security Administration.
2. The number is short, consisting of only nine digits.
3. Under the Tax Reform Act of 1976, federal, state, and local governments were authorized to require social security numbers for identification purposes from any person affected by any tax, general public assistance, or motor vehicle laws. It should be noted that this Act repealed in large part a section of the Privacy Act of 1974 wherein Congress had declared a moratorium on increased use by the government of the social security number as a personal identifier.

However, use of the social security number has become quite controversial in recent years, especially with the increasing proliferation of data banks across the country containing records on various groups of individuals. A major concern has been that the use of a standard and unique identifier would facilitate the exchange of personal information between data banks and might consequently lead to disclosure of information that the Constitution indicates should be protected. Those concerned with the use of social security numbers as a potential source of invasion of privacy argue that:

1. Although information in a particular data bank pertaining to an individual may be accurate and relevant for the purpose of the agency or organization maintaining that data bank, it may be misinterpreted or taken out of proper context when entered into a data bank of a different agency or organization.
2. There is an increased likelihood of unauthorized access to and alteration of personal records as more and more data banks are linked together.
3. With the interchange of information among data banks, it is conceivable that incorrect or obsolete information pertaining to an individual may end up in some of the data banks and be used improperly to affect the credit rating or status of an individual.
4. Similarly, it is possible that the interchange of information among data

banks may result in public disclosure, either accidental or intentional, of information that is not only confidential, but which may prove to be embarrassing or cause difficulties for some of the individuals involved.

As can be seen, the "advantages" of the social security number—uniqueness, universality, conciseness—may, in fact, be inherent disadvantages when considering the issue of privacy. Another point to be considered is that the number is not completely reliable as an identifier. It has been estimated by the Social Security Administration, for example, that over 4 million individuals have two or more numbers. In addition, there is no built-in check feature, such as a check digit, to help verify the validity of a given number.

14.1.6   The Privacy of Medical Information

The widespread use of computers in the health care field has raised many questions about the privacy of personal medical records. Recently, for example, government researchers investigating the long-term effects of abortions examined the medical records of 48,000 women, without their consent. The invasion of privacy here was compounded when some of the women's names were inadvertently disclosed in a preliminary report.

Medical information is frequently used by insurance companies, credit bureaus, welfare agencies, employers, government agencies, and numerous other organizations. The health insurance industry, for example, maintains its own data bank, known as the Medical Information Bureau.

A recent study funded by the Institute for Computer Sciences and Technology of the National Bureau of Standards has revealed that there are numerous privacy problems in the medical record-keeping area that require solutions. The study analyzed the use of medical records by various agencies. It produced the following conclusions:

1. In the area of primary health care, an individual typically seeks help from a medical professional. It is expected that the traditional doctor-patient privilege of confidentiality will prevent the disclosure of personal information. The study shows that for many reasons observance of strict confidentiality has been seriously eroded and that patient information is regularly disclosed without consent. The requirement of "informed consent" by patients for the release of their medical information is not very well observed today. In many instances consent is obtained because the patient fears, or has been threatened with, loss of services. This can occur, for example, when third parties, such as insurance companies, are involved in paying for the medical care; the fear of nonpayment exists. "Informed" consent is often nonexistent because a patient does not usually have the right to see his or her medical records.

2. With regard to payment for medical services, the private insurance companies as well as the government medical programs contribute to the threat of invasion of privacy. An unresolved issue is how much personal data from medical records really needs to be disclosed to medical insurance companies in order to determine eligibility, assess claims, and detect possible fraud. The issue of privacy is especially acute when psychiatric conditions are involved. Two other key questions that have been raised in this area are:
   a. How long should personal data be retained by the insurance carriers?
   b. Should individuals who receive benefits have the right to examine their records?

3. Health data is also used by many social agencies for various research projects with a wide range of objectives. These studies can shed considerable light on medical trends in this country. The challenge is to adjust the balance between the right to privacy on the one side, and the needs of legitimate social programs on the other. Often, the use of personal health data leads to what one study terms "stigmatizing and discriminatory judgments" about individuals. This arises especially when the individuals involved have had psychiatric treatment, or are homosexuals, or have undergone drug or alcohol rehabilitation. The problem, as the study notes, is that traditional laws and institutional policies have not kept pace with the expanded uses of health information in our society. Standards necessary to resolve many of the key issues are lacking in various sectors of the national health care system.

An interesting conclusion of the study was that most cases of *actual* harm to individuals resulting from invasion of privacy arose from manual methods of handling medical records. The main problem today with the use of computerized medical records involves *potential* harm—the creation of health information systems that many believe may be *threats* to basic rights.

Some of the major recommendations presented in the report suggest that health data systems should provide:

1. Procedures for issuing a public notice and privacy-impact statement whenever a computerized health care system is created and for communicating the statement to the population of individuals whose records will be affected.
2. Socially acceptable standards of relevance in the collection of personal data which would be established through public discussion and appropriate policy-setting mechanisms.
3. Information to individuals as to how their medical data will be used, together with the procedures to be followed before the data is used for any purpose other than that originally specified.
4. Patients with a right to review information about their medical conditions, where feasible. Where health data is to be used for making judgments about claims for payment, for example, an individual should

have an absolute right to inspect the information to be disclosed from his or her medical record.

5. Special training programs for the medical staff to alert them to possible threats to individual rights.
6. A handbook for each health data system that specifies patients' rights.
7. Special procedures for disseminating information for medical research or health care evaluation programs so that these activities can be carried on without jeopardizing an individual's rights.

14.1.7 Privacy Legislation

There are numerous state and federal laws that deal with the issue of privacy. A review of some of the major federal laws will provide a perspective on legislative attempts that have been made to prevent the erosion of an individual's privacy.

1. **The Right to Financial Privacy Act of 1979** deals, for example, with the type of personal information that federal agencies can obtain from financial institutions. Ordinarily, unless an individual consents in advance to the release of the information, the federal agency must follow certain procedures:
   a. It must be able to demonstrate that the information sought is relevant to a legitimate law enforcement investigation.
   b. It must subpoena the information from the financial institution and send a copy of the subpoena to the individual involved with forms and instructions, indicating how a court challenge may be initiated to prevent the agency from obtaining the information.
   c. It must certify in writing to the financial institution that the individual has been advised of his or her rights and that either (1) a court has overruled the person's objections, or (2) the time has expired in which a challenge could be raised.
   These procedures require prior notice to be given to people before personal information can be released. There are exceptions to this prior notice rule, but these exceptions require court approval. If, for example, the agency is concerned that prior notice may lead to tampering with evidence or may hamper an investigation, the agency will seek the court's permission to override prior notice.
2. **The Privacy Act of 1974** is concerned with data banks of personal information that are maintained by federal agencies. Some of the highlights of the act are:
   a. An agency can release information only with the individual's written consent or through a legal process (e.g., court order).
   b. One agency is not to convey personal information to another agency unless the latter is conducting a law enforcement action against the individual involved.
   c. Each agency must publish at least once a year in the *Federal Register* the kind and location of every data bank it maintains, with instruc-

tions on how an individual can obtain a copy of his or her personal file. This provision is intended to ensure that no federal agency maintains secret files about specific people.

    d. The act provides an individual with not only the right to inspect his or her personal information in a data bank but also the opportunity to have erroneous information corrected.

3.   There are laws that pertain to *private* data banks as well as federal ones. **The Fair Credit Reporting Act of 1971** is concerned with consumer credit information that is maintained and disseminated by various credit agencies. Some of the major provisions under this act include the following:

    a. A credit agency ordinarily can only provide information on an individual's credit standing to an organization to which the individual has applied for such things as credit, employment, and insurance.

    b. An individual is given the right to see any portions of the credit agency's files that were used as a basis for the denial of credit. Here again, the individual is provided with the opportunity to have erroneous information corrected.

    c. If a credit agency intends to contact neighbors or friends of the person being investigated about his or her character or life-style, the agency must first notify the person.

It should be noted that there are numerous state privacy statutes as well as the federal laws indicated above, many of which have similar provisions (see Figure 14.1).

Notwithstanding the numerous privacy laws that currently exist, the concern for ensuring privacy continues to be of such paramount importance that new and revised laws are constantly being considered by various legislative bodies throughout the country. Recently, Congress has been considering proposals aimed at increasing privacy protection for millions of individuals who either use credit cards or have insurance policies. Under the proposed legislation, credit card companies would be required to inform their cardholders of the kind of personal information collected. Moreover, cardholders would be given the right to challenge a request for disclosure of the records to any organization. Insurance companies would be required to advise applicants for insurance of the kind of information that would be collected about them. Policyholders would be given the right to see information in their files and, as in the prior instances, an opportunity to have erroneous information corrected.

All of these laws point to the government's appreciation of the potential threat to privacy that exists as a result of the computer revolution and the consequent establishment of large data banks. Although these laws have made tremendous inroads toward protecting an individual's privacy, there is still much work that needs to be done in this area. It must also be noted that no matter how well intentioned

Summary Status of State and Federal Privacy
Laws and Rulings Pertaining to Personal Information Records

	Banking	Criminal Justice	Employee Personnel	Government Files	Health Medical	IRS, Tax	Personal Credit	Student
Alabama								
Alaska								
Arizona								
Arkansas								
California								
Colorado								
Connecticut								
Delaware								
Florida								
Georgia								
Hawaii								
Idaho								
Illinois								
Indiana								
Iowa								
Kansas								
Kentucky								
Louisiana								
Maine								
Maryland								
Massachusetts								
Michigan								
Minnesota								
Mississippi								
Missouri								
Montana								
Nebraska								
Nevada								
New Hampshire								
New Jersey								
New Mexico								
New York								
North Carolina								
North Dakota								
Ohio								
Oklahoma								
Oregon								
Pennsylvania								
Rhode Island								
South Carolina								
South Dakota								
Tennessee								
Texas								
Utah								
Vermont								
Virginia								
Washington								
West Virginia								
Wisconsin								
Wyoming								
Federal Law								

Figure 14.1.

some companies may be with regard to preserving privacy, at some point cost factors become a major consideration. Just how much is a company willing to expend to ensure the confidentiality and integrity of personal information contained in its data banks? A case in point involves the Right to Financial Privacy Act passed in 1979. When bankers found that it would cost the banking industry approximately $1 billion to comply with a minor section of the law, they appealed to Congress; the costly provision was subsequently repealed. The unknown costs in terms of dollars and employee hours of complying with various privacy laws have also tempered some of the enthusiasm with which companies attempt to protect their customers' privacy.

Another serious problem is that not all companies are affected to the same extent by the various privacy laws. Consider Interbank, for example, which is a switching agent for bank card transactions such as Master Card. Interbank handles approximately 2 million charge card transactions each day for over 1100 financial institutions throughout the United States and in 120 foreign countries. Since Interbank provides merely a financial communications link between member companies and does not itself maintain a data bank of personal information, it is not subject to many of the privacy laws currently in effect.

It is interesting to note that at least 17 states have enacted privacy laws that specifically address the issue of how state agencies are to maintain information on individuals. The effectiveness of these laws in protecting an individual's rights is, however, yet to be established. According to the National Association for State Information Systems, there are still serious obstacles to preserving the privacy. Although the states have implemented various plans in this area, it has been found that not all the states *enforce* them. There is the added problem that many of the states do not *audit* the plans to evaluate how effective the laws really are. The main reason proffered for the lack of attention by the states to the issues of privacy and security of data is the limited financial resources of the agencies involved.

14.2 OTHER LEGAL ISSUES

Now that we have examined computer crime and the issue of privacy, we will briefly explore other legal issues that have emerged as the impact of the computer becomes more pervasive in our society.

An important and, as yet, unresolved issue is: From whom, if anyone, can an individual seek recovery if he or she has suffered damages as a result of a computer error? Many questions of computer negligence and liability are not easy to resolve since there are virtually no legal precedents to guide the way. It is very common in the computer industry for software or consulting companies to supply programs to a company for a fee. Let us assume, for example, that a program has been supplied to a hospital to monitor a patient's vital signs and to alert the hospital staff when certain changes occur. We will assume that due to an error in the program, the staff is not alerted when a particularly critical condition occurs, and consequently the patient dies.

Whether or not the patient's family can successfully sue the hospital depends on whether the hospital was justified in relying on the program. Moreover, it may be possible for the family to sue the company that supplied the program. There has been very little legal groundwork established in this area to date.

One approach to this problem hinges on whether programs are considered to be services or products. The distinction has major legal ramifications. For example, under the Uniform Commercial Code, which has been adopted by virtually every state, if computer programs are considered goods then it is possible for third parties (e.g., outsiders to the original contract between the software house and the hospital) who are harmed by a program error to sue the software company for consequential damages.

Another approach to allowing third parties to sue a software supplier hinges on the issue of negligence. There are legal precedents involving accountants, for example, which have established that as a general rule accountants are *not* liable to third parties for their negligence. Whether or not this approach will carry over to the computer field remains to be seen.

It should be noted that software houses are obtaining insurance to protect themselves in the event that they are held liable for consequential damages arising out of errors in their software.

In a related development, at least one court, a federal district court in New York, has ruled that computer specialists and their clients have a special relationship which makes the computer specialists liable for malpractice claims, in much the same way as doctors and lawyers are liable for malpractice claims. One consequence is that software houses that supply erroneous programs may be subject to liability even years after the contracts under which the programs were supplied have been terminated.

Another interesting legal development is related to the leasing of computers. Recent advances in semiconductor technology have resulted in smaller and more powerful computer circuitry. Consequently, computer prices have dropped sharply. Many businesses that originally acquired computer systems by leasing them have been attempting to cancel their leases so that they can acquire better and less expensive systems. This presents a major problem to leasing companies. Leasing companies buy computer equipment from various manufacturers; they then lease it out to businesses. A typical seven-year lease affords the user the opportunity to cancel the lease after the first three years. Starting in 1973, the leasing companies were able to procure insurance from Lloyd's of London to provide them with full payment in the event leases were canceled. If a lease is canceled by the user, Lloyd's, an insurance exchange comprised of over 350 insurance syndicates, is obliged to pay the leasing company any revenue it loses as a consequence of a lease being broken. Under the insurance contract, the leasing company must attempt to find a new user for the equipment, thereby minimizing the losses involved.

It has been estimated that the syndicates could lose perhaps as much as $1 billion, which would be a record loss. Already, Lloyd's has been sued for almost $600 million. It should be noted that Lloyd's stopped writing this type of insurance contract in 1978 after it became painfully aware of the extent of the risk it was underwriting.

There have not been many lawsuits to date involving computer-produced libel, false written statements that injure one's reputation. An interesting lawsuit was brought in New Jersey where a credit bureau was sued for issuing a defamatory consumer credit report. It was held by an appellate court that the credit agency had a privilege that freed it from liability "provided the information was given under an honest belief in its truth and without express or actual malice."

As we have seen, although many laws have been enacted concerning computer crime, privacy, and other computer-related activities, there is still a need for legislation at the federal level to provide uniform procedures and protection to individuals.

KEY TERMS

Fair Credit Reporting Act of 1971
National Crime Information Center (NCIC)
National Security Agency
Privacy Act of 1974
Right to Financial Privacy Act of 1979

DISCUSSION QUESTIONS

1. The Census Bureau is required by law to keep all material collected for the census confidential. Is this feasible? What controls would need to be incorporated to ensure that this law was not violated?

2.   If home computers are used with increasing frequency, as predicted, and they are employed to communicate with central data bases, can you see any privacy issues that might arise?
3.   What are some of the differences between privacy and security?

APPLICATION

What are the key issues raised by the following article?

Perspective:
Managing DP Security[a]
By Michael J. Keliher

Establishing a security and privacy system is not enough today. You have to *manage it*, no more and no less than you manage manufacturing, engineering or any other business function.

More and more members of the public are gaining access to terminals and computers. We must ensure that the sophistication of our safeguards grows along with this trend. Otherwise, our opponents—the violators—will get ahead of us.

But what is the *user's* commitment to security? What is the computer user's role in security and privacy protection? If I were a data processing manager, I would want three things from my top management.

My first recommendation would be to assign *high-level responsibility* for security and privacy. This move would demonstrate to employees that a firm is serious. Then the *employees* would take it seriously. As long as I can remember, employees have followed the management style of their leaders. The employees may not like to think of it as imitation. We leaders may not like to think of it as imitation. But imitation it is.

Employees aren't blind. They know the difference between executive *words* and executive *actions*. Because security and privacy are *social* concerns—just like equal employment opportunity, business ethics and on-the-job safety—our employees know we must show concern. They're on the lookout for the empty gesture. So let's show them we're *serious*.

Let's identify respected, high-level employees as security and privacy chiefs. And let's write this responsibility into their job characters and objectives. Otherwise, our employees will quickly perceive these appointments as window-dressing, just like some executive memberships on ethics and safety committees.

The security chief's very first task should be to analyze the current safeguards in each department. Perhaps they're adequate already. But if they're inadequate, then the security chief should develop a program *for the entire organization*. He should get top management approval of the program. Then he should *manage it*. No exceptions. No compromises. This is a top-down program, not a democracy.

My second recommendation then would be to develop a *full-time security and privacy program* to monitor, audit and review the activities of the entire organization. To *manage* security and privacy. And incidentally, you and I know that security and privacy are not data processing problems. They're not problems for the data processing manager to solve all by himself.

We need a *systems* approach—an analytical approach. And we need to fund it properly. Let's not shoe-string this project to death. Let's give it the resources it must have in order to work properly.

We must learn to *think system*. We must begin to think in terms of the organization of data and the impact of that organization on security and privacy. Just establishing a system isn't good enough. We need to *manage it*.

My third recommendation would be to exercise more care in selecting and screening the *personnel* who will have access to computers and terminals. When you boil it all down, the greatest threat to security and privacy in our companies is the intentional violation by our own employee. We really must get tough on selection of employees and prosecution of violators.

There's really no point in spending any time or effort on security and privacy if we as business people don't make an attempt to keep potential and actual criminals off our own payrolls.

And let's not be tempted to make exceptions at the top. Let's make sure we have the guts to fire our fellow executives who stray beyond legal and ethical boundaries.

I believe our employees see these incidents as the ultimate test of top management ethics. Whenever these incidents occur, let's show our people what we stand for.

[a] *Information Systems News*, May 5, 1980, p. 31. Copyright 1980 by CMP Publications Inc., 333 East Shore Road, Manhasset, NY. Reprinted with permission.

15

Computers in the arts and the humanities

This text has pointed to the traditional "two cultures" that exist in our society, where students of the sciences and students of the humanities view the world in very different ways. We have further indicated that the gap which exists between these so-called "two cultures" has resulted in areas of specialization within each that are far too insulated and that fail to benefit from alternative perspectives provided by other disciplines.

Because the computer has become such a common tool for many different applications, it needs to be understood by both the scientist and the humanist, not simply in terms of the technology but in terms of how that technology can best serve society as a whole.

The use of computers in the humanities could help to bridge the communication gap that tends to separate scientific disciplines from the humanities, and which keeps each from understanding the perspectives of the other. That is, the application of computers to the humanities requires:

1. Computer scientists with the ability to understand the needs of people in the liberal arts
2. People in the liberal arts with a willingness to experiment with computers in an effort to add a dimension to their work and to understand better the creative process

In short, the applications of computers to humanities subjects, begun about 1965, have a great deal of potential for bringing the "two cultures" closer together.

15.1 COMPUTERS IN THE ARTS

The application of computers to the fine arts is only one application area in the humanities, but it is a major one and is emphasized in this chapter. Later, we focus on other applications of computers to the humanities. Although we center our discussion on computers as an aid to the artist and musician, "Computers in the Arts" actually means the use of computers in the following areas:

1. Art
2. Music
3. Poetry
4. Creative composition
5. Sculpture
6. Film
7. Ballet and other choreography

In discussing computer utilization in the arts we emphasize two principal ways in which computers can be used effectively:

1. As a device that, given a set of basic rules or structures, can produce an artistic product. This has two potential advantages:
   a. The computer can shed light on the artistic process itself.
   b. A personal or micro computer can also enable amateur or would-be artists to experiment or "tinker," and to derive some satisfaction from their own creations produced with the assistance of a machine.
2. As a tool to assist artists in designing, structuring, and expressing their final product.

15.1.1 The Computer as Artist

15.1.1.1 The Use of Computers to Produce a Form of Art

When the computer is used to provide the actual art form, the following elements are typically included in the program:

1. Reading in a library of traditional art forms.
2. Using preprogrammed rules of the artist to have the computer manipulate the data in the library at random and create an art form of its own.
3. Producing output in the form of a drawing on a graphics display terminal.
4. Providing the artist (or amateur user) with the option of making specific changes or transformations to the computer-produced art form. Experimentation of this kind can lead to a combined artist-computer creation that neither could have produced alone.

Figure 15.1. Computer-generated abstract art (moiré pattern).

For a computer to function as if it were an artist, it must possess the following characteristics:

Features of a Computer Necessary for Producing Art Forms

1. The ability to accept art forms as input
2. The ability to process and change these input forms according to prescribed rules
3. The ability to process input randomly
4. The ability to enable users, or artists, to make changes in a real-time environment
5. Graphics display ability

(See Figure 15.1 for an illustration of computer-generated art.)

This last feature, graphics display ability, has only been available on a large-scale basis in recent years. Many graphics display terminals now have the capability of generating numerous forms and figures in a wide variety of colors and for a minimal cost. The main disadvantage is that programming a computer to produce graphic output is very difficult and requires high-level mathematical ability. There are, however, packages available that minimize the effort required to generate computer graphics and these packages will undoubtedly proliferate in the coming years. The following chart provides an analysis of computer graphics as it relates to the art field:

Advantages and Disadvantages of Computer Graphics and Art

Advantages

1. Computer scientists and humanists work together to achieve this end.
2. Many systems, even small ones, can be adapted to include graphics display.
3. Personal expression by amateur or would-be artists is now available.
4. Light can be shed on the creative process itself.
5. Artists can be assisted in the more tedious aspects of their job.

Disadvantages

1. Large-scale sophisticated computer graphics systems are expensive.
2. It is difficult to learn the mathematics and advanced programming techniques for computer graphics software.
3. The end costs sometimes cannot be justified.

Computer-generated art has met with considerable success. There have been, for example, numerous displays in art museums of this type of work. Many artists are enthusiastic about the prospects for non-professionals to experiment with art and to produce their own art forms, with the use of personal computers:

> Home computers will be as commonplace as television sets in the not-too-distant future. Wall displays under computer control will allow the whole family to create its own visual environment. The direction and very nature of art under such conditions might well be radically different from what we know as art today. The artist in our society cannot escape the profound influence that the rapidly expanding technology exerts on every facet of our daily existence.[1]

15.1.1.2 The Computer as an Artist's Tool

Thus far, we have focused on the computer as a device for producing an art form which the user, either artist or amateur, can then transform or adjust. Computers can also be used by artists as tools in much the same way as a scientist uses a scientific instrument. That is, the artist can program his or her own creation into the computer and then use the machine to:

Transform
Rotate
Magnify
Distort
Reflect
Change color

[1] Lillian F. Schwartz and Charles B. Rubinstein, "Film-Making with Computer: Adapting a New Technology for Art," *Interdisciplinary Science Reviews*, Vol. 4, No. 4, p. 305.

In this case, the computer is used as a kind of "black box" to facilitate the artist's task.

Many artists have begun to rely upon the computer as a tool of the trade:

> In handling the visuals, the artist need not constantly monitor the program controls and instead can concentrate on making the emotional and intellectual decisions to structure the images. The tools in this system become second-nature and do not impose upon, or interrupt, the creative process.[1]

The main areas of success in the art field rest with applications such as:

1. Computer-aided design (CAD), discussed in Chapter 8, which is a practical art form that has met with considerable success.
2. Sculpture, where the ability of the computer to provide cross sections and transformations can save the sculptor considerable time and effort.

Yet in other other areas, we have not yet reached the level where the computer can provide the user, either artist or would-be artist, with art of consistently high quality. The reason for the slow progress in this field is mostly a result of the same communication gap mentioned so many times before:

1. Artists view computers with a certain amount of distaste, fear, or resistance.
2. Computer professionals are usually less attuned to aesthetics and the humanities than is desired.

Jeff Bangert, a computer professional who is active in the art field, sums up this dichotomy as follows:

> Let me see if I can identify what I think the nature of the problem is. First, I have to point my finger at artists and say, of this group of people, that one of the characteristics is a certain antagonism toward the aesthetics of the man on the street, the ordinary person. . . . Now we are not all technologists. Most artists who want to do art with technology have to work with someone else. If a person is an artist and says: "Hey, I'd like to do computer stuff," most of the time she/he needs a programmer and here is the problem. . . . The aesthetic sensibilities of the programmer are likely to be those of the person in the street. . . . If we focus on collaboration between the artist and the technologist, the solution is

[1]Lillian F. Schwartz and Charles B. Rubinstein, "Computer Graphics as Art; Variation on Reality," unpublished paper.

obvious. Artist and technologist must agree to collaborate aesthetically.[1]

15.1.1.3 The Significance of the Computer as Artist

Many humanists fear that the use of computers in the fine arts will lead to the computer replacing people as artists. If, indeed, computer-generated art is as creative and satisfying as forms of art produced by the best artists, this fear may be well founded.

Note, however, that the computer requires *rules* for manipulating input. On the other hand, many of the greatest works of art transcend the common rules employed by contemporary artists. In short, based on the level of sophistication of existing computer art and the direction in which it has moved, it is unlikely that machines will replace the artist, now or in the future.

What, then, is the significance of computer-generated art? First, the use of computers can assist the artist in understanding the creative process, in analyzing existing techniques or "rules," and in demonstrating the potential of new techniques or rules.

Second, computers can be used by ordinary lay people to express their own creativity, even if that creativity is amateur or unsophisticated. That is, personal computers have an added benefit for people: they can be used to translate an individual's creative, albeit unsophisticated, ideas into drawings, paintings, music, short stories, and so on, from which people can derive great pleasure. The individual enters the ideas as input; the computer then translates them into actual creations.

15.1.1.4 Computers and Research in the Art Field

Bell Laboratories has undertaken a series of computer experiments in the visual arts. One such experiment is designed to determine the least amount of visual information that a picture may contain and still be recognizable. Such studies of the "information content" of a picture may be useful for designing future visual communications systems, and for devising techniques for computer storage of pictures.

The picture in Figure 15.2 is divided into approximately 200 squares, with each square rendered in an even tone from 1 through 16 intensities of gray. The figure is that of Abraham Lincoln, but it may take some rotating, or squinting, to "see" the portrait (see also Figure 15.3).

---

[1]Jeff Bangert, "Art and Technology—The Future Was Yesterday," *Proceedings of the 9th International Sculpture Conference, New Orleans,* published by the University of Kansas Press, p. 193.

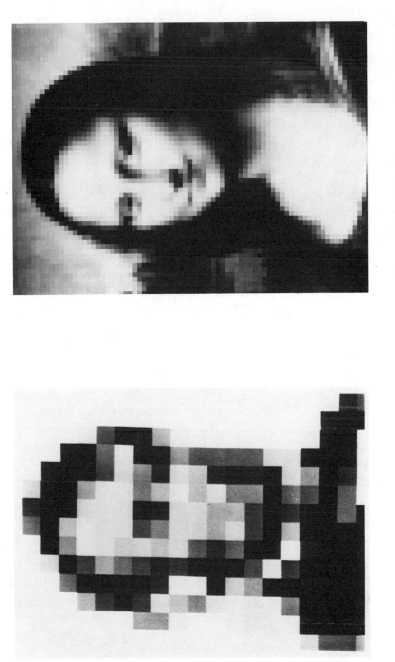

Figure 15.3. Computer-generated portrait.

Figure 15.2. Computer-generated portrait.

Figure 15.4. Computer-generated picture of a woman's face.

There have also been experiments designed to derive a form of computer-generated art from photographs (see Figure 15.4). Using a digitizer (see Figure 15.5), the computer has converted a photo of a young woman into a series of numbers and then transformed the numbers back into a graphic display. By measuring the levels of dark and light and then almost eliminating grays, the woman's face has been turned into what looks like a contour map.

15.1.1.5 Conclusion

Despite the existence of graphics packages, the artist who wishes to utilize a computer must have some knowledge of programming. This factor, together with the computer professional's general lack of understanding of art remain serious obstacles:

> Since there is no natural way of communicating with the equipment, a better than average understanding of programming and graphic algorithm is necessary to produce a computer image. This

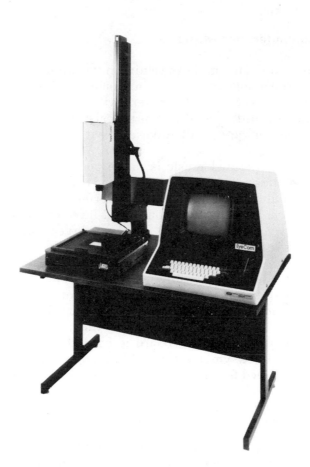

Figure 15.5. Picture digitizer and display system.

alone keeps a large number of people from being involved in the practice of computer art. Another noteworthy point is that not all engineering-scientists who have programming and image generating skills are capable of generating computer aesthetics; their images blatantly lack visual awareness. Conversely, those that are visually literate cannot grasp the technical language of the computer, or simply abhor the complexity of programming.[1]

Although the proliferation of packages in recent years has minimized the need for knowing advanced programming languages, the dilemma described above remains.

[1] William J. Kolomyjec, "Introduction to Computer Aesthetics," paper presented at the International Conference on Visual Literacy.

15.1.2 Computers and Music

Although one would not make the claim that computers are commonly used tools of the musician, there are areas in which such devices have played a significant role. Moreover, with the decreasing cost of hardware and the anticipated decline in resistance to this device by the humanist, the computer will have a great deal of potential as a musician's tool.

Computer-generated music is made possible with the use of a **music synthesizer**. This device is attached to a computer and utilizes a digital-to-analog converter. The converter makes it possible to depress numeric keys on a keyboard and have them converted to a corresponding voltage level that can be "played back" as musical notes. These synthesizers are available with microcomputers, providing the amateur with the ability to generate music.

As indicated in the preceding section, computer-generated art has been made possible by the graphics capability of computers.

The graphics capability of a computer is also important in music to print the notes on a printer or to display them on a cathode ray tube (CRT) (see Figure 15.6). A keyboard is used that has had the keys relabeled with music symbols. Special languages, such as SCORTOS, have been developed for processing of musical information.

15.1.2.1 The Computer as a Production Tool in Music

Musical compositions are frequently published and then sold or distributed to a wide audience. The process of printing, or typesetting, a musical work so that it can be mass produced is very complex and prone to errors. Computers are an effective tool to facilitate this typesetting operation. They function in exactly the same manner as text editing systems.

An operator, or in this instance a composer, keys in the notes. The computer can display the arrangement and play it back so that the composer can check for accuracy and make changes as necessary. The final, edited version would then be transformed to some coded form and stored in a computer medium such as punched paper tape, cassette tape, or floppy disk. A punched paper tape is commonly used because it can effectively "drive" a print mechanism. That is, the punched tape functions just like it does on a piano roll, but instead of driving a player piano it drives a print device that can then print music.

This use of the computer to facilitate the production process has been very effective. In general, it results in fewer errors in the music. Moreover, it makes future revisions much easier. If the composer wishes to make some minor changes, the computer-produced medium

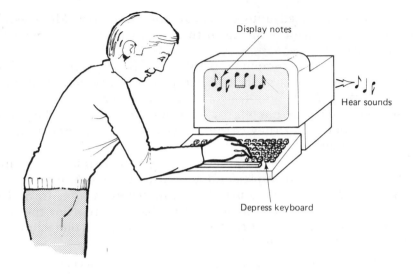

Figure 15.6.   Displaying music on a CRT.

need only be patched so that the rest of the work will remain unchanged and error-free.

Note that the graphics package for producing music by computer is very complex. The programming of half or quarter notes and other musical configurations requires advanced techniques.

15.1.2.2   Computers as a Tool
for Musical Composition
or Amateur "Tinkering"

Just as the artist can use a computer as a tool for facilitating the creation of a work, a computer can be used as a musician's tool.

The musician can attach a musical instrument to the computer or simply use a standard keyboard to create notes. In both cases, a music synthesizer would be attached to the computer.

The musician plays the notes and the computer stores the results. Changes, additions, and deletions can be made easily as well.

The musician can test the sounds by requesting the computer to transform them to different keys or play them back using the sounds of different instruments or of an entire orchestra. Frequently, a composition sounds fine when played on a single instrument but is not suitable for an entire orchestra. The computer can be used to test the sounds as necessary.

Once the musician is satisfied with the composition, there is no need to spend time developing final copy because the computer has stored the edited final version. Thus the composition can be automatically transcribed onto paper by the computer. Moreover, the computer can score the music so that it is suitable for a variety of instruments.

The use of the computer in this way is of particular value to musicians, who may be excellent composers but who have difficulty writing music. Many guitarists, for example, cannot read or write music very well but are highly respected composers. They would certainly benefit from a device that transforms their compositions into the proper notation.

Note that the use of computers to print or score music is no simple task. The software is complex and not without flaws. Moreover, many musicians are reluctant to use the computer even as a transcriber, because it is so difficult, if not impossible, to program the actual rendering of a musical piece that might be desired by a musician. As an expert in the field has stated:

> You cannot go from a performance to a score, or vice versa, in any easy fashion, while preserving the qualities that make the notation of music readable to most musicians and the properties of a performance that make it worthwhile listening material.
>
> A score is a highly idiomatic rendering of a piece of music, and a piece of music is a unique instance of the composition that the composer had in mind when the score was written.[1]

This limitation also affects the ability of a computer to print music as part of a production process, as described above. The computer, then, will never be *perfect* as a transcriber or as a musician's tool but it can be effective in many instances. Raskin, however, and many others remain skeptical as to whether the computer will ever be "good enough":

> The building of a perfect music transcriber is literally impossible. Whether it is possible to make the composer's aid good enough for most practical purposes remains to be seen.[2]

In summary, computers have been used to assist musicians, like artists, in achieving their objectives. Just as transformations and editing of artistic works can be performed with the use of computer, the computer can play back or transform a musical score in various ways. This ability is not only useful for the professional but also for the amateur artist or musician, who enjoys creating an art form or musical composition, but is not expert at it. The computer can be programmed to provide stylistic structure and direction to any work.

The availability of music synthesizers with low-priced micro-

[1] Jef Raskin, "Using the Computer as a Musician's Amanuensis," *Byte*, May 1980, p. 128. Adapted with permission. Copyright 1980, Byte Publications, Inc.

[2] Jef Raskin, "Using the Computer as a Musician's Amanuensis," *Byte*, May 1980, p. 128. Adapted with permission. Copyright 1980, Byte Publications, Inc.

computers has enabled many computer hobbyists and home users to "tinker" with music. They depress keys on a keyboard which correspond to musical notes and the computer plays back the results as sounds. This technique is very similar to electronic games such as Merlin, which are hand-held devices that provide children with the ability to "play" music.

15.1.2.3   The Computer as a Creative Instrument in Music

As in the art field, there have been experiments conducted to test the computer's ability to compose original works. The method used relies on a random number generator to select notes randomly. A program then tests the random notes generated and eliminates all incompatibilities or cacophonous arrangements. The result is a creative work that may or may not be pleasing to the ear.

Another way in which computer-produced music can be generated is to combine, in a systematic way, previously used musical bars or excerpts considered to be particularly harmonious. This, too, may or may not produce a work with sufficient consistency or originality.

In either case, the composer may begin with a computer-generated arrangement and make adjustments that will result in an interesting and aesthetic work. The first musical compositions of this genre were produced by Lejaren Hiller and Leonard Isaacson at the University of Illinois. Their first computer-produced composition was developed in the 1950s and was called "Illiac Suite," named after the University of Illinois' first electronic digital computer, the Illiac. Their second composition was called "Computer Cantata." Both works were published in a 1959 book entitled *Experimental Music*.

Such experiments with computer-produced music, although interesting, will probably not have a very significant effect on those who study or write music. Although there are isolated cases of limited success in this field, the entire concept of computers as creative instruments in music, as well as in art, remains controversial. It is hoped, however, that the use of computers in this way will, in the future, shed some light on the creative process itself.

Note that the computer's starting point, a random number generator, is not really a revolutionary concept. Rather, classical composers have been known to begin their composition with random arrangements as well:

> Mozart once composed music with a pair of dice. Presumably he used the dice to select notes at random from the scale and then constructed a melody and its supporting harmony from that selection. He might also have used a random number pattern in composing the rhythm. Of course, this was done as a novelty and

never became a common practice in music composition in that time. In the past 30 years, however, a growing number of composers have taken up an interest in what they call "stochastic music;" that is, music composed from random numbers.

This interest in random music has grown largely as a philosophical outgrowth of the avant-garde movement, and its practice is facilitated by the introduction of the digital computer to the arts.[1]

Computers are used in the other art fields mentioned—poetry, creative composition, sculpture, film, and ballet—in ways that are very similar to those discussed for art and music. Art and music, however, have been the two artistic fields where computers have been most extensively used with the greatest success.

15.1.2.4 The Computer as a Research Tool in Music

With the use of computers to evaluate various musical patterns, it is possible for scholars to analyze the works of classical composers and to ascertain the influence of one composer on another. These devices can also be used to help determine authorship of some music. Consider the following illustration:

> Dr. Franklin B. Zimmerman, professor of music (at the University of Pennsylvania) is in the middle of a complex program which utilizes a "full core arrangement." It is called the Melodic Indexing Program—Melind for short.
>
> "My ambition," Zimmerman said, "is to set up a very detailed index of baroque composers." This index is being done in three steps, the first being compilation of thematic indexes by first lines. "The theme of most works is revealed in the first 10 tones." Step two is to trace thematic usage and borrowing. Handel, for example, whose index is complete, used some 26,000 themes and borrowed repeatedly from himself.
>
> Step three, according to Zimmerman, is "letting the computer analyze the stylistic 'finger prints' of melodics" to help determine authorship.[2]

15.2 RESEARCH IN THE HUMANITIES

Students in the humanities are most likely to encounter the computer as a research tool. In this capacity, the ability of computers to perform high-speed literary searches is most evident.

[1] Wayne Bateman, *Introduction to Computer Music* (New York: Wiley, 1980), p. 223.
[2] *Computerworld*, Apr. 7, 1980, p. 47.

Many libraries currently subscribe to one of a variety of **information banks**. These banks maintain data on a very large number of articles, books, or other resources. Some of these information banks cite or abstract material in a specific discipline. There are legal banks, medical banks, historical banks, and so on. Other information banks abstract or cite all articles in a fixed set of journals.

For some information banks one can enter a key word or phrase. The computer scans the file and prints the names of articles relating to the key word or phrase; sometimes the machine will also print an abstract of each article.

Some information banks require the user to enter one of a fixed number of codes. Others permit free-style words which are then compared against the file; when a match occurs, the corresponding record is printed.

The computer as a research tool can save the user many hours in the library. Several minutes at a terminal in a library will usually provide users with a wide range of articles pertinent to their research.

The main limitation of these information banks is still cost. Large university libraries with substantial subsidies will provide access to information banks free of charge. Most others charge the user and the cost can sometimes be substantial, depending on the size of the data base and the number of items actually accessed. It is not unusual for a 3-minute search at a terminal to cost a user $30 or more. But as the technology advances, the cost is likely to decrease.

Still another potential of personal computers is the ability to link up with information banks using one's home telephone. Such services are currently available. That is, for a fixed monthly fee, a user can have personal access to a specific information bank. This obviates the need for going to a library, waiting for a free terminal, and so on. Here, again, as the number of home computers continues to increase and the cost of technology continues to decrease, such services will become very common.

In short, a computer is a very useful research tool for humanists. It provides the user with the ability to retrieve data from centralized information banks as necessary.

But a computer can also be used by humanists for analyzing data. Historians use computers as a kind of "number cruncher" for analyzing demographic data (see Figure 15.7).

Scholars use computers for determining authorship of given literary works. The computer stores a text or portion of a text and is programmed to compare phrases to those whose authorship is known. When statistical evidence indicates the likelihood of a match, the computer prints the result.

Electronic devices can also be used for dating a work of art, determining the influence of one humanist on another, and so on.

Zero-Base History:
Accounting for a Social Interpretation at Colonial Williamsburg[a]

By CARY CARSON
Director of Research
With Harold Gill, Kevin Kelly, and Linda Rowe

You, the puzzle solver, have as your assignment to pick through the barrel one piece at a time until you fit together enough of them to guess the subject of a picture that can never be completed.

Impossible? Historians at Colonial Williamsburg do it every day. Most historical research is a matter of careful sifting through whole archives in search of precious puzzle pieces associated with a particular person, topic, or event. It is tedious work, doing it one piece at a time.

Now there is promise of a better, faster way. The National Endowment for the Humanities has recently announced that the Research Department at Colonial Williamsburg will receive a gifts-and-matching grant for $250,000 to be used, in effect, to turn the barrel upside down and spill the puzzle pieces out where historians can study them all together. Over the next five years members of the Research Department staff will empty the records of York County, Virginia. They will comb out an estimated 900,000 to one million bits of information about some 60,000 men, women, and children whose names appear in public and private documents between 1630 and 1830. Fitting the pieces together with help from a computer at the College of William and Mary, the project's co-directors, Cary Carson, Harold Gill, and Kevin Kelly, expect to reconstitute the populations of Williamsburg, Yorktown, and rural York County and reconstruct the entire social order from slaves and servants to the county's planters and patricians.

[a] *Colonial Williamsburg Today*, Vol. 1, No. 4, p. 2.

Figure 15.7.

15.3 COMPUTERS AND MUSEUMS

Another area in which computers have been used with some success in the humanities is in museums. Several museums have utilized computers for cataloging, storing, and retrieving information concerning their respective inventories. Data is cataloged and made available through either a batch or on-line system to a network of museums.

The Museum Computer Network, Inc., is an international association of museums and related institutions working together to index collections.[1] It is a nonprofit membership organization. Its goals are to make collections and documentation more accessible, to assist in controlling inventories, and to help disseminate information about

[1]Information excerpted from a Museum Computer Network publication called *GRIPHOS*, by David Vance.

collections. To accomplish these goals, it makes use of a computerized system called GRIPHOS.

GRIPHOS stands for General Retrieval and Information Processor for Humanities Oriented Studies. It is a system that, offers a data storage format suitable for the large inventories of museums. GRIPHOS is a full data base management system supported by the Center for Contemporary Arts and Letters at the State University of New York at Stony Brook. It supports catalog storage, indexing, and retrieval of museum data.

The GRIPHOS system is *content independent*. Catalog entities may be anything that can be described in words and numbers.

Summary:
Advances in Hardware That Are Relevant to the Humanities

1. Graphics display terminals
2. Digitizers for artists
3. Synthesizers for musicians
4. Light pens for drawing
5. Word processing equipment for text editing

KEY TERMS

Cathode ray tube (CRT)
Computer-aided design
Graphics display terminal
GRIPHOS
Information banks
Museum Computer Network
Music synthesizer

DISCUSSION QUESTIONS

1. Do you think the computer can develop an art form that would be viewed by the experts as highly creative and sophisticated?
2. Is it possible for computers used in the humanities to result in very significant changes to these subjects?
3. Indicate some of the ways in which computers can be used for research in the humanities. Provide examples not discussed in the text.
4. Do you think that using a computer for identifying author, date, or influence on a creative work is a reliable technique? Explain your answer.

APPLICATION

Consider the application below and then answer the questions that follow it.

At University of Pennsylvania:
Humanists Nudged Toward DP for Research[a]

PHILADELPHIA—The University of Pennsylvania here is planning to replace its IBM 360/65 with a 4341 this year as part of a program to increase the use of computers in the humanities.

But while the increased power will help, the university hasn't been standing still up until now.

"I'm trying to 'rev up' the use of the computer in the humanities," Dr. Howard Brody, associate dean for computing in the Faculty of Arts and Sciences, said. "I assume a lot of humanists have little card files and they keep lots of notes. Well, when you get 40 boxes of those card files, you can start losing control of what you are doing."

Here the computer can help, if only for sorting and remembering. But computers can also be used to correlate exhaustive research findings, saving time and money, he added.

Going for Baroque

The departments of music, religion and linguistics all have found interesting uses for the computer in the humanities, Brody said. Dr. Franklin B. Zimmerman, professor of music, is in the middle of a complex program which he said utilizes a "full core arrangement." It is called the Melodic Indexing Program—Melind for short.

"My ambition," Zimmerman said, "is to set up a very detailed index of baroque composers." This index is being done in three steps, the first being compilation of thematic indexes by first lines. "The theme of most works is revealed in the first 10 tones."

Step two is to trace thematic usage and borrowing. Handel, for example, whose index is complete, used some 26,000 themes and borrowed repeatedly from himself.

Step three, according to Zimmer-

man, is "letting the computer analyze the stylistic 'finger prints' of melodics" to help determine authorship.

In the religion department, Dr. Robert A. Kraft, chairman and professor, is trying to apply the computer to concordance, or indexing work, on ancient Greek texts. Kraft is developing a system to reduce the prodigious amount of hand copying and paper shuffling involved in producing critical texts of the Bible.

"The computer also makes it possible to format the text in different ways"—Greek and Hebrew side by side, for example, or interlinear, he added.

Dr. William Labov, professor of linguistics and director of the Urban Language Survey, has his own Digital Equipment Corp. PDP-11, which has been churning out data on linguistic variables.

According to Gregory Guy, a graduate student in linguistics who is watching the Linguistics Lab while Labov is away for the semester, the computer is "primarily used for vowel analysis. An analyzer gives you an acoustic analysis of speech sounds as they are being spoken."

In Labov's study of black English, the computer was used "for statistical analysis of linguistic variables . . . like the verb 'to be,'" Guy said. "The occasions on which [the verb] is used are often influenced by linguistic and social context."

Not Suited for Job?

In his office at the David Rittenhouse Laboratories, Brody pointed to an advertising flyer he received, noting that "you can now buy the complete works of Virgil in machine-readable form for $30."

436

What about the objection, sure to be raised, that the computer is an anonymous machine, not suited to the study of the humanities?

"It's an anonymous machine, like a typewriter," Brody said, "but I don't see people rebelling against the typewriter."

Through financial inducements, loans of equipment and lavish attention Brody hopes to make the humanists' first experience with the computer "so sweet, so painless and so costfree" that they will continue to use it regularly.

Brody explained the reason for the 4341 is that the old computer is down too often and that maintenance costs have been rising "at an alarming rate."

DP Experience

Brody and his colleagues in the physics department have had lots of experience with computers. In fact, the department is the largest user of computer time on campus, using most of that time for high energy physics—a popular specialty among the faculty.

One of the world's leading authorities on the subject, Dr. Alfred Mann, explained that high energy physics needs the time because the discipline is heavily dependent on probability and statistics. To design a detector to verify whether protons ever decay, for example, one must run off a large number of complex calculations, called Monte Carlo calculations, which describe the interaction of the products of the proton decay with the material of the proposed detector.

"It is a geat deal of computing," Mann said, looking over a thick printout. "If you did it on a little hand calculator it would take forever. On the computer it is a few-minute job."

Application Questions

1. Is the computer used in this application as a creative tool? Explain your answer.
2. How is the computer in this application used by the departments of music, religion, and linguistics?

IV

COMPUTERS: THE YEARS AHEAD

16

The computer professional

16.1 OPPORTUNITIES IN THE COMPUTING FIELD

As a result of the great proliferation of computers, there are a wide variety of career opportunities for those interested in the computing field.

16.1.1 Programming

Most entry-level positions are in the programming field. The types of opportunities include the following:

Application Programmers: those who are provided with the requirements of a job and are asked to develop the logic and then code, debug, and document the program. Application programmers usually apply their skills to either commercial problems in areas such as payroll, inventory, sales, accounting, and so on, or to scientific problems.

Maintenance Programmers: those responsible for revising, amending, or updating existing programs. These people frequently serve as "trouble shooters," finding and fixing errors in existing software.

Systems Programmers: highly skilled programmers who are responsible for maximizing the overall efficiency of the computer system. They write enhancements to existing software, as well as new software that improves the quality of the operating system.

16.1.2 Job Requirements for Programmers

Because the computing field is so dynamic and so new, there is no real consensus on skills required for programmers or on the best method for hiring them. Among the most common characteristics that companies look for in entry-level positions are:

Programming experience—obtained either from on-the-job training, college courses, or data processing institutes.

College degree—most frequently, companies look for a B.S. in computer science or a B.B.A. in information processing.

A logical mind, an interest in problem solving, and an ability to think quickly and to express oneself well.

For scientific programming, some scientific training is required; for commercial applications, some business experience is preferred.

16.1.3 Programming Languages

There are, of course, a wide variety of programming languages which are available. Organizations commonly look for people with expertise in one or more of the languages specified in Chapter 5. These include COBOL, FORTRAN, BASIC, APL, Pascal, assembler language, RPG, and PL/1.

16.1.4 The Next Step

There are essentially two career paths for programmers: a programmer can follow either the technical path or the managerial path.

16.1.4.1 The Technical Path

Like engineers, researchers, and scientists, a programmer can continue as a technical expert and enhance his or her skills by learning more and more about new programming techniques and languages. Since the field changes rapidly, career programmers can always find new fields to explore to keep current. Opportunities in compiler design, software engineering, and the like are always available, especially when new hardware is introduced.

16.1.4.2 The Managerial Path

Other programmers, particularly those who have an interest in business, are apt to want to become more involved with management-level decision making. Beyond the obvious position of programming manager, the career choices in this sphere are numerous. We will consider the following: programming manager, systems analyst or systems consultant, DP manager, data base administrator, EDP auditor, and VP or director of information services.

a. *Programming Manager.* This is the person who supervises the activities of a group of programmers.

b. *Systems Analyst or Systems Consultant.* A systems analyst is a person responsible for analyzing existing business procedures, determining the basic problem areas or inefficiencies, and designing a more efficient computerized set of procedures or system. An analyst may work for an organization in an advisory capacity or may work for a consulting company hired to determine a given organization's needs.

A systems analyst is sometimes responsible for making recommendations as to which computer system a company should acquire.

In some organizations with fewer computer applications, an analyst is often responsible for programming as well as designing a system. Such analysts are referred to as programmer analysts.

c. *DP Manager.* A DP manager is responsible for the overall operations of the computer center. The DP manager supervises the data-entry procedures, control procedures, and equipment operations at the center. He or she is held accountable for the efficient and effective utilization of computer equipment. A DP manager must see to it that computer errors are kept to a minimum and that the computer system is relatively secure.

d. *Data Base Administrator.* A data base administrator is responsible for organizing and designing the data base and associated computer files used by the organization. The data base administrator is held accountable for the efficient design of the data base and for implementing proper controls and techniques necessary for accessing the data base.

e. *EDP Auditor.* These are accounting and computer specialists who are responsible for assessing the effectiveness and efficiency of the computer system. They evaluate the system control features and determine if there is any need for additional controls.

f. *VP of Information Services* (Director of Management Information Systems). This person is responsible for all computer operations and applications. This is a top-level management position. This individual supervises all of the types of programmers and systems-level computer professionals discussed above.

See Table 16.1 for typical salary ranges for these professionals.

There are numerous ways in which the information processing department can be organized.

Figure 16.1 illustrates an organization in which programmers report directly to systems analysts. This puts analysts in a supervisory

Table 16.1 *Average Salaries by Computer Installation Size*[a]

Job Title	Average Salary When Monthly Equipment Rental Is:		
	Up to $50,000	*Up to $150,000*	*$150,000 Plus*
1. Corporate Director of DP/MIS	$39,200	$44,997	$36,996
2. Systems Analyst-Manager	31,833	27,280	30,815
3. Systems Analyst	21,188	21,959	19,798
4. Senior Programmer	21,833	22,587	24,073
5. Programmer	19,748	19,302	18,925
6. Manager of Computer Operations	23,504	23,786	28,796
7. Data Base Manager	32,400	26,442	31,750

position where they assign programs to be coded for new systems to members of their staff and then monitor the progress.

Figure 16.2 illustrates an organization in which programmers and analysts report to different supervisors. In this type of organization, programmers and analysts work together in the design of programs for a new system, but there is no supervisory relationship. It makes for less control, but for a freer exchange of ideas between the two groups.

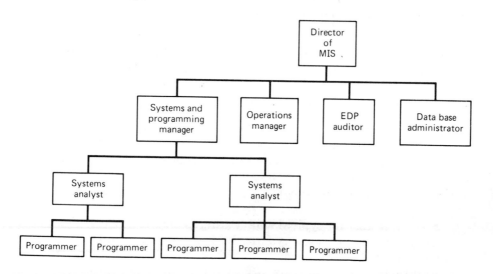

Figure 16.1. Organization in which programmers report directly to systems analysts.

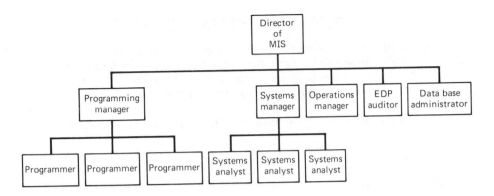

Figure 16.2. Organization in which programmers and analysts report to different supervisors.

It should be noted that the relative position of the information processing department itself within the company's organizational structure often dictates how effectively the company's information needs will be met. In some companies, for example, the director of management information systems reports to the vice-president of finance or to a comptroller.

Frequently, this hierarchical structure results in a priority system in which the development of accounting-oriented computer applications is emphasized. This often works to the detriment of other areas within the organization that deserve equal attention. Many companies have resolved this problem by having the information processing department report directly to the president or to the executive vice-president of the organization. In this way, each department's request for computer services is more objectively evaluated.

16.2 THE COMPUTING FIELD: SCIENCE OR ART?

Here, again, there really is no consensus as to the nature of the computing task. Some view computing as primarily involving the following skills:

1. The ability to be creative and to provide a unique solution to a problem.
2. The ability to communicate with users so that their needs can be better understood. The computer professional must be able to allay all fears of the user relative to automation, and project an image of confidence, understanding, and capability. These skills are consistent with those necessary for humanists or liberal arts-oriented professionals who focus on creativity and human concerns.

Others view computing as focusing on the following skills:

1. The ability to think logically, objectively, and rationally.
2. The ability to be able to communicate with others in a scientific manner. That is, the computer professional must be nonjudgmental, gather all the facts, and then make objective recommendations for solving problems.

This approach, of course, focuses on the computer professional as a scientist.

As in most cases, the best professionals are those who are neither at one extreme nor the other, but who properly balance both approaches. Those who can blend these two approaches, knowing precisely when each should dominate, are apt to be the most successful professionals. Nonetheless, controversy remains in many circles as to which approach is most desirable.

16.3 STRUCTURED DESIGN AN EFFORT TO FORMALIZE COMPUTING AS A SCIENCE

One of the main reasons for computer errors, system failures, and the general dissatisfaction that management sometimes feels toward computer projects is the lack of standardization. A dearth of standards exists in both hardware and software.

Many I/O devices, for example, are not compatible with one another. In addition, software methods and hardware interfaces used by manufacturers are not always consistent, making it extremely difficult to evaluate or assess equipment.

Moreover, there exist very few standard techniques in programming, systems, or data base design. Thus each package produced becomes a kind of individual achievement, and management finds itself unable to assess or compare such achievements. For those who aim to make computing more scientific and less "ego oriented," this represents a very serious problem.

Structured programming is a method of modularizing or segmenting a program into distinct blocks. These modules or blocks can be written by individual programmers, can be exchanged or copied from one program to another, and can be evaluated on their own merits. Moreover, it is much easier to debug a modularized program than one that has numerous entry and reentry points. To enable each module to function as a stand-alone entity, branches or GO TO instructions are not used. These are replaced by DO . . . WHILE loops or subroutines (FOR . . . NEXT loops in BASIC). In fact, structured programming is sometimes referred to as "GO TO-less" programming.

Another technique used in structured programming is called the **top-down approach**. The top-down approach basically involves defining a problem, program, or even system in most general terms, and then successively refining each module or segment in more and more specific terms.

The main advantages of structured programming then are as follows:

1. Standardization is achieved.
2. Program design and debugging are made easier.
3. Interaction of different segments is facilitated.
4. The computing function is made more scientific.

Systems and data base design concepts have come to incorporate these top-down, modularized, and structured features.

From a management perspective, structured design provides an additional advantage over those listed above: it improves management's ability to evaluate technical design features. By standardizing procedures and thereby eliminating some unique or creative elements, management can better evaluate programming and systems design.

It has been suggested that structured concepts are applied to computing not simply to improve standards, but to reduce the creativity and independence of the computing specialist. This view, taken by one of the very few sociologists who has studied this field, places structured techniques in a very different light:

> To make the production of programs independent of individual programmers—in much the same way cars are produced independently of individual automobile workers—various schemes had been proposed from time to time to standardize what programmers did. Generally, these were without lasting impact. They were the software equivalent of helpful hints to the homemaker, focusing on specific coding problems, organizational structures, personnel techniques, and so on. Unlike such piecemeal approaches, structured programming offered an entirely new way of writing programs, elegant in theory and unambiguous in principle. Indeed, the principle was simple: if managers could not yet have machines which wrote programs, at least they could have programmers who worked like machines. Until human programmers were eliminated altogether, their work would be made as machine-like—that is, as simple and limited and routine—as possible.[1]

Another result of implementing structured design in programming is the "team effort." Heretofore, programmers worked independently, some say reclusively. With this new structured approach,

[1] Philip Kraft, *Programmers and Managers*, (New York: Springer-Verlag), p. 57.

sometimes called "egoless" programming, the relationships among programmers will be altered. Some have predicted that this will substantially change peer relationships:

> The first two decades of programming history gave us the image of the introverted, isolated programmer surrounded by stacks of output. . . .
>
> Fortunately this image is becoming caricature. The lonely days of programming are giving way to community, interdependence and stability. This passage is happening gradually—the settler groups are still resented by the pioneers who seek to preserve their freedom and independence. Personality studies of programmers still show that programmers' need for social interaction is significantly lower than for people in many other professions. The concept of the programmer as a "loner" has some validity, but it is changing.
>
> As organizations become more dependent on computerized systems, production schedules cannot be violated, maintenance must be fast and error rates must be low. To satisfy these needs, managers are turning to team organization strategies such as egoless democratic teams . . . and to group review processes such as structured walkthroughs.[1]

The commonly held view that programmers are loners who work best in isolation is slowly being eroded. **Structured walkthroughs** have become common at many installations; groups of programmers "walk through" or evaluate each other's structured programs. This technique enables each program to benefit from a group perspective. It also minimizes the computer time required to debug a program.

16.4 ETHICS WITHIN THE COMPUTING FIELD

Most professionals have a code of ethics to which members of that profession are expected to abide. The computing field has been attempting to establish such a professional code of ethics for many years.

Because of the implications of computerization and the potential areas for unethical behavior, such a code is imperative. Issues which have arisen that require a code of ethics include the following. Note that in each instance, the courts will need to decide the legal issues, but we are focusing here on the ethical or moral issues:

1. To what degree should a computer professional be responsible for the output produced by his or her system?

[1] Ben Shneiderman, "Group Processes in Programming," *Datamation*, Jan. 1980, p. 138.

a. If, for example, the system results in invasion of privacy and a programmer was aware of this potential, is he or she responsible?
b. If, for example, a system produces erroneous results, is the computer professional ethically responsible?
c. Is it reasonable to expect software packages to be totally free of errors?
2. Do computing professionals have the right to utilize computer equipment whenever they desire?
a. Should computing professionals be permitted to use computers for game playing, printing Snoopy calendars, and the like?
b. Should computing professionals be permitted to use computers to place them in an advantageous position (e.g., in gambling casinos)?
c. If a time-sharing facility is available, does a programmer have the right to use it for non-job-related activities?
d. Should a programmer copy a software package without appropriate permission?
3. Should computing professionals take some social responsibility for the ways in which their products are utilized?
a. If, for example, a computer system is to be used to replace a labor force, is this, at least in part, the computer professional's responsibility?
b. Is it the computer professional's responsibility to ensure the integrity of a system and its protection from invasion of privacy even if these are not part of the system's objectives?

There are, of course, no simple answers to any of these questions. Moreover, many very ethical people have argued against the need for computer professionals to assume social responsibility for their systems. They claim that the utilization of a system is not the computer professional's responsibility. Just as Alfred Nobel cannot be held accountable for the immoral use of dynamite, computer professionals should not be held accountable for programs that are used illegally or unethically.

As the debate over these ethical issues goes on, there are many leaders of the field who believe that a code of ethics is of primary importance. As computers become prevalent and as their unethical use increases, more and more citizens will call upon their government to pass laws that will clearly specify the legal responsibility of computer specialists. Leaders in the computer field insist that it would be far better for professionals to police themselves, before the government finds it necessary to pass laws.

16.5   CERTIFICATION OF COMPUTER PROFESSIONALS

One method that is frequently used to minimize the abuses in a field and to maximize professional behavior is to require certification or licensing of professionals in that field.

A license is a legal document that permits an individual to practice in a certain specialty; doctors, for example, are licensed by a medical board. A certification, on the other hand, is a credential which indicates that the profession recognizes the individual as possessing a specified set of skills. The main difference between a license and certification is that legally one cannot practice without a license, but one can practice without certification. There are, for example, accountants who are not Certified Public Accountants (CPAs) but who maintain a practice. Similarly, some engineers are certified, others are not.

Both licensing and certifying usually require an applicant to meet certain criteria and to pass an examination. There may also be subsequent examinations to make certain that the individual maintains his or her skills. Most computer professionals would prefer to see an industry-wide certification system as opposed to government licensing.

In 1960, the Data Processing Management Association began a program to certify data processors. The certificate called CDP, Certificate in Data Processing, required an applicant to have some college training and some experience. The first exam was offered in 1962, and since then thousands of people have taken it and about two-thirds have passed.

In 1973, an effort was made to build on the CDP and to make it more comprehensive. The Institute for Certification of Computer Professionals (ICCP), which is supported by eight computer organizations, has established its certification program with the following stated purposes:

> ICCP is a non-profit organization established for the purpose of testing and certifying knowledge and skills of computing personnel. It is a coordinated, cooperative, industry-wide effort.
>
> A primary objective is the pooling of resources of constituent societies so that the full attention of the information processing industry will be focused on the vital tasks of development and recognition of qualified personnel.
>
> The Institute will foster, promote and encourage development and improvement of standards of performance and good practice. It will become an authoritative source of information for employers, educators, practitioners and public officials.[1]

Unlike the CDP, CCP eligibility requirements are as follows:

> Although any interested individual may take this examination, it is intended for senior-level programmers. No specific educational or experience requirements must be met in order to take the examina-

---

[1]Brochure, Institute for Certification of Computer Professionals.

tion, but a candidate who does not have broad experience will find the examination extremely difficult to complete successfully.[1]

Many leading figures in the computing field have promoted the use of the CCP test as a formal basis of certification for professionals. They anticipate that the CCP will be for the computing field what the CPA is for accounting: a credential which indicates that the person is highly qualified. With such self-policing within the computing industry itself, there will be less need for governments to impose restrictions and to pass laws regulating the proper use of computers. A

[1]Brochure, Institute for Certification of Computer Professionals.

ACM FORUM

The Value of Certification[a]

☐ Does certification of computer skills have real value to an employer? In order to have value, the certificate must say something about the work-performance capability of the holder of the certificate. It is doubtful that the certificate can convey such information. Why is this doubtful? Here are a few things to consider:

1. A prime characteristic of those who do well in the certification process is that they are good at taking tests. Repeated studies of other occupational tests show that the correlation between test performance and occupational performance is rather weak. This is to be expected, because many other factors such as motivation, general intelligence, knowledge outside the specific questions asked in the test, and work habits all contribute to job performance.

2. The actual work capabilities possessed by the person who is a CDP may not be suitable to the job. Relying on a CDP to say that a person has knowledge of the computer field which will be of value on a job does not come anywhere near guaranteeing that the knowledge will be of value.

3. The personal temperament which leads a person to seek a CDP may or may not be desirable for a particular job. For example, I do not want to have working for me people who are too eager to have a third party attest to their capability. I prefer a more self-reliant type. However, there are people who want exactly the kind of employee who hungers after a CDP. For these employers, voluntary CDPS give a reading on temperament, as well as the test-taking capability of the holder of a CDP.

In summary, the voluntary CDP has its value. This value ought not to be blown out of proportion by zealous proponents. Those eager to inflate the importance of a CDP have not presented persuasive evidence to show that the CDP has significant relevance to the elements of job performance. Until they can present such evidence, dedicated advocates of the CDP would do well to be more restrained in the claims and demands they make.

THOMAS L. GERBER
Gerber Associates
419 E. Railroad Ave.
Aberdeen, SD 57401

[a]*Communications of the ACM*, Vol. 22, No. 8.

Figure 16.3.

past president of the Association for Computing Machinery, Dan McCracken, stated the following on the subject:

> I have written before of the need for those who claim to be professionals to demonstrate their competence to the general public who can be hurt by the misuse of specialized knowledge and who cannot judge that competence. Certification is not the whole answer to this highly complex issue but it is one useful part. Governmental licensing may come, perhaps it is another useful part, too, although I am not enthusiastic about the prospect. . . .
>
> I do not equate certification with professionalism, but the two do overlap. The public asks, reasonably enough, that we demonstrate our proficiency to carry on work that has tremendous potential for good or bad impact on the public. Certification is one of the important ways we can show that we do accept the responsibility that goes with the exercise of specialized knowledge. That we can grow and benefit individually in the process is a pleasant plus.[1]

[1]*Communications of the ACM.*

2.2: **Social Responsibility:** One is expected to combat ignorance about information processing technology in those public areas where one's application can be expected to have an adverse social impact.

2.5: **Integrity:** One will not knowingly lay claims to competence one does not demonstrably possess.

2.8: **Protection of Privacy:** One shall have special regard for the potential effects of computer-based systems on the right of privacy of individuals whether this is within one's own organization, among customers or suppliers, or in relation to the general public.

  Because of the privileged capability of computer professionals to gain access to computerized files, especially strong strictures will be applied to those who have used their positions of trust to obtain information from computerized files for their personal gain.

  Where it is possible that decisions can be made within a computer-based system which could adversely affect the personal security, work, or career of an individual, the system design shall specifically provide for decision review by a responsible executive who will thus remain accountable and identifiable for that decision.

3.1: **Education:** One has a special responsibility to keep oneself fully aware of developments in information processing technology relevant to one's current professional occupation. One will contribute to the interchange of technical and professional information by encouraging and participating in education activities directed both to fellow professionals and to the public at large. One will do all in one's power to further public understanding of computer systems. One will contribute to the growth of knowledge in the field to the extent that one's expertise, time, and position allow.

3.5: **Discretion:** One shall exercise maximum discretion in disclosing, or permitting to be disclosed, or using to one's own advantage, any information relating to the affairs of one's present or previous employers or clients.

Figure 16.4.   Selected codes of ethics, conduct, and good practice of the Institute for Certification of Computer Professionals.

See Figure 16.3 for a different perspective on the value of certification.

Currently, the CCP is a voluntary certification program. As you can see, many hope that it will begin to carry the same weight as the CPA does for accountants. The ICCP also requires candidates to subscribe to its Codes of Ethics, Conduct and Good Practice. See Figure 16.4 for selected sections of these codes.

16.6 MAJOR COMPUTER SOCIETIES

The charter member societies of the Institute for Certification of Computer Professionals are among the most important computing societies in the United States. A brief synopsis of the objectives of each is included in Figure 16.5.

ACM: The **Association for Computing Machinery** was founded in 1947 and is the oldest society of the computing community. Dedicated to the development of information processing as a discipline and to the responsible use of computers, ACM has over 40,000 members. ACM publishes seven major periodicals, offers 31 special interest groups and recognizes over *300* chapters and student chapters. ACM sponsors a variety of national, regional and local conferences, seminars and programs.
11 W. 42 St · New York, New York 10036

ACPA: The **Association of Computer Programmers and Analysts** is an international organization of professionals dedicated to providing service to its membership, the profession and to the public. ACPA offers its members a voice on professional issues, and opportunities to develop professional skills through seminars, workshops and conferences. ACPA provides informative national and chapter publications, and promotes interchange of ideas with other professionals at chapter activities.
P.O. Box 95 · Kensington, Maryland 20795

AEDS: The **Association for Educational Data Systems** is a private, nonprofit educational organization founded in 1962 by a group of professional educators and technical specialists in educational applications of computers. It provides a forum for the exchange of ideas and information about the relationship of modern technology to modern education. This is accomplished through its monthly magazine, THE MONITOR and its quarterly JOURNAL, annual conference and frequent workshops and seminars. It also conducts an annual computer programming contest for secondary school students.
1201 Sixteenth Street, N.W. · Washington, D.C. 20036

A1A: The **Automation 1 Association** is dedicated to the professional growth of its members through monthly technical seminars, monthly dinner meetings and monthly field trips to a variety of computer installations. A corollary to the

---

Figure 16.5. Institute for Certification of Computer Professionals: charter member societies.

professional growth offered through A1A is the opportunity for lasting friendships with people of similar interests.
2425 San Diego Avenue · San Diego, California 92110

CIPS: The **Canadian Information Processing Society** was formed in 1958 to bring together Canadians with a common interest in the field of information processing. The current membership of over 2,000 persons includes scientists, businessmen and others who make their careers in computing and information processing.
Suite 214 · 212 King Street West, Toronto, Ontario, Canada M5H 1K5

DPMA: The **Data Processing Management Association** is the largest professional association in the field of computer management with over 24,000 members in the United States, Canada, and other countries. The purpose of DPMA is to engage in education and research activities focused on the development of effective programs for the self-improvement of its membership. It seeks to encourage high standards of competence and promotes a professional attitude among its members.
505 Busse Highway · Park Ridge, Ill. 60068

IEEE: The **Computer Society of the Institute of Electrical and Electronics Engineers,** by charter, definition and action, is the leading professional association in advancing the theory and practice of computer and information processing Technology. The Society promotes cooperation and interchange of recent and relevant information among its 40,000 members in all parts of the world.
P.O. Box 639 · Silver Spring, Md. 20901

SCDP: The **Society of Certified Data Processors** is an organization formed to represent exclusively the interest and wishes of the holder of the Certificate in Data Processing. Formed in 1971, the SCDP has pursued its goals at ICCP, ANSI, CODA SYL, and among the industry groups. The SCDP is a "grass-roots" society wherein the members control what positions, actions, and directions the organization takes. It is the only organization exclusively representing the CDP holders in these forums.
2670 Union Extended, Suite 532 · Memphis TN 38112

Figure 16.5   (Continued)

KEY TERMS

APL
Application programmer
Assembler language
Association for Computing Machinery (ACM)
Certification
COBOL
Data base administrator
Director of information services
DP manager
FORTRAN

Institute for Certification of Computer Professionals (ICCP)

Maintenance programmer

PL/1

RPG

Scientific programmer

Structured design

Structured programming

Systems analyst

Systems programmer

Top-down approach

DISCUSSION QUESTIONS

1. What attributes would you expect to find in someone who was a programmer? Would you expect to find the same attributes in someone who was a structured programmer?
2. Many organizations promote applications programmers by making them systems analysts. What are the advantages and disadvantages of this policy?
3. Do you think computer professionals are more scientific or creative in approach? Explain your answer.
4. Do you think programmers have the responsibility for ensuring that their programs do not infringe on the privacy of individuals? Explain your answer?
5. Do you think computer programmers, in general, should possess strong mathematical skills? Explain your answer.
6. The job of EDP auditor is one of the fastest growing in the field. Can you explain why?

APPLICATION

What is the message to programmers and systems analysts in the following article?

Law Leaves DPers Open to Criminal Liability[a]

BOSTON—Thrown in jail for a programming error? That's neither a 1984-ish prediction nor a Soviet propagandist horror story.

The possibility for criminal liability in programming exists here and now. It stems from the ever-increasing number of state and federal regulations promulgated every year that affect computer operations in industry, according to a recent issue of "Computer Law and Tax Report" (CLTR).

To avoid potential criminal status, DPers in industry must become aware of new regulations and make appropriate adjustments to their systems, the newsletter advised.

A newly enacted rule regulating

computer operations affects programmers in the drug industry,
CLTR noted. U.S. code states that
anyone who causes "the adultera-
tion of any drug . . . in interstate
commerce" faces imprisonment of
up to a year or a $1,000 fine.

Role in Adulteration

The law considers a drug adul-
terated if the methods, facilities or
controls used in its manufacture,
processing, packaging or storage
do not meet "current good manufacturing practice."

Effective March 28 were new
Food and Drug Administration
(FDA) rules that set forth "current
good manufacturing practices"
for human and veterinary drugs.
Among the rules was a section
dealing with the operation of computer systems.

When computer equipment is
used in drug preparation, FDA
regulations require that:

- Routine calibrations, inspec-
  tions and checking be done in
  accordance with written programs designed to ensure
  proper performance.
- Written records of these calibrations, checks and inspec-
  tions be maintained.
- Appropriate controls be exercised to make sure that changes

in production and control records are made by authorized
personnel only.

- The input or formulas and
  other record or data into the
  computer be checked for accuracy.
- Backup files of data entered
  into the system be maintained
  (except when certain data,
  such as calculations, is eliminated in the automated process, in which case written records of the program must be
  maintained with appropriate
  validation data.
- Hard copy or alternative systems such as duplicates, tapes
  or microfilm be maintained to
  ensure that backup data is
  exact, complete and secure
  from "alteration, inadvertent
  erasures or loss."

Open to Prosecution

The failure of a drug manufacturer to set up and enforce these
security, backup, access and documentation controls "will certainly
lay it open to possible prosecution," CLTR warned.

In addition, the systems analysts who ignores these controls
or the programmer who fails to
document his program may also
be liable.

[a] *Computerworld.* Copyright by CW Communications/Inc., Framingham,
MA 01701. Reprinted with permission.

17

A look to the future

17.1 INTRODUCTION

This text has provided a summary of basic computer concepts in an effort to provide students with "computer literacy." Of equal importance has been our attempt to demonstrate how computers are actually used in a wide variety of disciplines.

But it is no longer necessary for a text to emphasize the effects of computers on society. There are virtually countless ways that computers affect our daily lives. Rather, we have focused on the potential benefits to be derived from the computer's impact as well as the potential difficulties. It has been our intention to provide a balanced picture of the impact of computers on society.

This chapter focuses on areas of computer utilization that have great potential for the future. These are areas in which computers are currently being used, but the expectation is that tremendous growth will occur in the near future. This growing utilization of computers, and in some cases dependence on them, will result in sociological, economic, political, and environmental changes that, although difficult to assess, may well be revolutionary.

17.2 THE "OFFICE OF THE FUTURE"

As we proceed toward the end of the twentieth century, there is every expectation that the growing use of computers will transform the office into a totally new structure, both organizationally and economically.

It is reasonable to expect that the "office of the future," certainly of the immediate future, will contain computer hardware and telecommunications equipment already familiar to the user; but this equipment will be more efficient, more compact, and less expensive than that of previous generations.

Some of the features of this office of the future have already been discussed. Some offices have already begun to acquire the more advanced hardware and software that promise to dramatically change businesses in the future. Among these are facsimile devices and word processing systems.

17.2.1 Facsimile Devices

Facsimile devices make it possible to transmit documents, reports, correspondences—indeed any messages—from one location to another instantaneously.

With the use of a facsimile device and a telephone, it is possible to enhance greatly the speed, quantity, and hopefully the quality of both interorganizational and intraorganizational communications. So-called "electronic mail" is just one aspect of facsimile systems. This means that organizations will have the ability to receive and transmit mail on-line, if they wish. In addition, facsimile devices minimize the need for secretarial assistance in placing calls and leaving messages when the individual being called is unavailable. These functions can be handled automatically, by electronic devices. Moreover, facsimile devices can reduce the dependence on two-party communications. The transmission and receipt of messages can be distributed to numerous individuals.

Note that although such devices are currently available, they are still somewhat expensive. Thus only larger organizations have been able to make use of them. With hardware costs decreasing each year, it is likely that increasing numbers of organizations will be able to afford these devices, making it possible for more and more interorganizational communication using facsimile equipment. One can reasonably expect facsimile devices to become as prevalent as telephones in the future, thereby greatly improving the ability of individuals and organizations to communicate with one another.

17.2.2 Word-Processing Systems

The "office of the future" will undoubtedly rely heavily on word-processing equipment for processing written communications. Many large organizations already use such equipment for the production of large volumes of repetitive-type letters, promotional material, and various types of notices and statements. Text editing can also be achieved using this equipment. A document is keyed in, or typed, using the system and the author can alter, append, or delete sections as necessary. A hard copy can be created any time it is required. Such an application will, in the future, rely on sophisticated voice recognition devices. Here, again, the decreasing cost of hardware will no doubt make even more sophisticated equipment available to most organizations and probably to small businesses and individual users as well.

Word-processing systems will have a dramatic effect on secretaries. To begin with, equipment is currently being developed that will enable a user to dictate into a machine that will *automatically* create the text. The user can view the text on a screen, make changes as necessary, and obtain a hard copy at the press of a button.

This type of word-processing system will virtually eliminate a major aspect of the typical secretary's work load. As you might expect, most secretaries do not view this prospect with much enthusiasm. Note, however, that it is unlikely that this truly revolutionary use of word processing will result in mass unemployment. Rather, it is more likely that such ability will greatly increase the amount of communication and information in an office. The secretary's role, then, is likely to change from clerk-typist to manager of information. The resultant change in the secretary's role is a feature of the "office of the future" that should be given adequate attention *now* to ensure a smooth transition, one that will not cause unnecessary difficulties in the work force.

17.3   MANAGEMENT INFORMATION SYSTEMS

In its ideal form, a management information system requires a central computer system used to maintain a data base on the company's entire operations. With proper controls and security procedures, this data base will be made available to authorized personnel for inquiry-response, on-line updating, and providing management with required reports.

In addition, the CPU will serve as a "host" computer to a network of minis located at each office. The mini handles local needs and serves as a front-end processor, making it possible for all local terminals to communicate with the central processor.

Communication with terminal devices will be in a conversational mode. This minimizes the need for any computer expertise on the part of the user.

Although there have been numerous attempts to establish a management information system that functions as described, the fact is that most of these attempts have fallen short of expectations. Many have failed entirely. With an increased need for proper data base management and growing attention to the problems that have arisen, there are apt to be MIS systems in the future that function as originally envisioned. This means that within the organization, both users and computer specialists will need to work very closely to design, implement, and update the system as required.

17.4 THE CHANGING NATURE OF THE WORKPLACE

Throughout this text we have considered the impact that terminals, minicomputers, and microcomputers have had, and will continue to have, on small organizations and home users who in the past were not able to afford computer equipment. Small-scale users now have the ability to acquire such devices and to link up with data bases, remote locations or branch offices, and virtually any other user who has access to similar equipment.

As we approach the end of the twentieth century, we will undoubtedly find increasing numbers of such users. The effect of this equipment for personal use will be explored in the next section. In this section we explore the effect of inexpensive, readily available computing equipment and communications links on the work force.

You will note that a large percentage of the operations performed in a typical organization involve information flow. The utilization of computers and data communications networks can provide a company with its informational needs, even when office employees are not physically in the office. Why, then, is it absolutely necessary for employees to be physically present in the office when performing their tasks? With the use of a terminal in one's home, it would be possible and perhaps more efficient for many functions to be performed at home and linked on-line to a main computer in the office. Alvin Toffler has suggested that "telecommuting"—using the telephone at home for communication with the office—may replace commuting in the near future. Several companies have already implemented this type of arrangement. A large Chicago bank, the Continental Illinois National Bank and Trust Company, for example, has part of its word-processing staff working at home with on-line terminals.

Executives can also make use of computer technology to work at home. Even though these executives would be located remotely from their offices, they would be able to maintain control over their organization's operations. With the use of an on-line terminal it would be relatively simple for an executive to supervise and to communicate with various managers in the company. In addition, he or she could also access a central data base and inquire about the status of any phase of the company's operations and thereby make appropriate decisions—remotely.

17.4.1   Effects on the Workplace and the Worker

The state of the art in the computer field is currently advanced enough to enable ideas such as these to become a reality. What is necessary now is an acceptance of the concept by both management and workers; but one must also realize that a new approach to employer-employee relations will be required. New techniques for measuring employee performance may also be necessary.

Consider the fact that it may be more difficult for supervisors to evaluate the quality of work performed by employees located remotely from the office. The performance of an employee who works in an office environment is more easily measured.

There may be other communication problems to be considered as well:

1.   Since source documents would physically be removed from the office and located in an employee's home, there may be potential security and privacy problems relating to the data.
2.   What happens if the employee's terminal is inoperable and requires maintenance? If the employee were in the office environment, he or she could easily use another terminal.
3.   What happens if the employee encounters a problem in interpreting a source document? In the office, a supervisor could easily be asked to resolve the problem.
4.   What insurance problems, if any, will need to be resolved? When an employee is located in an office, he or she is ordinarily covered by Workmen's Compensation, for example, for injuries occurring on the job. How will an employee who works at home be covered for injuries? In addition, how will it be determined if injuries sustained in the home are really job related?
5.   How will an employee's morale and social well-being be affected? In an office, employees interact with one another, conversing about various company and personal matters. Will an employee working at home feel alienated? It is difficult to determine the actual effects of group dynamics and the difficulties that might be encountered if people are asked to work in separate quarters.
6.   Will an employee working at home be less productive than at the office because of interruptions and distractions, such as the telephone ringing, people knocking at the door, and children coming home from school?

In general, if workers begin to use computing equipment in the home for communicating with the office, the entire concept of "work" and "the office" may be affected.

Alvin Toffler predicts that the worker at home, in an "electronic cottage" setting, will not only be common in the coming years but will be effective as well.

> Given such equipment, who might be the first to make the transition from centralized work to the "electronic cottage"? While it would be a mistake to underestimate the need for direct face-to-face contact in business, and all the subliminal and nonverbal communication that accompanies that contact, it is also true that certain tasks do not require much outside contact at all—or need it only intermittently.
>
> Thus low abstraction office workers for the most part perform tasks—entering data, typing, retrieving, totaling columns of figures, preparing invoices, and the like—that require few, if any, direct face-to-face transactions. They could perhaps be most easily shifted into the electronic cottage.[1]

17.4.2   Effects on Society as a Whole

Thus far, we have considered the *organizational* effects of workers using terminals or computers at home as a primary tool to perform their jobs. It is obvious, however, that such a dramatic change in people's lives will have tremendous ramifications for society as a whole.

1. There would be quite an impact from an ecological and energy point of view. By working at home, for example, those employees who normally drive to work would conserve energy and consequently reduce the amount of pollution caused by the exhaust from cars.
2. The mass transportation needs that have become evident in recent years would diminish considerably. Moreover, people would no longer need to live near large cities. Thus the structure of urban and suburban areas may change. This may result in a more even population distribution.
3. Workers would have more flexibility in being able to arrange their working hours to accommodate their personal needs. This would be especially true if the central computer were accessible around the clock, thereby allowing the entry of data at nontraditional office work hours such as during the night.

Employees working at home would presumably gain more leisure time as a consequence of the advantages listed above. Family life may well become more meaningful and rewarding.

Whether or not companies will be encouraged to implement this new type of work arrangement remains to be seen. What is clear at this

---

[1] Alvin Toffler, *The Third Wave* (New York: Morrow, 1980), p. 213.

point, however, is that the lines that separate where and how we live, work, and shop are already being slowly eroded by the prevalence of computer technology.

17.5   THE FUTURE OF PERSONAL COMPUTERS

By the end of the 1980s, it is estimated that several million microcomputers will be found in homes, businesses, and schools. Currently, several hundred thousand microcomputers are sold each year. The predictions are that these numbers will increase dramatically and that in the near future microcomputers will have a profound impact on various segments of society. Indeed, the term "personal computer" to describe these devices is itself becoming obsolete since its use is no longer limited to the hobbyist who was said to "tinker" with such electronic devices.

We have already considered some of the current applications of microcomputers. In this section we consider some additional applications that have already made an impact but which promise to have an even more profound effect on society in the future.

17.5.1   Microcomputers in the Home

We have previously considered the use of microcomputers for entertainment, education, and financial management in the home. But with the use of an appropriate interface, microcomputers can serve as on-line terminals and can be made to communicate over telephone lines. Using a terminal in this way provides people with access to a wide variety of services, such as:

1. News wire services
2. The latest stock prices
3. Hotel and air reservations systems
4. Computer-assisted instruction packages
5. Ticket availability at various shows and entertainment centers

The services listed above are currently available, but the list of potential services is relatively limitless—and the cost is inexpensive. Typically, there is a one-time initial membership charge to provide the user with access. Each time a service is accessed, charges are based on actual usage time. One can find such services available for less than $3 per hour for off-peak usage to more than $15 per hour for usage during regular business hours.

Other consumer-oriented services are also available, but to a more limited degree. Some retail establishments make an item's price and its quantity on hand available to users in an on-line environment. This enables consumers to check the price of items, to comparison shop while at home, and in some instances to place orders using the microcomputer.

Banks have also begun limited projects to enable customers to access their bank records and to make certain types of transactions using their microcomputer. Such applications require very strict security procedures.

Microprocessors which are built into microcomputer systems are ideally suited for providing some form of centralized control. With increasing frequency, microsystems have become available to monitor energy use, for example. Such a system provides automatic control of various energy sources in an effort to maximize the efficient use of energy. These systems have met with great success in large industrial organizations and are now available for home use as well.

Similar control systems are available to provide fire and burglar alarm services. A microcomputer can be programmed to detect any movement in the user's house when it is supposed to be vacant, to detect any movement near entrances at night, to turn lights on and off at fixed hours, and so on.

In addition to providing the services mentioned, a home computer has one other major advantage—it enables people to communicate with one another. This has great potential for social change. It can provide handicapped people with services heretofore unavailable to them, and it can permit many more people to do at least some of their work at home. It can revolutionize our political system by enabling legislators to poll their constituents on key issues.

The microcomputer is usually a separate unit. But it is possible to adapt standard television sets into microcomputers as well by adding on components such as chips and keyboards. This concept greatly increases both the potential and the applicability of a microcomputer. Network and closed-circuit television could be used for interactive educational purposes in ways that would not otherwise be feasible.

In short, the potential of the microcomputer in the home is virtually limitless. In the years to come, it is likely that these devices will be as commonplace as a radio or a dishwasher. This will have a profound effect on the way people obtain information and communicate with one another.

17.5.2 Microcomputers as Educational Tools

It is likely that in the near future, students will need to access a microcomputer to do their homework, in much the same way that students today need easy access to typewriters or encyclopedias.

It is common today for students on all levels to use textbooks that are designed to reinforce classroom learning. A microcomputer with CAI modules could serve the same purpose. The CAI modules could be individual cassettes or disks that each student accesses on a stand-alone device.

Or, CAI modules could be made available in an on-line environment to numerous users at the same time. Students would do their homework by accessing the appropriate module perhaps by using a home computer. The question and answer segment could be graded automatically and the teacher could receive a printout of the student's progress and performance each day.

Some textbook publishers have already begun projects for converting educational material from traditional textbook form into CAI modules that make use of graphics capability and can monitor a student's progress.

Microcomputers that become a tool for doing homework would serve to augment the use of computers in the classroom, which has already proven to be very effective for learning.

It is evident that microcomputers as well as other CAI equipment will continue to play a significant role in the educational process in the future.

17.5.3 Microcomputers in Business

We have already discussed the fact that microcomputers, because of their relatively low cost, are being used increasingly by many small businesses. The applications are as numerous as they are diverse.

A company in New York, for example, markets a microcomputer system together with a program specifically designed to assist those involved in managing real estate. This is particularly advantageous for owners and managers of apartment complexes that have at least 300 units. The system can keep track of such items as:

1. Rents paid and those tenants in arrears
2. Vacancies
3. Security deposits
4. Lease renewals and expirations
5. Garage space allocation and rent
6. Credits due individual tenants

The system can produce a variety of reports, including a profit-and-loss statement for a particular building, in addition to rent statements, dispossess notices, and checks.

In another application, an owner of a dry-cleaning store in Connecticut has a microcomputer with a disk drive in his house that is used to keep track of his business records. Once a week, the owner takes home the business records and enters the data into the computer. The system utilizes an ordinary TV set for a display screen. The owner can enter payroll data, such as each employee's name and hours worked. The computer has been programmed to retrieve the appropriate information from tax tables stored on the disk in order to prepare payroll checks on a printer that is part of the system. The system also has a general ledger program that keeps track of the cost for supplies, rent, expenses for operating the store's vehicles, and other expenses as well. The system can produce a variety of reports, showing totals for income and expenses, trends, and other information about the store's operations.

The uses of microcomputers extend to nonprofit organizations as well. In Westport, Connecticut, for example, a volunteer fire department maintains a mailing list on a magnetic disk. Since a printer has not yet been acquired for the microcomputer, the disk is brought to a local computer store, which prints the mailing labels on its system for $2.

Undoubtedly, we will continue to see many small business operations in the future using microcomputers for a variety of applications.

17.6 HARDWARE AND SOFTWARE IN GENERAL

With hardware costs decreasing and software costs increasing, there will probably be a shift in the types of systems that will be developed.

Various input/output units that were once considered too expensive will become commonly used devices. These include optical character recognition (OCR) devices that can read bar codes, typed documents, or even handwritten data. OCR units are currently much less expensive, smaller in size, and more versatile than in previous years.

Voice recognition devices capable of interpreting the spoken word have great potential in the computing field. These, too, will be used with greater frequency.

Computer output microfilm devices can produce at very great speeds a high volume of information on microfilm. This saves time, storage, and costs, and enables a user with a microfilm reader to access a document very rapidly. The computer industry has recognized the potential of these devices for many years, but until recently, cost has been an obstacle. With the cost of these devices decreasing, COM will most likely become far more prevalent in the future.

In terms of computer systems, in general, the tendency of most users is to think small. Many organizations have traded in large and medium-sized systems for a series of minicomputers that can be operated in a distributed environment. Frequently, this change results in greater computer power at less cost.

It is likely that many of the applications and issues considered in this text will remain relevant in the future. Point-of-sale and electronic funds transfer systems will continue to grow.

The future of computer-assisted instruction using large-scale systems is somewhat precarious. In general, more and more schools will discover the potential of low-cost microcomputers for limited CAI.

There is evidence to suggest that many computer manufacturers and software houses will begin to offer many more packages in the health care field. The future of computer applications in this area seems very bright. There are now computer-aided design (CAD) devices being used for simulating limb movement in an effort to develop better artificial limbs.

But despite the anticipated growth in computer utilization, many of the basic problems remain. There have been attempts to standardize programming and systems work using structured techniques, but progress is slow. The government is attempting to deal with the issue of privacy but here, again, changes in legislation come slowly. Users are currently more attuned to the need for proper controls and security measures, but unless full attention is given to this problem, difficulties will remain. And finally the effort to bridge the communication gap between users and computer professionals is showing signs of success. In ever-increasing numbers, humanists and other nonspecialists are beginning to recognize the great potential of computers, if used and controlled properly.

17.7   THE FUTURE OF THE COMPUTER PROFESSION

By all accounts, the computer field in the years to come will offer one of the best employment opportunities of all the professions. *Money* magazine recently analyzed data from the Bureau of Labor Statistics, as well as data from colleges, professional associations, and recruiting firms.[1] The 18 occupations studied included doctors, lawyers, architects, dentists, and computer systems analysts, to name just a few. The job of systems analyst was ranked *first* among the occupations, partly because of the excellent prospects for getting jobs and promotions. Surprisingly, doctors were ranked second because of a projected surplus, especially in major cities. It is interesting to note that a comment in the chart in *Money* next to the category of systems analyst had the following notation: "Add management skills and you can write your own program for advancement."

[1] *Money*, May 1980, p. 76.

Similarly, a recent article in *The New York Times* began as follows:

> Never before in the . . . history of the data processing industry has there been such an acute shortage of computer programmers. In California, for example, the Security Pacific National Bank has put a $1,000 bounty on these most sought after of computer professionals. And the Connecticut General Insurance Corporation recently rewarded employees who were successful in recruiting programmers with an ounce of gold and $700. These examples are by no means atypical.[2]

The article continued by pointing out that job opportunities in the field of programming had more than doubled over the preceding year and that future prospects were likely to remain very favorable.

Studies have shown that the annual turnover rate in this field is approximately 30%. This makes it critical for employers to provide appropriate incentives to both attract and keep qualified professionals.

The outlook for job opportunities in the computer field thus appears very encouraging for the future. It must be noted, however, that the computer field is dynamic rather than static. There are always new developments in hardware and software. Consequently, the computer specialist has a professional obligation to keep abreast of the state of the art. As we have already discussed, many professionals have been arguing for certification of computer specialists in an effort to provide the appropriate incentives for keeping informed.

17.8 HUMAN–MACHINE INTERFACE

There have been, and will continue to be, a series of problems associated with human beings interacting with machines. As machines become more capable of performing tasks traditionally undertaken by people and as more people are placed in positions where they must interact with these machines, the problems will become even more critical.

It is imperative that computer professionals and users alike assume the responsibility of educating people on the ways in which appropriate human-machine interaction is achieved. It is equally important that these users and professionals assist people in adapting to situations that require human-machine interaction and that the fear and resistance with which many people react to computers be allayed.

---

[2] Peter J. Schuyten, "Programmers in Short Supply," *The New York Times*, Nov. 22, 1979, p. D2.

The philosophical issues relating to intelligence in machines, and to the fear that machines will take over, must also be addressed. If the problems associated with human-machine interaction are dealt with appropriately, James Martin's optimistic predictions for the future may well prove to be correct:

> Computers act as a storage battery for human intellect, and data networks provide the means of distributing the resource. As time goes by, more and more human intellect will be stored in the machines. It will become unnecessary, for example, to do many forms of mathematics by hand; a machine can integrate, differentiate, and solve complex equations. Mathematicians will go on to more creative pursuits, and as they do so the machines will become still more capable. Doctors, generals, architects and scientists will likewise have the computer network taking over the routine work, providing them with better information, and allowing them to concentrate on the more creative or human parts of their jobs.[1]

17.9   OTHER ISSUES TO BE CONSIDERED

There are numerous issues surrounding computer utilization that remain unresolved and will undoubtedly not be completely resolved for years to come, if at all. We have already discussed in great detail some of these issues relating to privacy and security. It must be emphasized that many of the controversial societal issues concerning computer technology are extremely complex. For example, although the maintenance of various government data banks, do, in fact, serve legitimate governmental needs, the mere existence of some of these data banks infringe on an individual's right to privacy.

It is not easy to draw a line that clearly delineates those computer applications that, on balance, provide society with more benefit than harm. Indeed, *who* is to say what constitutes a benefit, from a societal viewpoint, and *how* it can be measured?

Consider the issue of electronic mail. The U.S. Postal Service has for some time proposed that it be permitted to become involved in the electronic mail system.[2] Essentially, the proposed plan would allow businesses that produce large volumes of computer-generated bills or other mailings to transmit them electronically from their computers to post offices in certain major cities throughout the country. The post offices would then print the messages, enclose them in envelopes, and deliver them to the intended recipients. A major controversy surrounding this plan involves the desire of the Postal Service to have a

[1] James Martin, *Human-Machine Interface* (Englewood Cliffs, NJ: Prentice-Hall, 1981), p. 85.
[2] *The Wall Street Journal*, Feb. 25, 1980, p. 8, col. 1.

"significant" role in the electronic transmission process. As could be expected, telecommunications carriers, private companies that provide transmission network facilities, want to restrict the Postal Service's involvement. It would seem that the Postal Service, as a quasi-governmental agency, might have a competitive advantage over private carriers. In any event, it appears likely that whether private carriers or the Postal Service, or both, provide electronic transmission service, electronic mail utilizing Postal Service delivery facilities will become widespread.

One of the biggest controversies involving computer technology concerns the issue of human dependence, perhaps overdependence, on these devices. Frequently, so much faith is put into these machines that backup systems are not adequately designed. Recently, for example, two commercial jetliners almost collided over North Carolina. There had been a brief computer failure at the Washington Control Center immediately prior to the near collision. In the process of switching to a backup system, during an interval of less than one minute, confusion developed as to which controllers were monitoring the two planes, which were, at that time, on a direct collision course. Fortunately, an accident was averted just in time.

There are numerous problems that result from an overdependence on computers. Recently, within a period of three days, the U.S. Strategic Air Command received *two* incorrect computer messages indicating that the Soviet Union had launched a nuclear missile attack. On both occasions, approximately 100 B-52 bombers armed with nuclear weapons were prepared for takeoff. Fortunately, both alerts, which lasted less than three minutes, were called off when it was determined that the computer had malfunctioned. Perhaps what is most astounding about these incidents is that they occurred within three days of each other. Certainly, this type of incident should never have happened at all.

There is no question that, in balance, computers can well help to meet many of society's needs. It must be remembered, however, that there is nothing mystical about these machines. They are merely electronic devices that serve as tools. How well they are programmed and thus meet our needs depends, to a large extent, on what types of controls society at large puts on their use. There is no question that more legislation, especially at the federal level, will be needed in the future to provide the proper controls for EFT systems, electronic mail, maintenance and use of governmental data banks, and numerous other computer applications, many of which are still in the design stages.

Jacques Ellul, a noted humanist and philosopher, claims that technology no longer aims at the appropriate objectives of improving a society's life-style:

The aims of technology, which were clear enough a century and a half ago, have gradually disappeared from view. Humanity seems to have forgotten the wherefore of all its travail, as though its goals had been translated into an abstraction or had become implicit; or as though its ends rested in an unforeseeable future of undetermined date. . . . Even things which not long ago seemed to be immediate objectives—rising living standards, hygiene, comfort—no longer seem to have that character, possibly because man finds the endless adaptation to new circumstances disagreeable.[1]

It is the responsibility of computer professionals and users alike to keep technology in touch with humanity and to make certain that the tools of computing do not overpower those that rely on them.

KEY TERMS

Electronic mail
Facsimile devices
Management information system
Microcomputers
Word-processing system

DISCUSSION QUESTIONS

1. What changes can be expected in the "office of the future"?
2. Why is it likely that management information systems will be more successful in the future?
3. How will executives be able to make use of computer technology to work at home?
4. What problems may arise for employees who use computer technology in their homes to perform their work?
5. What changes can be expected in computer hardware and software in the years to come?
6. What are some of the controversial societal issues involving computer utilization that will probably continue to exist for many years to come?

APPLICATION

Based on the following article, what can we expect in the way of new computer technology within the next few years? How will this technology affect our daily lives?

[1] Jacques Ellul, *The Technological Society* (New York: Knopf), p. 430.

Futurist Maps Course of Coming Technology[a]

By Bruce Hoard

SAINT-PAUL-DE-VENCE, France—Tomorrow's decision makers can look forward to a host of electronic marvels including libraries on a chip and factories on a wafer, according to Earl Joseph, a staff futurist for Univac.

Joseph imparted his predictions to a skeptical and questioning audience here at Sperry Corp.'s International Executive Centre as part of a four-day seminar focusing on decision making and its relationship to information technology.

"The technology we currently have in place is at least 100 years behind what it could be," he told a group of largely British journalists and publishers, who came to listen, learn and luxuriate on the Cote d'Azur.

The futurist sketched out his perception of the future information processing order by using a "future map." The map started with the development of the microprocessor on a chip and moved through miniprocessors, minicomputers, medium-scale computers and eventually large-scale computers on a chip by the mid-1990s.

Increasingly large memories will be condensed to chip size, leading to the advent of the library on a chip in conjunction with large-scale computers, he claimed. Joseph's micro-sized reduction list read like a menu of the absurd: book on a chip, MIS on a chip, doctor on a chip and, for those with iron stomachs, politician on a chip.

Wafer-wise, he tossed out visions of the office on a wafer, the factory on a wafer, culture on a wafer and future world on a wafer.

'Awareness Machines'

Intelligent and sensor-perceptive machines that will volunteer knowledge to users based on key words are also within technological grasp, Joseph noted. Primitive models of these "current awareness machines" are now in limited use in such areas as the military, large corporations and other governmental agencies, he said.

"That's a different system, and you can imagine how helpful it would be," the futurist commented.

Advanced communications capabilities will allow other machines to listen to specially broadcast programming aimed at a specific orientation, Joseph said. Farm machines, for example, will listen to information on farm futures and implement it in daily operations.

Of the current state of artificial intelligence, he said. "We have a long way to go," but noted humanity learned more about the brain during the '70s than it had in all the rest of history.

Today's management information services (MIS) systems are complicated and difficult to use, so top-level decision makers are eschewing them, the futurist said. In the future, however, they will be supplanted by deductive reasoning systems and general domain knowledge systems; "these are things that are beginning to come out of the laboratory and will be put in a form decision makers can use," Joseph said.

Just as agricultural and industrial development was marked by a unique set of tools, the information age must "grow" its own set of tools, according to Joseph, who is an advocate of microprocessor-based farming. Those tools include the smart office, books on a chip and videodisks which are "beginning to be integrated with a long list of other things."

Joseph did designate a human role in his new age. People are needed to guide the technology revolution.

One problem is debugging. In the past, technologies have become obsolete by the time they were debugged, but in the future, debugging should be done in parallel with the design process, he asserted.

Call for Cooperation

Joseph also called for less "non-cooperative confrontations" between technologists and societal designers. Once that cohesion is reached, humanity will find itself in an "all-win situation," he claimed.

During the question period, Joseph's vision of the future was called "appalling" by one participant who openly wondered how such a depersonalized society could enhance the human existence. Wouldn't the information order Joseph was espousing lead to a considerable amount of unemployment? he asked.

The speaker replied that such technology would actually create more jobs than it eliminated because of the tremendous influx of knowledge. Future jobs that will arise as a result of technology include knowledge engineering and space mining, he said.

[a] *Computerworld*, Aug. 11, 1980, p. 11. Copyright 1980 by CW Communications/Inc., Framingham, MA 01701. Reprinted with permission.

Glossary

Abacus. A computational tool using beads that dates back to about 3500 B.C.

Ada. A programming language that encourages structured program design.

Aiken, Howard. A mathematician at Harvard University who developed the idea for an electromechanical computer which used relays for completing circuits and adding to specific counters; designed the Mark I.

Analog Computer. This device measures or processes data in a continuous form.

Analytical Engine. A device developed by Charles Babbage that is similar in concept to modern digital computers; used cards to indicate the specific functions to be performed and to specify the actual data.

APL. A high-level symbolic programming language; an acronym for A Programming Language; best used for interactive programming using a terminal.

Application Programmers. The individuals who develop the logic, then code, debug, and document a program.

Arithmetic-Logic Unit. The unit of a CPU that performs arithmetic operations and comparisons.

Artificial Intelligence (AI). A scientific field concerned with simulating the process of reasoning in order to shed light on the nature of rational thought.

ASCII. A common computer code; an abbreviation for American Standard Code for Information Interchange.

Assembler Language. A low-level programming language; similar to machine language; does not require complex translations.

Association for Computing Machinery (ACM). A major computer society.

Atanasoff, John. Designed an electronic digital computer developed to solve some specific mathematical problems.

Authorization Code. A code that permits a terminal user to access a particular computer system.

Automatic Teller Machine (ATM). A machine that provides 24-hour banking services.

Auxiliary Storage. A separate storage unit that supplements primary storage in the CPU.

Babbage, Charles. Frequently considered the father of the modern computer; in the early 1800s he outlined the ideas that have become the basis for modern computational devices.

BASIC. A high-level symbolic programming language; an acronym for Beginner's All-purpose Symbolic Instruction Code; similar to FORTRAN; best suited for programming with the use of terminals.

Batch Processing. The processing of data in groups or batches, as opposed to the immediate processing of data.

Binary Number. A number represented by a combination of 0's and 1's; ideally suited for use in computers, where 0 represents the "off" state and 1 represents the "on" state.

Business Data Processing. A field of study that focuses on the computer as a business or management tool.

Byte. A sequence of bits, usually 8, used to represent a character in storage.

CAI. *See* Computer-Assisted Instruction.

Card Punch. A device in a computer system that punches card information which has been transmitted from the CPU.

Card Read/Punch. A device in a computer system that houses a card reader and a card punch unit.

Card Reader. A device in a computer system that reads punched card data and transmits it to the CPU.

CAT Scanner. A diagnostic device used for producing cross-sectional X-rays of a person's internal organs; an acronym for computed axial tomography.

Cathode Ray Tube (CRT). A terminal device that prints messages on a television-like tube; output is said to be "soft copy" since it is not retained as a permanent record.

Central Processing Unit (CPU). The device that controls the actual operations of the computer system; these include input, data transfer, arithmetic, logic, and output operations which are part of each user program.

Centralized Data Base. Contains all data that pertains to the operations of the organization.

Centralized Data Processing. The performance of the data processing function by a single computer center within a company. *Contrast with* Decentralized Data Processing.

Certification. A credential which indicates that the profession recognizes the individual as possessing a specified set of skills.

Charge-Coupled Device. A variation of a metal-oxide semiconductor that includes packets of electrical charges in a small slice of silicon; provides very high speed memories with large capacities at a relatively low cost.

Chip. A component used in many modern CPUs; can contain thousands of integrated circuits.

CMI. *See* Computer-Managed Instruction.

COBOL. A high-level symbolic programming language; an acronym for Common Business Oriented Language; English-like; most suited for business-type problems.

Coding a Program. The writing of instructions in a program after the logic flow has been mapped out using either a flowchart or pseudocode.

Collection of Data. That aspect of a systems analyst's job associated with acquiring data on how a given system operates; includes reading procedures manuals and discussing the present system with managers and operating staff.

Compatibility. When software prepared for one computer can be utilized by another without a rigorous conversion, the two systems are said to be compatible.

Compilation (Compiler). The translation process that produces a machine-language equivalent of a high-level symbolic programming language; more complex process than an assembly. The program that performs this translation is called a compiler.

Computer. A device that operates on data at high speeds, can store data, and needs to be programmed. The term "computer" is most frequently used to denote a digital device.

Computer-Aided Design (CAD). A technique used in industry for the design, development, and testing of any kind of equipment.

Computer-Assisted Instruction (CAI). An educational tool by which the computer usually prints textual information on a terminal and then asks the student to respond to a series of questions. Depending on the accuracy of the responses, the computer will either proceed to a more advanced topic or else repeat the material.

Computer Crime. The act of stealing, embezzling, or otherwise defrauding an organization with the use of a computer.

Computer-Managed Instruction (CMI). The use of computers to maintain records on the effectiveness of CAI.

Computer Output Microfilm (COM). Microfilm output from a computer system.

Computer Science. A course of study that focuses on understanding computer technology and theory and on techniques used for maximizing the overall design efficiency of the machine; frequently emphasizes numerical analysis and mathematical programming.

Computer Security. The techniques used for minimizing unauthorized use of a computer.

Computer System. A series of devices that read input data, process the data, and produce output information.

Control Unit. The part of the CPU that supervises or monitors the functions performed by the computer system; a program called a supervisor controls the operations.

Conversion of Source Documents. The process of creating machine-readable input from incoming source documents.

Core Storage. A form of CPU memory that uses magnetic cores in on-off states to represent characters.

COURSEWRITER. An English-like programming language for CAI systems.

Cybernetics. The study of control and communication in machines and in living organisms.

Data. Raw facts that are entered as input, processed, and transformed into meaningful information.

Data Base Administrator. The individual responsible for organizing, designing, and maintaining the data base and associated computer files used by the organization.

Data Transfer. The movement of data from one area of storage to another.

Debugging. Eliminating from a program any syntax and/or logic errors or "bugs."

Decentralized Data Processing. When data processing is performed by various centers within a company. Each department may hire its own computing staff and maintain its own computer facility.

Dedicated Computer. A computer that is used as a special-purpose device designed to satisfy the needs of a specific user in a specific way.

Detail File. Can be stored on various computer media; is used to update or revise the master file.

Difference Engine. A device developed by Charles Babbage to produce astronomical tables accurately and quickly; was powered by a steam engine.

Digital Computer.   This device operates on data in discrete form.

Direct Access.   A method of processing that is independent of the location of the data in a file. The most common method for accessing magnetic disk records directly (or randomly), for example, is with the use of an index. *Contrast with* Sequential Processing.

Director of Information Services.   The individual who is responsible for all computer operations and applications; a top-level management position.

Distributed Data Processing (DDP).   Each department has its own computer facility, but there is one central computer controlling, coordinating, and integrating the data processing activities of all departments; combines the advantages of both the centralized and decentralized approach and minimizes the disadvantages.

DP Manager.   The person responsible for the overall operations of the computer center.

EBCDIC.   *See* Extended Binary Coded Decimal Interchange Code.

Eckert, J. Presper, Jr.   The chief engineer on ENIAC.

Edit Procedure.   The process of validating a file of data to ensure that records do not contain obvious omissions, inconsistencies, or errors.

EDVAC.   The first electronic digital computer designed to have stored-program capability.

Electromechanical Computer.   This device used moving parts, as compared to an electronic computer, which uses solid-state components.

Electronic Cash Register.   A device that functions like a traditional cash register except that it has greater capability and can perform many tasks automatically.

Electronic Computer.   Initially an electronic computer made use of vacuum tubes, transistors, and then other solid-state components; there are no moving parts—therefore, these devices are fast and experience few breakdowns.

Electronic Data Processing (EDP).   In current terminology, EDP refers to the processing of data by electronic digital computers.

Electronic Funds Transfer System (EFT).   A system that eliminates the exchange of cash or checks by automatically transferring funds from one account to another.

Electronic Mail.   The use of facsimile devices to transmit information from one location to another.

ELIZA.   A program that simulates human responses and provides some insight into language analysis.

ENIAC.   An electronic computer designed by J. Presper Eckert, Jr., and John Mauchly and completed in 1946; an acronym for Electronic Numerical Integrator and Computer.

Erasable Programmable Read-Only Memory (EPROM).   A chip is not only programmable to include a set of functions, but the program can be "erased" or overlayed with another program through a micro-code procedure.

Exception Report.   A listing of records that do not fall within established criteria.

Execution.   The operating cycle during which a program is actually being run.

Extended Binary Coded Decimal Interchange Code (EBCDIC). A computer code used to represent characters.

Facsimile Devices.   Devices that make it possible to transmit copies of documents, reports, correspondences, and messages from one location to another instantaneously.

Fair Credit Reporting Act of 1971.   Is concerned with consumer credit information that is maintained and disseminated by various credit agencies.

Feasibility Study.   A study used to determine (1) the computer equipment that a company should select for its data processing department, and/or (2) whether writing a particular software package can be justified as compared to buying one.

Field.   A group of consecutive positions used to represent an item of data.

File.   A collection of individual records that are treated as one unit. A payroll file, for example, is a company's complete collection of employee records.

File Maintenance.   An update procedure that makes a master file of data current.

Firmware.   Prewired hardware that has been preprogrammed to perform specific functions.

Floppy Disk.   A direct-access form of storage that is also known as a diskette or flexible disk; a floppy disk is similar to a standard magnetic disk which is used to store data and programs using random-access methods of processing.

Flowchart.   A pictorial representation of the logic to be used in a program or a system.

FORTRAN.   A high-level symbolic programming language; an abbreviation for Formula Translator; most suited for scientific or mathematical problems.

Front-End Processor.   A minicomputer that can organize, control, and process data from a series of terminals, and then transmit the output to a large-scale system which integrates the data from a network of minis.

General Problem Solver. A program designed to simulate a wide range of human problem-solving techniques.

General-Purpose Computer. A device that can be programmed to perform a wide variety of functions.

Graphics Display Terminal. A CRT that typically has the capability of generating numerous forms and figures in a wide variety of colors.

GRIPHOS. An acronym for General Retrieval and Information Processor for Humanities Oriented Studies; a system that offers a data storage format suitable for the large inventories of museums.

Hard Copy. A permanent record of output from a computer system. *Contrast with* Soft Copy.

Hardware. The physical devices that constitute a computer system. *Contrast with* software.

Hawthorne Experiments. Industrial management experiments conducted in New Jersey which demonstrated that human relations and human factors are of considerable importance in increasing productivity and in obtaining cooperation.

Health Information Systems. Computers are used for both record keeping and medical diagnosis.

Heuristics. A technique for solving a problem by making educated guesses; frequently used in AI applications.

Hierarchy of Operations. The order of operations performed by the computer when an instruction involving calculations is executed.

High-Level Languages. Symbolic programming languages that require compilation; they are easier to code than low-level languages but more difficult to translate because they are English-like and not machine-like.

Hollerith, Herman. Developed tabulating machines that utilized the punched card concept.

Hollerith Code. The system of punches used on a card to represent data; named for Herman Hollerith.

Hospital Information Systems. Computers are used primarily for record-keeping purposes. *Contrast with* Medical Information Systems.

Host Processor. A mainframe that controls the transmission of data from and to a series of minis or terminals.

Index. A direct-access feature that provides the computer with the capability of "looking up" disk records, just as one looks up subjects in the index of a book.

Industrial Revolution. A period (1760-1830) of changes and displacement caused by rapidly expanding technologies; resulted in an era in which laborsaving equipment was seen as related to success in business and scientific pursuits.

Information. Processed data.

Information Banks. These banks maintain data on a very large number of articles, books, or other resources on particular subjects.

Input. Incoming data read into a computer system for processing.

Input Unit. The device that reads data from a specific form and converts it into electrical pulses which are transmitted to the CPU.

Institute for Certification of Computer Professionals (ICCP). An organization established for the purpose of testing and certifying knowledge and skills of computing personnel.

Integrated Circuit. Consists of hundreds of electronic components on a thin silicon wafer.

Intelligent Terminal. A terminal device that contains a built-in facility for editing incoming data even before the data is transmitted to the computer.

Jacquard, Joseph Marie. Built an attachment to the weaving loom that resulted in automated pattern weaving; used a system of punched holes in cards to direct the movement of threads so that a specific design could be produced.

Job Control Language (JCL). The language in which the programmer and/or operator communicates job requirements to the operating system software (supervisor). JCL specifications include the type of translation desired, input/output equipment to be used, end-of-data indicators, and so on.

Keypunch Machine. A typewriter-like device that an operator uses to punch data into a card, usually from a source document.

Key-to-Disk Encoder. A typewriter-like device used by an operator to enter data on a magnetic disk from a source document.

Key-to-Tape Encoder. A typewriter-like device used by an operator to enter data on a magnetic tape from a source document.

Large-Scale Computers. These are high-level machines that have storage capacities in the several megabyte (million byte) range. They usually contain full control systems with minimal operator intervention, are capable of linking up with dozens of sophisticated I/O devices, have high-level teleprocessing capability, and can perform operations at very high speeds.

Laser Beam Reader. A device that uses an electric eye mechanism to read the Universal Product Code.

Leibniz, Gottfried. An important figure of the Scientific Revolution; designed a calculator that could perform addition, subtraction, multiplication, and division.

Light Pen.   A device used with some CRT terminals to make changes to the data displayed on the screen.

Line Printer.   A computer output device that prints one line at a time.

Linguistics.   The study of languages, how they have evolved, and how they compare with one another.

Log–On Procedures.   The procedures necessary to gain access to a computer system with the use of a terminal.

Loop.   A sequence of steps in a program to be executed a specified number of times.

Lovelace, Augusta Ada.   Worked closely with Charles Babbage in developing ideas for the Analytical Engine; wrote a demonstration program for the device; published articles on Babbage's work; considered the first programmer.

Low-Level Languages.   Symbolic programming languages that require assembly; they are harder to code than high-level languages but easier to translate since they are machine-like and not English-like.

Machine Language Program.   Is machine dependent; involves the use of special codes and the assignment of actual storage addresses.

Magnetic Bubble Memory.   Consists of magnetized spots on a thin film of semiconductor material; is nonvolatile, which means that data is retained even if power is shut off.

Magnetic Core.   Used to represent data or instructions in memory; a tiny doughnut-shaped ferrite element.

Magnetic Disk.   An input/output medium that can be used for high-volume, high-speed storage where data is stored as magnetized bits. A disk has the added feature of random or direct accessibility.

Magnetic Ink Character Recognition (MICR) Devices.   Computer hardware capable of reading characters imprinted with magnetic ink, such as on checks.

Magnetic Ink Characters.   The figures found on the bottom of checks which indicate the account number, and a code to designate the bank where the account is located.

Magnetic Tape.   A high-speed input/output medium that stores data in the form of magnetized bits. It is commonly used to store high-volume files.

Mainframe.   *See* Central Processing Unit.

Maintenance Programmer.   The individual responsible for revising, amending, or updating existing programs.

Management Game.   A simulation technique used to train management. Management personnel are asked to make executive-level decisions for hypothetical firms in an effort to improve their decision-making ability.

Management Information System (MIS). A systems approach that treats business departments as integrated parts of one total system rather than as separate entities. This approach aims at facilitating the flow of information and at providing management with greater decision-making power.

Mark I. An electromechanical computer designed by Howard Aiken of Harvard University.

Mark-Sense Reader. Detects the presence of pencil marks on predetermined grids of source documents.

Mass Storage Device. An auxiliary device that can greatly enhance the memory capacity of a computer system.

Master File. The main data file that holds all current information for a specific department or system; the major file in a particular application; the file that contains all the data fields used to create required output. A master accounts receivable file, for example, is a collection of records that includes all customer account information.

Mauchly, John. Conceived the original idea for the ENIAC, the first operational electronic digital computer built in the United States.

Mechanistic View. A belief of some people that all matter can be explained in terms of computable, mechanical entities.

Medical Information Systems. Computers are used primarily for diagnostic and evaluating purposes. *Contrast with* Hospital Information Systems.

Medium-Scale Computers. These devices are capable of high-speed and complex operations. They can use a large number of sophisticated I/O devices. They do require some operator intervention even though they utilize complex software to handle most typical control procedures.

Megabyte. One million bytes of storage.

Memory Size. The number of storage positions that can be accessed in a computer system; can vary widely, depending on the category of computer.

Microcomputer. A small computer that can be acquired for as little as several hundred dollars in its basic form.

Minicomputer. A small computer with most of the same features as a standard-sized computer; frequently used as a front-end processor in a data communications network.

Mini Medical Systems. Small computers used by some doctors and drugstores to assess their own diagnostic or treatment abilities.

Multiphasic Screening. The computer assists the physician by giving a preliminary analysis of the patient's history and current medical symptoms.

Multiprocessing. The simultaneous operating of two or more CPUs linked together.

Multiprogramming. The ability of a computer system to execute two or more programs simultaneously; this is a common feature of time-sharing and data communications systems.

MUMPS. A programming language designed for use in the health care field; an acronym for Massachusetts (General Hospital) Utility Multi Programming System.

Museum Computer Network. Several museums utilize computers for cataloging, storing, and retrieving information about their respective inventories.

Music Synthesizer. A device attached to a computer which utilizes a digital-to-analog converter to create musical sounds.

Nanosecond. One billionth (10^{-9}) of a second.

National Crime Information Center (NCIC). A computerized information center maintained by the FBI which serves agencies throughout the United States.

National Security Agency. This agency protects U.S. communications from intrusion by foreign powers, and collects intelligence data to be disseminated to other agencies for their use.

Numerical Control. The use of computers to produce machine tools automatically to required specifications; typically, a punched paper tape with codes in it is used to control the operations of a machine.

Object Program. A machine-language equivalent of a source program. Object programs are the only ones that can be executed without being translated first.

Off-line Processing. The processing of data that is not directly under the control of the CPU.

On-line Processing. As data is collected, it is immediately used as input to a computer system with a device, such as a terminal, that is directly connected to the CPU. *Contrast with* Batch Processing.

Operating System. A series of control programs that enables a computer to handle tasks automatically that would otherwise require operator intervention. These tasks include compilation, scheduling, input/output control, and so on.

Optical Character Recognition (OCR) Devices. Computer hardware capable of reading typed or handwritten documents.

Output. Data that has been processed by a computer system.

Output Unit. The device that transmits information from the CPU and converts the electronic pulses to an appropriate output form.

Page Printer. A computer output device that prints an entire page at one time.

Pascal. A high-level symbolic programming language, named for the mathematician Blaise Pascal, that facilitates the use of structured programming techniques.

Pascal, Blaise. A French scientist who was one of the first modern scientists to develop and build a calculator.

Pattern Recognition. The ability of a computer to identify or classify shapes, forms, or relationships.

Picosecond. One trillionth (10^{-12}) of a second.

PLATO. The largest available CAI system; an acronym for Programmed Logic for Automatic Teaching Operations.

PL/1. A high-level symbolic programming language; an acronym for Programming Language/1; combines the features of FORTRAN and COBOL.

Plug-Compatible Machine (PCM). A device that adds storage capability or additional input/output as needed.

Point-of-Sale System (POS). A system that enables sales clerks using special terminals to automatically update computer files at the same time as they prepare sales receipts.

Powers, James. Developed his own version of punched card tabulating equipment in the early twentieth century.

Primary Storage. The storage capacity of a computer system that is located within the CPU; *contrast with* auxiliary storage.

Privacy Act of 1974. This is concerned with data banks of personal information that are maintained by federal agencies.

Problem Definition. Formal document prepared by the systems analyst which defines the current system and its basic inadequacies.

Process Control. A computer continuously measures the key variables of a process, such as the flow of fluid, pressure, and temperature, and makes necessary adjustments.

Production Control. Assembly-line activities can be monitored and controlled by computers.

Program. A series of instructions that reads input data, processes it, and converts it to output.

Program Documentation. Specifications that fully describe a program after it has been completely tested; includes a source listing, input/output specifications, flowcharts, test data used, schedules, and so on.

Programmable Read-Only Memory (PROM). A chip (or chips) that contains a programmed set of functions; either the user or the manufacturer writes the code for the chip.

Programmed Instruction. A typical CAI sequence consists of text material, test questions requiring student responses, additional backup instructional material, and an analysis of progress.

Programmer. The computer professional who writes and debugs the program, or set of instructions, which operates on input and converts it to output.

PROMIS. An acronym for Problem-Oriented Medical Information System; designed to alleviate some major record-keeping problems in the health care field.

Protocol. The log-on procedures used to access a computer system.

Pseudocode. A tool used for depicting logic; widely used for applications that have complex logical control procedures, where a structured approach is most useful; utilizes a code similar to a program code.

Punched Card. A card punched with holes used to represent data.

Punched Paper Tape. A paper tape which is punched with holes that represent specific characters.

RAM (Random-Access Memory). That part of memory that can be accessed or altered as needed by each program; used for storing programs and data.

Read-Only Memory (ROM). The part of memory that contains prewired functions; cannot be altered by programmed instructions.

Read/Write Head. A feature of a magnetic tape or magnetic disk drive that enables the device to read magnetic data or to record magnetic data, depending on the application.

Real-Time System. A system designed to update files immediately upon the entry of input data; provides management with information fast enough to affect the decision-making process.

Record. A collection of related fields, such as an employee's time card.

Right to Financial Privacy Act of 1979. This law deals with the type of personal information that federal agencies can obtain from financial institutions.

ROM. *See* Read-Only Memory.

RPG. A high-level program generator; an acronym for Report Program Generator; most suited for printing simple reports.

Scientific Programmer. A person who writes the set of instructions so that the computer will perform technical or scientific tasks.

Scientific Revolution. During the sixteenth and seventeenth centuries, scientific values changed radically; a new model emerged for science which was machine oriented and which focused on the application of science to real-world situations.

Sequential Processing. The method of processing data consecutively as it appears on the input medium. This method is most commonly used with card and tape processing. *Contrast with* Direct Access.

Serial Printer. Functions like a typewriter, printing one character at a time; used primarily for interactive keyboard-print terminals.

Simulation. An operations research technique that produces a model of a system, one that can be manipulated and studied to understand the system better and to make predictions about the future.

Small-Scale Computers. These computers are designed to perform functions in far less time and with greater accuracy than mechanical tabulating equipment. They frequently utilize punched card input and are basically used to produce printed output.

Soft Copy. Output from a computer system that is in the form of a visual display. *Contrast with* Hard Copy.

Software. Programming support that enables the computer system to operate effectively; includes the supervisor and user programs.

Source Data Automation. The methods devised to reduce the conversion from source documents to input in machine-readable form.

Source Document. The originating report or document which when converted to a machine-readable form is used as input to a computer system.

Source Program. A program written in a symbolic programming language; source programs must be translated before they can be executed.

Special-Purpose Computer. A device that performs a specific set of functions. These are devices that are frequently designed for a manufacturing environment.

Stibitz, George. Designed electromechanical, relay computers (Models I-V) for wartime use.

Stored-Program Concept. A program must be stored or located inside the CPU in order for various operations to be performed.

Structured Design. A method for standardizing programming and systems work.

Structured Programming. A term used to describe an efficient programming technique that can facilitate the design and coding of programs; referred to as GO TO-less or modular programming.

Supercomputers. These are machines that have capabilities far beyond even the large-scale systems. Their speed is in the range of 100 million instructions per second.

Supervisor. A component of the operating system; a special program that resides inside the CPU to control the operations of the entire system; calls in each application program and integrates the processing of each step.

Symbolic Program. A program written in a symbolic form which is easier for the programmer to understand than the machine's own code; requires a translation process.

Syntax Error. A violation of a programming language rule that is detected during the translation process.

System Resident Device. The entire operating system, which consists of a library of compilers, assemblers, interpreters, and other programs in addition to the supervisor, is stored on an auxiliary storage device such as a disk.

Systems Analyst. The computer specialist responsible for analyzing current procedures and designing the most efficient and economical systems or procedures that will better accomplish given tasks within a company.

Systems Programmer. One who designs programs that will be utilized by computer installations to maximize the efficiency of the computer itself.

Tape Cartridges. These devices are used to store data and programs that are processed sequentially in a batch mode; similar to mini magnetic tapes.

Tape Cassettes. These devices operate like miniature magnetic tapes; they are used to store data and programs that are processed sequentially in a batch mode.

Tape Labels. An *external label* is used to identify the tape for the operator. An *internal label*, called a header label, is the first record on the tape and identifies the tape to the computer.

Tape Librarian. A computer center employee responsible for maintaining control of magnetic tapes.

Template. Used to draw a flowchart; contains symbols that represent specific operations.

Terminal. A device that can typically be used at remote locations to enter data and programs into a CPU and/or receive responses to inquiries.

TICCIT. An acronym for Time Shared Interactive Computer Controlled Information Television; a CAI system.

Time-Sharing. Term used to describe a central processing unit that is shared by several users, usually with the use of terminals. Small companies that cannot afford to rent or buy their own computer find this particularly advantageous.

Top-Down Approach. Defining a problem or program or system in most general terms, then successively refining each module in more and more specific terms.

Transaction File. A file that contains records that will be used to update a master file. *See* Detail File.

Translation. The process of converting a source program into machine language.

Turing, Alan. A British mathematician who, among other things, attempted to determine if machines can be made to function in ways similar to the way in which human beings behave when they are "thinking."

Turing Test. A person asks questions, and on the basis of the answers, must determine if the respondent is another human being or a machine.

Turnkey System. A complete hardware and software package designed by the manufacturer to perform a given set of tasks; the user "turns the key" and the system operates automatically.

TUTOR. An English-like programming language for CAI systems.

Uninterruptible Power Supply. A unit that functions as a control unit monitoring the supply of electricity and can also function as a generator if there is a sudden loss of electricity.

Universal Product Code (UPC). A bar code that appears on virtually all consumer goods; can be read by a scanner or wand device; used in point-of-sale systems.

Update Procedure. The process of making a master file of data current.

Virtual Storage (VS). A computer control system that maximizes the efficient use of storage by using overlay techniques.

von Neumann, John. A mathematician who contributed to the logical design theory for the stored-program concept.

Wand Reader. A device that is passed over a Universal Product Code to record the item purchased.

Weizenbaum, Joseph. Author of a program called ELIZA, which not only simulates human responses but provides some insight into language analysis.

Word Processing. A type of data processing that attempts to automate secretarial tasks performed in most offices; instead of typing documents, reports, and letters using a standard typewriter, a secretary uses a terminal to print the document, make changes where appropriate, and store the information for future printing.

B

Resources in the computing field: a bibliographic review

I. Books and Journals Categorized by Subject Matter
II. Periodicals
III. Prominent Computer Societies

This bibliographic review focuses on books, monographs, and proceedings. Articles and scholarly papers have been cited in the text. Rather than providing a comprehensive list of timely articles that may become obsolete in several months, we have included instead a list of journals that can be consulted. A brief description of each journal is also provided.

B.1 BOOKS AND JOURNALS CATEGORIZED BY SUBJECT MATTER

ARTIFICIAL INTELLIGENCE

BANERJI, RANAN, *Artificial Intelligence: A Theoretical Approach.* Amsterdam: North-Holland, 1980.
Provides an analysis of heuristics by focusing on several studies at a number of research centers.

BELLMAN, RICHARD, *An Introduction to Artificial Intelligence: Can Computers Think?* San Francisco: Boyd & Fraser, 1978.
This is a comprehensive book on AI.

DREYFUS, HUBERT L., *What Computers Can't Do*. New York: Harper & Row, 1972.
A philosophical evaluation of the problems inherent in artificial intelligence research.

JACKSON, P. C., *Introduction to Artificial Intelligence*. Princeton, NJ: Petrocelli Books, 1974.
Provides a survey of AI from both a technical and a nontechnical viewpoint.

MICHIE, DONALD, *On Machine Intelligence*. New York: Wiley, 1974.
A well-written account of the main ideas of AI. It includes a collection of articles written for the nonspecialist by Michie, who is regarded as one of the leading authorities on AI in Great Britain.

SLAGLE, JAMES R., *Artificial Intelligence: The Heuristic Programming Approach*. New York: McGraw-Hill, 1971.
A classic work in AI. Provides a fully-documented, articulate account of the development of the subject.

WEIZENBAUM, JOSEPH, *Computer Power and Human Reason*. San Francisco: W. H. Freeman, 1976.
A refreshing view of the problems inherent in AI research from the point of view of an insider.

Journals Specifically Related to Artificial Intelligence

American Journal of Computational Linguistics
American Society for Cybernetics — Forum
Artificial Intelligence: An International Journal

COMPUTERS: FROM THE PAST TO THE PRESENT

Annals of the History of Computing. Arlington, VA: AFIPS Press.
This is a quarterly publication that focuses on the history of computing. It includes articles by computer pioneers themselves as well as by historians.

BELL, C. GORDON, and ALLAN NEWELL, *Computer Structures: Reading and Examples*. New York: McGraw-Hill, 1971.
This book discusses first-, second-, and third-generation computers. It also includes reprints of some classical articles.

BURKS, ARTHUR W., HERMAN H. GOLDSTINE, and JOHN VON NEUMANN, "Planning and Coding Problems for an Electronic Computing Instrument," Part 1, in John von Neumann, *Collected Works*, Vol. 5, ed. A. H. Taub. New York: Oxford University Press, 1963.

GOLDSTINE, HERMAN H., *The Computer from Pascal to von Neumann*. Princeton, NJ: Princeton University Press, 1972.
This book considers the history of digital and analog calculating devices as well as those computers with which the author was involved: ENIAC, EDVAC, and John von Neumann's Institute for Advanced Study computer.

GOLDSTINE, HERMAN H., and JOHN VON NEUMANN, "Planning and Coding Problems for an Electronic Computing Instrument," Parts 2 and 3, in John von Neumann, *Collected Works*, Vol. 5, ed. A. H. Taub. New York: Oxford University Press, 1963.

LUKOFF, HERMAN, *From Dits to Bits*. Portland, OR: Robotics Press, 1979.
This work is an autobiography written by a computer pioneer who worked on ENIAC and UNIVAC.

METROPOLIS, N., ed., *A History of Computing in the Twentieth Century*. New York: Academic Press, 1980.
This is a series of papers presented by computer pioneers at a 1976 History of Computing Conference at Los Alamos, New Mexico.

MORRISON, P., and E. MORRISON, eds., *Charles Babbage and His Calculating Engines: Selected Writings by Charles Babbage and Others*. New York: Dover, 1961.
This book includes material on Babbage's life and two engines.

RANDELL, BRIAN, "An Annotated Bibliography on the Origins of Computers," *Annals of the History of Computing*, Vol. 1, No. 2, Oct. 1979.
Includes the most extensive bibliography of historical sources currently available.

RANDELL, BRIAN, *The Origins of Digital Computers: Selected Papers*. New York: Springer-Verlag, 1973.
This book contains 32 original papers and manuscripts relating to the origins of digital computers.

REDMOND, KENT C., and THOMAS M. SMITH, *Project Whirlwind*. Bedford, MA: Digital Press, 1980.
This book discusses the intellectual and sociological factors influencing the development of M.I.T.'s first electronic digital computer.

STERN, NANCY, *From ENIAC to UNIVAC*. Bedford, MA: Digital Press, 1981.
This book discusses the development of the ENIAC, BINAC, and UNIVAC, as well as the academic, governmental, and commercial forces that influenced these developments.

COMPUTERS AND AUTOMATION

BROOKS, FREDERICK P., *The Mythical Man-Month*. Reading, MA: Addison-Wesley, 1975.
This book discusses some of the problems associated with computerization.

LANDON, K. C., *Computers and Bureaucratic Reform*. New York: Wiley, 1974.
This book focuses on the impact of computers on society bureaucracy, in general.

PYLYSHYN, ZENON W., *Perspectives on the Computer Revolution*. Englewood Cliffs, NJ: Prentice-Hall, 1970.
Consists of a series of readings on the impact of the computer revolution; pp. 402-405, 480-496 deal with issues relating to automation.

SIMON, HERBERT A., *The New Science of Management Decision*. New York: Harper & Row, 1960.
A classic work on management science.

TOMESKI, EDWARD A., and HAROLD LAZARUS, *People-Oriented Computer Systems: The Computer in Crisis*. New York: Van Nostrand Reinhold, 1975.
This book focuses on how and why computer systems have failed people and organizations, and what can be done to make these systems better serve society.

WINNER, LANGDON, *Autonomous Technology: Technology Out-of-Control as a Theme in Political Thought*. Cambridge, MA: MIT Press, 1977.
An ideological critique of technology as it affects political systems.

COMPUTERS AND THE FUTURE

ELLUL, JACQUES, *The Technological Society*. New York: Knopf, 1974.
A humanist's analysis of our technical civilization and of the effect of an increasingly standardized culture on the future of human beings.

MARTIN, JAMES, *The Wired Society*. Englewood Cliffs, NJ: Prentice-Hall, 1978.
A work that focuses on the effects that the technology of communication is likely to have on society in the not-so-distant future.

TOFFLER, ALVIN, *Future Shock*. New York: Bantam Books, 1971.
A sociological view of the effects of technology on society.

TOFFLER, ALVIN, *The Third Wave*. New York: Morrow, 1980.
The book focuses on what the author describes as the "third wave" of change in history, the first being the Agricultural Revolution and the second being the Industrial Revolution. It provides an analysis of the forces that are influencing society.

COMPUTERS AND THE HUMANITIES

BATEMAN, WAYNE, *Introduction to Computer Music*. New York: Wiley, 1980.
This book focuses on how digital computers may be used to generate new and interesting musical sounds.

ERNST, D., *Electronic Music*. New York: Macmillan, 1977.

HIGGINS, D., *Computers for the Arts*. New York: Abyss Publications, 1977.

HILLER, L. A., and R. A. BAKER, "Computer Cantata." New York: Theodore Presser, 1968.
A classic musical work.

HILLER, L. A., and L. M. ISAASON, *Experimental Music*. New York: McGraw-Hill, 1959; "Illiac Suite for String Quartet," New York: Theodore Presser, 1957.
Two classic works in the field, the first a book, the second a piece of music.

LEAVITT, RUTH, ed., *Artist and Computer*. New York: Harmony Books, 1974.
A series of articles written by people who have experimented with computer art.

MORGAN, CHRISTOPHER P., *The Byte Book of Computer Music*. Petersborough, NH: Byte Publications, 1979.
This book is designed for people who wish to experiment with computer music.

Journals Specifically Related to Computers and the Humanities

Computer Graphics and Art (monthly)
Computers and the Humanities

COMPUTERS IN EDUCATION

ALDERMAN, DONALD L., *Evaluation of the TICCIT Computer-Assisted Instructional System in the Community College*. Princeton, NJ: Educational Testing Service, 1978.
Report on a research project to determine the overall effectiveness of the TICCIT system on the college level.

ANASTASIO, ERNEST J., and JUDITH S. MORGAN, *Factors Inhibiting the Use of Computers in Instruction*. Princeton, NJ: Educom, 1972.

DAVISSON, W. I., and F. J. BONELLO, *Computer-Assisted Instruction in Economic Education: A Case Study*. Notre Dame, IN: University of Notre Dame Press, 1976.
An analysis of one CAI project.

ELLIS, ALLEN, *The Use and Misuse of Computers in Education*. New York: McGraw-Hill, 1974.

HUSSAIN, KHATEEB, *Development of Information Systems for Education*. Englewood Cliffs, NJ: Prentice-Hall, 1973.

OETTINGER, ANTHONY, G., *Run, Computer, Run*. Cambridge, MA: Harvard University Press, 1969.
This is a classic work that summarizes the basic issues relating to CAI.

ROCKERT, J. F., and M. S. SCOTT-MORTON, *Computers and the Learning Process in Higher Education*. New York: McGraw-Hill, 1975.
An in-depth view of computers used at the university level.

SEIDEL, ROBERT J., and MARTIN RUBIN, eds., *Computers and Communications: Implications for Education*. New York: Academic Press, 1977.
A sociological and technological evaluation of CAI.

Journals Specifically Related to Computers in Education

ACM (Association for Computing Machinery) Bulletins:
- SIGCSE (Special Interest Group for Computer Science Education) (quarterly).
- SIGCUE (Special Interest Group for Computer Users in Education) (quarterly).

Data Processing for Education (monthly)

Educational Technology (monthly)

Journal of Educational Data Processing (bimonthly)

The Journal: Technical Horizons in Education (monthly)

COMPUTERS IN THE SCIENCES AND MEDICINE

COLLEEN, M. F., ed., *Hospital Computer Systems*. New York: Wiley, 1974.
This is a collection of papers on the use of computers in hospitals.

FERNBACH, S., and A. H. TAUB, eds., *Computers and Their Role in the Physical Sciences*. Urbana, IL: University of Illinois Press, 1972.

This is a collection of articles that indicate the various ways computers are used in society.

PERKINS, W. J., ed., *Biomedical Computing*. Baltimore, MD: University Park Press, 1977.
This is a collection of technical articles that describe the state of biomedical computing.

ELECTRONIC FUNDS TRANSFER

American Institute of Certified Public Accountants, "Audit Considerations in Electronic Funds Transfer Systems," 1978.

COLTON, K., and K. KRAEMER, *Computers and Banking: Electronic Funds Transfer Systems and Public Policy*. New York: Plenum, 1980.
A series of articles focusing on EFT.

Communications of the ACM, December 1979.
The entire issue is devoted to the impact of EFT on society.

GENERAL WORKS

ABSHIRE, GARY M., ed., *The Impact of Computers on Society and Ethics: A Bibliography*. Morristown, NJ: Creative Computing, 1980.
Contains 1920 alphabetic entries of books, magazine articles, news items, scholarly papers, and other works dealing with the impact of computers on society and ethics. Covers 1948 through 1979.

PERSONAL COMPUTING

AHL, DAVID, ed., *Basic Computer Games*. Morristown, NJ: Creative Computing, 1979.
A listing of numerous games in BASIC that can be played on a microcomputer.

ALBRECHT, B., et al., *What to Do After You Hit Return*. Menlo Park, CA: People's Computer Co., 1975.
This book includes a survey of games written in BASIC for microcomputer users.

CAPECE, R. P., ed., *Personal Computing: Hardware and Software Basics*. New York: McGraw-Hill, 1979.
A series of writings on the hardware and software available with microcomputers.

McGLYNN, DANIEL R., *Personal Computing: Home, Professional and Small Business Applications*. New York: Wiley, 1979.
This book provides a basic introduction to personal computers, their capabilities and limitations.

OSBORNE, A., *An Introduction to Microcomputers*. New York: Osborne Associates, 1976.
A technical work on the features and circuitry of microprocessors.

JOURNALS SPECIFICALLY RELATED TO PERSONAL COMPUTING

The prices are effective as of 1981.

BYTE 70 Main Street Peterborough, NH 03458	Monthly $15/year
Creative Computing P.O. Box 789 Morristown, NJ 07960	Monthly $20/year
Dr. Dobb's Journal of Computer Calisthenics and Orthodontia Box 310 Menlo Park, CA 94025	Monthly $12/year
Interface Age 16704 Marquerdt Avenue Cerritos, CA 90701	Monthly $15/year
Personal Computing Hayden Publishing Co., Inc. 50 Essex Street Rochelle Park, NJ 07662	Monthly $14/year

PRIVACY AND SECURITY

GOLDSTEIN, R. C., *The Cost of Privacy*. Brighton, MA: Honeywell, 1975.

HSIAO, DAVID K., DOUGLAS S. KERR, and STUART E. MADNICK, *Computer Security*. New York: Academic Press, 1979.
Provides a review of recent research in computer security, together with a critical assessment of this research.

PARKER, D. B., S. NYCUM, and O. S. OURA, *Computer Abuse*. Springfield, VA: National Technical Information Service, 1973.
Includes case histories of computer abuse.

PARKER, DONN B., *Crime by Computer*. New York: Scribners, 1976.

WESSEL, MILTON R., *Freedom's Edge: The Computer Threat to Society*. Reading, MA: Addison-Wesley, 1974.

Discusses the effect of computerized data bases on individual privacy.

WESTIN, A., and M. BAKER, *Databanks in a Free Society*. New York: Quadrangle, 1972.

WESTIN, A. F., *Privacy and Freedom*. New York: Atheneum, 1967.
An authoritative, although somewhat dated study of privacy problems.

THE COMPUTER PROFESSION

BRANDON, DICK H., *Management Standards for Data Processing*. New York: Harper & Row, 1963.
This book focuses on a management approach to data processing.

CHURCHMAN, C. WEST., *The Systems Approach*. New York: Dell, 1968.
Takes an honest look at the science-versus-art dichotomy intrinsic to systems analysis.

DRUCKER, PETER F., *Technology, Management and Society*. New York: Harper & Row, 1970.
This book considers the interaction of technology and management and its effect on society.

GREENBAUM, JOAN M., *In the Name of Efficiency*. Philadelphia: Temple University Press, 1979.
This book looks at the origins and techniques of modern management science and its use in the data processing workplace.

KRAFT, PHILIP, *Programmers and Managers: The Routinization of Computer Programming in the United States*. New York: Springer-Verlag, 1977.
This book considers the interrelationships between programmers and managers.

PARKER, DONN B., *Ethical Conflicts in Computer Science and Technology*. Arlington, VA: AFIPS Press, 1979.
This book considers the ethical problems and conflicts generated by scientific and technological developments as they affect both the technological community and society in general.

SHNEIDERMAN, BEN, *Software Psychology: Human Factors in Computer and Information Systems*. Cambridge, MA: Winthrop Publishers, 1980.
This book considers motivational, stylistic, and language design factors influencing programmers. It also describes current research techniques and indicates practical guidelines for programming and systems design.

WEINBERG, GERALD, *The Psychology of Computer Programming.* New York: Van Nostrand, 1971.
This book was one of the first to consider the human element in computer programming. It considers in detail the actual behavior and thought processes of programmers as they carry out their daily activities.

YOURDON, EDWARD, *Techniques of Program Structure and Design.* Englewood Cliffs, NJ: Prentice-Hall, 1975.
Focuses on the structured approach to programming and systems analysis.

B.2 PERIODICALS

This list is by no means exhaustive, but it does include some of the best known journals in the field. The prices are effective as of 1981.

Publication:	*Communications of the ACM* (Association for Computing Machinery)
Organization:	ACM
Address:	1133 Avenue of the Americas New York, NY 10036
Frequency:	Monthly
Cost:	Free with ACM membership; $12.50 per year for nonmembers
Orientation:	Computer science publication. Focuses on topics such as computer architecture, artificial intelligence, operating systems, programming languages, social impact of computers, management science, operations research.
Publication:	*Computer*
Organization:	IEEE Computer Society
Address:	IEEE Computer Society 5855 Naples Plaza Suite 301 Long Beach, CA 90803
Frequency:	Monthly
Cost:	Free for IEEE Computer Society members; $3.00/issue for nonmembers
Orientation:	For technical and computer science people, technology oriented, some attention to social applications.
Publication:	*Computer Decisions: The Management Magazine of Computing.*

Organization: Hayden Publishing Company
Address: 50 Essex Street
                Rochelle Park, NJ 07662
Frequency: Monthly
Cost: Free to qualified executives with active professional and functional responsibility in organizations that use computers and computer based services. Available to others at $26.
Orientation: This is a relatively nontechnical, management-oriented magazine which focuses on major computer issues such as security, word processing, minicomputers. The articles tend to be of general interest but provide only an introduction to some of the major topics.

Publication: *Computerworld*: The Newsweekly for the Computer Community
Address: 375 Cochituate Road
                Framingham, MA 01701
Frequency: Weekly
Cost: $25 per year
Orientation: This is a newspaper that addresses itself to events and occurrences in the data processing industry. It is relatively nontechnical and can serve the beginning data processing student as well as the data processing professional. Some of the categories that appear in each issue are: news, editorial, software and services, communications, systems and peripherals, miniworld, and computer industry. This is an excellent source for reviewing the most recent advances in all facets of the computer field.

Publication: *Data World*
                4 volumes
Organization: Auerbach Publishers, Inc.
Address: 6560 North Park Drive
                Pennsauken, NJ 08109
Frequency: This is offered by yearly subscription, which includes monthly updates.
Cost: $535 per year
Orientation: This work, like *Datapro*, provides a reference on computer developments which is comprehensive and current. This service provides coverage of the world's most widely used and actively marketed EDP products and service. It indicates vendor information, product specifications and prices, and independent product evaluations. Major topics include general-purpose computers, minicom-

puters, peripherals, data handling, software, and data communications. This work is an invaluable reference.

Publication:	*Datamation*
Address:	666 Fifth Avenue New York, NY 10019
Frequency:	Monthly
Cost:	No charge to qualified individuals who are employed by companies involved with automatic information-handling equipment. Available to others by subscription at the annual rate of $32; U.S. students, $16.
Orientation:	This journal features many interesting articles on the data processing industry. The articles are usually written by top-level DP professionals. Many of the articles are technical in nature, but a large number would be of interest to DP students. Most of the recent advances in the industry are covered in this journal.

Publication:	*Datapro*
Organization:	Datapro Research Corp.
Address:	1805 Underwood Boulevard Delran, NJ 08075
Frequency:	This reference is offered by yearly subscription, which includes monthly updates.
Cost:	$475/year
Orientation:	This is a first-rate reference providing a comprehensive and current analysis of the performance of computers, data communications, office systems, software, and so on.

Publication:	*Information Systems News*
Organization:	CMP Publications
Address:	333 East Short Road Manhasset, NY 11030
Frequency:	Monthly
Cost:	Free to qualified management and professional personnel involved in the information systems industry. Subscription rate for all others in the United States and Canada is $17.50 per year.
Orientation:	This publication is an MIS newspaper which includes editorials and news on software, computers, data communications, MIS strategies, and so on. Lists career opportunities as well.

Publication:	*Infosystems*
Organization:	Hitchcock Publishing Co.

Address: Hitchcock Building
Wheaton, IL 60187

Frequency: Monthly

Cost: No charge to qualified individuals; $30.00 per year for others

Orientation: This is a nontechnical applications-oriented journal which focuses on various uses of DP equipment. Frequently, an entire issue is devoted to a specific application—for example, word processing, computer-aided manufacturing, or micrographics, just to name a few.

Publication: *Journal of Systems Management*

Organization: Association for Systems Management

Address: 24587 Bagley Road
Cleveland, OH 44138

Frequency: Monthly

Cost: $15.00 per year

Orientation: This is a systems-oriented journal that focuses on management concerns. Topics include those relating to systems analysis and design, data base management systems, management information systems, cost/benefit analysis, and human resources management.

Publication: *Mini-Micro Systems*

Organization: A Cahners Publication

Address: 221 Columbus Avenue
Boston, MA 02116

Frequency: Monthly

Cost: Circulated without charge by name and title to U.S.-based corporate and technical management, systems engineers, and other personnel who meet qualification procedures. Available to others at the rate of $30.00 per year in the United States.

Orientation: The mini-micro articles focus on recent advances in the computing field and tend to be relatively nontechnical. Some of the feature articles, however, are somewhat technical.

Publication: *Security World*

Organization: Cahners Publishing Company

Address: 5 South Wabash Avenue
Chicago, IL 60603

Frequency: Monthly

Cost: $24.00 per year

Orientation: Features issues that are central for the security professional. Includes features on catastrophe protection, methods to prevent and detect crime, security systems, and personnel.

Publication: *Small Systems World*
Organization: Hunter Publications
Address: 53 West Jackson Boulevard
Chicago, IL 60604
Frequency: Monthly
Cost: Without charge to any EDP system per site; $15 annually for personal subscriptions
Orientation: Each issue contains three or four articles on various computer topics, not necessarily specific to small computer systems. Some articles are general and some are rather technical in nature. There are a relatively small number of pages per issue.

B.3 PROMINENT COMPUTER SOCIETIES

American Institute of Aeronautics & Astronautics
1290 Sixth Avenue
New York, NY 10019

The American Society for Information Science
1010 Sixteenth Street, N.W.
Second Floor
Washington, DC 20036

American Statistical Association
806 Fifteenth Street, N.W.
Washington, DC 20005

Association for Computational Linguistics
SRI International
333 Ravenswood Avenue
Menlo Park, CA 94025

Association for Computational Linguistics
Queens College
Flushing, NY 11367

The Association for Computing Machinery, Inc. (ACM)
1133 Avenue of the Americas
New York, NY 10036

Association for Educational Data Systems
1201 Sixteenth Street, N.W.
Washington, DC 20036

Association for Systems Management
24587 Bagley Road
Cleveland, OH 44138

Data Processing Management Association (DPMA)
505 Busse Highway
Park Ridge, IL 60068

The Institute of Electrical and Electronics Engineers, Inc. (IEEE)
345 East Forty-Seventh Street
New York, NY 10017

The Institute of Electrical and Electronics Engineers, Inc. (IEEE)
Computer Society
1109 Spring Street
Suite 202
Silver Spring, MD 20910

Instrument Society of America
International Headquarters
67 Alexander Drive
P.O. Box 12277
Research Triangle Park, NC 27709

The Society for Computer Simulation, Inc.
P.O. Box 2228
La Jolla, CA 92038

Society for Industrial and Applied Mathematics
1405 Architects Building
117 South 17th Street
Philadelphia, PA 19103

Society for Information Display
654 Sepulveda Boulevard
Los Angeles, CA 90049

Index

A

Abacus, 29-30, 474
ABC computer, 46-47
Access time, 183
Accuracy, of computers, 18
ACM (*See* Association for
    Computing Machinery)
Acoustic coupler, 196
ACPA (*See* Association of
    Computer Programmers and
    Analysts)
Acquisition, methods of
    computer, 238-39
Ada (language), 148, 474
Address:
    disk, 105
    machine, 135
    storage, 62
    symbolic, 138
AEDS (*See* Association for
    Educational Data Systems)
AI (*See* Artificial Intelligence)
Aiken, Howard, 44-45, 474
American Standard Code for
    Information Interchange
    (ASCII), 77, 474
Analog computer, 14, 474
    device, 13
Analysis, systems, 241
Analytical Engine, 38, 474
APL, 144, 474
Apple computer, 184

Application packages, 245
Application program, 128-52
Application programmer, 441,
    474
APT (A Programming Tool),
    212
Arithmetic-Logic Unit, 62, 474
Arithmetic operation, in
    BASIC, 202
Arithmetic operations, 59-61
    hierarchy of, 207
Army Ordnance Department,
    45-48
Array, in BASIC, 226-229
Artificial Intelligence (AI), 331-
    52, 474
Arts, computers in, 419-37
ASCII (*See* American Standard
    Code for Information
    Interchange)
Assembler, 139, 474
Assembler language, 139, 474
Association for Computing
    Machinery (ACM), 475
    and certification, 451-52
    as computer society, 453
Association for Educational
    Data Systems (AEDS), 453
Association of Computer
    Programmers and Analysts
    (ACPA), 453
Atanasoff, John V., 46, 475
Atari computer, 187

ATM (*See* Automatic Teller Machine)

Audio responses, and CAI, 277

Audit procedures, in hospitals, 310-11

Audit trail, 241

Augusta, Ada Lovelace, 39-40

Authorization code, 197, 394, 475
  security measures and, 376

Automated clearinghouse, for banks, 366

Automated factory, 262

Automatic Sequence Controlled Calculator (*See* Mark I)

Automatic Teller Machine (ATM), 365, 475

Automation:
  computers and, 266-70
  and hospital information systems, 312
  and workers, 461

Auxiliary storage, 54-55, 63-65, 475

B

Babbage, Charles, 36-39, 475
  and Ada, 148
  ideas and modern computers, 45

Backspacing, using terminal, 198

Back-up file, 375

Back-up tape, 103

Badges, for security, 394

Banking, and computers, 363-77

Bar code reader, and UPC, 361

BASIC, defined, 144-45, 475

BASIC programming, 194-233

Batch application, in Electronic Funds Transfer, 364
  in Point-of-Sale Systems, 355-56

Batch processing, 65-66, 242-43, 475
  of tapes, 99

Batch updating, 119

BCD (*See* Binary Coded Decimal)

Bell Telephone Laboratories, and computers, 45

Billings, John Shaw, 41

Binary Coded Decimal (BCD), 77

Binary numbers, 70-77, 475

Biological systems, and computers, 342-43

Bit, defined, 74
  digit, 75
  zone, 75

"Black box" computer, 350

"Black box" concept, 423

Blank lines, printing in BASIC, 206

Burst, paper, 108

Business, computers in, 237-53
  microcomputers in, 465-66

Business data processing, 5-8, 9, 237-53, 475

Business-oriented problems, 145

Business system, defined, 240

Byte, and bits, 75, 475
  of memory, 168
  of storage, 62

C

CAD (*See* Computer-aided design)

CAI (*See* Computer-assisted instruction)

Card punch, 95, 475

Card reader, 96-97, 475

Card read/punch, 475

Career opportunities, in computing, 441-56

Carnegie Institute of
Technology, and Artificial
Intelligence, 336-38
CASE, 323
CAT scan, 324, 475
Cathode Ray Tube (CRT), 116-
17, 475
advantages in education,
277-78
CCP (*See* Certificate of
Computer Professional)
CDP (*See* Certificate of Data
Processing)
Central Intelligence Agency,
406
Centralized data base, 476
Centralized data processing,
246-51, 476
Central Processing Unit (CPU),
10-11, 54-55, 56, 61-63, 475
Certificate of Computer
Professional (CCP), 450-53
Certificate of Data Processing
(CDP), 450-53
Certification, of computer
professionals, 449-53, 476
Character, of data, 70, 93
Character printer, 110
Charge-coupled device, 80, 476
Check float, 372
Check guarantee services, 366
Chess-playing machine, 336-38
Chip, 78-79, 476
CMI (*See* Computer-Managed
Instruction)
COBOL, 145, 476
Coding programs, 133-35, 476
Coding sheet, 133
Collection of data, 476
COM (*See* Computer Output
Microfilm)
Commodore PET computer, 184
Communication gap, 4
Communication theory, 342-43

"Community Practice,"
standard, 327-28
Compatibility, of computers,
169, 476
Compiler (compilation), 139, 476
Computer, analog, 13
digital, 14, 478
electromechanical, 44-45
electronic, 45-46
Computer, dedicated, 177
defined, 19-20, 476
general purpose, 177
large-scale, 172-73
medium-scale, 172
small-scale, 171-72
special-purpose, 177
stand-alone, 177
super, 174
turnkey, 177
Computer-aided design (CAD),
263-66, 423, 476
Computer-assisted instruction
(CAI), 275-309, 476
in medicine, 323-24
and micros, 185
Computer-based security
system, 397-98
Computer crime, 476
Computer graphics, 420-22
Computerized blood bank, 326
Computer literacy, 3, 275
Computer-Managed Instruction
(CMI), 295-97, 477
Computer Output Microfilm
(COM), 117-19, 466, 477
Computer professional, 441-56
in the future, 467-68
Computer science, 6-8, 477
Computer security, 477
Computer societies, 453-54
Computer system, 10, 54-87, 477
Conditional statement, in
BASIC, 212-20
Console terminal, 156

Constant, alphanumeric, 204-5
  numeric, 202
Constants, in BASIC, 202
Consultants, 128
Consumer, and computer, 353,
  380
Consumer acceptance, of EFT,
  371-72
Continuous forms, 108
Control key, in BASIC, 198
  on terminal, 197
Control list, 243
Control unit, 62, 477
Conversion of source
  documents, 477
Core memory, 77
Core storage, 477
Cost, of computer system,
  167-69
  of computers, 17-18
  of data processing services,
  153
  of large-scale system, 173
Countess of Lovelace, 148
COURSEWRITER, 300
COURSEWRITER,
  programming language, 288,
  477
CPU (*See* Central Processing
  Unit)
Creativity, and computers, 20
Crime, and computers, 21-22,
  381-99
CRT (*See* Cathode Ray Tube)
Cybernetics, 342-343, 477

D

Data, 9, 477
Data Bank, financial, 407-8
Data base, defined, 246-48
  in hospitals, 307-8
Data Base Administrator, 443,
  477

Data collection, in systems, 241
Data communications, and
  CAI, 277
Data entry devices, in CAD, 203
Data entry operator, 120
Data layout, 131
Data manipulation, 12
Data processing (*See* Business
  Data Processing)
Data processing, costs, 153
Data Processing Management
  Association (DPMA), 454
  and certification, 450
Data representation, 70-77
DATA statement, in BASIC,
  220-22
Data transfer operations, 59-61,
  477
DDP (*See* Distributed Data
  Processing)
Debit card, 373
Debug, 141, 477
Decentralized data processing,
  248-51, 477
Decimal numbering system, 71
Decision-making capability, of
  computers, 16
Dedicated computer, 177-78, 477
Dehumanization, and
  computers, 20
DEL key on a terminal, 198
Density, of tapes and disks, 182
Department stores, and
  computers, 353-63
Design, of systems, 241
Detail file, 242, 477
Detail report, 244
Diagnosis, and computers,
  314-19
Dial-up, computer, 196
Difference Engine, 36-37, 477
Digital, computer, 14, 478
Digital Equipment Corporation
  (DEC), 177

Digital-to-analog converter, 428
Digit bits, 75
Digitizer, 427
Digit punch, on a card, 94
DIM statement, in BASIC, 229
Direct access, 478
Director of Information
   Services, 478
Director of Management
   Information Systems, 443
Direct processing, 105
Disk (*See* Magnetic disk)
Diskette, 106, 182
Distributed Data Processing
   (DDP), 178-79, 250-51, 478
DOCTOR (*See* ELIZA)
Documentation, systems, 241
Documenting a program, 143-44
Dot matrix printer, 110
DO-WHILE, and structured
   programming, 147
DPMA (*See* Data Processing
   Management Association)
DP manager, 443, 478
Dreyfus, Hubert, 346-48
Drill-and-practice, in CAI, 280,
   285-86

E

Ear surgery, and
   microcomputers, 321-22
EBCDIC (*See* Extended Binary
   Coded Decimal Interchange
   Code)
Eckert, J. Presper, Jr., 45-48,
   478
Eckert-Mauchly Computer
   Corporation, 48
Editing data, 242
Edit procedure, 478
EDP (*See* Electronic data
   processing)
EDP Auditor, 443

Education, computers in,
   275-309
   microcomputers in, 464-65
EDVAC, 45-48, 478
EFT (*See* Electronic Funds
   Transfer)
Electromechanical computers,
   44-45, 478
Electronic cash register, 353-63,
   478
Electronic computer, defined,
   45-46, 478
   development of, 45-47
Electronic data processing
   (EDP), 9, 237-53, 478
Electronic Funds Transfer
   (EFT), 363-77, 478
   and financial data banks,
   407-8
Electronic mail, 253, 458, 478
   and U.S. Post Office, 469
Electrophotographic printer,
   110-11
Electrosensitive printer, 110-11
Electrostatic printer, 110-11
Elements of computer system,
   55
ELIZA, 343-46, 478
Ellul, Jacques, 470-71
Encryption codes, 394
END statement in BASIC, 202,
   221
Enhancements, programming,
   195
ENIAC, 45-46, 478-79
EPROM (*See* Erasable
   Programmable read-only
   memory)
Equity funding fraud, 383-84
Erasable Programmable read-
   only memory (EPROM), 159,
   479
Errors, computer, 15
Ethics, and computing, 448-49

Exception report, 244-45, 479
Executing a program, 138-41, 479
Experimentation, and computers, 349
Extended BASIC, 195, 229
Extended Binary Coded Decimal Interchange Code (EBCDIC), 75-77, 479
External tape labels, 101-2
Eye surgery, and microcomputers, 321-22

F

Facilities management, 128
Facsimile device, 253, 458, 479
Fair Credit Reporting Act of 1971, 479
Fast-food establishments, and computers, 353-63
Feasibility study, 17, 479
Federal Bureau of Investigation, 405-6
Federal computer matching programs, 407
Federal government, and computer crime, 391-93
Feedback mechanism, 255-56
Field, 94, 479
Field name, variable, in BASIC, 201
File, 92, 94, 241, 479
File maintenance, 242-44, 479
File protection ring, 102
Financial data bank, 407-8
Fire systems, 376
Firmware, 83, 159, 479
Flexible disk, 106
Floppy disk, 106, 184, 479
Floppy disk drive, 181
Flowchart (*See* Program flowchart)

FOR . . . . NEXT, in BASIC, 222-26
FORTRAN, 145-46, 479
Fraud, computer, 376
Front-end processor, 159, 479-80
and networks, 178

G

Gates, 62-63
and binary numbers, 70
General problem solver program, 338, 480
General-purpose computer, 14, 177, 480
Generations of computers, 49
GO (game), and computers, 336
GOTO, in BASIC, 202
GOTO—less programming, 446-48
Grandfather-father-son tapes, 103
Graphics, and CAI, 280
Graphics display terminal, 480
in CAD, 263
Greek view of science, 28-29
GRIPHOS, 434-35, 480

H

Handicapped people, and computers, 321-22
Handicapped students, and CAI, 292-93
Hard copy, 480
Hard-copy terminal, 115-16
Hardware, 54, 91-125, 166, 480
Hard-wired terminal, 196
in schools, 275
Harvard Business School Management Game, 287
Harvard University, and computers, 44-45

Hawthorne Experiments, 267, 480
Hazeltine Corporation, and TICCIT, 300-301
Head crash, on disk, 375
Header label, 102
Health, computers in, 305-30
Health information system, 306, 319-20, 480
Heuristics, 335-37, 480
Hexadecimal code, 75-77
Hierarchical data processing, 178
Hierarchy of arithmetic operations, 207
Hierarchy of data, 94
Hierarchy of operations, 480
High-level languages, 480
Hollerith, Herman, 41-43, 480
Hollerith code, 94, 480
Honeywell v. Sperry Rand litigation, 46-47
Hooper, T. J., case, 327
Hospital information system, 305-14, 480
Host processor, 174, 459, 480
Humanities, computers in, 419-37
Human-machine interface, 468-69

I

IBM (*See* International Business Machines Corporation)
IBM system, 3, 93
ICC (*See* Integrated circuit chip)
ICCP (*See* Institute for Certification of Computer Professionals)
Identification problem, with tape and disk, 101
IEEE, Computer society, 454

IF-THEN, in BASIC, 212-20
IF-THEN-ELSE, and structured programming, 147
Illinois, University of, and CAI, 276, 297-300
Imitation game, and Alan Turing, 333-34
Impact printer, 109
Implementing, a program, 142-43
Index, disk, 105, 480
Individualized instruction, and CAI, 290-91
Industrial Revolution, 33-35, 40-41, 480-81
Industry, computers in, 253-66
Information, 9, 481
Information banks, 481
Information sciences, 6
Information system, and hospitals, 306-7
Ink Jet printer, 110-11
Input, defined, 9, 481
  device, 10
  errors, 15
  operations, 59-60
  statement in BASIC, 209-10
  unit, 54-55, 56-57, 481
Inquiry-response, 247
Institute for Advanced Study Computer, 48
Institute for Certification of Computer Professionals (ICCP), 450-53, 481
Integrated circuit chip (ICC), 177
Integrated circuits, 49, 77-78, 481
Intelligent terminal, 252, 481
Internal tape label, 102
International Business Machines (IBM) Corp., 43, 184
  and first electronic computers, 48

International Business
Machines (IBM) Corp. (cont.):
and Mark I, 44
Interpreter, 141
BASIC, 229
Iron oxide coating, of disk, 97,
103-4

J

Jacquard, Joseph Marie, 35, 36,
481
JCL (*See* Job Control
Language)
Job Control Language (JCL),
156, 481
Job requirements, for
programmers, 441-42

K

K, 62, 168
Kaiser Foundation Hospital,
and multiphasic screening,
318
Key field, on disk, 105
Keypunching a program, 134
Keypunch machine, 95, 481
Key-to-disk encoder, 107, 481
Key-to-tape encoder, 98, 481

L

Label, tape, 101-2
Language, and artificial
intelligence, 340-42
Large-scale computer, 481
Laser beam reader, 481
and UPC, 361
Laser-xerographic printer,
110-11
Laws, computer crime, 389-91
Leasing computers, 238-39

Legal issues, and computers,
404-18
Legislation, privacy, 411-14
Leibniz, Gottfried, 32-33, 481
LET statement, in BASIC, 202,
210-11
Letter-quality printer, 110-11
Liability issue, and computers,
372-73
Libraries, and computers, 433
Library retrieval system, 322-23
Light pèn, 482
and CAI, 277
Line number, in BASIC, 198,
201
Line Printer, 108, 482
Linguistics, 482
and artificial intelligence,
340-42
List, in BASIC, 226-29
LIST command, 199
Listing, source program, 139
Literacy, computer, 275
LOAD command, 200
Logical control operation, 12
Logical design theory, of
computers, 47-48
Logical test, in BASIC, 212-20
Logic error, in a program, 142
Logic operations, 59-61
Logic theorist program, 338
Log-on procedures, 196-98, 482
Loop, in BASIC, 214-15, 222-26,
482
Lovelace, Countess of, 39-40,
482
Low-Level programming
languages, 482

M

Machine address, 135
Machine language, 135-36, 482

Magnetic bubble memory, 80-81, 376, 482
Magnetic core memory, 77, 482
Magnetic disk, 103-7, 482
Magnetic Ink Character Recognition (MICR), 120, 482 and EFT, 368
Magnetic Ink Characters, 482
Magnetic tape, 97-103, 482
Mail, electronic, 458
Mainframe, 54, 482
Maintenance programmer, 441, 482
Malpractice, and computer professionals, 381
Management game, 287, 482
Management Information System (MIS), 246-48, 483 and future, 459-60 and hospital information system, 306-7
Management-level positions, in computing, 442
Manufacturing, computers in, 253-66
Mark I, 44-45, 483
Mark-sense devices, 122-23, 483
Martin, James, 469
Massachusetts General Hospital, and MUMPS, 318
Mass storage, 64-65
Mass storage device, 483
Master file, 98, 241-42, 483
Mauchly, John, 45-48, 483
Means-end analysis, 339
MECC (*See* Minnesota Educational Computing Consortium)
Mechanistic view of the universe, 343
Medical information, and privacy issues, 409-11
Medical information system, 306, 314-19, 483

Medical research, 322-23
Medicine, computers in, 305-30
Medium-scale computer, 483
MEDLARS, 323
Megabyte, 62, 168, 483
Memory size, 63, 168, 483
Menabrea, 39
MICR (*See* Magnetic Ink Character Recognition Equipment)
Microcomputers, 166-93, 483 and BASIC, 196 and CAI, 279-80 and the future, 463-66
Microprocessor, 182
Microsecond, 18
Mill, (Babbage), 39
Million instructions per second, 171
Millisecond, 18
Minicomputers, 19, 166-93, 483 and disks, 106 and EFT, 364 and front-end processor, 159 and medical system, 320-21, 483 and off-line processing, 68
Minnesota Educational Computing Consortium (MECC), 301
Minsky, Marvin cf, 346
MIPS (*See* Million instructions per second)
MIS (*See* Management Information System)
MIT, and robotics, 339-40
MITRE Corporation, and TICCIT, 300-301
Modem, 196
Modern era, in science, 30-31
Modules, of computers, 178
Moore School of Electrical Engineering, 45-48

Multiphasic screening, 315-18, 483
Multiprocessing, 158-59, 484
Multiprogramming, 156-57, 484
MUMPS, 318, 484
Museum Computer Network, 434, 484
Museums, computers and, 434-35
Music, computers and, 428-32
Music synthesizer, 428, 484

N

Nanosecond, 18, 169, 484
Napier, John, 32-33
National Crime Information Center (NCIC), 405-6, 484
National Library of Medicine, 323
National Security Agency, 406, 484
NCIC (*See* National Crime Information Center)
Negligence, in hospitals, 327-28
Network, of computers, 174
of minis, 459
Newell, Allen, 336-38
Newswire services, and computers, 463
Nonimpact printer, 109-10
Nonvolatility of memory, 80-81
"Number cruncher," 349, 433
Numerical analysis, 6
Numerical control, 258-62, 484

O

Object program, 138-39, 484
OCR (*See* Optical Character Recognition)
Oettinger, Anthony, 340-42
Office automation, 251-53, 457-59

Office of Management and Budget, 407
Office of the future, 457-59
Off-line processing, 68-69, 484
and MICR, 120
Ohio State University College of Medicine, 323-24
One-dimensional array, in BASIC, 226-29
ON—GOTO statements, in BASIC, 226
On-line applications, Electronic Funds Transfer, 364
Point-of-Sale System, 355-56
On-line processing, 66, 242-43, 484
and disks, 106
On-line updating, 119
Operating system, 152-60, 484
Operating system software, 128-29
Operation code, actual, 135
symbolic, 135
Optical Character Recognition (OCR), 119-23, 466, 484
Optical scanner, 120
Organization chart, 249, 444
Originality, and computers, 20
Output, defined, 9, 484
device, 10-12
operation, 59-61
reporting, 244-45
unit, 54-55, 56, 58, 484

P

Packaged application programs, 128, 152
Page printer, 108, 484
Papert, Seymour cf, 346
Parentheses, in BASIC, 208-9
Partition, of CPU, 157
Pascal, Blaise, 31-32, 147, 485
Pascal, programming language, 146-47, 484-85

Pattern recognition, 331-52, 485
PCM (*See* Plug-compatible machine)
Pedagogy, and CAI, 294-95
Personal computer, 185
  and the future, 463-66
Picosecond, 18, 169, 485
PL/1, 147, 485
Planning tools, for programs, 132-33
PLATO, 276, 297-300, 485
Plug-compatible machine (PCM), 169-70, 485
Point-of-Sale System (POS), 353-63, 367-77, 485
Portable bar code reader, and UPC, 361
POS (*See* Point-of-Sale System)
Power outages, and computers, 375-76
Powers, James, 43, 485
Preauthorized banking, 366
Pre-modern era, 27-29
Primary storage, 61-62, 485
Printer, 108-14
PRINT option, in BASIC, 204
Privacy, and computers, 21, 312-13, 404-18
  and EFT, 369-71
Privacy legislation, 411-14, 485
Problem definition, 143-44, 485
Problem-solving tasks, and Artificial Intelligence, 332-33
Process control, 254-57, 485
Processing operations, 59-61
Production, computers in, 253-66
Production control, 257-58, 485
Professional, computer, 441-56
  in the future, 467-68
Professional Standards Review Organization, 311
Program, 5, 12, 15, 485
  and computer system, 54
  and Jacquard, 35

Program (cont.):
  logic error, 142
  object, 138-39
  source, 139-41
Program documentation, 143-44, 485
Program errors, reasons for, 132
Program flowchart, 133, 479
Programmable read-only memory (PROM), 159, 485
Programmed instruction, 485
  and CAI, 283
Programmer, 5, 15, 152, 485-86
Programmers, types of, 441
Programming, and heuristics, 335-37
  in BASIC, 194-233
  structured, 147
Programming error, 15
Programming manager, 443
Program preparation, 129-30
Program sheet, 133
Program specifications, 132
PROM (*See* Programmable read-only memory)
PROMIS system, 318-19, 486
Protocol, and computers, 195, 486
Pseudocode, 133, 486
Psychology, and Artificial Intelligence, 332
  and computers, 346-48
Pulses, electronic, 70
Punched card devices, 41-42
Punched cards, 92-97, 486
Punched paper tape, 123, 486
Purchasing computer, 238-39

R

Radar, and computers, 44
Radio Shack computer, 184
RAM (*See* Random access memory)

Random access memory (RAM), 82-83, 486

Random processing, and disk, 106

Read-only memory (ROM), 83, 159, 486

READ statement, in BASIC, 220-22

Read/write head, of disk, 104, 486
of tape, 97

Real-time processing, 66-68, 106, 486

Recombinant DNA studies, and computers, 350

Record, 94, 486

Record size, on tape and disk, 99

Register, 62

Relays, and electromechanical computers, 44-45

Reliability, of computers, 18

Remington Rand, 43, 48

REM statement, in BASIC, 219

Renting computers, 238-39

Reporting, 244-45

Research, computers and art, 424-26
computers and humanities, 432-34
computers and medical, 322-23
computers and music, 432

Retention cycle, of tape, 101

Return key, on a terminal, 197

Robot, and Artificial Intelligence, 332
industrial, 258-62

Robotics, 339-40

ROM (*See* Read-only memory)

Row, on a card, 94

RPG, 147-48, 486

RUN command, 199

S

Salaries, of computer professionals, 444

Santayana, George, 26

SAVE command, 200

Scheutz, Pehr George, 37

Sciences, computers in, 348-50

Scientific management, 267

Scientific problems, 146

Scientific programmer, 6, 486

Scientific revolution, 28, 486

SCORTOS, 428

Scrambling, data, 394

Sculpture, and computers, 423

Secondary storge (*See* Auxiliary storage)

Sector, on a disk, 182

Security, and computers, 381-99
and EFT, 371
and POS, 374-77

Semiconductor, 80

Sequential processing, and disk, 105, 486
and tape, 99

Serial printer, 108, 486

Shannon, Claude, 336

Simon, Herbert A., 336-38, 347

Simulating human behavior, with computers, 343-46

Simulation, and CAI, 287-88, 487
and computers and medical, 323-24

Small-scale computer, 171-72, 486

Snow, C. P., 4

Socialization, CAI effects on, 295

Social security numbers, and computers, 408-9

Soft copy terminal, 117, 486

Software, 127-69, 486
and legal issues, 390

Software (cont.):
protection, 396-98
supplier, 152
Source data automation, 252-53, 486
Source document, 487
Source program, 138-39, 487
Special-purpose computer, 14, 177, 487
in manufacturing, 262
Speed, of computers, 17-18, 169
Sperry Rand, 43, 48
"Stand-alone" CAI device, 280
"Stand-alone" computer, 177
Standards, in programming, 446-48
Stanford Research Institute, and robotics, 339-40
Stanford University, and robotics, 339-40
Stibitz, George R., 45, 487
Stock service, and computers, 463
STOP command, 203
Storage capacity, 19
Store (Babbage), 39
Stored-program concept, 12, 47-48, 487
String variable, in BASIC, 209-10
Structured design, 446-48, 487
Structured programming, 133, 147, 446-48, 487
Structured walkthrough, 448
Student-machine interaction, 291
Stuttering, and computers, 322
Subscript, in BASIC, 226-29
Summary report, 244
Supercomputer, 174, 487
Supermarket, and computers, 353-63
Supervisor, 62, 128, 154, 487
Surface, on a disk, 182

Surgery, and microcomputers, 321-22
Symbolic program, 138, 487
Syntax error, 139, 141, 229, 487
Synthesizer, music, 428
System, and programming, 130
System, business, 240
System command, 199
System concept, 91, 170-71
System resident device, 154, 488
Systems analysis, 245-46
Systems analyst, 6, 130, 239-40, 443, 488
Systems design, 130, 241
Systems programmer, 6, 156, 441, 488

T

Table handling, in BASIC, 226-29
Tabulating machine, 42-43
Tabulating Machine Company, 43
Tape (*See* Magnetic tape)
Tape cartridge, 180, 488
Tape cassette, 181, 488
Tape label, 101-2, 488
Tape librarian, 102, 488
Telecommuting, 460-62
Television, as a personal computer, 187
Template, flowcharting, 133, 488
Terminal, 114-17, 488
and BASIC, 195
intelligent, 252
Test data, 141
Text editing, 458-59
Thermal printer, 110-11
TICCIT, 300-301, 488
Time-sharing, 238, 276, 488
Toffler, Alvin, 460-62
Top-down approach, 247-51, 488
Top-down programming, 447-48

Tower of Hanoi problem, 338-39
Track, on a disk, 182
Trailer record, 217
Transaction file, 119, 242, 488
Transfer rate, 181
Transistor, 49
Translating a program, 138-39,
  340-42, 488
Transportation control, 262-63
Turing, Alan, 333-34, 488
Turing test, 333-34, 489
Turnkey computer, 177-78, 489
  in manufacturing, 262
TUTOR, 228, 300, 489
Tutorial instruction, with CAI,
  286-87
"Two Cultures," 419
Typewriter terminal, 115-16
Typing, a program, 134
Typographical errors, in
  BASIC, 198-99

U

Unconditional branch, in
  BASIC, 202
Unemployment, and computers,
  20
Uninterruptible power supply,
  376, 489
UNIVAC, first, 47-48
Universal Product Code (UPC),
  359-63, 489
UPC (See Universal Product
  Code)
Update procedure, 119, 242-44,
  489
Upward compatible, 169
User, defined, 7
U.S. Post Office, 469

V

Vacuum tubes, 44, 49
Variable field name, in BASIC,
  201

Variable string, in BASIC,
  209-10
Vermont, University of, and
  PROMIS, 318-19
Virtual storage (VS), 158, 489
Visual display terminal, 116-17
Voice recognition device, 466
von Neumann, John, 47-48,
  346-48, 489
VP, of Information Services,
  443
VS (See Virtual storage)

W

Wand reader, and POS, 361, 489
Wartime, and computers, 44-46
Watson, Thomas J., Sr., and
  MARK I, 44
Weizenbaum, Joseph, 343-47,
  489
Wiretapping, 394
Wirth, Niklaus, 146
Word processing, 185, 251-53,
  458-59, 489
Workplace, changing nature of,
  460-61
World War II, and computers,
  44-45

X

X-ray technology, 324

Y

"Yankee ingenuity," 40-41

Z

Zone bit, 75
Zone punch, on a card, 94
Zuse, Konrad, 45